THE POLITICS OF REFUGEE POLICY
IN THE GLOBAL SOUTH

MCGILL-QUEEN'S REFUGEE AND FORCED MIGRATION STUDIES

Series editors: Megan Bradley and James Milner

Forced migration is a local, national, regional, and global challenge with profound political and social implications. Understanding the causes and consequences of, and possible responses to, forced migration requires careful analysis from a range of disciplinary perspectives, as well as interdisciplinary dialogue.

The purpose of the McGill-Queen's Refugee and Forced Migration Studies series is to advance in-depth examination of diverse forms, dimensions, and experiences of displacement, including in the context of conflict and violence, repression and persecution, and disasters and environmental change. The series will explore responses to refugees, internal displacement, and other forms of forced migration to illuminate the dynamics surrounding forced migration in global, national, and local contexts, including Canada, the perspectives of displaced individuals and communities, and the connections to broader patterns of human mobility. Featuring research from fields including politics, international relations, law, anthropology, sociology, geography, and history, the series highlights new and critical areas of enquiry within the field, especially conversations across disciplines and from the perspective of researchers in the global South, where the majority of forced migration unfolds. The series benefits from an international advisory board made up of leading scholars in refugee and forced migration studies.

10 The Right to Research
   Historical Narratives by Refugee and Global South Researchers
   Edited by Kate Reed and Marcia C. Schenck

11 Kingdom of Barracks
   Polish Displaced Persons in Allied-Occupied Germany and Austria
   Katarzyna Nowak

12 Urban Refugees and Digital Technology
   Reshaping Social, Political, and Economic Networks
   Charles Martin-Shields

13 Migration Governance in North America
   Policy, Politics, and Community
   Edited by Kiran Banerjee and Craig Damian Smith

14 Write to Return
   Huguenot Refugees on the Frontiers of the French Enlightenment
   Bryan A. Banks

15 The Politics of Refugee Policy in the Global South
   Ola G. El-Taliawi

The Politics of Refugee Policy in the Global South

OLA G. EL-TALIAWI

McGill-Queen's University Press
Montreal & Kingston • London • Chicago

© McGill-Queen's University Press 2024

ISBN 978-0-2280-2117-9 (cloth)
ISBN 978-0-2280-2118-6 (paper)
ISBN 978-0-2280-2172-8 (ePDF)
ISBN 978-0-2280-2173-5 (ePUB)
ISBN 978-0-2280-2192-6 (open access)

Legal deposit second quarter 2024
Bibliothèque nationale du Québec

Printed in Canada on acid-free paper that is 100% ancient forest free (100% post-consumer recycled), processed chlorine free

This book has been published with the help of a grant from the Canadian Federation for the Humanities and Social Sciences, through the Awards to Scholarly Publications Program, using funds provided by the Social Sciences and Humanities Research Council of Canada. Funding was also received from the University of Twente and the Local Engagement Refugee Research Network.

We acknowledge the support of the Canada Council for the Arts.
Nous remercions le Conseil des arts du Canada de son soutien.

McGill-Queen's University Press in Montreal is on land which long served as a site of meeting and exchange amongst Indigenous Peoples, including the Haudenosaunee and Anishinabeg nations. In Kingston it is situated on the territory of the Haudenosaunee and Anishinaabek. We acknowledge and thank the diverse Indigenous Peoples whose footsteps have marked these territories on which peoples of the world now gather.

Library and Archives Canada Cataloguing in Publication

Title: The politics of refugee policy in the Global South / Ola G. El-Taliawi.
Names: El-Taliawi, Ola G., author.
Series: McGill-Queen's refugee and forced migration studies ; 15.
Description: Series statement: McGill-Queen's refugee and forced migration studies ; 15 | Includes bibliographical references and index.
Identifiers: Canadiana (print) 20240299280 | Canadiana (ebook) 20240299299 | ISBN 9780228021186 (paper) | ISBN 9780228021179 (cloth) | ISBN 9780228021728 (ePDF) | ISBN 9780228021735 (ePUB) | ISBN 9780228021926 (open access)
Subjects: LCSH: Syria—History—Civil War, 2011—Refugees—Jordan. | LCSH: Syria—History—Civil War, 2011—Refugees—Lebanon. | LCSH: Refugees—Government policy—Jordan. | LCSH: Refugees—Government policy—Lebanon.
Classification: LCC HV640.5.S97 E48 2024 | DDC 956.9104/231—dc23

This book was typeset in 10.5/13 Sabon.

"Home is where all our attempts to escape ... finally cease."
(Naguib Mahfouz)

This work is dedicated to the thousands of people who have lost their lives crossing seas or borders in search of "home," in the hope that it will help alleviate human suffering, if only marginally.

Contents

Tables and Figures   ix

Keywords, Definitions, and Abbreviations   xi

Acknowledgments   xv

1 Rising Forced Displacement in the Global South:
A Complex Policy Problem   3

2 A Complexity Approach to Analyzing Variation
in Refugee Policy in the Global South   30

3 Syria's Civil War and Ensuing Humanitarian Disaster:
Eleven Years On   67

4 From Home to Hosts: Jordan's and Lebanon's Refugee
Policy-Making Contexts   90

5 Syrian Refugee Displacement in Jordan:
A Descriptive Narrative   103

6 Unpacking Jordan's Policy Response to Syrian Displacement:
"If We Can't Win, Then We at Least Shouldn't Lose"   115

viii Contents

7 Syrian Refugee Displacement in Lebanon:
A Descriptive Narrative 142

8 Unpacking Lebanon's Policy Response to Syrian Displacement:
"Policy of No Policy" 152

9 One Displacement, Two Responses:
Comparative Analysis and Discussion 176

10 Similar but Different: Understanding Refugee-Policy
Variation in the Global South 191

Notes 217

References 231

Index 285

Tables and Figures

TABLES

1.1 Select host-country background facts   15

2.1 Breakdown of refugee-policy output by elements and degree of restrictiveness   57

3.1 Syrian refugee population in neighbouring countries (at 30 November 2022)   82

6.1 Jordan's policy choices on Syrian displacement and their evolution   129

8.1 Lebanon's policy choices on Syrian displacement and their evolution   165

9.1 Comparative tabulation of Lebanon's and Jordan's policy responses to Syrian displacement (2011–22)   178

9.2 Differences and similarities in Lebanon's and Jordan's system inputs, process, and outputs   184

FIGURES

2.1 Refugee-policy elements   35

2.2 Drivers of host-policy responses to mass influx situations   44

2.3 A systemic view of the refugee policy-making process 60

3.1 Map of Syria. Source: CIA World Factbook 68

4.1 Map of Jordan. Source: CIA World Factbook 92

4.2 Map of Lebanon. Source: CIA World Factbook 96

6.1 Jordan's institutional framework for the Syrian refugee response 124

6.2 Phases of Jordan's policy evolution on Syrian displacement (2011–22) 127

6.3 Systemic visualization of Jordan's key response drivers (2011–22) 139

8.1 Phases of Lebanon's policy evolution on Syrian displacement (2011–22) 164

8.2 Systemic visualization of Lebanon's key response drivers (2011–22) 173

9.1 Evolution of Lebanon's and Jordan's input arena interactions and responses (2011–22) 186

10.1 Hypothesized typology of host behaviour 203

Keywords, Definitions, and Abbreviations

ARDD	Arab Renaissance for Democracy and Development
asylum seeker	an individual who seeks asylum in another country but whose refugee status has not yet been determined[1]
country of first asylum	used in this study as a synonym for *country of first entry*[2]
EU	European Union
Geneva Convention	1951 Convention Relating to the Status of Refugees
GoJ	Government of Jordan
GoL	Government of Lebanon
GSO	General Security Office (Lebanon)
HBB	home-based business
HRW	Human Rights Watch
IDP	internally displaced person
IGO	intergovernmental organization
ILO	International Labour Organization
IMCC	Inter-ministerial Coordination Committee
INGO	international non-governmental organization
IO	international organization
JHCO	Jordan Hashemite Charity Organization
JRPSC	Jordan Response Plan for the Syria Crisis
LCRP	Lebanon Crisis Response Plan
LDCs	least-developed countries

xii Keywords, Definitions, and Abbreviations

Leb4Refs	Lebanon for Refugees
mass influx	a situation in which a large number of people, usually thousands, arrive at or cross an international border suddenly or in a relatively short period of time, thus incapacitating states' ability to conduct individual refugee-status-determination procedures[3]
MENA	Middle East and North Africa
MOI	Ministry of Interior (Jordan)
MOL	Ministry of Labour (Jordan)
MOPIC	Ministry of Planning and International Cooperation (Jordan)
MORA	Ministry of Refugee Affairs (Lebanon)
MOSA	Ministry of Social Affairs (Lebanon)
MOSD	Ministry of Social Development (Jordan)
MOU	memorandum of understanding
NGO	non-governmental organization
non-refoulement	the duty of states, as enshrined in customary international law, not to return refugees to countries where they face potential threat[4]
NRC	Norwegian Refugee Council
OAU	Organisation of African Unity
prima facie refugee	the determination by a state or UNHCR of a refugee on the basis of readily apparent and objective circumstances in the country of origin that led to exodus[5]
PRS	Palestinian refugees from Syria
refugee	an individual who is outside the country of their nationality and is unable or unwilling to return owing to a well-founded fear of persecution on the basis of race, religion, nationality, membership of a particular social group, or political opinion[6]
Refugee Convention	1951 Convention Relating to the Status of Refugees; also known as the Geneva Convention
resettlement	the transfer of refugees from a country to which they sought asylum to another country, which has agreed to grant them permanent settlement[7]

Keywords, Definitions, and Abbreviations

RSD	refugee-status determination
SRS	Syrian refugees from Syria
3RP	regional refugee and resilience plan
UNDP	United Nations Development Programme
UNHCR	United Nations High Commissioner for Refugees, responsible for ensuring that the Refugee Convention is adhered to
UNICEF	United Nations Children's Fund
UNRWA	United Nations Relief and Works Agency for Palestine
URDA	Union of Relief and Development Associations

Acknowledgments

In the spring of 2017, I travelled to Lebanon and Jordan to conduct part of the fieldwork for this book. The experience helped me find answers to my research questions, but it also gave me first-hand a feel for what it was to be displaced and what it meant for small countries grappling with problems of their own to host another significantly large population. During that time I enjoyed the hospitality of Ghada Shawky, to whom I am very grateful. I also owe much thanks to Ambassador Nabil Fahmy, and my friends at the Egyptian embassies in Beirut and Amman, who helped me immensely. I am also indebted to the Center for Arab and Middle East Studies (CAMES) at the American University of Beirut, the Center for Middle East Studies at the University of Columbia, and the Center for Migration and Refugee Studies at the American University in Cairo, where I was hosted as a visiting research fellow. The warmth and generosity of the Lebanese and Jordanians are a testament to the many wonderful aspects of the Middle East, which are seldom reported in the news.

In the course of writing this book I have also come across many people to whom I owe much gratitude, including the Local Engagement Refugee Research Network (LERRN) at Carleton University, for supporting me in ensuring this work comes to light. Special thanks should be made to Luiz Leomil, whose research assistance was nothing short of invaluable. I am deeply indebted to the stakeholder respondents, who have lent me their insights and knowledge and have amplified refugees' voices. I hope I have done your insights justice.

I would like to thank my colleagues at the Lee Kuan Yew School of Public Policy, who have been there for me through thick and thin and imparted considerable knowledge and wisdom to me: J.J. Woo, Mehmet Kerem Coban, Maria Lourdes Montenegro, Yifei Yan, Aubrey Tabuga, Jingru Zhang, Stuti Rawat, Kidjie Saguin, and many others. I also find it especially relevant to mention my support system of the wonderful women who inspire me with their grit and passion every day: Dina El-Ghandour, Rana Essam, Manar Marzouk, Ranya Mahmoud, Aya Al-Gawish, Malak El-Far, Dina Hany, Menna Shoman, Abeer El-Kayaty, Samaa Abdel Khalek, Nahla El-Okda, Heba Ghannam, and members of the lovely writing group that kept me going: Lama, Rawan, and Stephanie.

This book began in 2018 at the National University of Singapore. While writing the book I relied on the help of exceptional mentors who supported and guided me throughout the process: Dr Ibrahim Awad, Dr Zeger van der Wal, Professor Michael Howlett, and Dr Caroline Brassard. It is also especially important to thank my "invisible" peer reviewers and the regional scholars who read various versions of this book. Special thanks go to Dr Alaa El-Din Awad, Dr Asya El-Meehy, Dr Joseph Daher, and Farah Ismail for their valuable contributions. I am also grateful for the loving support of Philip Jansen, who turned out to be a brilliant book-cover designer.

Above all, this book would not have seen the light without the encouragement of my family, who never doubted my abilities. Their unconditional love is unmatched, and it would be a lost cause to try to put my gratitude and love for them into words. Finally, I would like to thank Dr James Milner, who manages to lead with so much humanity.

THE POLITICS OF REFUGEE POLICY
IN THE GLOBAL SOUTH

I

Rising Forced Displacement in the Global South: A Complex Policy Problem

Refugees fleeing from violent conflict represent a complex and intractable policy challenge to the countries of destination. This is especially the case in developing countries of the Global South, where refugee movements predominantly originate and settle, and where political stability is often volatile and the capacity to provide assistance to refugees and asylum seekers is limited (Feller 2006). Such a situation is compounded when countries face a sudden influx of refugees. In these cases, assistance becomes a humanitarian necessity that requires the collaboration of state and non-state actors. Mass refugee situations affect not only refugees and host governments but also local host communities, aid workers, non-governmental organizations (NGOs), and other actors. They are "wicked policy problems" that transcend several policy sectors, such as migration, health, social policy, and foreign policy (Miller 2014; Head 2008).[1]

Over the past few years, global displacement numbers have increased substantially, reaching 101.1 million people by the end of 2022 (UNHCR 2022c).[2] Refugees make up 27.1 million of this global, forcibly displaced population,[3] and contrary to alarmist media images that suggest otherwise, the majority of the world's refugees are not situated in the Global North, but they tend to originate from states in the Global South and to move en masse across borders into neighbouring states in the same region. An estimated 83 per cent of the world's displaced population is, in fact, hosted in the Global South, including in low-income countries. Least-developed countries (LDCs) alone host 27 per cent of the total refugee population (UNHCR 2022c). Not only do refugees hosted in the Global South tend to be mass refugee populations, but they are also becoming increasingly urban (Crawford 2022). Refugees are no longer being contained at borders, or "safe havens," but are instead settling amidst host populations in urban and pre-urban areas. The high degree of urbanization tests local host communities' infrastructure, resources, and sense of social and cultural cohesion (Crawford 2022; Sanyal 2021; UNHCR 2012a). Hence, refugees are often seen as a threat to a country's demographic, economic and social equilibrium, as evidenced by the surge in anti-refugee rhetoric in many parts of the world.

The imbalanced geographic distribution of refugees in countries of the South, their exponential increase in number, and their increasing urbanization all pose particular governance challenges for host governments and the international humanitarian community. While an international regime exists to govern the treatment of refugees, not all states are party to it. Furthermore, those that are party to it are accorded considerable discretion in defining who a refugee is and what they are entitled to. There is also absence of clear parameters to describe how states should help each other in shouldering the burden of hosting refugees. Therefore, the perceived need for international solidarity is often driven by the politics and visibility of each refugee crisis rather than by the host country's actual needs (UNHCR 2012a). This international regime first emerged with the establishment in 1950 of the Office of the United Nations High Commissioner for Refugees (UNHCR) and with the creation of the 1951 Convention Relating to the Status of Refugees ("Geneva Convention"). The latter defines refugees as an individual who "owing to well-founded fear of being persecuted for reasons of race, religion, nationality, membership of a particular social group or political opinion, is outside the country of [their] nationality and is unable or, owing to such fear, is unwilling to avail [themself] of the protection of that country." This regime also established the principle of non-refoulement, which indicates that refugees and asylum seekers cannot be forcibly returned to their countries of origin if doing so would put their lives in danger.

The international regime was originally designed to govern refugee affairs in Europe and has since been unable to move beyond its European origins to address current displacement realities. Despite the fact that 149 countries are party to the Geneva Convention and its 1967 Protocol Relating to the Status of Refugees, refugee protection still appears to be embedded in the context of the post–Second

Rising Forced Displacement

World War era, which limits the regime's ability to deal with the reality of Southern displacement. As the founders of this global refugee regime were focused on refugee movements occurring in Europe, and considered the "refugee problem" a temporary situation, they set temporal and geographical restrictions for international protection, making it only available to those fleeing the European continent in the aftermath of the Second World War. While refugees receive statutory international protection (either from countries of asylum or from UNHCR), mass movements, or displaced individuals who flee due to reasons not prescribed in the Geneva Convention, do not have access to the same protection mechanism (Landau 2014). More comprehensive refugee definitions that recognize mass movements resulting from massive violations of human rights as having grounds for international protection, have emerged in regional contexts such as Africa and the Americas.[4] However, the global picture for refugee protection is still very narrow (Betts 2010a). The global refugee regime seems out of sync with realities in the world today and the changing context of forced displacement. One of the regime's key structural limitations lies in its lack of a clear and concrete mechanism for ensuring international cooperation and responsibility sharing on the part of states that are not hosting mass refugee movements – predominantly countries in the North.

I pose here a key question: why is there a need to pay particular attention to the South? There are several reasons that it is imperative to understand refugee-policy processes in the South as distinct from those of the North. Firstly, refugee policy-making in the Global South usually happens in the context of mass displacement rather than the resettlement of individual asylum seekers. Secondly, countries of the Global South are host to the vast majority of the world's refugees. Thirdly, policy-making processes in developing and developed economies differ, owing to their differing contexts (Colebatch and Radin 2006). It is not unusual for governments, developing or developed, to be reluctant or parsimonious when spending their scarce resources on foreign nationals. Global South countries largely face pre-existing unfavourable economic realities and must cope more often with mass influxes. Therefore, the question tends to be intensified, thus generating different outcomes than those experienced in the North.

Moreover, Global South countries tend to be sites of the unique dynamics created through their distinct relationships with donor states and international organizations (IOs), which generate bargaining processes and variations in refugee protection. In many cases, such as those examined in this book, religious affiliations and sectarian politics may also play an important role in shaping policy outcomes for different refugee populations. As this study will outline, developing countries may not follow the statutory international protection norms primarily set in the Global North. Instead, they navigate mass refugee influxes according to domestic interests and more flexible bilateral agreements with donor states and IOs. In some instances this has paradoxically led to increased protection, rather than the other way around, as local norms of hospitality and refugee-hosting allow for an expansion in the refugee-protection space (as in the cases of Latin America, Africa, and the Middle East). However, the lack of a binding and consistent regulatory framework makes the granting of refugee protection highly uncertain.

Developed countries, however, with a wider capacity for covering unexpected public expenditures, tend to be geographically distant from epicentres of forced displacement and to impose more sophisticated border- and visa-control mechanisms. Often, Global North countries are not countries of first asylum but countries of resettlement. This involves a durable solution offered to select vulnerable refugee groups that is completely discretionary to states. If resettlement places are offered, refugees are identified (usually by UNHCR) and have their profiles submitted to national immigration authorities, who make the final decision whether or not to admit these refugees to their country. When resettling refugees, countries are not bound to statutory obligations and tend to have wider discretion to enact policies that fit their national interests (e.g., by establishing resettlement quotas). This, in turn, results in distinct pressures and allows Global North countries to be faced with different policy options. I will be discussing durable solutions and the dynamics of resettlement more in chapter 2.

The complex factors facing host governments that are witnessing mass displacement in the South also overlap to make the granting of asylum and the provision of services to refugees a highly complex policy issue. This is evident in the diversity of responses adopted during incidences of mass refugee flows even within the same region. Given this situation, I contemplate the reasons for governments' decisions to admit or reject refugees. When do governments decide to grant refugees temporary protection or treat them as "aliens"? What makes a government collaborate with international organizations in the management of refugee flows, or restrict their operations? Such questions, and others, point to a compelling need to understand how and why governments in the South choose to respond to mass influx situations.

Given the lack of burden sharing and the differences in the capacity of the hosting states, there is variation in how they respond. This is important because the norms of the regime are supposed to be universal, but we are seeing great differences. We need to understand the variation between states, and we need to understand the particular conditions of states in the Global South, because that is where the majority of the world's refugees are to be found. However, the field of refugee- and forced-migration studies has yet to systemically engage in explaining the complexities of the refugee policy-making process in major refugee-hosting countries in the Global South. This gap in the refugee studies literature exists because it is disproportionately produced by scholars in the Global North.

There are differing contexts of refugee policy-making dynamics and processes in the North and the South. Therefore, there needs to be an adequate comparative framework for understanding what Adamson and Tsourapas (2020) have referred to as "the Migration State," beyond the Global North. This book aims to address this important gap in the literature by presenting an analytical framework and methodology for analyzing refugee policy-making in the Global South. It highlights the political and economic dynamics and power relationships that influence that policy-making. It also draws on a body of literature across the forced migration and policy science disciplines to propose a theoretical framework that examines refugee-policy formulation and implementation from a complex systems perspective.[5] The key argument this book makes is that refugee policies are the result not of a single overriding factor but of a constellation of factors that interact with each other and evolve over time. It presents a typology of host-government behaviour for further testing, an agenda for research, and a set of policy implications for host governments witnessing mass refugee displacement.

KEY QUESTIONS

This study seeks to contribute to our understanding of refugee governance and policy-making by comparing the policy responses of two developing countries of first asylum in the Global South, namely

8   The Politics of Refugee Policy in the Global South

Lebanon and Jordan, to the Syrian refugee crisis. More precisely, in this book I seek to answer three main research questions.

The first question is: How do we come to analyze and understand the way in which governments in the Global South respond to mass refugee movements? As noted previously, this book addresses a gap in scientific literature and introduces a unique longitudinal study to the body of scholarly literature. Notably, while states in the Global South host the majority of refugees, the biggest share of research on refugee affairs still originates from the Global North and does not match both the realities experienced in the developing world and the perceived rise in what Samaddar (2020) terms the "postcolonial age of migration." Moreover, current research on policy-making in response to mass-influx situations tends to neglect relevant indirect causes and their dynamics, such as processes and system-level factors. Therefore, this book proposes a more holistic framework for analyzing responses to mass refugee influxes in the South. It encompasses the nuances of these policy contexts and allows us to explore a wider range of direct and indirect factors as well as their effects on policy outcomes over time.

The second question this book aims to answer is: How have the governments of Lebanon and Jordan responded to the mass influx of Syrian refugees over time, and what has influenced their policy decisions? This is followed by the third question: What explains the variations in policy outputs between them, despite the similarities in the displacement features and their contexts? I will explore this by applying the proposed analytical framework for understanding refugee policy-making in the Global South to the cases of Lebanon's and Jordan's policy responses to Syrian displacement from 2011 to 2022.

KEY ARGUMENT

While a refugee "crisis" narrative has become widespread in certain developed regions of the world, most displaced people who cross international borders tend to remain within their regions and look for international protection in neighbouring countries. Currently, countries of the Global South host the vast majority of the forcibly displaced worldwide. Such countries, which are more prone to becoming countries of first asylum to mass refugee movements, also often face pre-existing socio-economic challenges of their own, and their systems are more likely to become overburdered because they frequently lack the capacity to respond alone to mass refugee movements. Given the structural limitations of the global refugee regime, countries in the Global South also have less influence on the workings of the regime. Despite this, they carry the greatest burden of hosting the world's refugees.

Global South countries are, then, often loci for unique dynamics and realities in refugee protection that are distinct from those experienced in the North. Such realities may encompass poor bureaucratic capacity, inadequate economic and environmental management, and diminished power relations with foreign actors and within the international refugee regime, among others. Religious affiliations and sectarian politics may also play a role in policy-making processes, as will be demonstrated clearly in the Lebanese scenario (in chapters 7 and 8). This leads to distinct protection realities for different groups even within the same migratory movement.

Nonetheless, the field of refugee studies predominantly engages with the question of policy in the context of the industrialized Global North. It is also still dominated by scholars from the North, who tend to engage with forced-migration problems in the South as mere "observers" rather than as insiders. This book advocates for the expansion of studies that engage with policy and governance in the South by scholars from the South. This does not mean that scholars from the North are not capable of making significant contributions to the field but that the analysis of refugee policy needs to be undertaken by scholars who are closest to the context and who are less likely to analyze the issues using an outsiders' perspective. Scholars from the South are also more prone to having their findings and recommendations accepted by practitioners because they are considered to have a better grasp on the complexities and nuances of policy environments in their regions. This study contributes to overcoming the current imbalance in knowledge production, through presenting cases of displacement in the South and through amplifying the voices of scholars in such local displacement contexts, including the author's voice. Special attention was given to this by conducting interviews, and having case chapter consultations, with other regional scholars from Syria, Lebanon, and Jordan. This book also relies heavily on the works of regional scholars and those from the Global South whenever appropriate (cf. Arar and Fitzgerald 2022; Betts, Memişoğlu, and Ali 2021; Fakhoury 2020, 2021; El-Hariri 2020; Beaujouan and Rasheed 2019; El-Chemali 2019; Yassen 2019; Geha and Talhouk 2019; Janmyr and Mourad 2018).

In addition to calling for a quantitative expansion of studies conducted on questions of refugee policy and governance, particularly in the Global South, this work argues for a qualitative change in how policy research should be conducted in contexts of mass displacement in the South. Rather than adopting reductionist notions of asylum, it calls for refugee studies to adopt "complexity" as a conceptual tool. Among the different analytical models, complex systems thinking is capable of refining our ability to understand and analyze refugee policy-making, specifically in cases of humanitarian emergencies or crises, because developments tend to be rapid, volatile, complex, and hard to predict. It is also useful to apply complex systems thinking to contexts characterized by more informal policy processes. Non-signatory countries of the South are a specific case in point.

Complex systems thinking enables a more nuanced and holistic understanding of refugee policy-making by allowing researchers to move beyond direct causal analysis to an exploration of systemic factors and processes that shape policies. This approach also allows for a dynamic rather than a static perspective by accounting for changes in contexts and/or policies over time as the situation and responses evolve. By situating host policy responses to mass refugee movements within the context of their larger complex systems, this book expands upon existing studies that take an exclusively sociological, anthropological, or bottom-up perspective (cf. Arar and Fitzgerald 2022; Tobin, Momani, and Al-Yakoub 2022; Göransson, Hultin, and Mähring 2020). It also addresses those studies that reduce policy output to one or two factors in isolation (cf. Betts, Memişoğlu, and Ali 2021; Aras and Mencütek 2015). It provides a tool kit and research manual for the future generation of forced-migration and refugee-policy scholars who are interested in understanding refugee-policy processes in refugee-hosting states across the Global South. This book does so by applying and testing the use of complexity to the case of Syrian displacement in Lebanon and Jordan.

WHY SYRIAN DISPLACEMENT IN LEBANON AND JORDAN

While global forced displacement is on the rise, and contemporary history provides us with various cases of mass displacement, I chose Syrian displacement as an empirical demonstration for three key reasons: its scale and intensity, its contribution to the literature, and its instrumental nature.

Regarding the first of these, *scale and intensity*, recent UNHCR (2022c) figures indicate that, in 2021, 69 per cent of all refugees worldwide came from five countries, the largest being the Syrian Arab Republic (6.8 million). By utilizing the standard measurement in refugee studies, which is the proportion of refugees compared to the local population, the report showed that in 2021 Lebanon ranked second worldwide in hosting the largest number of refugees in relation to its national population (one in eight inhabitants being a refugee), followed by Curaçao (one in ten), Jordan (one in fourteen), and Turkey (one in twenty-three) (UNHCR 2022c).[6] In terms of absolute numbers, Turkey was the largest refugee-hosting country worldwide (3.8 million), followed by Colombia (1.8 million), Uganda and Pakistan (1.5 million each), and Germany (1.3 million) (UNHCR 2022c). The Syrian refugee crisis is considered to be one of the largest refugee movements since the flight of around fifteen million East Bengalis from Bangladesh in 1971 (*The Economist* 2015). Therefore, it is imperative to examine the governance of such a widespread movement of forced migrants and to infer lessons for the field of refugee studies, and specifically for the study of refugee policy.

To do so, I move to the second key reason, *contribution to the literature*. An extensive literature has emerged over the past few years covering this specific refugee movement. However, it tends to be dominated primarily by grey literature rather than by scientific studies. That literature is, for the most part, largely descriptive, does not have an analytical or scientific character, and is often produced by NGOs, think tanks, and other non-scholarly sources. In a dissection of the scholarly literature that has emerged on the Syrian refugee movement in recent years, it is evident that most of it is primarily concerned with investigating bottom-up perspectives related to refugee- and host-community livelihoods, coping mechanisms, and others (cf. Hultin et al. 2022; Tobin, Momani, and Al-Yakoub 2022; Göransson, Hultin, and Mähring 2020).

Furthermore, while the past few years have seen an increase in literature investigating refugee reception in the South and paying particular attention to Syrian displacement in various countries of the Middle East, such scholarship is mostly dominated by single case studies (cf. Mencütek 2022; Kikano, Fauveaud, and Lizarralde 2021; Mccarthy 2021; Belanger and Saracoglu 2020; N.S. Singh et al. 2020; Geha and Talhouk 2019; Akgündüz, Van den Berg, and Hassink 2015). Studies of a comparative nature are less prevalent. Although this literature has helped improve our understanding of the dynamics of mass refugee governance, it lacks explanation of the variation in policy outcomes across policy-making contexts and over time –particularly because of its over-reliance on single-case studies. This body of scholarship also tends to concentrate on a specific dependent variable or policy element, such as integration, employment, or education (cf. Fakhoury 2021; Fakhoury and Ozkul 2019; Janmyr 2018; Morris 2019; Badalič 2019; Memişoğlu and Yavçan 2022; Unutulmaz 2019; Hamadeh 2019). Much of the literature also tends to isolate a specific explanatory variable for study, such as foreign policy, geopolitics, or the role of UNHCR (cf. Abdelaaty 2021a; Tsourapas 2019; El-Hariri 2020; El-Chemali 2019; Mencütek 2022). Therefore, it misses a much-needed perspective that takes into consideration the complexity of policy-making under conditions of deep uncertainty and crisis. What is unique about this book is that it compares two countries and does so in a historical context and with detailed policy analysis, using a framework adapted from the field of public policy. It also provides a detailed account of the political and legal landscapes and pays close attention to both the social and the political relations between Syria and the other countries under examination. The study employs the most up-to-date empirical data on the governance of Syrian displacement, including the impact of COVID-19 on host behaviour, and recent important innovations such as the Jordan Compact.

The third key reason is the *instrumental nature* of the Syrian refugee crisis. The case of Syrian displacement in Lebanon and Jordan provides an opportunity to analyze the refugee policies of two bordering host governments in response to the same refugee crisis (exogenous shock). Both countries have been subject to the same shock at the same time, and combined with their varying contexts, this acts as a "natural experiment." The displacement also mixes emergency and protracted features and includes subgroups within the same refugee population (Syrians fleeing Syria, and Palestinians fleeing Syria).[7] This instrumental nature provides richness to the analysis and the results. Specifically, this book utilizes the case of Syrian displacement in Lebanon and Jordan to advance our understanding of refugee policy-making in Global South settings in several ways. Firstly, it develops our ability to understand and comparatively analyze policy processes and outcomes by applying to the cases of Lebanon and Jordan a framework that adopts the notion of complexity. This lens goes beyond reducing the phenomenon of asylum provision to static or reductionist simplifications. Rather, it incorporates change-and-factor interaction. Secondly, this book provides a template for scholars aiming to study refugee policy-making in other contexts of the Global South, and adds a key comparative and rich empirical study to the body of scholarship.

For the purpose of this book, Lebanon and Jordan also serve as instrumental cases. Not only do they rank second and third, respectively, in hosting the largest number of Syrian refugees, but, following the emergence of the Syrian conflict, they have been among the five countries in the world with the largest number of refugees per capita. They rank second and fourth, respectively, in hosting the largest number of refugees compared to the local population, including non-Syrians. Therefore, Lebanon and Jordan are clearly important to study. Both countries also represent a crucial under-examined subset of countries in the Global South that are non-signatory to the Geneva Convention. Hence, they are not bound by the set of "hard laws" of refugee protection that are enshrined in the Geneva Convention and its Protocol. Scholars should, then, distinguish these countries from the remainder. We should also expand our studies of them if we are to advance refugee protection in such unique contexts.

Lebanon and Jordan were also specifically chosen as cases for this book because they allow the exploration of policy variation across space and time, while having a comparable nature from a research perspective. These states are similar in terms of being countries of first entry for Syrian refugees and having shared borders with Syria. They also have witnessed the same refugee influx at the same time and share the same regional context of the "Arab Spring." However, despite the similar experience, policy outcomes in these countries are dissimilar and have changed over time. My analysis attempts to link differences in the policy responses to the systemic factors and processes related to Lebanon's and Jordan's distinct arrangements and conjectures. This involves, *inter alia*, their political regime types; geopolitical positions in the Middle East and North Africa (MENA); involvement in and stance on the Syrian conflict; relations with the Syrian regime; and relationship with the international donor community and humanitarian agencies operating in their territories. While leading humanitarian agencies appear to have a significant role in assisting Syrians in these countries, the relationship of the latter with these organizations is characterized by several nuances, leading to complex dynamics and differences in refugee assistance and protection.

Comparative cases from the MENA region can be advantageous in explaining variation, as researchers can hold some variables constant and concentrate on others that may be linked to variation in their refugee responses (Mencütek 2020). In this sense, Lebanon's and Jordan's responses to Syrian displacement were specifically chosen for this book owing to their comparable nature from a research perspective. In particular, the research design of a most- similar comparative case study approach, which will be explicated further in the section "A Guide to Methods and Research Design." Table 1.1 presents some select background facts of the host countries under examination.

Lebanon and Jordan are also countries of interest because they have become loci for innovations in refugee assistance, including through special compacts negotiated with donor states in recent years. Nonetheless, despite great enthusiasm on the part of the international community, these agreements have had questionable impact in both countries over time. It is, therefore, pertinent to understand how the refugee policies in these host countries were constructed and to reflect on their policy successes and failures. This comes at a significant time, when Syrian displacement is entering its thirteenth year. The practical implications that can be inferred from this monumental event are key to effective governance of future refugee movements. They also solidify our call to bridge theory with practice and go beyond analysis of the norm of refugee protection to engage with actual practice.

Furthermore, in examining the governance of Syrian refugees in Lebanon and Jordan, I perform a key task of bridging the current gap between two important fields – forced migration studies and

Table 1.1 | Select host-country background facts

	Lebanon	Jordan
Proportion of refugees to population (including non-Syrians)	142 per 1,000 inhabitants	67 per 1,000 inhabitants
Ethnic composition	Arab (95.0%); Other (5.0% including Armenian)	Arab (97.4%); Other (2.6% including Armenian and Circassian)
Religion	Muslim (63.1% [31.9% Sunni, 31.2% Shiite]); Christian (32.4%, majority Maronite); Other (4.5% including Druze)	Muslim (97.1%, predominantly Sunni); Christian (2.1%); Other (0.8%)
Political regime	Parliamentary republic; partly free	Parliamentary constitutional monarchy; partly free
Economic and human development performance	Lower middle-income country with high human development	Upper middle-income country with high human development
Party to 1951 Geneva Convention	No	No
Has an MOU with UNHCR	Yes	Yes
History of refugee hosting and/or refugee outflows	Yes	Yes

Sources: Compiled from Bidinger et al. (2014); CIA (2022a, 2022b); UNDP (2022); UNHCR (2020i); World Bank (2022a, 2022b); Freedom House (2022a).

public policy – and their connection is a necessary intervention that is currently lacking (El-Taliawi, Nair, and Van der Wal 2021). Thus, through its comparative engagement with the question of Syrian refugee governance, and its utilization of a complexity approach, this book makes a significant interdisciplinary and empirical contribution to scholarship. In addition, the longitudinal nature of the cases in this study – covering an eleven-year period between 2011 and

2022 – is unique and has allowed for more robust examination of the politics of variation across time. This book not only analyzes the initial period of the displacement of Syrians but also sheds light on changes that have occurred along the way, including effects of the COVID-19 pandemic, something that has yet to be properly encompassed by scholarship.

While Turkey and Iraq also share borders with Syria, their exclusion from this book is mainly motivated by the most-similar comparative approach. This is particularly the case for Turkey, despite its inclusion in other studies, sometimes along with Lebanon and Jordan (Badalič 2019; Içduygu and Nimer 2020; Mencütek 2018; Tsourapas 2019). The comparison between Lebanon and Jordan allows for a focus on important variables of interest, including the Arab Spring dynamics, previous Palestinian refugee-hosting experiences, geographic size and resources, and power relations vis-à-vis Europe and UNHCR. In contrast, most of these variables are different in the Turkish context. Moreover, while the Turkish case is relevant for research on forced migration, the country's position in the global architecture of power, its public-service-provision capacities, its degree of institutionalization of international refugee norms, and its reliance on international humanitarian aid are all significantly different from those of Lebanon and Jordan (Mencütek 2020). As such, Jordan and Lebanon are most comparable from a research methods and design perspective. By focusing on these two countries only, this study outruns the risk of conflating distinct contexts and provides an in-depth study. A further exclusion criterion involved selecting countries where I am a native speaker. This is relevant because I rely on field observations – a valuable source of primary insight. As an Arabic-speaking scholar, I had the advantage of conducting interviews in the native language without reliance on a translator, which significantly enhances the validity of results.

In addition to having some of the same dissonances as the Turkish case, Iraq had data-collection difficulties that made its inclusion in the research unfeasible. The book does not, however, discount the importance or relevance of Turkey and Iraq as host countries and does reflect on them in the concluding chapter. Although Israel also shares borders with Syria, it did not host mass Syrian refugees, and hence it was excluded from the study. Finally, while the addition of more cases is often desirable, a large number of cases may compromise the in-depth nature and quality of analysis. By providing a two-case study, this book was able to maintain the significant longitudinal time frame (2011–22) and to base the findings on several rounds of fieldwork (in 2017 and 2021).

The Syrian case also provides an opportunity to amplify the voices of female and regional scholars. My role as a researcher from the region was beneficial in allowing me to engage with the case as an insider rather than as a mere observer. This is especially relevant to the uniqueness of this book because in general the majority of research on refugee affairs originates in the Global North (El-Taliawi, Leomil, and Milner 2021; Neang, McNally, and Rahim 2022), which limits the ability of those researchers from outside the region to grasp the nuance of policy contexts in the South, and the ability of their findings and recommendations to be viewed as more localized and acceptable by actors in the Global South.

WHY DO WE NEED THIS BOOK?

Mass refugee situations are mostly the problem of the developing countries of the Global South. Despite this, the set-up of the global refugee regime, and the disparities between the North and South, allow countries in the North to have more influence on the regime, although they are the remotest from the problem. The first step to correcting this imbalance may lie in our understanding and recognition of the changing context of global forced displacement, the specificity of refugee governance and policy-making in the South, and the prevalence of variation in policy approaches even within the same region. Advancing our understanding of these issues can happen through incorporating complexity and bridging the gap in knowledge production on refugee issues between the North and South.

This book contributes to the field of refugee studies by laying the foundation for future scholarship on refugee policy-making in the context of the Global South. In this way it provides a point of reference for scholars and links the fields of refugee studies and public policy. Although much work has been done on refugee and asylum policies in the context of industrialized countries as countries of resettlement (Bashford and McAdam 2014; Andrew and Lukajo 2005; Alink, Boin, and T'Hart 2001), less attention has been given in the literature to countries in the Global South, which tend to witness the majority of mass refugee movements. Hence, this book also plays a role in challenging the dominant Western-centric character of comparative refugee studies (Mencütek 2020) and advances the current literature on refugee policy in the Global South and on global refugee policy generally (Milner 2014). It also makes the case for the need to distinguish between the context of the Global South and that of the Global North in analyzing refugee policy responses. In addition, it advances the current knowledge production by scholars from the South on refugee policy issues in the South.

The importance of differentiating between the North and the South with regard to refugee-regime dynamics has already been noted in the scholarly literature, and studies highlighting the unique factors at play in these countries are now abundant (FitzGerald and Arar 2018; Freier, Micinski, and Tsourapas 2021; Harrell-Bond 2008). Nevertheless, we still have not had work that problematizes the Global South as a unit of analysis. This book argues that such a category is useful and important, and it offers a foundation and a method for thinking about host states in the Global South. Importantly, it is a method that does not homogenize them. This book also makes an existential shift within the literature away from painting states in the Global South as pathological subjects. In this way, it aims to lay a solid and robust foundation for a manner of thinking about host states that can be replicated in other cases.

Furthermore, while the field of forced migration and refugee studies has traditionally drawn upon various disciplines, it has rarely made use of public policy frameworks and tools to inform its analysis. In a recent analysis of journal articles engaging with refugee-policy issues published between 2011 and 2020, it was found that the vast majority of publications (91.2 per cent) did not employ any specific analytical or theoretical framework in their analyses. The minority that did so, tended to employ frameworks originally linked to the disciplinary field of public policy (El-Taliawi, Leomil, and Milner 2021). In its use of complex systems thinking for the analysis of refugee policy-making processes, my study provides an important example of analytically sound scholarship that engages with refugee policy and governance. It lays the foundation for the distinct study of refugee policy as a subfield of forced migration and refugee studies.

This book is also needed to advance our understanding of the complexity of policy-making in response to mass refugee movements. If the refugee studies literature has long recognized important drivers and factors influencing public policies in the context of mass refugee influxes, these tend to be linked in terms of their direct causality, and less attention is paid to processes and indirect factors at the systemic level. Government responses to refugee movements are influenced by increasingly complex and interdependent causes, which may not be directedly related to the refugee movement. Moreover, responses to mass refugee movements tend to be marked by rapid fluidity as highly dynamic situations evolve. Therefore, it is important to realize the complexity at play while analyzing national policy responses to refugee movements, and avoid presenting overly simplistic and static notions of asylum. Complex systems thinking is a conceptual tool that enables a more nuanced and holistic understanding of refugee policy-making, allowing researchers to move beyond analysis of direct causality to explore the processes and systemic factors driving responses. Furthermore, complex systems thinking provides a more adequate approach for understanding change than many other analytical angles. Finally, policy-making that occurs in emergency settings tends to differ from policy-making that occurs in non-emergency times (El-Taliawi and Hartley 2021).

Therefore, when attempting to understand policy processes that occur during humanitarian emergency situations, it makes sense to use an approach that takes such complexity into consideration. Additionally, a complexity approach allows us to account for interactions between the global and the domestic policy spheres, specifically with regards to refugee policy. Over the past few years the field of public policy has begun to utilize tools to transcend "the domestic-international cleft" prevalent in the disciplines of international relations and comparative politics and that allow us to theorize the interplay and intersections of both the domestic and the global sources of influence on policy (Stone and Moloney 2019). In this way, the book proposes a new analytical framework based on complex systems thinking and encourages its use by a new generation of scholars seeking to understand and explain the refugee policy-making process in refugee-hosting states across the Global South. It also provides a research manual for scholars and researchers by outlining in detail the research design, data collection, and analytical techniques used.

This study also contributes to the literature through knowledge accumulation by adding to the body of literature the most up-to-date and comprehensive empirical examination of policy responses in Lebanon and Jordan to one of the twenty-first century's largest refugee movements, namely the Syrian refugee movement. It is especially relevant in its discussion of cases in the Middle East, since almost 40 per cent of the world's forcibly displaced peoples emanate from the region (Yahya and Muasher 2018). Although countries in the Middle East are at the crossroads of recurrent refugee movements, many states in the region have been adamant about not joining the Refugee Convention (aka the Geneva Convention). Paradoxically, and mainly due to reduced capacity, these countries request assistance from the international refugee regime to be able to meet the needs of refugees and their own local communities. Thus, they themselves are members of such a regime, albeit in an exclusionary manner. Therefore, it is important to understand how and why refugee policies are formulated in such contexts and what mechanisms are utilized by global refugee-policy actors to navigate this complex policy terrain.

In addition, given the state of the global refugee regime and the many constraints on protection for the world's refugees, this book has significant practical implications. As Musarat-Akram (1999, 216) argues, "the expectations, enshrined in the 1951 Refugee Convention, that the burden of the world's refugee flows would be shared and that there will be a universal humanitarian response to the plight of forcibly displaced persons, have been replaced with the reality that the refugee burden is being borne overwhelmingly by those least able to cope with it." This broken system is leading to increased incidences of illegal migration and boat crises, as countries are closing their borders and imposing restrictive policies. Thus, understanding how global refugee policies are negotiated and implemented can help bridge the current divide between normative expectations and actual practice. Additionally, understanding such dynamics can help inform our understanding of how to reduce the negative human consequences of displacement and how to raise refugees' protection standards (Betts and Loescher 2011). In my concluding chapter I reflect on lessons learned for practice, while highlighting the need to respect contextual specificity. I also reflect on what Ukraine's refugee movement can tell us about the workings of the global refugee regime, in contrast to Syrian displacement.

A GUIDE TO METHODS AND RESEARCH DESIGN

My study adopts a methodological approach that is meant to refine our theoretical understanding of refugee policy-making in the context of mass refugee displacement, specifically as applied to countries of the Global South. It relies on a comparative qualitative case study approach, which allows for the description and analysis of contemporary events over which the researcher has no control, and it also allows for *context* to be taken into consideration. As a method, the use of case studies is especially relevant when the boundaries are not clear between the phenomenon in question and the context in which it takes place (Van Evera 1997). Case studies allow us to answer "how" and "why" questions (Yin 2009; Gerring 2006); they provide the researcher with high conceptual validity, generate new hypotheses and potentially overlooked variables, and address causal complexity (George and Bennett 2005).

Specifically, this book applies a most similar, most different comparative method, which chooses systems that are as similar as possible with regard to the research phenomenon of interest (Anckar 2020; Geddes 1990).[8] While a most different, most similar method is appropriate for studying systems that generate similar or identical outcomes, a most similar, most different comparative design is more suitable for explaining cases of variance among similar systems. Since this book is concerned with understanding policies and variations among them, it adopts a most-similar design. However, it is important to note that most similar, most different does not mean completely similar and completely different, but as similar and as different as possible (i.e., Lebanon and Jordan were chosen for their most different policy outcomes with regard to Syrian displacement, and most similar refugee-policy contexts). This means neither that their outcomes completely vary nor that their contexts are completely similar. It means that for the purpose of this study I pay special attention to isolating the similar factors to uncover those that may be behind the puzzling variation. In the coming chapters I discuss the relevant variables of similarity and difference in more detail.

My research relied on the collection of primary and secondary qualitative data. For the primary data, in-depth elite interviews were conducted in Beirut (Lebanon) and Amman (Jordan) in 2017 and 2021 – prior to and during the COVID-19 pandemic. Although the pandemic outbreak was unexpected and disruptive, it helped shed light on the impact of such a public health crisis on the Syrian refugee policies of both countries. To conduct the interviews, I developed a question guide tailored to three sets of respondent groups: (1) government officials, policy-makers, and political actors; (2) representatives of international, intergovernmental, and non-governmental organizations; and (3) informed observers. The semi-structured nature of the interviews was specifically designed to allow respondents to recount their experiences and opinions, while allowing the researcher not to lose sight of the overall focus of the interview.

With regard to sampling and respondent recruitment, I adopted convenience sampling, followed by snowballing. Non-probability convenience sampling was considered to be the best method for the purposes of this study because it includes drawing a sample of the key players who had the most involvement with the events and processes being studied (Tansey 2009). In other words, the quality of an interview, and the insight it could provide into the policy process, were deemed more important than the quantity of respondents recruited. The initial list of respondents was created based on secondary sources. Respondents were contacted by telephone or email. Interviews were conducted in government buildings, field offices, and/or other public spaces depending on the interviewee's preference. In 2017 nineteen in-depth elite interviews (W. Harvey 2011) were conducted in Lebanon, and twenty-two interviews were conducted in Jordan. Furthermore, eighteen follow-up interviews were conducted in 2021 in Lebanon, Jordan, and Syria. Interviewing continued until a point of data saturation was reached or respondents were unreachable.

The range of actors interviewed were diversified both vertically and horizontally. This involved including the main organizations in charge of refugee affairs; executive and legislative branches of government; central and local levels of government; different tiers of organizational positions (leadership, managerial, and administrative); current as well as past government cabinets that existed during the period of examination (2011–22); international, intergovernmental, and non-governmental organizations; and international and local informed observers.[9] This diversification served the purpose of triangulating (i.e., validating) the insights provided by respondents. Furthermore, whenever separate agencies existed for Syrian Refugees from Syria (SRS) and Palestinian Refugees from Syria (PRS), they were both interviewed. A full list of the respondents interviewed, including their organizational affiliations, was kept on file, with names excluded for confidentiality purposes.

Interviews were conducted in either English or Arabic, depending on the interviewee's preference. My command of both languages minimized any potential confusion in the relaying of concepts. I also relied on my own observations in the field, as well as on the use of secondary sources, to supplement and validate interview data. Such secondary sources included over three hundred government documents and speeches, international NGO reports. United Nations (UN) policy documents, scholarly articles, books, and newspapers. This methodology and analytical technique may be replicated in other studies aiming to investigate the same set of questions.

The following analytical techniques were used to analyze the data in this study: event process tracing (Bennett and Checkel 2014) and chronologies (Yin 2009). Event process tracing was specifically chosen as an analytical technique to allow for backtracking (i.e., tracing in retrospect the process by which the policy decisions came about). This helped in determining the mechanism by which key factors may have, directly or indirectly, influenced governments' policies. Process tracing is especially relevant as an analytical technique for examining complexity, which is the chosen approach for this book, because it allows for the investigation of intervening variables (George and Bennett 2005).

The chronologies technique was useful in tracing the major junctures and policy changes over the course of the crisis. It is a technique often used in case studies to allow the researcher to trace events over time using specific time markers. During data coding, facts mentioned by respondents were coded according to the following nodes: event, decision, and action, followed by date mentioned and actors involved. Additional nodes used during the analysis are explicated further in the case chapters. All facts were further checked through data and source triangulation, which will be discussed shortly.[10]

While conducting research of any kind, it is important to maintain the reliability and integrity of the process so that the conclusions are robust and replicable. Moreover, similar to other research approaches, case studies present us with some drawbacks, which need to be adequately addressed and minimized. Case studies are particularly vulnerable to validity threats due to the sheer volume of data that needs to be managed, organized, and analyzed systematically (Heale and Twycross 2018; Yin 2009). Case studies that did not devote adequate attention to designing robust data collection and analysis methods have had their validity and reliability called into question (Meyer 2008; Yin 2009).

Thus, to reduce potential threats to the validity and reliability of this research study, a series of measures were undertaken. Firstly, respondent validation of interview drafts was obtained, whenever possible, to ensure that subjects' self-reported views were not misinterpreted. Secondly, I relied on standardized explanations of key terms, which were prepared beforehand, to facilitate understanding during interviews and to minimize ambiguity in the use of terminology (Yin 2009). Thirdly, the transcribing of interviews took place on the same day as the interview, whenever possible, to shorten the recall period.[11] To raise the study's reliability and replicability, the following techniques were adopted: (1) documentation of all steps in a research journal; (2) creation of a database, divided into both primary and secondary data; and (3) reliance on semi-structured interviews. Such techniques were used to minimize errors and biases and to ensure that the same case study could be replicated, with the researcher arriving at the same results (Yin 2009).

To overcome the possibility that convenience and snowball sampling might result in the exclusion of some relevant actors, an initial map of the main actors in charge of refugee affairs in both countries was created by relying on secondary sources. This map was continuously updated as more interviews were conducted, by asking respondents to recommend further relevant actors. This was done to ensure that representatives of the key actors were included in subject recruitment. It was especially important because ensuring representation of the key policy actors was prioritized over the number of respondents interviewed, as mentioned earlier. During data collection and analysis I continuously searched for negative cases and discrepant evidence to test rival or competing explanations and to establish a chain of evidence (Yin 2009, 2014). Furthermore, to give a more balanced and accurate picture of the situation, the data was continuously cross-checked using multiple sources of evidence, including NGO reports and news sources, and through interviews of independent informed observers.

PROBLEMATIZING KEY TERMS AND CONCEPTS

It is paramount before moving further to note that while a mass displacement situation may be referred to in the context of this book as a "crisis" or an "emergency" situation, this is not meant to pathologize or sensationalize refugee movements. On the contrary, refugee movements may bring about positive effects if policies are designed to effectively harness their potential. However, researchers need not shy away from stating the reality that in countries with limited governance and administrative capacity (El-Taliawi and Van der Wal 2019) the mass arrival of any population, with the sudden and unplanned increase in population size, poses significant humanitarian and policy challenges that may be construed in this sense as an emergency crisis situation. Therefore, it is important that such key terms be understood from that perspective.

It is also important to note that the "developed versus developing country" dichotomy and categorization have important political and historical connotations and biases and are subject to great debate. For instance, during the Cold War the term *Third World* was originally intended to refer to a bloc of countries that did not align themselves during the West-East conflict (Kloß 2017) – that is, of the first and second worlds – but it was quickly conflated with another connotation that focused on their structural weaknesses and impoverishment (Tomlinson 2003). Later, building on the globalization and development paradigms, representations of the world as divided between "developed" and "developing" countries became dominant. Arguably, however, this approach was mainly invoked and set forth by the most rich and powerful nations. Hence, it has been criticized for being overly prescriptive and providing justification for interventions in the poorer parts of the world (Kothari 2005). Thus, whenever applied in this book, the term *developing country* is used to refer to a state of economic development, which is important to account for economic performance and resources.

Furthermore, as the Global South is the main locus of attention in this book, it is relevant to reflect on the use of this concept and terminology. Although the term *Global South* is now often used broadly in reference to less developed regions of Latin America, Asia, Africa, and Oceania (Dados and Connell 2012), the concept emerged with the objective of moving beyond the developmentalist discourses of the past, with their simplistic notions of impoverishment and biases (Kloß 2017; Lopez 2007). That is, the concept recognizes the clear structural differences between the North and the South. It is more critical and marks a shift towards emphasis on geopolitical relations of power caused by unequal global power relations, imperialism, and neo-colonialism (Dados and Connell 2012; Kloß 2017). Albeit more nuanced, the concept of the Global South still shares some of the same limitations of other terminologies and may often oversimplify the complex entanglements and uneven developments in the real world (Kaltmeier 2015). Moreover, while the terminology encompasses countries such as Brazil and India that usually fall within the group of "middle powers" (Alden and Vieira 2005), it also encompasses less powerful countries that have a distinguished set of capabilities, such as Kenya, Tanzania, and Uganda (Chorev 2023). Nonetheless, in the context of this book the Global South concept provides an adequate lens to understand shared historical processes of economic development and performance, colonial legacies, and postcolonial liberation struggles and state building, as well as global power relations, which are relevant to explain the governance of forced migration outside the North.

Although this book focuses mainly on the legal and political facets of refugee status, the social aspects are also relevant for policy and research. In particular, it is important for us to remain critical about homogenizing meanings and values that are frequently attached to those who are forcibly displaced. The contemporary "refugee" label often does not reflect the heterogeneity and complexities of the individual to whom it is attached. Therefore, it fails to provide nuance to the diverse historical, social, political, and cultural contexts that drive displacement and shape individual experiences (Malkki 1995). In fact, rather than adequately representing refugees, this label often reflects the interests and operational procedures of states and humanitarian actors involved in the governance of the international refugee regime (Zetter 2014). As such, although continually reshaped as a result of changes in state and humanitarian discourses (Vigil and Abidi 2018), this label tells us very little about refugee identities, which are replaced with categorical prescriptions of assumed needs (Zetter 1991). As a result, through this labelling process and the formation of a clear-cut refugee category, refugees are often treated as "blank pages," as if they had no education, no occupation, or no life before becoming refugees (Hajdukowski-Ahmed, Khanlou, and Moussa 2008). Admittedly, the discipline of forced migration studies has had a certain role to play in this process because in many works, refugee identities have been constituted through neutral, humanitarian, and apolitical discourses (Malkki 1992). In this process of objectification some see refugees as powerless victims without agency and voice, while others see them as threats. This is particularly the case in domestic contexts in which refugees are framed as job stealers or terrorists, for example (Vigil

Rising Forced Displacement

and Abidi 2018). Naturally this guides not only the way in which they are perceived by society but also the character and effectiveness of policies directed towards them.

Consequently it is important to realize the relevance of refugee identities, which interact with one another and often contradict previously established labels (Vigil and Abidi 2018). In the same vein, it should be recognized that refugees' multiple identities are fluid and context dependent and intersect with one another. The idea of intersectionality was first elaborated by Kimberlé Crenshaw in 1989 to challenge homogenizing and essentializing (initially women's) experiences and identities (Taha 2019). According to this view, identities (seen as fluid and context dependent) intersect due to their mutual influence on one another, generating different combinations and experiences of privilege and/or oppression across contexts and over time (Aberman 2013; Petersen 2016; Vervliet et al. 2013). That is, the interaction between several social categories can alter refugees' experiences (Vervliet et al. 2013). The approach that this book endorses highlights that refugees are an extremely diverse group, and refugee experiences are shaped by multiple identities such as (but not limited to) gender, race, national origin, class, age, disability, and sexual orientation (Taha 2019).

Finally, terms such as *mass influx* have been repeatedly used in the media and politicized in order to sensationalize refugee movements and to cast them in a threatening light. It is important to note that the use of such terms in this book is for purely technical reasons. A *mass refugee influx situation* is a term that is used, and defined by UNHCR policy documents, to guide the practice of refugee protection in conditions that fall outside of the Geneva Convention, and my use is to be understood in this sense, for scientific purposes only.

ROAD MAP OF CONTENTS

The remainder of this book is divided into nine chapters. Chapter 2 reviews the literature and outlines the study's key analytical framework. It performs two essential tasks. Firstly, it provides an overview and critical assessment of the state-of-the-art scholarship and debates surrounding how and why host governments formulate refugee policies, particularly in the case of mass displacement. Through an in-depth review of host policy responses, it discusses what scholars have said, and how they have engaged with this debate, as well as the potential drivers that shape the responses in theory and practice. While this chapter, and the book at large, is guided by the established formal and informal norms of refugee protection, it pays close attention to actual practices by host governments, which may often deviate from such norms (Landau and Amit 2014). In this sense it works to bridge the gap between the theory and norm of refugee protection and its actual implementation by host governments. Secondly, the chapter presents the book's analytical framework for the study of refugee policy-making in the Global South based on a complex systems approach. This chapter and its analytical framework are presented in such a way that they encourage replication by scholars seeking to understand and explain the refugee policy-making process in refugee-hosting countries of the South. Therefore, chapter 2 answers the book's first research question: How do we come to analyze and understand the way in which governments in the Global South respond to mass refugee movements?

Chapter 3 begins the process of applying the book's analytical framework to the study of Syrian displacement and refugee policy-making in neighbouring host states. This section first presents an overview of the origins of the Syrian civil war and its ensuing humanitarian disaster. It discusses the triggers of the war, and its chronological developments, situating the displacement in its geopolitical context. The chapter then details the humanitarian consequences of the conflict, including the makeup of the refugee movement and its characteristics, origins, and destinations. The chapter finally discusses the regional and international implications of the displacement and provides a synopsis of key regional and international community responses.

Chapter 4 transitions the reader from the "home" context, in this case Syria, to the "hosts" by providing an essential overview of Lebanon's and Jordan's refugee policy-making contexts. This chapter sets the stage for the reader by giving an important contextual background to the cases under study. Each country's policy-making context is unique in some ways and similar in others. The chapter discusses each of their contexts, including the demographic, socio-economic, and political terrain as well as the laws governing refugees. Thus, I provide a glimpse at the setting that preceded Syrian displacement to Lebanon and Jordan. I consider how the refugee policy-making contexts of each country appeared prior to the event in which we are interested. The variables discussed are derived mainly from the analytical framework and are chosen as potential factors of relevance to refugee policy-making processes in Lebanon and Jordan (i.e., factors that may influence each host government's refugee-policy decisions, specifically with regard to Syrian refugees).

Subsequently, chapters 5 to 8 apply the book's analytical framework to the cases under examination by discussing Jordan's and Lebanon's policy responses to the Syrian refugee movement. These key chapters are the empirical heart of the book. They answer the second research question: How have the governments of Lebanon and Jordan responded to the mass influx of Syrian refugees over time, and what has influenced their policy decisions? Each country case is divided into two chapters. The first chapter of each case provides a chronological descriptive account of the events of the displacement as they unfolded on the ground; the second chapter analyzes in depth each host government's policy response and the main drivers that shaped that response.

Chapter 9 then zooms out and compares the policy responses of Lebanon and Jordan across spatial geographies and over time from a holistic and dynamic perspective. To do so, it looks at the elements of convergence and divergence in both countries' policy approaches to Syrian refugees, using the book's analytical framework and approach. Therefore, this chapter contributes to answering the third research question: What explains the variations in policy outputs between Lebanon and Jordan, despite the similarities in the displacement features and their contexts?

Chapter 10 concludes by deriving theoretical and conceptual implications for the broader field of forced migration and refugee studies. This is particularly relevant for the study of refugee policy and presents a typology of host government behaviour. The chapter also reflects on the broader implications, derived from the cases of Lebanon and Jordan, for the practice of refugee governance by outlining key implications for effective governance of forced migration movements. It concludes with a discussion of the usefulness of applying the book's framework to other refugee-hosting cases across the Global South, and giving directions for future research.

2

A Complexity Approach to
Analyzing Variation in Refugee Policy
in the Global South

INTRODUCTION

Mass displacement is a multidimensional and complex phenomenon that has been studied widely since the creation of the field of refugee studies in the 1980s. Studies on mass displacement have been produced by various disciplines including sociology, anthropology, geography, political science, social policy, and social work. The understanding of mass displacement itself has evolved considerably to include causes other than armed conflict, such as environmental and development–induced displacement. In addition, displacement has come to be understood as manifestations of other than refugees and asylum seekers who cross international borders, including internally displaced people and diasporas.[1] Albert (2010) Scholars define *mass displacement*, also referred to as *mass influx*, as a situation in which a large number of people arrive at or cross an international border suddenly or in a relatively short period of time, thus incapacitating states' ability to conduct individual refugee status determination procedures (Albert 2010; Rutinwa 2002).

Scholarly work on mass displacement in the past decade has largely taken a bottom-up perspective by focusing on issues such as refugee livelihoods, coping mechanisms, and others (Alam, Siddique, and Akhtar 2022; Ruiz, Siegel, and Vargas-Silva. 2015; Baines and Gauvin 2014; Whyte et al. 2012; Fiddian-Qasmiyeh 2011; Rasmussen and Annan 2009). Less scholarly attention has been given to policy and governance issues. The existing scarce policy-centric scholarship has predominantly been in the context of European and Western countries of the Global North (Guild

2006; Kaunert 2009; Bloch and Schuster 2005; Barks 2008; Pirjola 2009). Countries of the South, which tend to be neighbouring or border-sharing countries to the country of conflict origin, have been comparatively under-examined from a policy and governance perspective (Blair, Grossman, and Weinstein 2022). This is problematic because the majority of the world's refugees are hosted in the Global South, and we cannot apply the lessons from the Global North to the Global South without considering the differences in structure and context that condition policy responses in the South. As countries of the Global South tend to be those that witness the massive and sudden flow of people, it is imperative to analyze their policy responses to such a large-scale phenomenon. They are faced with a complex policy problem, both normatively and practically. Furthermore, it is a problem laden with equally complex constraints, including expectations from the international community, citizens, and refugees, with economic, political, and social ramifications.

Additionally, it is important to conduct further studies on the Global South and to distinguish between it and the Global North for four reasons. Firstly, the hosting of massive refugee flows places burdens on a country's political economic system that differ from those of hosting individual resettled refugees. Therefore, it is to be expected that their policy considerations would be different. The Global South presents a dissimilar and distinct context in which to examine refugee-policy responses due to the fact that the majority of the world's refugees tend to originate from states in the Global South and to move en masse across borders into neighbouring states, whereas in the Global North the refugees tend to be individually resettled. Thus, there is a stark difference in the scale and mode of arrival and in the proximity of the receiving state to the country of conflict origin.

Secondly, countries in the Global South tend to be countries that have shared socio-economic, political, and historical specificities that are likely to make the context in which policy-making occurs highly fluid and more informal than that of the Global North. The historical context of the South varies from that of the North especially in terms of the history of borders and the affinities of groups that reside across shared borders (Pešalj et al. 2022). In terms of political dynamics and economic affluence, states in the Global South tend to be less powerful in influencing the international system. Such variations between the North and South contexts are also compounded by the lack of an existing mechanism for binding commitments to international cooperation within the refugee regime. This lack of commitment allows more affluent countries in the North to make contributions to burden sharing based on their discretion, which, in turn, creates significant inequalities within the global refugee regime.

Third, there exist important structural and sociological differences between the two global regions, given that states in the North constructed the global refugee regime to suit their needs and interests in responding to the refugee situation arising from the Second World War and then exported this regime to countries that may approach responses to refugees differently. This approach can take different forms, either by rejecting the 1951 Convention (e.g., in the Middle East and Asia) or by developing their own regional definitions (e.g., in Africa and Latin America). These various conditions create a different environment in which the objectives of the regime can be pursued, and often result in significant variation among states despite the universal claims of the regime. Therefore, there is a need to distinguish between the North and the South and to advance the policy-centric work on refugee policy-making in the Global South.

Fourth, when responding to mass refugee influxes, countries in the Global South tend to be loci for unique dynamics. These manifest as a result of factors such as dependency on humanitarian assistance, reduced state capacity, and limited adherence to international protection standards. This uniqueness calls for a framework that helps us analyze and understand responses in such specific contexts. Furthermore, even though previous literature has advanced our understanding of some of the key factors that influence asylum provision in mass influx situations, including in Global South settings (cf. Adamson and Tsourapas 2020; Milner 2009; Jacobsen 1996), such literature falls shorts of comprehensively explaining variation in responses between such countries across space and over time. Hence, understanding the shared characteristics among Global South countries, while very important, is not enough to predict dynamic policy outcomes. Countries within the same region, as will be seen in the cases presented by this book, may still exhibit variations. This study will fill a significant gap in our understanding of the nuances of refugee policy-making in the South, including variation between countries and over time.

A Complexity Approach to Analyzing Refugee-Policy Variation 33

Furthermore, previous studies have not taken into consideration the dynamic and complex nature of policy-making, especially in emergency and crisis situations. The analytical tool kit adopted in this book utilizes a complexity perspective that approaches asylum provision with an understanding of the existence of interdependence and variable interactions. This is in contrast to a clear-cut linear causal pathway that is often far from reality in such complex, fluid, and volatile crisis settings. The framework provided in this book can be applied to other case studies and used by the incoming generation of scholars who seek to understand and explain with more nuance the refugee policy-making process in refugee-hosting states across the Global South.

In this key chapter I answer the book's first research question: How do we come to analyze and understand the way in which governments in the global South respond to mass refugee movements? I begin with a discussion of policy responses to mass refugee displacement based on the scholarly and policy literature. Scholars wishing to understand the norm and practice of asylum provision can use this key discussion to inform their understanding of the main components of refugee policies in mass influx situations. This discussion is followed by a review of the predominant determinants and drivers that have been argued to influence policy responses in mass influx situations. I will then come to the heart of the chapter, presenting the conceptual framework proposed by this book. The framework will inform the coming chapters, and readers should keep it handy. Finally, a concluding section is presented, including a critique of our current understanding of refugee policy-making in mass influx situations in the Global South generally – and in the case of border-sharing countries, specifically – and ways to move forward.

POLICY RESPONSES TO MASS DISPLACEMENT: BETWEEN NORM AND PRACTICE

The way in which states respond to refugees has largely been approached from a normative and theoretical lens, which ignores the fact that on-the-ground practices tend to deviate from these norms. The argument is based on the grounds that refugee status is a privilege that entitles its holders to a set of rights, including civil, economic, social, and political rights and the right to the resolution of their plight with a sustainable or durable solution (Betts 2010a). Three key arguments tend to dominate the academic debate about the relationship between asylum seekers, refugees, citizens, and states and the way in which states should respond to refugees (Gill 2010). These arguments are put forth by cosmopolitans, particularists, and third-way proponents. Cosmopolitans argue that the state should not accord primacy to the rights of citizens over non-citizens, while particularists hold the contradictory belief that the state's very function is to further the interests of citizens, even at the expense of non-citizens if necessary. Third-way proponents argue that the state should extend asylum only to those in greatest need, to those geographically or culturally proximate, or indiscriminately but only up to the point at which an unacceptably adverse impact upon incumbent nationals' welfare is experienced. However, despite these debates, states do not in fact respond to refugees as is normatively prescribed, and variation in responses has been observed, even within states that share regional dynamics, socio-economic characteristics, political systems, and/or other features (Musarat-Akram 1999; Jacobsen 2014). Therefore, this section of the chapter will go beyond the restricted debate to discuss the norm and practice of asylum provision in response to mass influx situations.

Firstly, I need to clarify what *refugee policy* entails. A public policy is defined as "anything a government chooses to do or not to do" to solve a given problem on its institutional agenda (Dye 1992). Governments' asylum-policy choices can be analyzed in terms of their degree of adherence to international convention norms and prescriptions. A refugee who goes into exile normatively goes through what can be conceived of as a "life cycle." This cycle begins with the receiving of emergency assistance to meet their immediate needs, then the accessing of a set of rights including the right to protection and non-refoulement, and ending with a sustainable solution to their exile (Betts et al. 2017; UNHCR 2001a). Based on this conceptualization of a refugee life cycle, a government's refugee-policy choices can be divided into the following elements: (1) policy on entry and stay; (2) policy on livelihoods; and (3) policy on durable solutions (figure 2.1). In the following section I define and discuss each policy element in more detail, in normative terms and in actual practice.

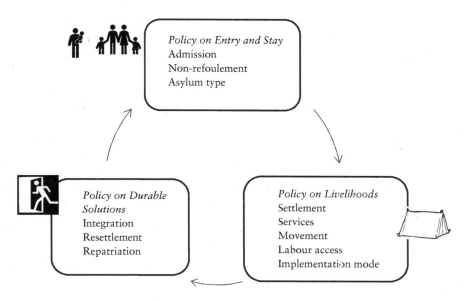

Figure 2.1 | Refugee-policy elements

POLICY ON ENTRY AND STAY

The policy on entry and stay adopted by a government can be analyzed in terms of admission choice, non-refoulement, and type of asylum granted.

In practice, states facing situations of mass influx have one of two options. Either they open their borders to admit those seeking refuge, or they close their borders and turn them away (referred to as refoulement). Normatively, governments are required to admit asylum seekers who are fleeing a well-founded fear of persecution from their country of origin on the basis of race, religion, nationality, membership of a particular social group, or political opinion (UNHCR 1981). States' obligations towards asylum seekers are triggered once they reach their borders to claim asylum (Betts and Loescher 2011). The principle of non-refoulement imposes on states not a duty to recognize refugees but a duty to not return them to countries where

36   The Politics of Refugee Policy in the Global South

they face potential threat (Hansen 2014). This notion is not only enshrined in the 1951 UN Convention on the Status of Refugees and its 1967 Protocol but also considered part of customary international law (UNHCR 2011; Gil-Bazo 2015). Therefore, it applies whether or not a government is party to such treaties.

However, and despite such normative provisions, instances of both border closures and openings have occurred in practice. The post–Cold War era is marked with incidents of border closures as governments have increasingly adopted "containment strategies." These include the creation of "safe zones" along a border to avoid admitting asylum seekers to their territories (Long 2012). Among the examples of border closures are Turkey's response to Kurdish Iraqis in 1991, and Tanzania's policy towards Burundians and Rwandans in 1995. In the former case the Turkish government adopted a closed-border policy in response to the large influx of mostly Kurdish Iraqis fleeing state reprisals in the wake of Iraq's Gulf War defeat (Lyman, in Long 2012). In the case of Tanzania the military chose to close its borders in the face of around forty thousand Burundian and Rwandan refugees fleeing genocide during the Great Lakes refugee crisis (Long 2012). There are also cases of violations of the non-refoulement principle through refugee rejections (Badalič 2019).

According to the provisions of the 1951 Geneva Convention, upon the admission of an asylum seeker to a country's territory, their claim for "refugee" status should be validated by authorities based on individual assessment and status determination (UNHCR 2011). However, in the case of mass influx, where the capacity to undertake individual status determination is limited, governments rely on an "objective inference" that such a group has a well-founded fear of persecution based on the condition that caused their flight from the country of origin, thus individual proof is no longer required (Albert 2010). This is predominant in the Global South because refugees tend to flee en masse across the nearest borders, whereas in the Global North refugees are predominantly resettled on an individual basis.

In this case of a mass refugee influx situation, governments are faced with two alternatives. They can either consider the incoming group as "prima facie refugees" or grant them temporary protection. The difference between the two lies in the type of asylum that is granted to incoming refugees. Prima facie status identifies its holders as refugees, has no predetermined duration, and entitles its holders to local integration and voluntary repatriation. This mechanism has so far been unique to countries of the economic South (Albert 2010). It was previously adopted, for instance, by Kenya in 2000, when it admitted 4,500 Sudanese asylum seekers on a prima facie basis (Kagan 2002). While prima facie is normatively the recommended treatment in the case of mass influx situations (UNHCR 2012b), an alternative mechanism has been practised, which is to grant the inflow temporary protection (also referred to as temporary stay or temporary asylum). In contrast to prima facie status, temporary protection is time constrained, and its holders are only allowed voluntary repatriation when conditions in the home country are deemed safe, or resettlement to a third country, but not local integration. Even though it has a predetermined duration, such as six months or one year, the duration may be renewed at the host government's discretion (UNHCR 2001b). Temporary protection is predominantly used by countries in the North, including Australia, the United States, and Germany (Albert 2010).

POLICY ON LIVELIHOODS

A government's policy choices do not end after the granting of asylum and the admission of refugees. The government needs to make choices regarding the refugee's type of settlement. This includes whether to restrict their movement and employment provisions, and the implementation mode through which their protection and access to services will be governed.

Type of Settlement Allowed

Regarding the type of settlement, scholarly and policy debate has evolved over the years from the classic thinking of housing refugees in camps to allowing them to self-settle in urban areas. Both practices have their respective proponents who advocate for their viability. On the one hand, proponents of encampment, which refers to the policy of confining refugees to designated areas that are set aside for their exclusive use, argue its necessity for two main reasons: (1) it is believed to be more logistically practical to provide large groups of refugees with relief and assistance when they are located in known and accessible locations; and (2) it is easier to secure their own physical safety and that of the host country when they are separated from the local community who may be hostile, and away from the border where they may cause a "spill over" effect of the conflict (Bakewell 2014; UNHCR 2000). Cases of encampment are more common in the South, including Kenya's Dadaab camps, which were created in 2011 in response to the crisis in the Horn of Africa and until 2022 continued to host around 350,000–400,000 Somalis (UNHCR 2015; Deng 2022).

On the other hand, opponents of the encampment model argue that it goes against the 1951 Geneva Convention provisions that point to the right of refugees to choose their place of residence. They argue that such "warehousing" of refugees undermines their human rights by placing them in often overcrowded, controlled areas (M. Smith 2004). It is also argued that it encourages idleness and dependence on aid, thus leading to health and social manifestations, such as domestic and gender-based violence (Crea, Calvo, and Loughry 2015; Aubone and Hernandez 2013). In their study on Syrian refugees in Lebanon and Jordan, Kikano and Lizarralde (2019) found that urban refugees, who were not confined to organized camps, lived in more favourable conditions. However, and despite this debate, housing refugees in camps, rather than allowing them to self-settle in urban areas, remains the more common practice in response to mass influx situations (Bakewell 2014).

Service Provision and Freedom of Movement

The type of settlement allowed may also be related to two other issues, namely freedom of movement and service provision. The 1951 Geneva Convention gives refugees the right to freedom of movement and the right to education, public relief, and assistance (UNHCR 2011). However, governments may choose to impose restrictions on both rights, in which refugees' movements are restricted to a designated camp area, and the provision of services is tied to camp residence. Both practices have occurred, sometimes simultaneously, such as in the case of Uganda's response to its Sudanese refugee population (Hovil 2007; Paul and Kuluthum 2022).

Access to the Labour Market

Another important decision a government has to make regarding the status of refugees is whether or not to allow them lawful employment and access to the labour market. Although in non-influx circumstances refugees should be granted the right to work, according to the provisions of the 1951 Convention, in the case of a mass influx it is left to the discretion of the host government to decide based on its own conditions (UNHCR 2012b). This discretionary clause allows those governments witnessing mass influx situations in the South to predominantly opt out of allowing refugees access to the labour market.

A considerable debate exists on the potential contribution of refugees to a host country's economy. On the one hand, it is often argued that refugees pose a threat to the economy by depressing local wage rates and overcrowding the labour market with low-wage earners. Thus, the provision of refugees with basic services and relief items, while excluding them from formal access to the labour market, is seen as necessary to protect citizens' employment opportunities (Zetter 2012). On the other hand, some scholars have contested this proportionately negative link between refugees and a host country's economy. It has been argued that granting them the right to work actually benefits both refugees and the host community (Milner 2009; Betts et al. 2017). This is based on the notion that allowing refugees to pursue productive lives makes them less dependent on aid and better able to overcome sources of tension and conflict in their host communities (Jacobsen 2002). In investigating the economic effects of the displacement of Syrian workers on the Lebanese economy, A. David et al. (2020) find that negative effects were mostly borne by the most vulnerable Lebanese workers, rather than by the highly skilled native workers. An empirical link between refugees and a host country's economy has not been sufficiently established (Ruiz and Vargas-Silva 2013), as evidenced by this discussion. In practice, governments predominantly prefer to restrict refugees' access to the labour market, such as in the example of the Slovenian government's response to refugees from Bosnia and Herzegovina in 1992 (Vrecer 2010).

MODE OF IMPLEMENTATION

The mode of implementation by which a government chooses to execute its policy is particularly relevant with regard to the bureaucratic structure to which refugee matters will be assigned and whether there will be collaboration with NGOs and IOs. Concerning the bureaucratic structure, a refugee crisis may lead to the creation of a new administrative body to handle the specific refugee population. An example is the case of Lebanon's creation of the Department of

Palestinian Refugee Affairs in 1959 to handle the registration and documentation of Palestinian refugees (Bianchi 2014). Alternatively, an already existing institution may be assigned responsibility for the refugee population, such as Turkey's Disaster and Emergency Management Authority with the mandate to manage the affairs of the Syrian refugee influx, which predated the creation of the Directorate General of Migration Management in 2013 (Içduygu and Aksel 2022). In mass influx situations the decision to allocate responsibility of refugees to a military or civilian state institution reflects the position of the refugee population on the government agenda, as a "high" or "low" policy issue, and it subsequently determines how public officials respond to refugees (Jacobsen 1996).

Another feature of a government's policy design in the face of a refugee crisis situation is its mode of collaboration with IOs and NGOs in the registration, service provision, and protection of refugees. Although collaboration during a crisis makes sense intuitively, varying practices have existed in which governments have taken the lead role in dealing with a refugee influx and restricted the work of international non-governmental organizations (INGOs) and NGOs, such as in the case of Turkey's early response to the Syrian refugee crisis (Bidinger et al. 2014). In other cases, governments either collaborate or "outsource" administrative procedures and/or service and relief provision to UNHCR and other voluntary and aid organizations (Muhammad 2011; Walzer 2008). The unique operational dynamics between UNHCR and host states in the Global South have been well documented. Host states may often defer to UNHCR as a manner of delegating or externalizing responsibility, or simply due to a reduced capacity to respond to the displacement on their own. They may also restrict UNHCR's operations, as a manner of bargaining or due to fears of refugees permanently settling in the host states.

Policy on Durable Solutions

Upon cessation of refugee or temporary protection status, refugees are no longer allowed to reside in their host country. At this point a solution that resolves their situation must be reached. Three conventional "durable solutions" exist, advocated by the international refugee regime: repatriation, local integration, and/or resettlement (Şengül 2022).[2] The type of durable solution allowed by a government may also be directly linked to the type of asylum granted to the refugee population, as previously discussed, or the decision may transpire later as the condition in the home country evolves. The three solutions, however, have spurred considerable debate as to their feasibility.

REPATRIATION

Repatriation refers to the return of refugees to their country of origin upon the cessation of the conflict that induced their flight (McConnachie 2022). It is also often referred to as voluntary repatriation. However, the "voluntary" aspect has been contested. For example, according to Moretti (2015), the 1951 Geneva Convention allows for involuntary or enforced return to take place subject to two issues: (1) there is a fundamental change in the conditions in the country of origin, and (2) the return takes place under conditions of "safety and dignity." Such provisions are said to be in place to ensure that repatriation will not be equated with refoulement (Androff 2022; Hammond 2014).

Over the years, repatriation has become the international community's "ideal" solution to the problem of mass refugee displacement in the South (Chetail 2004; Long 2014). However, this specific durable solution is not without its challenges. Voluntary repatriation is considered the solution where the international community and UNHCR have the "greatest limitations of mandate and influence" (Moretti 2015). Nevertheless, cases of repatriation have previously occurred, such as when 500,000 Burundians were returned to their country of origin in the 2000s after three decades of flight. Some of the largest repatriation efforts took place in the 1990s, which saw the return of hundreds of thousands of refugees to Afghanistan, Mozambique, Cambodia, Eritrea, and Ethiopia (Hammond 2014).

LOCAL INTEGRATION

Local integration refers to the permanent settlement and eventual naturalization of refugees (i.e., receiving citizenship) in the country of first asylum (Hovil and Maple 2022). It combines three elements: (1) a legal process that provides refugees with a range of rights in the host state; (2) an economic process whereby refugees are able to establish sustainable livelihoods; and (3) a social process of acceptance that allows refugees the opportunity to contribute to the social life of the host country without fear of discrimination (Crisp 2004).

The Politics of Refugee Policy in the Global South

While legal citizenship does not necessarily translate into inclusion and belonging, it is nevertheless a necessary step towards it (Hovil 2014). In some cases, refugees may attain all three elements of the local integration process without it necessarily culminating in naturalization (Crisp 2004). Observations such as this have given rise to the notion of intermediate integration, in which refugees are able to participate in the economic life of the host region without attaining the legal and political rights envisioned in local integration as a durable solution (Banki 2004). Such de facto integration may occur over time as result of the interaction between refugees and the local community, whereby refugees "negotiate" their livelihoods among the local community as a coping strategy (Hovil 2014). However, the difference between de facto integration and de jure integration is that the former does not represent a deliberate policy by the government but may result from a manifestation of other policy choices, including decisions on the type of settlement and economic access. An example of formally sanctioned local integration is Tanzania's offer to naturalize around 200,000 Burundians hosted since 1972 (Milner 2014).

Although local integration as a durable solution played a more prominent policy role in the past, especially during the 1950s (Meyer 2008), governments in the Global South soon became resistant to the notion of local integration. This particular durable solution is continually evaded by governments that "prefer an approach to citizenship that is both protectionist and exclusive," and where instances of naturalization are the exception rather than the rule (Hovil 2014). This restrictive attitude to local integration led some to consider it as the "forbidden solution" and the "non-solution" because of the rarity of its adoption in cases of mass influx in the world today (Fielden 2008).

RESETTLEMENT
Resettlement refers to the ordered movement of pre-selected refugees to a third country in which their settlement is expected to be permanent (Fee 2022; Van Selm 2014). While consideration for resettlement is a legal right, it might not occur if the refugee is not selected (Albert 2010). Resettlement countries almost exclusively comprise industrialized nations in the Global North (around twenty-eight countries) (Van Selm 2014). One of the largest resettlement programs to ever took place was the resettlement of around 1,315,000 Indochinese

from Laos, Vietnam, and Cambodia to thirty other countries during the period from 1975 to 1997 (Robinson 1998). However, although resettlement had been the preferred durable solution for the international refugee regime, its viability declined with the decline in resettlement opportunities (Moretti 2015). Currently, resettlement countries generally offer resettlement to less than 1 per cent of the world's refugees (Betts et al. 2017; UNHCR 2010). Therefore, it is less predominantly chosen as a policy on the part of governments in the South. Here, resettlement could also refer to the policy of denying local integration and only allowing resettlement to third country (or repatriation) as a durable solution.

DRIVERS OF HOST POLICY RESPONSES TO MASS DISPLACEMENT

The literature on forced migration and refugee policy is rife with determinant factors that are said to drive countries' policy decisions in mass influx situations. Such drivers can be grouped broadly into three categories of arenas: international arena, host arena, and displacement arena (figure 2.2).[3] This categorization is based on Kunz's model of refugee movements (1981), which groups the factors influencing refugees' integration upon resettlement into three categories: home-related, displacement-related, and host-related. This book is concerned with the study of refugee policy-making in mass influx settings, which tend to occur in the Global South. It argues for the need to distinguish between North and South contexts. Therefore, the drivers of policy responses discussed here are derived from cases in the Global South of mass refugee displacement that are specific to this context. In the following section a review of such factors takes place, including a discussion of how different scholars have debated the impact of these factors on governments' regulation and management of mass influx situations.

Drivers in the International Arena

The existence of refugees is a symbolic representation of the breakdown of the citizen-state relationship as a result of the inability or unwillingness of the state to ensure its citizens' physical security and fundamental human rights (Haddad 2008). Refugees fleeing their countries of origin are considered in need of "international

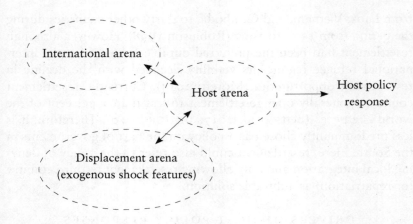

Figure 2.2 | Drivers of host-policy responses to mass influx situations

protection." They seek this from another state or the wider international community, inviting the influence of the international refugee regime (Betts 2010b). The purpose of the regime, which constitutes the institutions (norms and rules) and actors (donor governments, international organizations, and others) in the international community, is to regulate states' responses to refugees and ensure that refugees receive access to protection (Betts and Loescher 2011). However, the extent of influence of the regime on governments' responses to refugees is contested. Two streams of scholarship exist that debate the regime's extent of influence on states' asylum policies, with one arguing for significant positive influence, and the other skeptically undermining it. Both point to an array of reasons to support their respective positions.

The first stream argues that the international refugee regime has significant positive influence on government decision-making on refugee issues. This plays out through the setting of protection standards and regulations; the provision of international assistance, also referred to as burden or responsibility sharing; the propagation of humanitarian norms; and the use of advocacy (Owen 2020; Gottwald 2014). There are several international refugee instruments, including the 1951 Geneva Convention and its 1967 Protocol, the 1969 Organisation of African Unity (OAU) Convention, the 1984 Cartagena Declaration (Latin America), and the 2004 European Council Asylum Qualification Directive. These represent a solid institutional and legal underpinning for the protection of refugees that sets standards and rules of protection, with UNHCR as a monitoring body (Türk and Dowd 2014; Loescher, Betts, and Milner 2008). Not all countries are party to such international conventions. Nevertheless, these conventions help place standards for the treatment and protection of refugees, even if they are not perfectly followed (Khalil 2011). Additionally, UNHCR often co-signs memorandums of understanding (MOUs) with governments that are not party to the 1951 Geneva Convention to ensure that refugees are accorded protection. For instance, prior to the signing of an MOU with the Lebanese government, Iraqi refugees enjoyed very little protection and many lived in fear of refoulement and arbitrary detention (Harper 2008). Furthermore, the provision of international assistance, during and post emergency phases, gives the refugee regime added leverage in influencing countries to adopt more favourable asylum policies. Developing countries' lack of capacity to handle large refugee flows gives the international regime an advantage because it is relied upon to provide assistance during mass influx situations (Gordenker 2015). Such assistance aids countries in managing inflows of refugees but can also be used to pressure governments into adopting more favourable policies. For example, donor governments may threaten to cut off bilateral aid or contributions to UNHCR that are earmarked for the specific refugee situation. International assistance, often referred to as burden sharing, helped shape Africa's generous asylum policies in the early 1980s. The deal included African states' admitting refugees to their territories and providing the land required to accommodate them, in return for funding that would aid them with the provision of food, shelter, and health care to the refugees (Crisp 2000). Much of this aid, which was provided by donor governments and channelled through UNHCR, helped in mitigating the impact of hosting refugees. It also provided states and elites with a source of foreign exchange, employment, and commercial opportunities (Crisp 2000). Furthermore, the resettlement of refugees to third countries poses an additional leverage point in the hands of the international regime because countries of resettlement have discretion in the provision of resettlement opportunities (Van Selm 2014; Betts and Loescher 2011). In order to "persuade" governments to adhere to its normative protection agenda, UNHCR uses advocacy, diplomatic pressure, and critique to propagate its humanitarian norms and encourage governments to adopt more positive policies towards refugees (Hamlin 2022; Loescher 2014).

The opposing stream, however, argues against over-estimating the influence of the international refugee regime (C. Harvey 2015). One reason that the influence of the international regime may not translate into policy action is states' sensitivity to their national sovereignty, which may be perceived to be undermined by international pressure (Kaiser 2005; Gordenker 2015). While refugees have the right to seek asylum, there is no international obligation on states to actually provide it. The principle of territorial sovereignty allows them the discretion to determine whom they admit to their territories (Mogire 2009). Accordingly, and under that pretext, states have been increasingly interpreting convention provisions in restrictive terms, while citing "national interest" (Musarat-Akram 1999; Türk and Dowd 2014). Furthermore, domestic states may also use as a pressure card their discretion in admitting refugees and allowing international organizations to operate on their territory, which may counterbalance the international regime's ability to use negative publicity (Lee 2014). This is particularly the case when inadequate burden sharing and international assistance are received, which can lead countries to become less willing to host refugees (Ward 2014; Mogire 2009). States' discretionary power related to the implementation of international refugee norms in their territories has become an important tool in the bargaining processes with international donors (Tesfaghiorghis 2019). In the cases of Kenya, Tanzania, and Guinea, host countries looking to call on donors employed several strategies, such as reducing the number of refugees admitted, decreasing the quality of protection, and even "inflating" the number of refugees hosted (Milner 2009). Refugee encampment may also be used as a strategy for making the presence of refugees more visible to donors (Bakewell 2014). Countries may employ their positions as host states to extract revenue, or refugee rent, from other state or non-state actors, thereby acting as "refugee rentier states" (Tsourapas 2019). Refugee-rent-seeking strategies have been used by Jordan, Lebanon, Egypt,

Ethiopia, Kenya, Iran, Pakistan, Colombia, Ecuador, and Peru. Such practices are now diffused and often emulated across the Global South (Freier, Micinski, and Tsourapas 2021). In tandem, host governments may also pressure resettlement countries to increase their intake numbers by refusing to admit refugees. This was a tactic used by the Thai government in 1979 in response to the United States' reduction of resettlement quotas (Zeager 2002).

Furthermore, works in the literature have pointed to linkages between responses to refugees and foreign policy concerns, which may or may not lead states to conform with the international refugee regime. For instance, during the Cold War the United States differentiated between refugees and asylum seekers from Communist and non-Communist countries. Refugees from the Soviet Union, Cuba, and elsewhere in the East benefited from easier conditions for asylum as they played a valuable propaganda role in the power struggle of "migration diplomacy" (Seeberg 2022; Adamson and Tsourapas 2019; Loescher 2001). That is, the decision to recognize citizens from another country as refugees "implies condemnation of the relevant government for persecuting its citizens, or at least failing to afford them protection" (Zolberg, Suhrke, and Aguayo 1986). A similar logic was seen to be in play in the case of Venezuelan asylum seekers in Brazil. Poor relations between sending and host governments were identified as being a main driver in influencing Brazil's 2019 decision to recognize the refugee status of that population on a prima facie basis, in accordance with criteria of the 1984 Cartagena Declaration (Leomil 2022). Conversely, positive relations with a country of origin may also lead a host state to refrain from granting refugee status to the nationals of such country (Jacobsen 1996) and may even make it reluctant to take over UNHCR's role in refugee-status determination (RSD) (Abdelaaty 2020). Finally, refugee policy is also often driven by state diplomatic aims unrelated to the country of origin or the refugee movement itself. For instance, in a 2016 agreement Turkey agreed, *inter alia*, to host asylum seekers returned from Greece in order to obtain visa-free travel for its citizens to the European Union and accelerate its membership application to that bloc (Adamson and Tsourapas 2019). Moreover, states have also implemented less restrictive asylum policies to help sustain their own legitimacy (in terms of being seen to respect the rights of refugees) vis-à-vis the international community (Betts 2013, 191).

Drivers in the Host Arena

A plethora of host-country factors are said to influence policy responses to mass displacement. These include a country's considerations on foreign policy, national security, the economy and environment, politics, and society and its perceived outcome of the crisis.

Several scholars identified foreign policy considerations as one of the determinants of governments' responses to mass refugee flows (Oztig 2022; Mogire 2009; Camarena 2015). Massive refugee movements that cross international borders may lead to adverse effects on host- and sending-country relations. This can be reflected in asylum decisions about which refugees are to be admitted and how they are treated (Zolberg, Suhrke, and Aguayo 1986). For instance, relations between Arab host countries and the Palestine Liberation Organization, and other regional and international actors, greatly influenced the protection standards of Palestinian refugees in the region (Khalil 2011). Similarly, the mass flow of Iraqi refugees in 1991 posed a major foreign-policy challenge to Turkey, as the latter tried to balance its response amidst the growing tension between Iraq and the United States (Ihlamur-Öner 2013). The influence of foreign policy is especially evident in the different ways in which states respond to different refugee flows based on their country of origin. Citing the example of China, Song (2014) argues that China's treatment of refugee groups throughout the past years has consistently reflected the status of its relationship with the displaced peoples' country of origin. Scholars have also pointed to the potential use of refugees as a strategic "tool," with adverse effects on refugee protection (Greenhill 2011; Snyder 2011; Lischer 2008). Geopolitical and regional politics may also play a role, with host-country foreign-policy considerations acting as an interface between international and host arenas.

Another relevant factor mentioned by scholars is national security considerations (Rana and Riaz 2022). The Thai government's response to Karen refugees from 1984 to 2011 was characterized by oscillation between negative and positive responses depending on its assessment and prioritization of security concerns (Lee 2014). Thus, when security issues dominated the policy agenda, the government assumed a more restrictive stance towards both refugees and international relief organizations. A growing body of literature exists on the security implications of refugee migration (cf. Lischer

A Complexity Approach to Analyzing Refugee-Policy Variation   49

2005; Salehyan and Gledtisch 2006). Two specific sources of threat that can arise from refugee inflows are mentioned: a "spill-over" effect of the conflict (Salehyan 2008; Lischer 2008) and internal conflict arising from the presence of refugees (Mogire 2009). Such security threats have led scholars to point to a rising "securitization" trend of asylum among countries of the North and the South, with adverse effects for refugee policy (Hammerstad 2014). As a case in point, Messari and Van der Klaauw (2010) point to adoption by Middle Eastern and North African states of increasingly restrictive policies towards refugees in response to the perceived "terrorist threat." The decline in the provision of asylum in Africa over the years has also been correlated with the increasing portrayal of refugees as a "threat" to social and political security (Crisp 2000). Finally, while the "threat" posed by Iraqi refugees in Syria was one of socio-economic destitution, rather than violence, such destitution was a source of tension in relations between refugees, the host government, and the local host community (Leenders 2008).

Economic and environmental concerns have been cited as a determinant factor of asylum policy response. A burgeoning body of literature exists that discusses the economic and environmental impact of refugees on host communities (cf. Ronald 2022; Ruiz and Vargas-Silva 2016; Ongpin 2009; Berry 2008). Large refugee flows place considerable strains on natural resources, leading to adverse economic and social impacts on the host community. Refugees also tend to make resource-use decisions that prioritize current consumption over future consumption, which puts a strain on resources that local populations are competing for (A. Martin 2005). Deteriorating environmental and economic conditions caused by large refugee movements, and the failure of the international community to address the problem, have led to the reduced willingness of African countries to host refugees (Crisp 2000).

Economic, and environmental conditions, however, may not prove to be a sufficient factor in explaining governments' response to refugees, because cases exist where countries with low economic capacity have responded favourably towards refugee flows. For instance, Musarat-Akram (1999) cites Malawi's hosting of more than a million Mozambican refugees between the mid-1980s and the early 1990s despite its poor economic conditions and shortage of land. It is thought that refugee flows tend to bring international and national attention to previously politically and economically marginalized areas, thus reducing their economic depravity (Landau 2003). Economic concern may also compel a host government to take a more positive stance towards relief agencies in order to ensure their assistance, which in turn reflects positively on refugees' welfare (Lee 2014). In this way, refugees can be seen as an economic asset by governments (Betts et al. 2017; Milner 2009).

With regard to political considerations, host government policies are said to be influenced by the local community's receptiveness of, and attitude towards, the refugee population. Favourable local receptiveness is seen to be correlated with less political resistance to the adoption of progressive asylum policies. For instance, Walzer (2008) argues that the local support of the Pakistani population of the government's decision to offer asylum to Afghan refugees not only reduced potential local conflict but also created a conducive asylum environment. In contrast, rising local resentment towards Vietnamese refugees in Malaysia nearly created a legitimacy crisis for the government (Idris 2012). In her work on the use of blame as a political tool, Syrian American scholar Baylouny (2020) discusses the process of "scapegoating" that often happens when citizen grievances rise. This is often due to reasons unrelated to the presence of refugees, but may then be used by political elites to transfer the blame to refugees' presence. The result is a reduced quality of asylum driven by political considerations and host-community sentiments.

This debate points to the type of political regime being a mediating factor. According to Crisp (2000), growing evidence exists of a link between democratization and decline in refugee protection. Prior to the 1990s, authoritarian governments and one-party states in the Third World were free to offer asylum to large refugee populations when they considered such policy to be in their interest. However, with the end of the Cold War and the introduction of pluralistic systems of government in many parts of the world, the refugee question became the topic of political contestation, leading to decline in refugee protection.

Scholars have indicated three factors that influence a community's degree of receptiveness towards refugees: local norms, such as traditions of hospitality and faith; perception of treatment; and previous historical experience. In his analysis of African refugee protection, Crisp (2000) argues that African states' earlier generous treatment of refugees was deeply conditioned by the region's local traditions of hospitality. Additionally, Admirand (2014) points to the role that faith plays in influencing asylum, because most faiths ascribe high moral value to the assistance of deprived and displaced people (Clemot 2022; Alakoc, Göksel, and Zarychta 2022; Hollenbach 2014). Faith may also intersect with asylum provision in a variety of ways, including through notions of "deservedness" of assistance. Fiddian-Qasmiyeh and Pacitto (2019) found evidence of the relationship between faith-based responses in the Global South and conceptualizations of humanitarianism, through their study of faith-based support for Syrian refugees in Jordan and of evangelical humanitarian relief providers on the Thai Myanmar border.

Furthermore, Crisp (2010) argues that local communities' perceptions of refugees as receiving preferential treatment in the form of material assistance and services may fuel negative attitudes towards them. The local reactions of Syrians and Jordanians towards Iraqi refugees were negatively influenced by the region's protracted hosting experience of Palestinian refugees, who have been displaced since 1948 (Lischer 2008; Gibson 2015). In contrast, the historical experience of *being* refugees positively influenced the local Lebanese population's reaction to Syrian refugees in 2011 (Awad 2014).

In addition, a host government's perceived expectation about the potential outcome of a refugee crisis has not been a widely studied factor. It has been mentioned by Goodwin-Gill and McAdam (2007) as influencing asylum policy decisions. According to S.K. Smith (2013), a host government's expectation about the outcome of the displacement situation influences its educational policy approach towards the refugee population. Therefore, it is important to further investigate whether this factor plays a role in the shaping of asylum policy and the mechanism by which it does so. This is particularly relevant in light of the debate on the specific challenges posed by protracted refugee situations on host communities. The perceived expectation may thus be considered in light of the host's foreign-policy stance towards the conflict (i.e., perceived outcome of whether the sending country will win or lose) or the length of time the conflict will endure, with the potential of it becoming a protracted situation.

Drivers in the Displacement Arena

With regard to displacement, an array of factors related to the refugee population is hypothesized to influence asylum response towards them. These factors include the volume of the movement, the length of stay, the character of the movement, and the reason for flight.

The volume of the refugee movement plays a pivotal role in influencing governments' reception standards. However, we still do not have conclusive evidence of the direction. In many cases, evidence has pointed towards the increasing volume of a refugee movement as having a negative influence on reception standards (cf. Aras and Mencütek 2015; Idris 2012; Chatty and Mansour 2011; Mogire 2009; Walzer 2008; Harper 2008; Abuya 2007). This is demonstrated in several cases in the Global South, and predominantly in Africa, where a rise in refugee numbers over time has correlated with a more restrictive policy environment (Crisp 2000). In the mid-1990s, renewed conflict in Burundi and Rwanda led to a dramatic increase in the number of refugees in Tanzania. In response, the Tanzanian government closed its previously open border and adopted a series of restrictive measures, including limiting refugees' economic access to the labour market and identifying voluntary repatriation as the only viable durable solution (Milner 2014). In China the fear of creating a "pull factor" also consistently influenced the way in which the Chinese government designed its asylum policies (Song 2014). The idea of a negative link between volume and reception is based on the rationale that a trade-off exists between the number of refugees and the degree of rights granted to them by states (Talib 2012). States tend to interpret their responsibilities towards asylum seekers and refugees more restrictively when faced with a higher number of asylum applications.[4]

Moreover, the length of time a refugee population spends in a country is said to be negatively correlated with governments' asylum policies. Refugee groups whose stay is prolonged are likely to receive worse treatment. One of the reasons is "compassion fatigue" (Jesse 1998). However, the length of time a refugee population spends in a host country may also be a significant factor in the consideration of local integration as a durable solution (Fielden 2008). For instance, the protracted nature of the Sudanese refugee population in Uganda led the government to reconsider its previous rejection of local integration. Instead it adopted a "self-reliance" strategy in 1999, whereby refugees would be able to sustain themselves (Kaiser 2005). Protracted refugee situations have received considerable attention in the literature because of the challenge of finding sustainable durable solutions that are acceptable to both the host government and the refugee community itself (see, for example, Abdulrahim and Khawaja 2011; Bradley 2011; Chatty and Mansour 2011; Zeus 2011).

A Complexity Approach to Analyzing Refugee-Policy Variation   53

With regard to the character of the refugee population, several scholars have discussed features such as ethnic and religious makeup, as well as degree of militarization, as precursors to treatment. The degree of linguistic, religious, ethnic, and cultural similarities between the host population and the refugee population – otherwise referred to as psychological compatibility – may ease governments' consideration of local integration as a durable solution (Fielden 2008). Similarly, Song (2014) has argued that refugees' ethnic and cultural linkage to China played a key role in China's policy towards Indochinese refugees. Ethnic affinity may also explain countries' divergent policy approaches to different refugee groups residing on their territories at the same time; in some cases very different policies have been applied to different ethnic refugee communities (Abdelaaty 2021b; Jaji 2014; Fielden 2008).

Scholars such as Walzer (2008) and Fielden (2008), however, have noted that while ethnic affiliation may ease government responses towards a refugee population, it cannot be a sufficient predictor of asylum, because cases exist in which the large volume of refugees increased local resentment towards them even when ethnic ties were the same. Additionally, it has been argued that the degree of militarization, or the presence of armed elements among the civilian refugees, has influenced governments' treatment (Lischer 2008; Jubilut and Carneiro 2011). For instance, Kenya's and Tanzania's shifts in policies towards Somali and Southern African refugees were closely related to the existence of armed elements among the refugee populations (Mogire 2009).

Furthermore, the reason for refugee flight has been debated as an additional determinant factor. As Durieux (2013) notes in his conceptual analysis of asylum paradigms prevalent in the world today, the reason for refugee flight tends to affect the image of the refugee, which in turn reflects on the government's response. According to Durieux, when refugees flee disaster, they are usually perceived as "victims" triggering "compassion" on the part of the government to "rescue" them by providing temporary asylum. Additionally, Crisp (2000) argues that the reason for flight was a major impetus behind Africa's favourable policies towards refugees in the 1960s and 1970s because many of the continents' refugees were the product of independence struggles and wars of national liberation. Alternatively, later refugee movements in the 1980s and onwards, no longer the product of anti-colonial and liberation struggles, have not been met with the same generosity. Crisp's analysis thus suggests a link between the reason for flight and foreign policy considerations.

FRAMEWORK OF ANALYSIS: A COMPLEX SYSTEMS APPROACH TO ANALYZING REFUGEE POLICY-MAKING

Now that I have discussed how previous scholars debated and investigated the elements of a host government's refugee policy, as well as the determinant factors that help shape it, an analytical framework is needed to demonstrate the relationships between such concepts, and how they should be analyzed – to help make sense of the "chaos." The analytical framework used in the book (figure 2.3) serves this specific purpose. It provides a framework for analyzing host government policies in situations of mass displacement (Jesse 1998). This framework is based on two foundational pillars. Firstly, it suggests that dynamic refugee policy-making processes in mass influx situations can be better analyzed in terms of inputs, process, and outputs. Secondly, it adopts a complex systems approach to the study and analysis of refugee policy-making. Among the different analytical approaches to the study of public policy (Anderson 2001), complex systems analysis is specifically chosen because this book deals with a humanitarian emergency and crisis situation. Unlike policy-making in non-crisis times, emergency and crisis situations are often characterized by complexity, dynamism, fluidity, and the interaction of many interdependent arenas (Mitroff 2000; El-Taliawi and Hartley 2021). Therefore, to analyze policy-making in such exceptionally complex situations, researchers need to adopt an analytical lens that does justice to such specificity.

Complex systems thinking first found its way into the policy sciences field in the 1970s and gained momentum in the 1990s (Stewart and Ayres 2001) as a reaction to the increasing perceptions that the problems confronting modern governments were becoming much more complex, profound, and interdependent in a way that only a complex systems–based paradigm could begin to comprehend them (Forrester 1993). Furthermore, the factors affecting the policy-making process in such situations cannot be understood or analyzed in terms of direct linear causality (Checkland 1999), but need to be understood in terms of the multifactorial influence of various elements. Such elements may be of an interdependent nature and may belong to more than one policy domain (e.g., climate change and migration). According to this approach, a systemic cause may be one of a number of multiple direct or indirect causes. Such causes have to be taken into consideration to fully comprehend any phenomenon under examination. A complex systems perspective also posits that change is a continuous occurrence in any biological, social, or economic system (Holzer, Kastner, and Werron 2014). Therefore, utilizing a complex systems perspective allows for a non-reductionist, holistic, and dynamic perspective in the analysis of policy-making. Consequently, it serves the important purpose of allowing us to analyze change as a policy evolves over time.

In his examination of the multiplicity of causes and consequences of Dutch asylum policy over a decade, Grütters (2007) provides a rare demonstration of the use of complex systems thinking in the study of asylum policy, albeit in a Global North setting. The model presented in my book, while utilizing a similar analytical lens, is based on the set of policy elements and drivers specific to mass influx situations, which tend to occur in the Global South. Therefore, it is relevant to examining cases in these settings. This relevance and limitation is based on the rationale that while some factors may overlap in the North and South, such as economic or security considerations, the way in which such factors play out under conditions of mass influx is expected to have a very different effect than those influencing the policy-making that occurs under stable conditions (i.e., in individual-resettlement or asylum-seeking policy contexts). This is due to several factors, including the rapidity of events in a humanitarian crisis situation which makes the policy-making process more fluid. Furthermore, the specific characteristics of countries of the South – including administrative and governance capacity and political influence in the global refugee regime – set a different contextual environmental for refugee policy-making than those of countries of the North, as discussed earlier. The inputs, process, and outputs of policy-making are thus expected to be unique and should be treated as such.

Refugee-Policy Outputs

Policy outputs refer to the output of the policy-making process in a mass displacement situation. In order to analyze and assess the output, scholars need to have a measure. Here I use an analytical tool that breaks down the policy adopted by a host government in response to a mass refugee movement into three policy components and subcomponents (Jacobsen 1996). Table 2.1 outlines the various components and includes variations of the different practices of each policy component as identified in the policy and scholarly literature. In this way a spectrum of policy output exists and can be used to help us measure Global South government responses to a mass refugee situation. Policy responses leaning to the far left represent perfect adherence to normative prescriptions of how governments *should* respond, while those leaning to the far right represent perfect non-adherence to normative prescriptions (Jacobsen 1996). In this sense a government's policy response can be evaluated as to whether it is more or less restrictive in its response to a refugee population. The idea of a spectrum of adherence, rather than a simple dichotomy, allows mixed practices to be taken into consideration.

It should be noted, however, that the notion of *restrictiveness* used here is a descriptor that is not meant to suggest that responding restrictively to refugees is the normal practice in the South. Nor is it intended to suggest that a completely open response should be the standard policy approach of host governments from a normative standpoint. The purpose of this tool is to aggregate a host government's policy response and to be able to describe and assess it in comparison to other countries, rather than to make normative value-laden judgments. This is especially relevant in examining the responses of governments that are not party to the Geneva Convention, most commonly in the Global South; these governments may often exhibit more open responses than those laid out in the Convention.

Refugee-Policy Inputs

Refugee-policy inputs are inputs to the policy-making process in a given context. Such inputs exist in three arenas, namely the international, host, and displacement arenas. They have been derived from previous literature and empirical studies on refugee governance in mass influx situations.

INPUTS IN THE INTERNATIONAL ARENA

· *International legal framework*: soft and hard laws that govern refugee affairs, including the 1951 Geneva Convention and its 1961 Protocol, and other instruments (study example: Khalil 2011).

Table 2.1 | Breakdown of refugee-policy output by elements and degree of restrictiveness

		Less restrictive	↔	More restrictive
Policy on entry and stay	Admission choice	*Admission*	*Restrictions imposed on admission*	*No admission*
	Non-refoulement	*No refoulement takes place*	*Inconsistent refoulement*	*Systematic refoulement*
	Type of asylum	*Prima facie status*	*Temporary protection*	*"Alien" status*
Policy on livelihoods	Type of settlement	*Non-encampment*	*Choice of settlement type allowed*	*Imposed encampment*
	Labour market access	*Access to labour market allowed*	*Restrictions imposed on access*	*Access to labour market not allowed*
	Freedom of movement	*Freedom of movement allowed*	*Restrictions on movement imposed*	*No freedom of movement*
	Service provision	*Non-relief services provided*	*Restrictions imposed on service provision*	*Non-relief services not provided*
	Implementation mode	*Collaboration with IOs*	*Restrictions on work of IOs*	*IOs not permitted*
		Civilian agency in charge of refugee population	*Mixed features*	*Military in charge of refugee population*
Policy on durable solutions	Repatriation, integration, and resettlement	*Three durable solutions allowed*	*Some solutions allowed, but not all*	*Only repatriation allowed*

Source: Adapted from Jacobsen (1996).

- *Humanitarianism*: norms and values of refugee protection that are propagated by humanitarian organizations and enshrined in legal instruments and customary international law (study example: Jesse 1998).
- *International organizations*: including intergovernmental organizations, such as UNHCR, international NGOs, and other international humanitarian organizations involved in the response (study example: Harper 2008).
- *International assistance*: relief and non-relief assistance provided by the international community to share the burden or responsibility of refugee hosting with the host country; it may include resettlement and humanitarian aid (study example: Crisp 2000).

INPUTS IN THE HOST ARENA

- *Economic and environmental concerns*: the resource capacity of the host country's economy and ecology and its ability to withstand the population increase resulting from the sudden mass influx (A. Martin 2005; Berry 2008).
- *Political regime type*: the host country's political system type and the degree to which citizens' wills influence policy decisions (Crisp 2000).
- *Perceived outcome*: the host government's perception or expectation of how the conflict will end (S.K. Smith 2013).
- *National security*: considerations related to the host country's military and non-military security and stability (Lischer 2005).
- *Foreign policy*: the host government's relations with other foreign governments, including but not limited to those involved or with a direct or indirect stake in the conflict (Mogire 2009; Tsourapas 2019; Aras and Mencütek 2015).
- *Political demographic concerns*: fears of potential threat to political equilibrium in the host country, including demographic-balance considerations (Walzer 2008; Idris 2012).
- *Social receptiveness*: the degree to which a society is accepting of the refugee movement (Jacobsen 1996).
- *Local norms*: values governing the treatment of refugees and those fleeing dangers, as derived from local religions and/or customs (Admirand 2014; Crisp 2000).
- *Historical refugee experience*: the host community's previous experience as refugees or as hosts to previous refugee movements (Awad 2014).

A Complexity Approach to Analyzing Refugee-Policy Variation   59

- *Perceived treatment*: the host community's perception of the refugee movement's treatment by the host government and other humanitarian actors (i.e., being more or less preferentially treated than the local community in terms of services or assistance provided) (Crisp 2000).

INPUTS IN THE DISPLACEMENT ARENA[5]

- *Nationality*: citizenship of the refugee movement.
- *Composition*: features of the refugee movement, including militarization and socio-economic profile (Lischer 2008).
- *Reason for flight*: the source of conflict that led to the influx, such as independence struggles or civil wars (Durieux 2013).
- *Volume*: influx volume in terms of population size (Walzer 2008).
- *Length of stay*: the amount of time the refugee movement remains in the host country (Jesse 1998).
- *Ethnic affiliation*: the movement's linguistic, ethnic, cultural, and religious profile (Fielden 2008).

The Refugee Policy-Making Process

The refugee policy-making process refers to the interactions that take place between and among the policy input variables within and across the three arenas and over time. The framework (see figure 2.3) demonstrates such hypothesized interactions based on the literature. In this case the dotted arrows in the framework refer to indirect relationship and interactions, while the solid arrows refer to direct relationships and interactions. It is expected that the policy inputs, and the process of interactions that take place between them, ultimately shape the output of the policy-making process – in this case a host government's policy towards the refugee movement. In this sense the framework presented here allows for the analysis of variation between states, as there will be different policy outputs if there are different policy inputs. A key argument of this book is that scholars should be more comfortable with policy variations between states. The framework demonstrates that it is "natural" that not every state in the South or in the same region responds the same way to mass refugee movements. In addition, difference does not necessarily mean deviance, so long as states are meeting their obligations under international refugee and human rights law. Variation

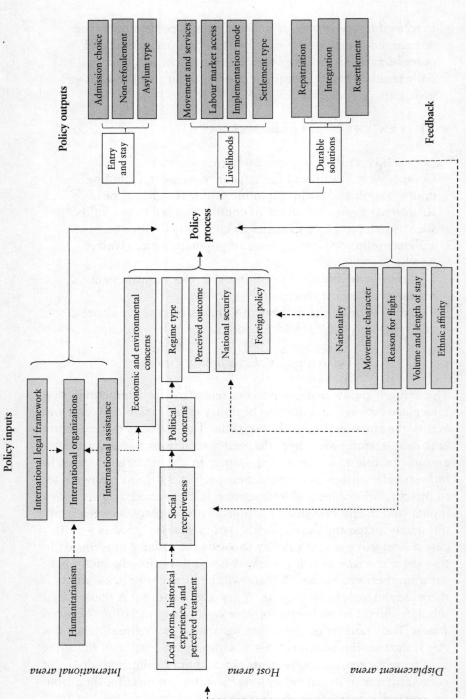

Figure 2.3 | A systemic view of the refugee policy-making process

is not, on its own, a problem. If we are to move beyond normative expectations of how states in the South should behave in mass refugee situations, to a better understanding of how and why they do so, then we need to be more comfortable with witnessing, and even expecting, variation across states.

From Key Questions to Hypothetical Propositions

To guide the data collection and analysis of the case studies used in this book, propositions were formulated to act as hypotheses. In qualitative case studies, propositions are used to direct the researcher's attention to potential angles or variables that should be examined within the scope of their study (Yin 2009). In other words, the propositions in this book are what would be expected to be found in answer to the book's key questions. Such propositions are based on the previous scholarly work and on evidence gathered in other cases discussed in this chapter.

Firstly, I expect the policy output adopted by host governments that are witnessing mass refugee displacement in the South – specifically their policies on entry and stay, livelihoods, and durable solutions – to be highly influenced by the international regime.

This is expected to take place through several mediating channels. These include the provision of international assistance (monetary or non-monetary) on the part of international regime players; the setting of protection standards by actors including (but not limited to) UNHCR; and international advocacy efforts. Hence, based on the previous empirical evidence gathered by scholars and discussed in this chapter, I assume that host governments are likely to be less restrictive of refugee movements as a result of more burden sharing provided by international regime players. This includes burden sharing by donor governments, as well as stronger advocacy efforts and the setting of protection standards on the part of UNHCR and other non-state actors. Such sharing is particularly expected as a state's position in the international regime becomes more marginal, as in the cases of Lebanon and Jordan. Inputs in the international arena are also expected to be mediated by features of the displacement itself. Due to the absence of a clear mechanism for responsibility sharing, international assistance is often driven by the visibility and politics surrounding each refugee crisis (UNHCR 2012a). Therefore, it is the proposition of this book that hosts' policy output will be highly conditioned by interactions between the international and displacement arenas.

Secondly, a host government's policy output is expected to be influenced by a series of domestic considerations. These include its own foreign policy and stance towards the conflict; previous refugee experience; and economic, environmental, demographic, and security considerations.

It is expected that empirical examination of the cases of Lebanon and Jordan would show that if the host government were supportive of the regime in the country-of-conflict origin, then an overall policy output that would be more restrictive of the refugee population would emerge. This is presumably in order not to signal hostility or embarrassment to the country of origin. How each country does so might vary in terms of the policy elements adopted, however. One host government may decide to encamp refugees as a way to contain the refugee situation in the hopes of a favourable conflict resolution being reached in the country of origin. Another host government might use the same rationale but apply it differently through allowing refugees to self-settle, and hence underplay the visibility of the refugee situation.

Furthermore, a country's previous refugee experience is expected to play a role in influencing a host government's policy output. In contrast, a previous experience of citizens themselves being refugees is likely to raise social receptiveness towards other refugees, whereas previous experience of hosting mass refugees may reduce such receptiveness and hence decrease the quality of asylum provided to new refugee movements, resulting in a more restrictive policy response. Social receptiveness is also conditional on the perceived treatment of the refugee population on the part of the host government and non-state actors, as well as features of the displacement itself and its compatibility with the host community. Perceived "preferential" treatment of the refugee population by the host community is likely to erode feelings of hospitality towards the refugee population. Local norms also play a role here: where refugee hosting and acceptance norms are prevalent in society, social receptiveness is likely to be higher. The extent of a host community's social receptiveness to the incoming refugee movement is mediated by the displacement features themselves and the type of political regime in which policy-making is taking place. In a regime where public opinion affects policy decisions, higher social receptiveness is expected to translate to less restrictive policy output. In a regime where the host government is less likely to respond to social considerations and sentiments, higher social receptiveness of the refugee movement may not feature greatly in the decision-making processes.

Economic, environmental, demographic, and security considerations are also expected to play a vital role in shaping the policy output. Reduced economic and environmental resources (whether or not directly due to the refugee movement) is expected to result in more restrictiveness (such as prohibiting or restricting further entry of refugees and providing refugees with less services). Security spillovers, or the potential of demographic changes to occur as a result of the long-term presence of refugees, may result in a restrictive and less favourable policy response.

Thirdly, features of the refugee movement itself are expected to play a role in shaping a host government's response towards it, such as volume, nationality, ethnicity, length of stay, and character of the movement.

Following previous evidence and debates it is expected that the higher the volume of the refugee movement, as well as the more protracted the displacement becomes, the more restrictive a refugee-policy output would be. However, this would be mediated by interactions with domestic and international factors, such as the provision of international assistance and considerations of resource capacity. A host government that is resource strapped and witnessing humanitarian funding shortages is expected to adopt policy choices that are less favourable to the refugee presence. Other features of the displacement, including nationality, ethnicity, and character (such as militarization or socio-economic profile), are also expected to interact with drivers in the domestic host and international arenas to ultimately shape the policy output. Specifically, the extent to which a refugee population's nationality will influence the policy response will depend on the foreign policy considerations of the host government, as well as the international political weight of the conflict. A militarized movement or one that acquires a militant character is expected to result in a more restrictive overall response. The socio-economic profile of the refugee population may also influence specific policy choices such as resorting to encampment to support refugees who may be less socio-economically able to self-settle and independently sustain themselves in displacement.

It is expected that application of the framework to empirical examination of Lebanon and Jordan would produce a result that confirms the three propositions. In my analysis in the coming chapters I will examine the extent to which the aforementioned drivers have in fact influenced the policy choices of both countries on Syrian displacement, over time, and in what way. It is important to note here that how the policy output is shaped does not depend heavily on each of the drivers in isolation but on how they interact with each other. This is especially the case because governments tend to weigh the costs and benefits of the various factors, and the myriad policy constraints on their behaviour, as the mass influx situation evolves, and adjust their policies accordingly. This is where the framework presented here is key. It even allows for the analysis of variation in policy responses among host states responding to the same refugee movement. Adopting a complexity lens is important for taking into consideration the multifactorial interdependence of drivers, which is expected to be more prevalent in, and unique to, mass-refugee-policy contexts of the Global South.

CONCLUSION

This chapter has provided a brief classification of the scholarly literature on mass displacement. The results reveal a need to extend the policy-centric work on countries of the Global South that host the majority of forced migrants worldwide. Subsequently, it discussed the policy alternatives prevalent in responding to mass refugees, between norm and actual practice, based on the policy and scholarly literature. Furthermore, it reviewed the ongoing scholarly debate on the key drivers and determinants of host governments' policy responses to mass refugee flows. Finally, it introduced the analytical framework developed for the study of refugee policy-making during mass influx situations. This framework can be applied to understanding how and why governments in the Global South respond the way they do to mass refugee flows. The framework builds on previous literature but extends it to include a complexity perspective that avoids reductionist notions of asylum provision to mere dependent or independent variables and linear causality and incorporates dynamism and interdependence.

Although scholars' attempts to explain refugee-policy responses to mass influx situations have progressed over the years, there remains much to be done to take this body of scholarly literature further. Firstly, since mass influx situations are rare, there is a need to collect more empirical evidence by relying on comparative analysis. The literature is currently skewed towards the use of single or atheoretical case studies (cf. Beaujouan and Rasheed 2019; El-Hariri 2020; Fakhoury 2020, 2021; Janmyr and Mourad 2018; Lenner 2020; Lupieri 2020; Morris 2019; Snoubar and Tanrisever 2019).[6]

Secondly, there is a need to move beyond reductionist notions of asylum that examine asylum provision in terms of single independent or dependent variables (cf. Betts, Memişoğlu, and Ali 2021; Badalič 2019; Memişoğlu and Yavçan 2022; Unutulmaz 2019; Hamadeh 2019; Aras and Mencütek, 2015; Tsourapas 2019; El-Hariri 2020; El-Chemali 2019). Rather we need to incorporate a more dynamic perspective that realizes the complexity and multifactorial interdependency at play in such settings. This dynamic perspective is especially important in the analysis of an emergency crisis situation because changes in such contexts are expected to occur at a faster pace. According to Jacobsen (1996), the political marginality of refugees and asylum seekers often allows host governments to adopt rapid positive or negative policy changes with impunity. Hence, the evolution of the policy throughout the course of the crisis situation should also be examined. In addition, there is a need to move beyond the simplistic notion of the existence of a single overriding concern, which motivates governments to adopt a specific policy response, to a more complex analysis of how the constellation of factors and their continuous changes over time influence governments' decisions.

Thirdly, as explained previously, while existing literature has advanced our understanding of responses in the Global South, it does not adequately account for variations across space, even within the South, and across time. Although this literature lays important groundwork, it lacks the nuance for which this book aims to compensate by not assuming parsimonious generalizations about refugee policy-making in the Global South. This book also distinguishes between the dynamics of border- and non-border-sharing countries, contributing to our understanding of policy and governance in the former. Fourthly, as is apparent from this review of the literature, evidence of the influence of the different factors and the mechanism by which they influence the governments' responses remains elusive, which calls for further empirical investigation.

Finally, while the field of forced migration studies is said to be closely informed by policy practices and prescriptions, it has rarely drawn upon the analytical tools of public policy to inform its analysis. The use of such analytical tools would contribute to a more nuanced understanding of refugee policy-making. This book argues that complex systems thinking is a conceptual tool that enables a more holistic understanding of refugee policy-making. It allows researchers to move beyond direct causality analysis and to explore processes and systemic factors driving responses, as well as their effects on policy outcomes over time.

In conclusion, this chapter has performed a key task by outlining an analytical framework and methodology that can be used by scholars seeking to understand and explain the refugee policy-making process in refugee-hosting states across the Global South, where the majority of mass refugee movements occur. I have answered the book's primary question, How do we come to analyze and understand the way in which governments in the Global South respond to mass refugee movements? In the following chapters I will demonstrate how this analytical framework can be applied to a case of mass displacement in the Middle East. As we go through the chapters, readers are encouraged to reflect on how this can be applied to other cases of interest.

3

Syria's Civil War and Ensuing Humanitarian Disaster: Eleven Years On

INTRODUCTION

After eleven years of war the Syrian conflict has taken the lives of over half a million people and generated the world's largest displaced population, a total of 13.7 million both inside and outside Syria, at the time of this book's writing (Devi 2022). This chapter begins the process of applying the analytical framework from chapter 2 to the case of Syrian displacement, by first presenting an overview of the conflict and its ensuing humanitarian disaster. It serves as a stand-alone chapter that offers a comprehensive telling of how developments in the Syrian conflict reflected on events in the neighbouring countries of Lebanon and Jordan. In other words, the aim of this chapter is to help readers contextualize host countries' policy responses and their change over time in light of evolving conflict dynamics in the country of origin.

Syria, officially the Syrian Arab Republic, not only is the country of origin for this displaced population but also holds a significant and sensitive geopolitical position in the Middle East. It is located in Southwest Asia, with Turkey to the north, Iraq to the east, Jordan to the south, and Lebanon and Israel to the west (figure 3.1). It is important to know that historically the "Greater Syria" region also comprised Jordan, Lebanon, Palestine, Israel, and substantial portions of southeastern Turkey (Pipes 1990). This chapter seeks to highlight the key features of the Syrian civil war (including the complex and multi-layered character of the conflict) and its impact on neighbouring Lebanon and Jordan, an impact that is further complicated by Syria's intricate relationship with both countries. I will also

Figure 3.1 | Map of Syria

show other critical aspects that have shaped Lebanon's and Jordan's responses to Syrian refugees, namely the regional and global geopolitical aspects of the conflict, and the involvement of key non-state actors. Both aspects are especially critical, given the proxy nature of the conflict in Syria and the international community's inability to assist in its resolution so far. Finally, this chapter highlights how certain aspects of the humanitarian disaster, including displacement volume, composition, and protraction, have further complicated protection prospects in neighbouring host countries in a variety of ways.

Following this introduction, the chapter is divided into eight sections. The first two sections provide a background on the Syrian conflict, including its triggers and developments. The third section situates the Syrian conflict within its wider regional and geopolitical context, describing how neighbouring countries and global powers alike have been extrinsically linked to and involved, in direct and indirect ways, in the Syrian conflict. The fourth section sheds light on how multilateral peace and conflict-resolution efforts have emerged and then stalled. The fifth section then zooms in to analyze the human consequences of the conflict with a focus on the displacement of Syrians and impacts on the region. This is followed by the sixth section, which explores the global implications of the conflict, including how the wider international community has attempted to respond to the displacement and protection crisis. The seventh section then critically discusses the complexity of return as a solution for the plight of Syrian refugees, exploring the factors behind this and discussing whether or not the conditions for sustainable return are in place in the current climate. The last section provides a conclusion to the chapter.

SYRIA'S "SPRING" (2011)

On Tuesday, 15 March 2011, calling for "dignity, freedom, and social justice," pro-democracy protesters took to the streets in the town of Deraa, south of the Syrian capital of Damascus, (Gifkins 2012). The domino effect of popular uprisings, ignited by a street vendor in Tunisia, had quickly rippled through the Middle East, raising hopes of an "Arab Spring." The calls for change toppled authoritarian rulers in Tunisia and Egypt, and Syria's regime was not immune (Y. Ryan 2011; Zuber and Moussa 2018). Protests in Syria were attributed to the failure of the Assad regime to keep its promises of reform, to economic depression, and to worsening environmental conditions (Çakmak and Ustaoğlu 2015). However, in her book on the origins of the Syrian conflict, Daoudy (2020) argues that deteriorating environmental conditions were rather a consequence of the regime's overall mismanagement and poor economic policies, than a direct factor on their own in instigating the protests.

Perceived as having one of the region's most repressive regimes, the Arab Socialist Ba'ath Party had been ruling Syria since 1963 (Barnes 2009; Osman 2017). The Ba'ath Party was founded by Michel Aflaq and Salah-al-Din Bitar in 1943 and later merged with the Syrian Socialist Party, in 1953 (Britannica 2022). The Ba'ath Party maintained a monopoly on power in Syria by exploiting sectarian tensions and relying on minorities, and in particular Alawites, in the army and the political establishment (Gifkins 2012; Daher 2018),[1] despite the fact that a majority of Syrians belong to Sunni Islam (Holliday 2011). Although this policy of awarding disproportionate power and privileges to Alawites (and other minorities, such as Druze and Ismailis) was a remnant of the French mandate in the 1920s, it remained a key strategy for maintaining the Assad regime (Berti and Paris 2014).

Torture, corruption, and lack of political freedom were landmarks of the Syrian regime. Although Syria is officially considered a presidential democracy, selection of the president is not open to popular choice, and candidates nominated by the Ba'ath Party run unopposed. Following the passing of President Hafiz al-Assad, who ruled Syria from 1971 to 2000, power was promptly taken by his son, Bashar al-Assad, when constitutional amendments were made that allowed the deceased president's son to effectively inherit the presidency – a political manoeuvre that was unsuccessfully replicated in Egypt, thereby igniting the Egyptian revolution (Butt 2020). In 2010, Human Rights Watch (HRW) ranked Syria's human rights record as "among the worst in the world (HRW 2011). Since 1963 Syria had been operating under emergency martial law, the lifting of which was one of the protesters' key demands because it gave sweeping powers to state security courts to try political prisoners (BBC 2011).

Economically, soon after assuming power, Assad attempted to promote neo-liberal policies in a so-called effort to modernize Syria (Bhardwaj 2012). This was also in line with general political economic trends in the region and the world. However, such economic restructurings were faced with increasing opposition (Harris 2005). and the introduction of privatization and the transition to a social market economy increased income inequality, especially among the middle classes (Rafizadeh 2013; Heydemann 2020). In terms of economic and human development, Syria ranked as a developing low-income economy with medium human development (World Bank 2022d; UNDP 2022). Prior to the war the poverty head-count ratio at the national poverty line was 35 per cent (as a percentage of the population), and national debt in relation to gross domestic product (GDP) was 30 per cent (World Bank 2022e; O'Neill 2021).

Environmentally Syria suffers from water scarcity, which has highly affected its people and economy (Barnes 2009). This is especially the case because Syria's economy is highly dependent on agriculture.[2] While its population increased from three million to twenty-two million between 1950 and 2012, the availability of renewable water shrank. Moreover, according to Gleick (2014), ineffective watershed management and the impacts of climate change contributed to agricultural failures. Between 2006 and 2009, around 1.3 million inhabitants of eastern Syria were affected by these problems, as were their livelihoods and basic food supports (Solh 2010; ISDR 2011). A return of drought in 2011 worsened the situation and is hypothesized to have contributed to the worsening economic situation that preceded the revolution, alongside poor overall economic mismanagement.[2] By late 2011 the UN estimated that between two million and three million Syrians were affected by the drought, with one million driven into food insecurity as a result (Gleick 2014).

The protests that started in Deraa soon spread to the outskirts of Syria's capital, Damascus, and other key cities (Gifkins 2012). The Syrian government responded to the protests with force, fuelling them further and spreading them across the country. In his first address to the nation since the start of the protests President Bashar al-Assad blamed the uprising on a foreign plot (Black 2012). From this point, protests spread to marginalized towns and cities throughout Syria. Moreover, a cycle evolved with protests occurring each week after Friday prayers (Gifkins 2012). Syria began to witness a period of hopeful activism and organization, which was met with escalating retaliation and violent repression from the regime (Pearlman 2017; Yassin-Kassab and Al-Shami 2018).

As security forces continued to use excessive force against protesters, the first sign of an internal crack within the regime started to appear. In the summer of July 2011 military defectors formed the Free Syrian Army, a rebel army aiming to overthrow the government. From then on, Syria's peaceful protests began to deteriorate into an armed rebellion and later a full-scale war, which was considered by commentators to be the deadliest conflict seen so far in the twenty-first century (Al Jazeera 2018; Abouzeid 2018).

FROM PRO-DEMOCRACY REVOLUTION
TO CIVIL WAR

As Syria is considered to be one of the most diverse countries in the region, its conflict soon gained sectarian undertones. Ethnically 90 per cent of the Syrian population is Arab, about 9 per cent are Kurds, and 1 per cent are Armenians, Circassians, and Turkomans.

In terms of religious diversity the majority of Syrians are Muslims (87 per cent). Among them, 80 per cent are Sunni Muslims (65 per cent are Arabs, and 15 per cent are Kurds) and 12 per cent are Alawites (Balanche 2018).

Demonstrators, who mostly belonged to the Sunni Muslim denomination, had maintained a secular message at the start (Holliday 2011). While the Sunni Arab bourgeoisie maintained close ties with the clergy, financing pious foundations and charitable associations, it did not represent a unified alternative to the Assad regime. Mostly because of internal divisions and regional rivalries, some sections were in fact allied with the regime, while others remained mainly passive (Balanche 2018; Berti and Paris 2014). While Corstange and York (2018) argue that the government narrative focused on sectarian differences in an effort to garner support for the Assad regime among minority religious groups, Daher (2018) provides a more complicated picture. According to him, the government narrative did not focus on sectarian differences from the start but rather tried to demonize the opposition as being all "Islamic terrorist extremists." It was only later that it began to use sectarianism as a narrative and tool for division (Daher 2018).

As a result of the sectarian divide, the war in Syria led to the de facto dissolution of its territory into several different political entities: the state of ISIS (the Islamic State of Iraq and Syria or the Islamic Caliphate of Abu Bakr al-Baghdadi), located in eastern Syria and northern Iraq; the remains of the original Syrian state, led by the Assad regime and enjoying Russian and Iranian support, located in western Syria; the autonomous Kurdish enclaves, located in the eastern and northern parts of Syrian territory; and the enclaves held in significant portions of northern and southern Syria by rebel groups, headed by Fath al-Sham Front (formerly, the Support Front for the People of Syria, the Al-Nusra Front, or Jabhat al-Nusra), affiliated until late July 2016 with al-Qaeda (Zisser 2017). Control over Syria's oil and black-market trade of oil products has been a key element of this conflict. For instance, both ISIS and Kurdish forces are dependent on oil and gas resources as one of their main sources of funding (Almohamad and Dittmann 2016).

SYRIA'S REGIONAL PROXY WAR

As the opposition mushroomed and divided into various fighting groups with divergent views of what a post-Assad Syria should look like, the unrest proved a magnet for foreign militants, who started to pour into the country (Ferris, Kirişci, and Shaikh 2013). Fearing the unrest would spill over and disrupt power balances, regional and international players became increasingly involved, and the revolution that had started with fifteen young boys drawing anti-government graffiti on Deraa's walls, escalated into an outright proxy war (Laub and Masters 2013). Given, as mentioned earlier, that Syria is one of the Middle East's most religiously diverse countries, the conflict's sectarian undertones also led to the war becoming a regional and international proxy war, in which the opposition was backed by Gulf Arab states, Turkey, and Western powers, and pro-regime groups were backed by Iran, Iraqi Shiite militants, Russia, and Lebanon's militant group Hezbollah (Hokayem 2012, 2014), giving off a Sunni versus Shiite coalition effect.[4]

Geopolitical Complications in the Levant and the Middle East

TURKEY AND THE KURDISH QUESTION

After years of deepening relations with the Assad regime, Turkey reversed its policy towards Assad shortly after the Syrian conflict began. As violence in Syria escalated, the question of insurgents and civilians being persecuted by the Assad regime was criticized by the Turkish government (Carpenter 2013). In fact, Turkey took on a leading overt role against the Syrian regime by allowing both the diplomatic and the military arms of the opposition to organize in its territory. Further, Turkey imposed an effective arms embargo and a broad sanctions package against Syria (Holliday 2011). Nevertheless, despite its attempt to drive Bashar al-Assad out of power in Syria, Turkey has also been concerned about the growth and self-governing ambitions of Kurdish forces in the Syrian Kurdistan (James and Özdamar 2009). Kurdish forces in that region are closely linked to the Kurdistan Workers' Party (PKK), which is primarily based in southeastern Turkey and northern Iraq (Berti and Paris 2014). Turkey has long feared that the growth and cooperation among Kurdish forces in the region could become the foundation for a larger and de facto independent Kurdish state, which it finds worrisome (Carpenter 2013).

INVOLVEMENT OF GULF ARAB STATES, IRAN, AND NEIGHBOURING IRAQ

Besides Turkish involvement, the Syrian war represented geopolitical complications, bringing into the picture the Gulf Arab states,

74   The Politics of Refugee Policy in the Global South

including Saudi Arabia, the United Arab Emirates (UAE), Iran, and Iraq. Both Iran and Iraq have supported the Assad regime during the conflict (Holliday 2011). This is especially the case because Iran has always seen the Assad regime as its main strategic ally in the region. Iran and Syria also have a mutual defence pact, signed in 2006 (Alvarez-Ossorio 2019). Together with Russia, Iran also made an agreement with Syria, allowing Iran to make lucrative reconstruction investments in the country as a "payback" for its support (Asseburg 2020). However, until today, experts have reported that economic gains have been very limited.[5]

Meanwhile Iraq has been concerned that the downfall of the Assad regime could embolden the Sunni tribes of its Anbar province (which borders Syria) to resist the central government and make for an unfriendly Sunni-dominated neighbour (Holliday 2011). In tandem, despite previously sharing good relations with the Syrian regime (especially in 2008–11), Saudi Arabia has supported insurgent groups against Assad (Zuber and Moussa 2018). Saudi Arabia's participation can be explained by the country's fears over the expanding regional role of Iran. In this context Saudi Arabia sees the support of the anti-Assad opposition and regime change in Syria as a crucial tool for weakening Iran's influence in the region. Meanwhile, albeit trying to distance itself from a long-standing Saudi tutelage, Qatar has also supported various Islamist-oriented militias in Syria since the onset of the conflict (Berti and Paris 2014). Although Qatar had been Assad's most important Gulf ally in the past (particularly in the 1990s), this relationship has changed drastically, and estimates of Qatari aid to rebels in Syria have reached USD 3 billion (Hokayem 2012, 2014).

COMPLICATIONS ON THE PALESTINIAN-ISRAELI FRONT

Israel is the only neighbour with which Syria is officially at war. The country has occupied the Syrian Golan Heights since 1967 and annexed the territory in 1981, even though it is still recognized as Syrian territory by the international community (Asseburg 2020; UN 2021). While Israel was not particularly interested in seeing the end of the Assad regime, and some of its leaders dreaded its potential downfall, it considered the conflict as fertile ground for weakening Iran's influence in the region (Kenner 2018).[6] As a consequence, Israeli air forces have been conducting air strikes in Syrian territory with increasing frequency, often trying to weaken the stronghold of Iranian or Iranian-proxy militias (BBC 2023).

On another front, although in the past the Syrian regime had backed the Palestinian resistance group Hamas in the Gaza Strip in an effort to create a "resistance front" in the region, the organization cut ties with Assad following the start of the Syrian conflict. As a result, the Syrian regime has directed its support to Hamas's rival group, the Palestinian Islamic Jihad (PIJ), and explored rivalries and feuds between Palestinian armed groups. Consequently, rival Palestinian groups have clashed in Syria, while groups, such as the Popular Front for the Liberation of Palestine – General Command (PFLP-GC) faction, have fought on the side of the Syrian regime (Hughes 2014). In 2022 Hamas leaders met with Assad and restored ties with Syria, citing the need for "strengthening cooperation to consolidate an axis of resistance to Israel's threats" (Daher 2022a; France24 News 2022).

International Involvement

Notably, international powers, including Russia, China, the United States, and Europe, have contributed a steady stream of weaponry and resources to different sides of the Syrian conflict.

RUSSIA AND CHINA

Russia joined the conflict in 2015 and became the main ally of the Assad regime in its fight against the Islamic State of Iraq and the Levant (ISIL) and other opposition groups (Balanche 2018; Zuber and Moussa 2018). Despite its heavy involvement, Russia continues to argue that it only attacks "terrorist" groups acting in Syria (BBC 2023; Pearson and Sanders 2019). This is, of course, contrary to the reality that Russia has many interests in the Syrian conflict. Firstly, according to Gifkins (2012), Russia is the main supplier of arms to Syria, accounting for approximately 10 per cent of Russia's arms sales. Secondly, Tartus naval base (in Syria) is Russia's last remaining military base outside the former Soviet Union. Albeit there have been disputes on the current military significance of this base, it holds political and symbolic significance for Russia. Thirdly, Russia's "resistance" to Western pressure over Syria is aimed at garnering recently faltering domestic support (Gifkins 2012). Russia has also repeatedly used its veto power in the United Nations Security Council to impede resolutions directed at Syria (Al Jazeera 2020). An expert on Russia's stakes mentioned the following: "Syria is one of Russia's few remaining allies in the region. Despite this, Russia expects to be compensated and to benefit from economic opportunities arising from reconstruction – but in the long run. Currently, the main objective is to maintain its geopolitical position by supporting the Syrian regime."[7]

Meanwhile China's relationship with the Assad regime, while maintaining a lower profile, is far from trivial (Carpenter 2013). Although China has not been directly involved in the conflict militarily and has only supported Assad's struggle against rebels at the ideological level, much has been said about China's interests in postwar Syria, including Syria's potential for advancing the Belt and Road Initiative (BRI) (Calabrese 2019; Chulov 2021; Wang 2021). While Chinese firms are interested in participating in Syria's infrastructure projects, Syria (together with Lebanon) represents a route to the Mediterranean that is an alternative to the Suez Canal and is thus strategic for the BRI (Giorgio 2020). In 2011–21 alone, China – along with Russia – voted three times in the Security Council against UN intervention in Syria (Ferdinand 2013).

WESTERN INTERVENTIONS: THE UNITED STATES AND EUROPE

Western interventions in the Syrian war, in military and diplomatic ways, have been substantial (Mandić 2022). The end of the Assad regime, as Iran's major ally in the region, is considered by Western powers to be a gateway to undermining this alliance and weakening Iranian influence in the Middle East (Hughes 2014). The United States has intervened on behalf of fighting rebels by providing training to vetted groups, such as the Free Syrian Army (FSA) (Gilsinan 2015). Fearing rising fundamentalism, it simultaneously led an international coalition of nearly sixty countries against ISIL (Pearson and Sanders 2019; Zuber and Moussa 2018).

Furthermore, in 2017, American warships engaged in a direct attack on the Syrian regime, launching a series of cruise missiles against an airbase in Syria. This occurred a few days after the regime had been accused of using chemical weapons against civilians in the Syrian Province of Idlib (Henriksen 2018). However, the United States called this attack "a specific response to a specific action," and otherwise the US government has generally refrained from countering the Syria regime directly (Barron and Barnes 2018). Europe has also been directly involved in the conflict, including the United Kingdom (since 2012) and France (since 2015). In addition to direct engagement and fighting alongside the United States, the United Kingdom, France, and Germany have assisted Syrian rebels and Syrian Kurds since the early stages of the conflict (Apps 2012; Stelzenmüller 2019).

In addition to military engagement, many Western countries have imposed sanctions on the Syrian regime. US sanctions against the Syrian regime outlive the war, starting in 1979 as retribution for "Syria's support of militant terrorist groups, occupation of Lebanon, pursuance of weapons of mass destruction and missile programs, and undermining of US and international efforts to stabilize Iraq" (Daher 2020; OFAC 2013). In 2011 Europe imposed a ban on Syrian oil, which reduced the country's production by 75 per cent (Holliday 2011), followed by a new set of direct and secondary sanctions imposed by the United States in 2019 (referred to as the Caesar Syria Civilian Protection Act or the Caesar Sanctions), warning others against cooperating with the Assad regime or with individuals responsible for grave human rights violations (Asseburg 2020). An expert on this matter cited the following: "The Caesar Act includes sanctions on key individuals, including the Syrian president, his wife and his sons and other key individuals in the government, as well the Syrian Central Bank. The US accuses the Central Bank of Syria of being a money-laundering mechanism, and so it has also been sanctioned."[8]

MULTILATERAL AND INTERNATIONAL PEACE EFFORTS

Beyond direct and indirect bilateral involvement in the war, multilateral efforts to hold government and opposition forces accountable and to resolve the conflict were part and parcel of the decade-long journey. In 2011 the UN established the Independent International Commission of Inquiry on the Syrian Arab Republic (IICISAR) to investigate war crimes committed on all sides of the conflict (Edwards and Cacciatori 2018). Alongside this, in early 2012, the United States and France proposed the creation of the Friends of Syria group, an initiative that also found support in the Arab world. The group's first meeting in February 2012 included representatives from around seventy states. However, considering the Syrian government was not invited to the meeting, Russia and China refrained from participating. At the time, the Friends of Syria group called for the immediate halt of all violence and for humanitarian agencies to be permitted to deliver humanitarian aid (Küçükkeleş 2012).

78   The Politics of Refugee Policy in the Global South

The year 2012 also saw other initiatives emerging at the UN-level. In February former UN secretary-general Kofi Annan was appointed as joint special envoy to solve the Syrian crisis. This resulted in a conference and agreement (referred to as the Geneva Agreement) led by Kofi Annan and the UN Security Council, which stipulated the establishment of a transitional governing body in Syria. Nevertheless, disagreements between the United States and Russia rose over the role that President Bashar al-Assad could play in this transition government. This prevented negotiations from moving forward and resulted in Kofi Annan's resignation from his role in August (ACRPS Policy Analysis Unit 2014). Negotiations only restarted in early 2014 (in a process known as Geneva II), after the United States and Russia assumed a more programmatic posture vis-à-vis the rise of ISIL and Assad's use of chemical weapons in 2013. However, with the exception of limited agreements on the delivery of humanitarian aid, Geneva II generated little progress. Both sides persisted in inflexibility on the central issues, such as Assad's role in a future transition government. With neither side budging from their positions, the UN process again failed (Lundgren 2016). In 2015 over twenty states and international organizations created the International Syria Support Group (ISSG), with the United States and Russia as co-chairs, along with an office run by the UN (Sasnal 2016).

Within the realm of the UN Security Council, the situation in Syria, as mentioned earlier, revived the use of the veto power by some of its permanent five members, namely Russia and China. Repeated vetoes of draft resolutions and even the mere threat of a veto stalled negotiations and rendered the Security Council largely inefficient. As a consequence, the Security Council only managed to pass modest resolutions calling on all parties to cease any violence, demanding access for humanitarian personnel, and deploying teams of unarmed observers (Webb 2014).

Role of the Arab League

The first conflict-management efforts in the Syrian conflict were undertaken by the Arab League, the leading intergovernmental organization in the Arab world. Although the league is customarily non-interventionist and even framed the conflict as a matter of domestic politics at the initial stage, it sent a mediation mission to Syria in 2011, which met with Assad and opposition members on several occasions (Lundgren 2016). However, after proposing a transition to a pluralistic democracy and that Assad transfer his powers to his deputy, the mission faced increased rejection by the Syrian regime (ACRPS Policy Analysis Unit 2014). Moreover, the league also faced internal disagreements, as Qatar and Saudi Arabia called for the adoption of tougher measures (Lundgren 2016). As a result, in 2012, mediation initiatives were handed over to the UN Security Council. Furthermore, Syria was suspended from the league, and economic and political sanctions were imposed (Bhardwaj 2012).

SYRIA'S HUMANITARIAN DISASTER

Eleven years into the war, an estimated 500,000 people have been killed, at least 1.5 million are living without access to humanitarian aid, and approximately 150,000 have been detained or forcibly disappeared (Bellintani 2021; MSF 2021; Walsh 2021). It was established by a UN commission of inquiry that both the regime and the rebels had committed grave human rights violations that amounted to war crimes, including the use of chemical weapons and sarin gas (Jasser 2014; OHCHR 2017). They were also accused of using systematic rape and civilian suffering, through the imposition of sieges and the blockade of humanitarian assistance, as methods of war (Ferris and Kirisci 2016). The fighting gave rise to a full-blown humanitarian crisis.

Syrian Refugee Movement Features

The violence, including gender-based violence, fears of military conscription, and the loss of means necessary for sustaining livelihood – such as jobs, access to health care, and basic services – led civilians to flee in large numbers (Freedman, Kıvılcım, and Baklacıoğlu 2017; Beaujouan and Rasheed 2019). By 2022, an estimated 6.6 million refugees had fled the country, and another 6.7 million were internally displaced (IDMC 2022; UNHCR 2022f). According to Ferris and Kirisci (2016), the refugee movement flowing out of the country was rapid, massive, and dynamic, with some displacements occurring several times both inside and outside Syria.

UNHCR does not record data disaggregated by ethnic or religious affiliation, but the refugee population is said to be composed mainly of Sunni Muslims fleeing anti-government controlled areas.[9] Further, women and children comprised more than two thirds of the displaced population (Karasapan 2022; Middle East Monitor 2020). The movement also included Palestinian refugees who had been residing as refugees in Syria but had to flee again with the rising violence, becoming twice displaced. According to UNRWA (2022), this group amounts to 137,234 Palestinian refugees who have fled Syria to neighbouring countries. Further, approximately 60 per cent of the 438,000 Palestinian refugees who remain in Syria have been displaced at least once, with a large majority having experienced multiple displacements (Beydoun, Abdulrahim, and Sakr 2021).

Syrian Refugees as a Regional Policy Challenge

While the choice of destination may have been based on a multiplicity of factors, such as social networks, financial ability, and physical condition, the majority of Syrian refugees have in fact settled in the direct vicinity of their country (Seven 2022; Ferris, Kirişci, and Shaikh 2013). According to an expert on this matter, although historic social ties likely influenced Syrian Kurds and Armenians to flee to specific countries, Sunni Syrians did not follow similar patterns. While they comprised the majority of those who fled, their choice of destinations likely varied by differences including gender, social class, and region of origin.[10] By November 2022 the number of registered Syrian refugees and asylum seekers in the neighbouring host countries had reached 3.6 million in Turkey, 825,081 in Lebanon, 669,483 in Jordan, 261,046 in Iraq, and 144,683 in Egypt (UNHCR 2022k). With the exception of Egypt and Lebanon, where no formal camps have been allowed, the majority of refugees are settled in non-camp settings in rural, urban, and peri-urban areas (table 3.1).

This massive displacement posed serious challenges for neighbouring countries that have struggled to cope with the burden placed on their economies, environment, infrastructure, and public service provision. In 2019 a deputy Turkish minister of foreign affairs reported that the country's budget expenditures on Syrian refugees since the start of the displacement had reached USD 40 billion (Sonmez 2019). Further, according to Lebanese president Michel Aoun, estimates showed that the country had spent approximately USD 25 billion on its response to Syrian refugees (Xinhua Net 2020). However, such figures are hugely contested by experts, for example: "Political actors in host countries generally blame Syrians for their socio-economic problems. They cite numbers, which are far fetched, as mere propaganda. All the while, some host governments have received international funding to support the Syrian displaced population but have not used the funding for this purpose."[11] In Iraq the Syrian conflict had a spillover effect as ISIL took control of key cities in the north and the west, posing an extra challenge to a country struggling with the consequences of its own protracted conflict (European Parliament 2017).

Despite the foregoing, governments in the region, including the Kurdistan Regional Government, adopted an open-border policy towards Syrian refugees that lasted until 2014 (IRIN 2015). Their entry requirements were not void of restrictions, but they were characterized by observers as "open and welcoming" (Ferris, Kirişci, and Shaikh 2013). Although none of these countries, with the exception of Turkey, is party to the Geneva Convention, they acted, for the most part, in accordance with some of the main contours of international norms of refugee protection, including non-refoulement.[12] As will be seen in chapters 5 to 8, their hospitality ebbed and flowed as dynamics of the Syrian conflict and factors in their internal and external policy environments changed. Exceptional policies adopted for Syrians generally did not apply, however, to Palestinian refugees from Syria (PRS), who were subject to stringent restrictions and sometimes denied entry altogether, as will be discussed in later chapters.

In 2014 a regional refugee and resilience plan (3RP) was put in place by the Office of UNHCR to coordinate humanitarian assistance efforts with national governments, NGOs, and UN agencies (UNDP 2020; Schillings 2018). According to the UN, over USD 50 billion in donor support was provided from 2013 to mid-2022 for the Syrian refugee crisis, through the 3RP and other funding appeals (OCHA 2021). However, as Freedman, Kıvılcım, and Baklacıoğlu (2017) note, the efficacy of the response was curtailed by the sheer scale of the displacement and the pre-existing political and economic fragility of the region.

A DISPLACEMENT WITH GLOBAL IMPLICATIONS

While neighbouring countries to Syria bore the major brunt of the humanitarian crisis, the rest of the world was not immune. In 2014 the extremist militant group ISIL invaded northern Iraq and eastern Syria (Hassan 2018). On Friday, 13 November 2015, a series of

Table 3.1 | Syrian refugee population in neighbouring countries (at 30 November 2022)

Country	Total	Camp population (%)	Non-camp population (%)
Turkey	3,577,714	7.7	92.3
Lebanon	825,081	0	100
Jordan	669,483	20	80
Iraq	261,046	36	64
Egypt	144,683	0	100
Other (North Africa)	41,742		

Source: Compiled from UNHCR (2022g)

coordinated attacks were carried out by the same group against civilians across Paris, killing 130 people and injuring 413. In response, a three-month state of emergency was declared in France, and coalition airstrikes were conducted against ISIL targets in Syria (Marcus 2015). The attacks signalled that whatever happened in Syria would have implications far beyond the region.

As the conflict intensified, refugees and asylum seekers sought other destination countries beyond the Middle East. In 2014, industrialized countries recorded the highest number of asylum applications made by a single group since 1992: an estimated 149,600 Syrians applied for asylum in Japan, the United States, Germany, and others (UNHCR 2014d). However, as neighbouring countries to Syria opened their borders to refugees, others were not so welcoming. As the European Union (EU) made it more and more difficult for refugees to arrive in Europe across a land border, many tried to make the journey by sea. Over the course of almost eight years (2014 to mid-2022), more than a million people, from Syria and other countries of origin, crossed the Mediterranean to seek asylum in Europe, and approximately 25,000 people drowned during the crossing (Sunderland 2022).

The refugee movement into European countries ignited a political storm that brought far-right parties to the fore and was the linchpin of the United Kingdom's exit from the European Union as

Europeans disagreed over what to do about the "migrant crisis" (Taggart and Szczerbiak 2018). With the rise in xenophobic sentiments and fears of a "Muslim exodus," European countries closed their borders, and the EU signed an agreement with Turkey in 2016 to return "irregular migrants" who were travelling through Turkey to reach Greece (Collett 2016). The United States, in turn, elected a far-right presidential candidate who was openly hostile to migrants (P. Martin 2017).

In the meanwhile the international community's efforts to respond effectively to the humanitarian crisis in the region and beyond were largely failing. Despite that several funding conferences, including the Helsinki and the Brussels conferences, were held to support regional host governments, funding appeals were coming short of host-country needs. Between 2012 and 2021, the 3RP was annually underfunded, with the largest gap occurring in 2021 (a 68 per cent gap) (OCHA 2021). Further, peace talks with the Syrian regime and the opposition were unable to reach a political solution to the conflict (Collin 2018). With no end in sight for the war in Syria, and the detrimental effects it was having on global peace and security, the question of refugees became one of the most pressing issues on the regional and global agendas.

With the sudden emergence of the COVID-19 pandemic and its human and economic impacts in Syria and neighbouring host countries, the situation of displaced Syrians was further complicated. Although international humanitarian funding appeals for both Syria and neighbouring countries have been amended to cover the impacts of the pandemic (i.e., to expand health access and cover the cost of vaccines), underfunding trends have remained, and health infrastructure in these countries continue to be overstretched (OCHA 2020a, 2020b, 2021, 2022). Moreover, although Syria and countries hosting Syrian refugees benefit from international vaccine distribution programs (i.e., COVAX), at the time of writing, full immunization rates were still below the 25 per cent mark.

A DECADE OF CONFLICT AND THE QUESTION OF REFUGEE RETURN

Durable solutions to the plight of refugees include local integration in a host state and third-country resettlement, but their voluntary return to countries of origin in conditions of safety is preferred,

The Politics of Refugee Policy in the Global South

being advocated by relevant actors within the international refugee regime, such as UNHCR. However, in the Syrian context the question of refugee return is both complex and volatile, particularly due to the myriad governance actors involved (both de jure and de facto). This is also exacerbated by lack of security, threats by the regime, and a dire economic situation.[13]

Statistics on Return

According to UNHCR (2022b), 336,496 self-organized or voluntary refugee returns to Syria took place between 2016 and October 2022. The majority of returns initiated from Turkey (153,306), followed by Lebanon (73,666), Jordan (64,644), Iraq (52,621), and Egypt (2,150) (UNHCR 2022h). However, considering that these figures are based on government sources and observation by UNHCR, the actual number may be significantly higher, and not all returns are accounted for (UNHCR 2020b). For instance, mass deportations have been denounced in the main countries hosting Syrians, even though at times their governments denied it (HRW 2017, 2019a). Starting in 2019, however, UNHCR noted a significant increase in returns. Although this trend was halted in the following year due to COVID-19 mobility restrictions, the number of returns started to regain traction in 2021 (UNHCR 2022h).

Challenges of Return

The instability of the situation in Syria, the myriad of actors and interests involved, and the difficulty of ensuring that return does not constitute refoulement make for a complex policy decision. Firstly, while return is considered the preferred policy solution to the refugee plight, conditions must be in place for successful return to take place. Such conditions should ensure that the principle of non-refoulement is upheld by guaranteeing voluntariness, safety, and sustainability (Crisp and Long 2016). In recent years surveys have shown that the majority of Syrians are favourable to returning to Syria but have not done so due to the ongoing conflict and political instability (Yassen 2019).

Secondly, while surveys have argued that most Syrians wish to return to Syria (UNHCR 2018a, 2019a, 2021a), it should not be presumed that all intend or are capable of doing so in the same conditions (Geha 2019a). For instance, Içduygu and Nimer (2020) have argued that the decision to return varies according to Syrians' socio-economic status, age, religious affiliation, level of knowledge of the host country's language, and region of settlement. Furthermore, perceptions on return are fluid and also reflect the changing conditions in Syria and host states over time.

PUSH FOR RETURN IN HOST STATES

At the time of writing, return to Syria was not deemed a safe solution by UNHCR, and the agency continues to call on states not to promote forced returns (UNHCR 2021c). Nevertheless, involuntary return has been triggered by the protraction of the situation and lack of alternative solutions, as well as the worsening in host-community relations and growing xenophobia (Içduygu and Nimer 2020). In this context and particularly after the stagnation of the conflict in favour of the Asaad regime in 2016, host governments started framing Syrians as a burden, and policy actors began introducing return into their discourses (Fakhoury 2021; Assi 2019).

During this period the idea of creating "safe zones" in Syria for refugees to return to became somewhat prominent (al-Makahleh 2017; Içduygu and Nimer 2020; El-Chemali 2019). In tandem, states have also constructed de facto return policy through use of informality to elude asylum norms and push refugees to return (Fakhoury 2021). According to Human Rights Watch, many Syrians returned under indirect pressure from harsh conditions, including lack of legal residence, fear of arrests, and restrictions on movement (HRW 2019). As stated by an expert, "indirect pressures can be considered forced return."[14] Return has also been used for political gain and as a bargaining tool to garner support from international donors (Içduygu and Nimer 2020). This includes not only host countries but also the Syrian government, which has promoted return in order to fuel the idea that the war is ending (Alfred 2018). According to an expert on this matter, "when Bashar talks about refugee returns, he does so for his own benefit, to get other countries to normalize relations with the Syrian regime, which needs international recognition and collaboration."[15]

CONDITIONS IN THE HOME STATE

For return to become sustainable, conditions in the home state need to be stable and conducive to return and reintegration (socially, economically, culturally, and politically). Although surveys indicate

86 The Politics of Refugee Policy in the Global South

that Syrians would like to return as soon as the situation in Syria improves (NRC 2018), the economic and infrastructure damage, as well as the destruction of social fabric, in Syria do not favour this solution. Syria's economy has deeply deteriorated since the conflict began in 2011, declining by more than 70 per cent in the period 2010–17 (CIA 2020). By 2018 it was estimated that the conflict had caused over USD 442.2 billion in losses for the country, including direct physical destruction and GDP losses (ESCWA 2020). Notably, physical destruction is unevenly distributed, and the worst damage is concentrated in areas that were previously contested by rebels and ISIL, such as the eastern suburbs of Damascus, East Aleppo, Al-Raqqa, Homs, and Hama *inter alia* (Asseburg 2020).

The lack of foreign investments, the barriers to international trade (including sanctions), the depreciation of the Syrian pound, and the collapse of the banking system have also highly affected the country's economy (Mehchy 2019). Inflation has reached unprecedented levels, standards of living have fallen sharply, and the economy has contracted by more than 60 per cent compared to its pre-war state (El-Taliawi, forthcoming; Alexander and Ahlam 2021; ESCWA 2016). Although in 2017 some economic indicators began to stabilize (including exchange rates and inflation), economic activity remains depressed (CIA 2020). As a result, human development outcomes have collapsed. It is estimated that more than 14.6 million people within Syria depend on some form of humanitarian assistance, and 12 million are food insecure (OHCHR 2022).

According to an NGO worker in Syria, the country presently experiences currency deflation; that is, the Syrian pound has lost its purchasing power.[16] As an expert on this matter argues, "the economic situation in Syria is so bad that families in Syria heavily rely on family members abroad ...all Syrians I know send money back home."[17] This situation was heightened during the COVID-19 pandemic. According to this same expert, while many Syrians in host countries (such as Jordan and Lebanon) "have lost their jobs and thus their ability to remit ... access to COVID-19 equipment in Syria is based on if citizens have relatives that can send them money to access COVID-19 care, meaning that the rising health needs are driving up the need to receive remittance."[18]

Since the beginning of the conflict, oil and gas production has also declined due to economic sanctions and the impacts of the war. Moreover, oil and gas fields are currently divided between the main players in the conflict, including the Syrian regime, Kurdish forces, and the ISIL (Almohamad and Dittmann 2016). At a time when the conflict seems to have tipped in favour of the Asaad regime, the implications of this for returnees are multifaceted (*The Economist* 2021). With most of Syria's oil and gas fields and agricultural land still outside the control of the regime, its strategy now concentrates on real estate and buildings (Asseburg 2020). Consequently the government has passed various laws to expedite the dispossession of properties and to deal with irregular settlements (EASO 2020). As a result, even though some areas have witnessed reconstruction efforts since 2017, many Syrians have lost their properties and are not able to return in a sustainable way (IDMC 2020). As argued by an expert on this subject, "there is no developmental process for 99 per cent of the Syrian population. The elites are the only ones who benefit."[19]

Finally, Syrians displaced outside and within Syria also need to interact with the Syrian security sector and receive permission or clearance to return. Many refugees who comprise opposition to the government and have been framed as "terrorists" may face persecution upon return. Moreover, the issue of mandatory military conscription also hinders their intentions to return (Devadas, Elbadawi, and Loayza 2019). According to an expert on this matter, "there are still arrests and some people are still leaving for fear of military conscription."[20]

NEED FOR STATE AND NON-STATE COLLABORATION

Within the international refugee regime, return is established as a mutually constitutive solution, involving countries of origin, host states, and the international community (Bradley 2009). Hence, although UNHCR is the key actor in charge of facilitating and overseeing return operations, sustainable return in conditions of safety and dignity will not be feasible without the cooperation of the Syrian regime – which holds power over the majority of Syria – international actors involved in the conflict (including Russia and the United States), host states, and local actors, including Hezbollah. Thus, in addition to the planning of logistics and the assigning of responsibilities outside and within Syria, political obstacles need to be surpassed, and general will to cooperate needs to be built.

At this moment the situation on the ground is still volatile, and political asymmetries appear to hinder chances of collaboration. An example of this is the UN Security Council's lack of unity for expanding humanitarian access to Syria. Currently only one border crossing remains active for humanitarian purposes, and Russia has continually threated to veto its continuity. The Lebanese government (especially parties with anti-Syrian regime sentiments) has avoided negotiating returns, due to fears that this may undermine the international community's support for Prime Minister Hariri. Meanwhile political parties and political figures in Lebanon, some with pro-Syrian regime allegiance, advocate for return (e.g., President Aoun) (Reuters 2017). Also, Hezbollah has "negotiated" the return of around ten thousand refugees from areas under its control without the involvement of the Lebanese government or the United Nations (Enders 2018).[21] In tandem, some external actors (i.e., Turkey and Russia) have also supported returns due to a desire to normalize the situation in Syria and benefit from its reconstruction (EUI 2022; Aslan 2019; Içduygu and Nimer 2020; Vohra 2019).[22]

Syria is still at war, and a peaceful resolution to the conflict remains elusive. Even though "safe zones" have been created, they are temporary and do not offer full protection. Notably, returns present challenges at the level of host and Syrian governments, at the supranational level, and at the level of individual refugees. Hence, return initiatives should be gradual, collaborative, and convincing to the refugee community (Içduygu and Nimer 2020). Although precise statistics and reliable information on returns are scarce, following the easing of COVID-19 mobility restrictions, data from UNHCR demonstrates that the number of self-organized returns has been in a growth trajectory since 2021 (UNHCR 2022h). As such, there is a need for increased cooperation and consensus among all parties involved in the conflict and its response.

CONCLUSION

Although fighting in Syria was not over at the time of this book's writing, by mid-2022 the Syrian regime and its allies had steadily regained control of around 60 per cent of the country's territory (Kaduri and Essa 2022). There appeared to be no real prospects for a peaceful settlement of the conflict, especially in areas where fighting rebels still held power on the ground. In this chapter, readers have been introduced to three key problematic complexities of the Syrian war: the complex and multi-layered character of the conflict, which is further complicated by Syria's intricate political and social relationship with its neighbours; the global and regional geopolitical aspects of the conflict, including the involvement of key non-state actors; and the protracted character of the conflict as well as the international community's inability to assist in its resolution.

Put together, these and other complexities linked to the conflict drive the responses of bordering host states to refugees and further complicate refugee policy-making at the national and local levels. For us to better structure and conceptualize how developments in the home country influence and shape host-country policies, we need not go further than applying the framework presented in chapter 2.

In more detail in the coming chapters I will show how each of the complex factors alluded to here have shaped Lebanon's and Jordan's responses to Syrian refugees on their lands. Some key factors discussed here, which will emerge as having been highly influential in shaping their policy responses, include the actors involved in the conflict and their evolving power dynamics. The coming chapters will demonstrate clearly how these factors have directly influenced Lebanon's and Jordan's perceived outcome of the conflict. Further, I will show how the conflict's protraction has conditioned the policies of both countries towards the Syrian displaced population.

The following chapters will show how factors, such as geopolitical relations, involvement of international actors, and global stances to the conflict, have affected Lebanon's and Jordan's foreign policy choices at the state level. At the social level, other factors, including the religious and ethnic composition of the displacement, have played a key role in conditioning host communities' social receptiveness of Syrian refugees. Finally, I will discuss the evolutions and restrictions in host border policies resulting from security and conflict spillovers from Syria. I will show how even economic sanctions imposed on Syria have had an impact on the policies and economic capacities of neighbouring host countries, particularly when economies are as intertwined as they are in this case.

4

From Home to Hosts: Jordan's and Lebanon's Refugee Policy-Making Contexts

INTRODUCTION

Introducing hosts in this key background chapter, I discuss Jordan's and Lebanon's refugee-policy environments. Based on the analytical framework described in chapter 2, I delve here into each host country's domestic arena to take a closer look at the context, or environment, in which the policies governing Syrian refugees are formulated and implemented. I highlight the key variables that are likely to shape and influence each country's policy response to Syrian displacement in particular and to mass refugee movements in general. Such variables include the host's socio-economic profile, administrative and political system, demographic and ethnic composition, previous refugee-hosting experiences as well as experiences of refugeehood, and relations with the "home" country (i.e., Syria). I also discuss the normative framework that governs refugees in each country, including laws, international agreements, and local norms.

This overview is necessary before showing, in the coming chapters, how each of these variables came into play and shaped Jordan's and Lebanon's initial policy responses and their evolutions over time. In this chapter I introduce Jordan's and Lebanon's refugee policy-making contexts, with emphasis on the pre-2011 era, prior to the arrival of Syrian refugees. Hence, this chapter provides, in many ways, an initial snapshot in the series of scenes that will unfold in this policy journey.

OVERVIEW OF JORDAN'S REFUGEE POLICY-MAKING CONTEXT

The Hashemite Kingdom of Jordan is an Arab country that lies at the crossroads of Asia and Africa. Geographically, the small kingdom is bordered by Iraq, Syria, Saudi Arabia, the Palestinian West Bank, and Israel (figure 4.1). Like many other Middle Eastern countries, its borders were drawn in the early twentieth century by European colonial powers (Milton-Edwards and Hinchcliffe 2009). It gained independence from the British in 1946, making it a nascent nation-state (Bacik 2007).

Jordan is a constitutional hereditary monarchy with a parliamentary form of government (UNPAN 2014). However, the king has traditionally held sweeping powers over both the executive and the legislative branches, especially on matters of foreign affairs (Lust-Okar 2009). The Democracy Index and Freedom in the World reports rank Jordan as an authoritarian regime that provides few political rights, civil liberties, and freedom to its citizens (Freedom House 2022a; *The Economist* 2022). Compared to other Middle Eastern countries, however, Jordan's human-rights record is relatively less blemished. According to Milton-Edwards and Hinchcliffe (2009), while Jordan does not appear to be a typical police state, this perception is relative in a region often portrayed in the West as having authoritarian rule.

Since the formation of Jordan its population has been on the rise, as a result of an exceptionally high birth rate by regional and international standards (ranging from 2.8 to 2.1 per cent between 2010 and 2020) and of several waves of regional displacement (Kumaraswamy and Singh 2017; World Bank 2022a). Between 2010 and 2021 Jordan's population increased from 7.2 million to 10.2 million, including Transjordanians and Palestinians who were granted Jordanian citizenship (DoS 2011; World Bank 2022a). The exact breakdown, however, is the subject of controversy. According to Kumaraswamy and Singh (2017), population statistics disclosed by the government are often blurred to reflect its desired demographic balance and to downplay the Palestinian component. As per government statistics, in 2011, Sunni Muslims accounted for 92 per cent of the population, while Christians made up 6 per cent, and Druze, a branch of Shia Islam, made up around 2 per cent. In terms of ethnicity, Arabs were reported to make up 98 per cent of

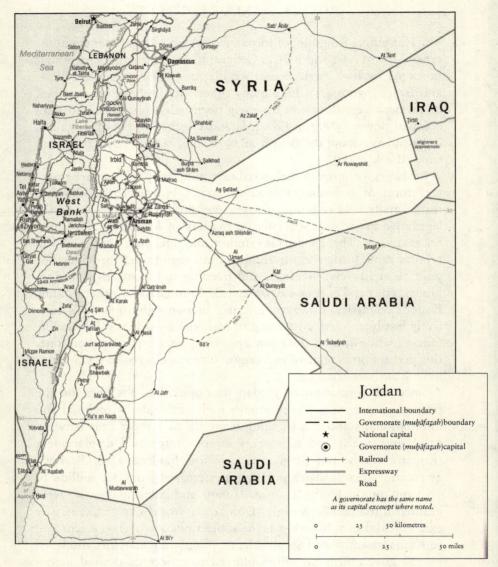

Figure 4.1 | Map of Jordan

Jordan's populace, while the other 2 per cent included Armenians, Circassians, and others (GoJ 2018). Comparing these figures to more recent ones reported in table 1.1 reveals no major difference. Jordan's non-citizen resident population also includes a large migrant population, including Egyptians; prior to the Syrian refugee movement those Egyptians made up 69 per cent of the kingdom's non-Jordanian labour force (Al Khouri 2007).

Jordan's economy is public sector heavy with a weak private sector (UNPAN 2014), and public-sector employment is reported by experts to be mostly dominated by and reserved for Transjordanians who are not of Palestinian origin. As a result, the private sector is primarily controlled by Jordanian Palestinians (Reiter 2004). Jordan is a semi-arid country that is almost land-locked and is short on natural resources, especially water and agricultural land. Between 2009 and 2022 Jordan was ranked as the fourth (Jordan Ministry of Water and Irrigation 2009) and the second (UNICEF 2022) most water-scarce country in the world. It is an upper-middle-income country of high human development, with a male unemployment rate that rose from 10.4 per cent in 2010 to 19.3 per cent in 2021 based on national estimates. Unemployment is especially rampant among the youth population (15–24 years), rising from 31.6 per cent in 2011 to 43.0 per cent in 2021 (national estimates) (UNDP 2018; World Bank 2022a). In 2010 its GDP per capita was reported as USD 3,736 and rose to USD 4,405 in 2021 (in current US dollars).

Since its inception Jordan has been heavily reliant on expatriate worker remittances and foreign aid (from the United Kingdom, the United States, and more recently from the oil-rich Gulf) (Issawi 1983). Following a severe financial and monetary crisis and food riots in 1989, the kingdom underwent several economic adjustment processes, with the support of the International Monetary Fund (IMF), to regain macroeconomic stability (Jadarat 2010). According to Bacik (2007), concern over budget security has always been a constant determinant of Jordanian domestic and foreign policies. In 2010 the kingdom had reported government gross debt of 59.4 per cent of GDP, as opposed to 91.0 per cent in 2022 (IMF 2022). Until recently the kingdom had a centralized system of government, with Amman as its administrative capital and most populous city. Jordan is divided into twelve administrative governorates, which are in turn divided into districts and sub-districts (UNPAN 2014).

Jordan: A Refuge Destination

Lying at the heart of the Arab world and having been relatively stable, Jordan has been receiving and hosting refugees from the surrounding region for decades (Chatelard 2010). In 2010 its overall refugee population was 2,450,381 (World Bank 2018). As Milton-Edwards and Hinchcliffe (2009) note, Jordan's proximity to Israel and its rule over the West Bank from 1948 to 1967 made it the most natural destination for fleeing Palestinians in the two great exoduses of 1948 and 1967. It also became a refuge destination for Palestinians fleeing other conflicts in the region, including the 1990 Gulf War and the 2003 invasion of Iraq (Davidson 2015). The Syrian crisis has added 14,000 Palestinian refugees to the pre-existing Palestinian population, as refugees fled the violence of the civil war (Salemi, Bowman, and Compton 2018). According to UNRWA (2022), an estimated 2.32 million registered Palestinian refugees currently reside in Jordan, making it the largest host of Palestinian refugees in the world. Their presence has altered and affected Jordan's political, social, and economic life in many ways as they came to constitute a large segment of the kingdom's population. Throughout its recent history Jordan was also host to other refugee populations, including Lebanese during the 1975–90 civil war, Bosnians during the 1990s conflict in Yugoslavia, and Iraqis during the Gulf War of 1991 and following the US invasion in 2003 (Davidson 2015).

Normative Framework Governing Refugees: Between Law and Local Norms

Like many countries in the Middle East, Jordan lacks a clear legal framework for refugees and asylum seekers. However, Frangieh (2016) argues that refugee protection does not operate in a complete legal vacuum. Jordan derives its legal framework for the governance of refugees from a multi-layered set of hard and soft laws. This mix is derived from international legal instruments, domestic legislation, and local norms. Although Jordan is not party to the 1951 Geneva Convention that governs the situation of refugees, in 1998 it signed an MOU with the UNHCR. This bilateral agreement regulates the main aspects of refugee protection (Olwan and Shiyab 2012). The major way in which the MOU diverges from the Convention's provisions, according to Al-Kilani (2014), is in prohibiting local integration as a durable solution for refugees. Otherwise, in line with the Geneva Convention, Jordan uses the same definition of *refugee* and generally abides by the principle of non-refoulement (Bank 2016). Other international and regional agreements that govern Jordan's treatment of refugees include the Universal Declaration of Human Rights, the Convention on the Elimination of All Forms of Racial Discrimination, the Convention on the Elimination of All Forms of Discrimination against Women, the Arab Charter on Human Rights, and the Convention on the Rights of the Child (CMRS 2018a).

With regard to constitutional provisions and domestic legislation, article 21(1) of the Jordanian constitution provides that "political refugees shall not be extradited on account of their political beliefs or for their defense of liberty" (WIPO 2023). It therefore offers refugee status for political asylum but, according to Al-Kilani (2014), only on an individual basis and in very exceptional situations. Therefore, it is not an option available for most refugees. Otherwise, refugees are governed by the 1973 Law No. 24 on Residence and Foreigners' Affairs (RefWorld 2023). Other than legal instruments, the norms of humanitarianism and generosity (as derived from tribal customs and religious beliefs) underpin Jordan's treatment of refugees. According to Chatty (2016), Jordanians' acceptance of refugees should be analyzed from an approach not based purely on rights but based on an analysis of local norms, specifically the institution of Karam, which is related to the social requirement to show hospitality to strangers. According to Akpinar (2007), the concept of hospitality to Muslims is a pillar of the Islamic ethical system. Showing hospitality is considered a moral duty towards strangers, guests, and/or refugees. Traditions of hospitality were also engrained in tribal culture in the Arabian Peninsula prior to the advent of Islam (Admirand 2014).

OVERVIEW OF LEBANON'S REFUGEE POLICY-MAKING CONTEXT

The Republic of Lebanon is a small country that lies in the Eastern Mediterranean region at the heart of the Middle East. It shares borders with Syria to the north and the east, and Israel to the south (figure 4.2). With the collapse of the Ottoman Empire, Lebanon passed into the hands of the French, who redrew its borders in 1920 to what constitutes present-day Lebanon (Traboulsi 2007).

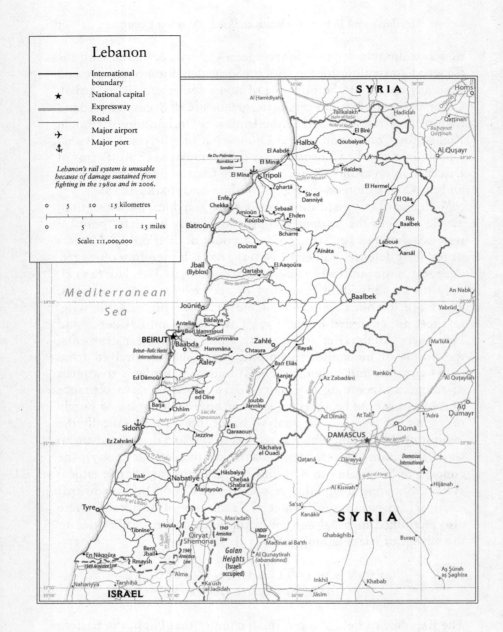

Figure 4.2 | Map of Lebanon

Jordan's and Lebanon's Refugee Policy-Making Contexts   97

Following independence from French mandate rule in 1943, the republic's parliamentary democracy adopted "confessionalism" as an overall framework, whereby the highest offices are proportionally reserved for representatives of the different religious communities in Lebanon (Nisan 2017). In 2022 the country fell in terms of political performance and was ranked for the first time as an authoritarian regime that is partly free (*The Economist* 2022; Freedom House 2022b). Religious sects and intersectarian rule had been the foundation of the Lebanese system, long before the creation of the Lebanese state (Salloukh et al. 2015). According to Cobban (2019, 11), "ideological parties and all other paraphernalia of Western democracy – even the appearance of democracy itself – come and go in Lebanon. Only the sects, and the politics of the sects, live on forever."

Today eighteen officially recognized sects make up the country's mosaic of religious community. Among them are six dominant groups that vie for political power. In order of population dominance they are Sunni Muslims (29.375 per cent), Shiite Muslims (29.375 per cent), Maronite Christians (19.313 per cent), Greek Orthodox Christians (6.750 per cent), Druze (5.479 per cent), and Greek Catholic Christians (4.375 per cent) (Salloukh et al. 2015; U.S. Department of State 2017).[1] However, demographic statistics are subject to controversy and discord due to the country's delicate sectarian balance and the political weight that is accorded to it. In terms of ethnicity, 95 per cent of the populace is of Arab origin (Cobban 2019).

Sectarian violence and power struggles have occurred repeatedly over the course of Lebanon's history. Most recently (1975–90), militias of the various political and religious groups fought a vicious and protracted civil war that entangled outside players including Palestinians, Israelis, and Syrians (Rabil 2003). The fifteen-year-long war led to the death of more than 2 per cent of the population and took a heavy toll on state authority, economic performance, and national development (Nisan 2017). According to Cobban (2019), the civil war also left a scar on the population's collective consciousness. In 1989 a reconciliation accord (dubbed the Ta'ef Agreement) was signed, thereby bringing an end to the armed conflict and paving the way for a redistribution of power among the country's various confessional communities. This power-sharing scheme constituted the following distribution of state posts: president (Maronite Christian); prime minister (Sunni Muslim); deputy

98   The Politics of Refugee Policy in the Global South

prime minister (Greek Orthodox Christian); speaker of parliament (Shiite Muslim); and armed forces chief of staff (Druze) (Salloukh et al. 2015).[2]

Since 1948 Lebanon has also been at the forefront of an enduring Arab-Israeli conflict, in which the Palestine Liberation Organization based in Lebanon launched military operations against Israel (Rabil 2003). As a result, Lebanon witnessed several rounds of invasions and major military hostilities with Israel in 1978, 1982, and finally in 2006 (Spyer 2009), which became Hezbollah's raison d'être in Lebanon.

In terms of economic performance, due to recent economic and financial downfall Lebanon was downgraded from an upper- to a lower-middle-income country, while retaining its high human development performance. Over the past years total unemployment rose from 6.84 per cent in 2010 to 14.50 per cent (of the total labour force). Between 2010 and 2021 GDP per capita fell from USD 7,761 to USD 2,670 (in current US dollars) (World Bank 2022b), and Lebanon's multidimensional poverty rate nearly doubled, from 42 per cent in 2019 to 82 per cent in 2021 (ESCWA 2021). However, literacy rates in Lebanon are considered among the most advanced in the region, standing at 95 per cent (World Bank 2022c).

Lebanon's administrative system is divided into eight governorates, which are in turn divided into twenty-six districts and 1,030 municipalities (UNPAN 2012). This territorial governance model is considered by experts to be integral to Lebanon's confessional and sectarian system. Administratively Lebanon suffers from a weak system of public service provision and fragile public institutions, in which sectarian interests take precedence over state interest, leading to frequent decision-making gridlock (Malaeb 2018). Faith-based organizations often compensate for state absence by providing social services and catering to their own religious groups, thereby sustaining political polarization in society (Kraft et al. 2008). Sectarian politics also manifests itself at the municipal level, and many districts are dominated by specific sects. According to Faour (2007), the districts of Beirut and North Lebanon are predominantly populated by Sunni Muslims (275,264 and 681,358, respectively), whereas Mount Lebanon comprises a majority Maronite population (511,942). The districts of South Lebanon and Nabatieh, and Beqaa Valley, are dominated by Shiite Muslims (839,862 and 359,947, respectively).[3]

Lebanon as a Refugee-Sending and -Receiving Country

Lebanon suffers from a chronic refugee problem. Owing to its geographic position and domestic political context, it has witnessed recurrent inflows and outflows of refugees over the years. In terms of refugee inflows, Lebanon hosts the largest refugee population per capita in the world, including a large Palestinian refugee community (European Commission 2018). In 2011 the Palestinian refugee population residing in Lebanon and registered with UNRWA stood at an estimated 433,000 (UNRWA 2011). The Syrian crisis also added an estimated 27,700 Palestinian refugees from Syria (PRS) to the pre-existing Palestinian population as refugees fled the violence of the civil war (LCRP 2021).[4] Almost 53 per cent of Palestinian refugees reside in twelve camps, which have been the site of recurrent violence, such as in 2007 when fighting broke out between the Lebanese army and militants in Nahr al-Bared refugee camp (Dakroub 2007). There are also approximately twenty-six unofficial sites, commonly referred to as "gatherings," where the remainder of Palestinian refugees live in Lebanon (United Kingdom Home Office 2018). Since May 2014 Palestinian refugees from Syria have only been allowed to enter Lebanon in limited circumstances for exceptional "humanitarian cases" (Lilly 2019), which drastically restricts the number of arrivals.

Palestinian refugee-hood has left a mark on the Lebanese socio-political landscape. The history of residence of these refugees in Lebanon is marred by sour feelings among Lebanese due to their prolonged stay, militant activism, and involvement in the civil war (Hudson 1997; Rabil 2016). They are also governed by a different set of laws and administrative practices than are all other refugee nationalities residing in Lebanon, such as Iraqis, Afghanis, and Somalis (UNHCR 2018f). In terms of refugee outflows, Lebanon witnessed mass displacement notably during its fifteen-year-long civil war (Tabar 2010).

Legal Framework Governing Refugees in Lebanon

Despite Lebanon's being one of the largest refugee-hosting countries in the world, no clear or comprehensive legal framework exists in the republic for the governance of refugee and asylum-seeker affairs. In fact, no legal definition of *refugee* is employed, and the country's consistent official position has been that Lebanon is not a country of asylum (Trad 2014). Instead, an array of legal instruments is relied upon, in a largely ad hoc manner, to compensate for this legal vacuum. Since Lebanon is not party to the 1951 Geneva Convention that governs the situation of refugees, or its 1967 Protocol, it considers that the granting of refugee status to individuals lies within its margins of discretion, and it implements some provisions of the Convention on a voluntary basis (De Bel Air 2017). For five decades UNHCR was operating in Lebanon based on an informal "gentleman's agreement" (Frangieh 2016). However, in 2003 an MOU was signed with UNHCR to clarify the main aspects of protection and assistance of non-Palestinian refugees in the country. According to this agreement, asylum seekers would be "tolerated" on an individual and temporary basis, subject to quick resettlement to a third country (OHCHR 2010).

Other international and regional agreements that govern Lebanon's treatment of refugees include the Universal Declaration of Human Rights, the Convention on the Elimination of All Forms of Racial Discrimination, the Convention on the Elimination of All Forms of Discrimination against Women; the Arab Charter on Human Rights, and the Convention on the Rights of the Child (CMRS 2018b). In terms of constitutional provisions, Lebanon's constitution does not include any legal articles that clarify the status of refugees and asylum seekers. Articles 26 and 31 of Law 1962 Regulating the Entry and Stay of Foreigners in Lebanon and Their Exit from the Country stipulates that "any foreigner who is subject of pursuit or has been convicted for a political crime by a non-Lebanese authority or whose life or freedom is threatened because of political considerations may ask for political asylum, and if a decision to expel a political refugee has been made, it is not permissible to deport such refugee to the territory of a state where his life or freedom are not secured." However, according to Dionigi (2016), this provision applies to political asylum only, and the institutional committee in charge of granting it largely exists on paper only. This is curious given that Lebanese nationality law allows for the naturalization of non-Lebanese.

Synopsis of Lebanese-Syrian Relations

Lebanese-Syrian relations are complex and intertwined at the economic, political, and social levels. Until the 1920s both countries were part of the Greater Syria region comprising Syria, Jordan, Palestine, and Lebanon. Consequently the vast majority of Lebanese share with the people of Syria not only their language and cuisine but also many of their social customs and traditions, including the courtesy of extending hospitality to strangers, a hallmark of Arab social life (Cobban 2019). Borders between the two countries were historically porous, and the Syrian interior was a destination of refuge to many Lebanese who had to flee Lebanon's own instability, including its most recent war with Israel in 2006 (Kalia 2006).

Following independence from French mandate rule, Syria refused to acknowledge Lebanon as a separate sovereign state, considering it a colonial creation. For decades Syrian hegemony and meddling in Lebanese internal affairs continued, including the entry of Syrian troops into Lebanon in 1976 during the events of the civil war (Geukjian 2016). The end of the war saw Syria holding overall strategic and military power in Lebanon. This power was faced by opposition that grew over the years and peaked with the assassination of former prime minister Rafiq Hariri allegedly by Syria and its allies. In response, thousands of Lebanese took to the streets, calling for independence from Syrian hegemony, and launched what came to be known as the 2005 "Cedar Revolution" (Knudsen and Kerr 2013). While these demonstrations were not unanimously representative of all voices as some of Syria's allies in Lebanon did not object to the presence of its forces, they nonetheless eventually led to the withdrawal of Syrian troops from Lebanon, but not to an end of Syrian influence. Lebanon's major political parties, according to Assi (2016), are polarized broadly into pro-Syrian (March 8 Alliance) and anti-Syrian (March 14 Alliance) factions.

Economically both countries are connected by way of trade and infrastructure. Highways link the heart of the Syrian interior to Lebanon's capital, and nationals of both countries were allowed entry without a visa based on a bilateral cooperation agreement signed in 1994 (CMRS 2018a). Consequently Lebanon was historically a destination of choice for many seasonal Syrian migrant workers who were traditionally employed in the agricultural and construction sectors (Chalcraft 2005). Banking sectors in both countries have historically also been tied together, dating back to the creation in 1919 of the Banque de Syrie et du Liban (Bank of Syria and Lebanon), and Lebanese banks continue to play a critical role for Syria's elite (Daher 2021).

CONCLUSION

In this key background chapter I discussed each host country's refugee-policy environment prior to the arrival of Syrian refugees in 2011. Starting with Jordan and then Lebanon, I discussed the key variables of relevance in each country's domestic policy-making arena, including their socio-economic profiles, administrative and political systems, demographic and ethnic composition, historical experiences (as refugees and/or refugee hosts), and relations to the country of origin (in this case Syria), as well as the normative framework that governs refugee affairs in each country, including laws, international agreements, and local norms.

This overview is based on the analytical framework developed in chapter 2, in which I outlined the key host variables that can directly or indirectly influence a host's policy response to a mass refugee movement. Thus, in this chapter I introduced the relevant variables in Lebanon's and Jordan's contexts, which will later influence their policies towards Syrian refugees. Understanding this policy context is key to understanding how and why a policy is formulated and implemented in response to a certain refugee population. Therefore, this application of the framework can be replicated in other refugee contexts and cases beyond the Syrian case. This chapter, thus, was an important prelude to the coming chapters, which will discuss the evolution of events in Jordan and Lebanon, as well as how each host responded to Syrian displacement and why.

5

Syrian Refugee Displacement in Jordan:
A Descriptive Narrative

INTRODUCTION

Since 2011 the Hashemite Kingdom of Jordan has grappled with a displacement of mass proportion as a result of the Syrian war. The response of the government of Jordan (GoJ) to this movement has evolved with the evolving dynamics of the crisis. This chapter provides a chronological and descriptive account of the events of Syrian refugees' displacement to Jordan as they unfolded on the ground. Using process tracing over the period from 2011 to 2022, and relying on primary and secondary data, I traced the evolution of the displacement, as well as the government's policy response, by creating a road map of events, actions, decisions, and major actors involved in the policy-making process.

This descriptive chronological account serves an important purpose for the book. It helps us unpack and analyze the GoJ's policy response, as well as its changes over time and the main drivers that shaped the response and its evolutions. While this chapter is descriptive, the series of unfolding scenes will be discussed more analytically in chapter 6 by applying the book's proposed framework. Before I can answer the why or how questions, I need to first ask and describe what happened.

SYRIAN DISPLACEMENT AND JORDAN'S POLICY RESPONSE EVOLUTION: A TIMELINE OF EVENTS

The winter of 2011 was an eventful time for the people of Jordan. For months they had been watching in disbelief as massive popular uprisings surged through the region. What many political analysts had failed to predict was in fact happening. But as uprisings spread across the Middle East, one uprising in particular drew the monarchy's close scrutiny – one that was close to home. Across the northern border, in neighbouring Syria, protests had erupted in the town of Deraa. Fleeing the regime's violent crackdown, the first trickle of what would later become a large-scale population movement crossed the Syrian border; seeking refuge in the nearby Jordanian town of Ramtha (Sweis 2017). The events of that year proved fateful for the small kingdom. The Jordanian regime found itself yet again caught at the crossroads of another regional turmoil. "We consider 15 March 2011 as the start of the crisis on our land. As opposed to the pre-crisis situation where Syrians came and went regularly, based on a pre-existing no-visa regime with Syria, this date signified the entry of a large number of Syrians – without exit."[1]

In the summer of 2017, I travelled to Jordan to interview government officials about Jordan's response to the Syrian refugee crisis. Most bureaucrats I interviewed talked about how they did not foresee how rapidly the situation would evolve. As early arrivers were from nearby Deraa, local Jordanians hosted them in their homes. Not only were there tribal and social relations between the border villages but also showing hospitality to guests was considered an important hallmark of tribal culture. The scene was one of easy border entry and informality as local Jordanians hosted the tens of fleeing Syrians in their homes. An expert described Jordan's response at the time to have been mainly societal. According to him, locals received Syrian refugees with "open arms" because they were fleeing for their lives. "It was the humanitarian thing to do," he said. "They are our brothers."[2] King Abdullah also became one of the first Arab leaders to call on Assad to resign (Kessler 2011). He was reported as saying, "The minute you get a Syrian coming across, there's no way you can turn them back and say our border is closed" (Goldberg 2013). However, what started as tens of Syrians crossing the border soon turned into thousands, and come 2012, reality started to set in, and the government realized it had an emergency on its hands. "The initial reaction of the government was that of panic," described a Jordanian expert. "Decision-making was more ad hoc than deliberate at that point," he added.[3] Having to deal with its own internal political unrest, the government was now faced with the question of what to do about the incoming flow of refugees.

As the numbers increased, the Jordanian government requested assistance from the main UN agency in charge of refugee protection.[4] UNHCR had been operating in Jordan under the provisions of the 1998 bilateral MOU. The MOU outlined the basis of cooperation between the GoJ and UNHCR, whereby UNHCR was responsible for registering refugees and finding them resettlement spots in third countries. While the GoJ realized it could not respond to such an emergency without assistance, it was reluctant to allow for the creation of camps, which became the first point of contention with UNHCR.[5] Previous experience with Palestinian refugee camps in Jordan had soured the public psyche, as Palestinian refugee camps metamorphosed over time into small cities of their own.[6] Speaking about the issue, a senior officer at Jordan's Ministry of Planning and International Cooperation (MOPIC) recounted the following: "It was not so much a strategic decision as much as a de facto situation. Because of the increase in numbers we were unable to deal with the situation. International NGOs were also pressuring us to make it logistically easier to provide aid."[7]

So construction of what would soon become the world's second-largest refugee camp went underway (Jamail 2013). Zaatari camp was built in the northern governorate of Mafraaq, and by the end of January 2013 it was hosting 56,666 Syrian refugees (UNHCR 2018d). "Zaatari was an open place at the start. It had no walls or fences," a Jordanian expert pointed out. Syrians were allowed to choose whether to settle in the camp or outside, the latter being a more favoured choice by most.[8] As more and more refugees continued to pour in, through both formal and informal border crossings, the government continued to implement an open-border policy towards them (HRW 2012). Children, who with women made up 71 per cent of the refugee movement, were allowed to enrol in Jordanian public schools free of charge (Al-Kilani 2014). To accommodate them, more school buildings were rented, double-shift classes were created, and more teachers were hired. Syrian refugees were also granted subsidized medical care.[9]

And with the refugees came another influx. As more funding was allocated to aiding Jordan in managing its refugee crisis, the number of international organizations working with Syrian refugees quickly mushroomed. Speaking on the issue, a UNHCR officer noted that because of the government's low capacity to deal with the refugee movement, NGOs were, more or less, leading the response.[10] As the conflict went on, the expectation that this would be a temporary situation and that Assad would soon fall started to dissipate. At Jordan's Ministry of Interior (MOI), a high-ranking official in the Refugee Affairs Coordination Office explained how a governance structure was set in place to deal with the crisis and be in charge of formulating Jordan's policy towards the Syrian refugee movement.[11] An official at the Ministry of State for Media Affairs and Communication stated: "The pressure of the crisis compelled us to plan. The huge influx of humanitarian organizations had to be managed. A lot of work was being done without coordination."[12]

Thus, MOPIC was tasked with leading the response and managing relations with international donors. All projects had to be studied by the ministry before being approved. An online system was also developed to track project implementation and fund usage. An inter-ministerial committee, led by MOPIC, was created to include representatives from the key ministries.[13] Two new security institutions were created at the MOI to handle the crisis. The Syrian Refugee Camps Directorate became responsible for regulating entry and exit to and from the camps, while the Syrian Refugee Affairs Directorate (SRAD) was tasked with regulating Syrian refugee affairs at large, acting as UNHCR's local counterpart.[14]

In an interview at the Humanitarian Assistance Unit at MOPIC, a key official recounted that the GoJ had decided that the response to this crisis had to be nationally led but based on a participatory approach.[15] International and local NGOs were planning and implementing partners but were mainly consulted through UNHCR.[16] The Jordan Hashemite Charity Organization, the monarchy's relief arm, changed its mandate, which was formerly to work on providing relief outside of Jordan, to becoming responsible for regulating all in-kind assistance earmarked for the Syrian refugee crisis.[17] Further, to assess the impact that the displacement was having on Jordan's key sectors, the government issued a needs assessment report (JRPSC 2013). This report paved the way for a consolidated plan, based on the government's consultations with donors and international and national NGOs on the main priority areas for work.[18] Coined the Jordan Response Plan for the Syria Crisis (JRPSC), it represented key actors' unified approach to the humanitarian response, but one in which the government took the lead (MOPIC 2015).

The government began scaling back its services to Syrian refugees and started requiring them to pay for health care at the same rate as non-insured Jordanians paid.[19] Stricter camp regulations were put in place, and sponsorships were needed for relocation outside camps or for temporary exit (Francis 2015). Several incidents of intense friction occurred between local police and Syrian refugees as the latter protested harsh camp and living conditions (*The Guardian* 2014). Meanwhile actors on the other side of Jordan's borders became problematic to the kingdom. They were overtly violent and vocally hostile to the Jordanian regime (Goldberg 2013). Fearing a security spillover and terrorists infiltrating the refugee movement, the government started imposing greater restrictions on entry.[20] Human rights groups reported cases of refoulement, especially of unaccompanied males. As a result, thousands of Syrians became stranded along the border in a desolate desert area called the berm, as the numbers allowed to enter started to dwindle (HRW 2014a). "This was not a closed border per se," recounted a Jordanian expert, "but more of a regulated one. Jordan was no longer allowing just anyone in."[21]

By 2016 the GoJ was reporting that Syrian refugees had reached an estimated 20 per cent of the population, including those who had been residing in Jordan prior to the crisis (Ghazal 2017). The crisis had become protracted, and there appeared to be no end in sight to the conflict in Syria. Three more camps had been added for Syrian refugees over the years, while the majority of the refugee population was self-settled in Jordan's municipalities.[22] Public services and resources became stretched (Francis 2015). Locals complained of overcrowded schools, lower supply of water, longer waiting time in hospitals, inflation in housing rents, and competition over jobs – all of which they associated with the refugee movement.[23] In an interview with Fox News (2016), the queen reflected on the situation by stating that "Jordan is reaching a breaking point. Kindness alone will not solve the problem anymore. Jordanians' generosity is wearing thin." In a survey conducted by Al-Momnei, Athamna, and El-Radayda (2016), 54.4 per cent of local respondents thought that Syrian refugees should be restricted to campgrounds. Further, in a meeting organized by SRAD, the UNHCR and other NGOs in attendance expressed concerns at the rising perception among locals that refugees were receiving preferential treatment by the international organizations that provided aid and services to the refugee population, while ignoring the host community.[24] Social tensions were mounting, and public anger was slowly replacing the initial hospitable reception (Francis 2015). "I can clearly see this influx causing

108   The Politics of Refugee Policy in the Global South

a demographic change in the Northern territory in ten years' time; it's almost inevitable. This a concern to us, of course," expressed an adviser to the royal court.[25]

The Ministry of Health reported an increase in communicable diseases that had been previously eradicated in Jordan, such as tuberculosis and measles (JRPSC 2013). The government reported that the cut-off of Syrian trading routes had led to a decrease in exports and an increase in imports, aggravating the country's pre-existing trade imbalance (JRPSC 2013, 23). Further, at a time that the kingdom's budget was under considerable fiscal strain, international assistance was waning (*Jordan Times* 2016b). Between 2014 and 2016, international assistance met only 60 per cent of the government's appeals (Kelberer 2017). The frustration that the monarchy was feeling was reflected in the king's address to foreign delegates at an international pledging conference held in London in February 2016. His speech stressed the point that "Jordan should not be penalized" for hosting the refugee population and that the international community had to share the burden (TRT World 2016).

As Jordan looked inwards at its own worsening and dire situation, its attention started to shift. Speaking on the issue, a Ministry of Interior official recounted to me how, as the crisis prolonged, the government had started to shift its response from one focused on humanitarianism to one centred on development. "If we cannot win from carrying this burden, then at least we should not lose the development gains we had acquired over the past years," he said. "We decided that assistance had to target both the Jordanian community as well as Syrian refugees."[26] As a result, negotiations took place between advisers in the royal court and European partners, and what came to be known as the Jordan Compact emerged.[27] According to this agreement, the government would ease regulatory barriers to Syrians' access to the labour market in return for better support of the JRPSC and the provision of preferential access of Jordan's products to the EU market. An official responsible for Syrian employment at the Ministry of Labour (MOL) pointed out that the ministry "agreed to offer 200,000 free work permits to Syrian refugees in sectors in which they would not be competing with Jordanian workforce. We also waived requirements for official documents. These are all concessions we were making for the first time for Syrian refugees only."[28] The Jordan Compact is hailed by international organizations as a progressive step towards securing refugees' livelihoods and host-community needs, beyond reliance on foreign aid. "This was something we, and other iNGOs, had been advocating for since 2014," recounted an officer working at the Danish Refugee Council.[29] "The Jordanian government is fairly responsive and open to discussion. They may stand their ground at first, but they become incrementally responsive to us," noted a UNHCR high-ranking official.[30] According to an MOPIC informant, "the London conference posed a turning point for the international community and Jordan's approach by turning the focus to the host community, not just the refugees."[31]

On the eve of 13 June 2016 an explosive-laden truck drove at high speed over the border from Syria and self-detonated beside a Jordanian military post.[32] The suicide attack, the first of its kind on Jordanian soil since the start of the Syrian civil war, left six military personnel dead and fourteen others wounded (BBC 2016). The violent attack shook both the government and the community. In a meeting at the Jordan Armed Forces headquarters, King Abdullah II said, "Jordan will respond with an iron fist to assaults or any attempts to tamper with the Kingdom's internal or border security" (*Jordan Times* 2016a). The events of that day shifted government policy and set in motion a series of actions, which would prove detrimental to thousands of Syrian refugees.

On 21 June the northern and northeastern borders were declared closed military zones, effectively marking the end of the movement into Jordan (Al Jazeera 2016). More and more refugees arrived at the border, but they were not allowed to enter. "We no longer had a managed border after the attack; it was effectively closed," recounted a Jordanian expert.[33] An estimated 80,000 refugees became trapped over time in the berm area, which acted as a de facto buffer zone. As a result of increasing restrictions, the government came under harsh attack from humanitarian organizations. The previously collaborative relationship became strained as they accused the government of punishing Syrian refugees who were fleeing from the same dangers that Jordan feared.[34] However, Jordanian officials refused to change course. In an interview with the BBC (2017), the king's response to a question regarding this was clear: "If you want to take the moral high ground on this issue, we will get them all to an airbase and we are more than happy to relocate them to your country."

In May 2016, following the passing of a new electoral law and in the context of growing popular economic demands, King Abdullah sought a fresh mandate and dissolved the Parliament, calling for new elections (M. Singh 2017). As a result, on 1 June, Prime Minister Abdullah Ensour resigned, and Hani Mulki was appointed by the king to serve as interim prime minister. An expert observed: "During the Abdullah Ensour government (2012–2016), Jordan was having energy problems because of the cut-off of Egyptian gas. The whole government narrative was about Syrian burden, which led to the demonization of Syrian refugees and the perception became negative – although from my opinion our problems are governance related."[35]

Following the elections held on 20 September, pro-regime members of Parliament retained the vast majority of seats in Parliament, and Hani Mulki was chosen once again by King Abdullah to form the next government (Magid 2016). Nevertheless, while the election of the new government was aimed at consolidating the regime and maintaining political stability, economic factors would undermine Mulki's administration. Since the start of his government, Mulki had been implementing IMF-backed austerity measures, aimed at controlling Jordan's growing public debt. As a result, public support for his government was progressively diminished, reaching its lowest point on 30 May 2018, amidst price hikes and following the submission of a new tax law to Parliament. A series of general strikes and protests were initiated in Amman and other regions of the country, gathering unprecedented large numbers (Eran 2018). On 1 June, King Abdullah attempted to intervene by ordering a freeze of the price hikes. Nonetheless, protests continued for four days, leading Prime Minister Mulki to resign on 4 June. As a consequence, Omar Razzaz, Mulki's education minister, was appointed prime minister, and a new government was formed; protests only ceased when Razzaz announced his intentions of withdrawing the new tax bill. Similar to his predecessor, however, Prime Minister Razzaz also sought to implement austerity measures and solve Jordan's fiscal problem (Razzaz 2019).

In mid-2018, important developments also occurred on the Syrian side of the border. In July the Syrian regime retook control of its border with Jordan (at the province of Deraa) (Reuters 2018b). As a result, in October the border crossing was reopened by Syrian and Jordanian authorities, and trade relations between the countries resumed (Al-Makahleh 2018; Morris 2019). However, following the border reopening, the admission of Syrians into Jordan started to be conditioned upon a "security clearance," which had to be granted by Jordanian authorities (Al-Khalidi and Barrington 2018). In tandem, the Jordanian government introduced new immigration pathways for foreign investors, including Syrians, through which naturalization and permanent residency were offered. However, access to citizenship would be restricted to larger investors, capable of investing amounts greater than USD 1 million (El-Taliawi, forthcoming; ERBD 2020).

In November 2018 there were strong signs of rapprochement between Jordan and Syriaas Jordan sent a parliamentary delegation to Syria. This was the first event of its kind since the start of the Syrian war, and the delegation was received by President Assad in Damascus. The trip was aimed at boosting the countries' bilateral relations, particularly when trade between the two countries was once again made possible by the border reopening (Al-Makahleh 2018). The prospects of resuming and increasing trade with Syria were discussed at the highest levels of the GoJ. However, these were put in jeopardy with the passing of the Caesar Act sanctions against Syria by the US government in 2019. Naturally, although these sanctions were aimed at punishing individuals in Syria, its fallout was also felt in Jordan, particularly in bordering towns. For instance, during pre-war times, in the city of Ramtha (eleven miles west of the border), 90 per cent of all trade came from Syria. As a result of the new sanctions package, Jordanian companies wishing to trade with Syria now had to apply to the US government for a special licence and go through cumbersome procedures (Bulos 2019). As one expert put it: "There is willingness from several countries, including Jordan, to open the borders and to normalize with the Syrian regime. There have been visits from parliamentarians and calls from businesspeople not to be targeted by Syrian sanctions."[36] Moreover, the sanctions affected not only trade between the two countries but also individuals' capacity to remit funds to and from Jordan via regular remittance channels. One Jordanian government official stated: "Jordanian banks do not allow transfers to go through the Central Bank of Syria or other Syrian banks which are on the sanctions list. Restricting such transactions applies even to Jordanians, not just Syrians."[37]

Meanwhile, also in 2019, the GoJ passed more restrictive regulations related to employment, which resulted in the closure of more sectors to non-Jordanians. An expert on the topic mentioned the following: "In 2019, Jordan created new regulations that increased closed jobs to around 50 jobs – mostly professional for Syrians."[38]

During the COVID-19 pandemic Jordan imposed one of the world's strictest responses to contain the spread of the virus. Starting on 19 March 2020, the government closed all borders and implemented a national lockdown. By mid-April, Jordan had started lifting restrictions on economic activity, ultimately lifting them altogether on 3 May while retaining a nightly curfew (Ben Mimoune 2020). Nevertheless, in August 2020 a surge in COVID-19 cases led the GoJ to close its border with Syria, which was only reopened on 17 April 2021 (Hardan 2021). As a result of its measures, the GoJ was able to flatten the curve and limit infections (Ben Mimoune 2020).

While Jordan was to some extent able to contain the spread of the COVID-19 pandemic, popular discontent vis-à-vis the government continued to grow. This was not only because of the country's worsening economic situation but also due to limits on civil and political freedoms imposed under emergency laws. In 2020, new parliamentary elections were held, and the regime expected to ease popular disenchantment (Al Jazeera 2020). The elections resulted in the appointment of Bisher Al-Khasawneh as prime minister. In an official statement Prime Minister Al-Khasawneh explained how he would attempt to deal with Jordan's two existential challenges – the pandemic and the economic crisis (Eran 2020).

On 3 April 2021 an alleged failed attempt at a palace coup led to the arrest of former Jordanian prince Hamzah bin Hussein and other key figures linked to the government (Millett 2021). Hamzah, who lost his royal title to King Abdullah's son, had been a strong critic of the government since 2018 (Saad and Hauser 2021). In July 2021 King Abdullah met with US president Joe Biden in order to discuss several issues, including the situation in Syria. On the occasion, the king was asked by reporters about the possibility of Syrian refugees returning to their homes and argued that this would not be possible any time soon as there was nothing for them to return to. He also argued that Bashar al-Assad "was there to stay" (Al-Khalidi 2021c). Two days following King Abdullah's words on Assad, Jordan and Syria announced that they had come to an agreement for fully reopening the border crossing between the two countries with loosened security requirements (*Enab Baladi* 2021). Nevertheless, on 29 July, Syrian rebels waged a spate of mortar attacks on Syrian army checkpoints in Deraa (Syrian side of the border) in the biggest flare-up of violence since the Syrian regime forces had retaken the region (Al-Khalidi 2021a). Considering this, on 31 July 31 the GoJ announced it would again close its border crossing with Syria, which was then reopened on 29 September (Reuters 2021, Al-Khalidi 2021b).

Although the return of refugees to Syria was for a long time seen as infeasible by Jordanian authorities, discussions on the topic gained momentum during 2022, particularly as relations between the GoJ and its Syrian counterparts continued to improve, and neighbouring countries such as Lebanon and Turkey publicly defended the idea. The international community, including UNHCR, however, still largely considers that conditions for safe and sustainable return have not yet been achieved (HRW 2022, Jordan, Akil, and Shaar 2022). In March 2022 the Jordanian and Turkish foreign ministers announced during a joint press conference in the Turkish capital, Ankara, that their countries had agreed to cooperate in the promotion of voluntary returns to Syria (Middle East Monitor 2022). Later, in September, the issue of promoting voluntary returns was also discussed by the foreign minister of Jordan and his Syrian counterpart during the sidelines of the seventy-seventh UN General Assembly, and coordination among the countries' intelligence services for that matter was made public (Intelligence Online 2022, The New Arab 2022).

By mid-2022, 1.75 million COVID-19 cases had been reported in Jordan, with 14,122 deaths. At the same time, 44.5 per cent of the population in Jordan had been fully vaccinated against the virus (WHO 2022b). Moreover, over 90 per cent of refugees residing in camps (including non-Syrians) had received one or more doses of the COVID-19 vaccine, and of Syrians living in urban areas the percentage of those who had received one or more doses stood at 50 per cent (Kheirallah et al. 2022). At the time (and since December 2021), refugees (including non-Syrians) living in urban areas who were fully vaccinated were entitled to a small cash compensation of JOD 7.5 , provided by UNHCR (UNHCR 2022a).

CONCLUSION

This chapter has provided a descriptive narrative of events as they unfolded on the ground in Jordan. Through the adoption of two analytical techniques, namely process tracing and chronologies, the events of Syrian displacement to Jordan were traced from 2011 to 2022. To construct this descriptive timeline of events, primary and secondary data were analyzed as to the key actions and reactions that took place in the three analytical arenas, presented in chapter 2, with respect to the Syrian refugee movement in Jordan. Key events, including the COVID-19 pandemic, that unfolded globally as well as in Syria and Jordan, interacted with each other, thus influencing the policies of the GoJ towards the Syrian refugee population present on its land.

Constructing this descriptive narrative is important for analytical purposes to help us unpack Jordan's policy response to the Syrian displaced population, not only as a snapshot but longitudinally as it evolved over time. Key events, such as the border attack of June 2016 and the change in conflict dynamics in Syria, signify guideposts for a researcher aiming to analyze how and why the GoJ responded to the displacement, by first taking a look at what happened. In the coming chapter I will thus proceed to answer analytically the former two key questions through an application of this book's proposed framework for the study of refugee policy.

6

Unpacking Jordan's Policy Response to Syrian Displacement: "If We Can't Win, Then We at Least Shouldn't Lose"

INTRODUCTION

The previous chapter provided a detailed account of the dynamics of Syrian displacement in Jordan as it unfolded on the ground over the course of eleven years, including a description of the interplay between the key policy actors and of the critical events that transpired as a result of the Syrian refugee movement. Chapter 6 builds on this descriptive account by applying the analytical framework proposed in chapter 2 to the Jordanian case. It aims to answer the book's second key research question by examining how Jordan responded to the Syrian refugee movement on its land, and why this policy response came about. Using process tracing and chronologies, and relying on primary and secondary data, I analyzed the GoJ's response over the period from 2011 to 2022.

This chapter is divided into three main sections, starting with an analytical breakdown of Jordan's policy response to Syrian displacement, followed by characterization of policy response evolution. In this sense, the first and second sections analytically answer our question on how Jordan responded to the refugee movement and presence over the eleven-year period. In the third section a discussion of Jordan's response drivers will take place.

ANALYTICAL BREAKDOWN OF JORDAN'S POLICY RESPONSE TO SYRIAN DISPLACEMENT

In this section, and relying on the literature on refugee-policy choices discussed in chapter 2, Jordan's policy is analyzed in terms of its three main components: entry and stay, livelihoods, and durable solutions.

For this analysis, Jordan's policy elements, and their evolution over the course of the displacement, have been derived from several sources of data. First, twelve in-depth elite interviews were conducted in 2017 and 2021 with government officials who were asked about the process by which each policy choice was made and how the policy evolved. Second, to triangulate government officials' answers and obtain an accurate picture of any unannounced policies being implemented, twenty-six in-depth interviews were conducted with NGOs and experts in 2017 and 2021. It is worth noting that both local and international NGOs were interviewed to increase the reliability of the data and because international governmental organizations, such as UNHCR, may be more involved in policy formulation, whereas local NGOs may be more involved in implementation. Therefore, both views had to be considered. Third, facts mentioned in the interviews were further checked through analysis of secondary data including reports of leading NGOs, scholarly articles, and grey literature.

Policy on Entry and Stay

One of the earliest decisions that a government witnessing a mass refugee situation must make is whether to open its borders to admit those seeking refuge on its territory or to close its borders and turn them away. While normatively governments are required by binding customary international law to admit asylum seekers who are fleeing a well-founded fear of persecution in their country of origin (UNHCR 1981), in practice instances of both border closures and openings have historically occurred. A government's policy on entry can be broken down for analytical purposes into three issues: its admission choice, its adherence to the principle of non-refoulement, and the type of asylum it grants to the refugee population.

Over the course of the displacement the GoJ's admission choice and adherence to the principle of non-refoulement went through three main stages. During the early emergency stage (2011–13), admission to Jordan was open to all refugees who entered through official or unofficial border entry points, whether or not they had official documents.[1] This open-border policy was facilitated by the pre-existing non-visa arrangement with Syria, which meant that Syrians customarily entered Jordan on a regular basis, mainly for seasonal employment in the construction and agricultural sectors.[2] However, as time went by and the displacement became mcre prolonged, admission became more selective, and entry restrictions started to be imposed, including the request for official documents (Su 2017; De Bel Air 2016). Cases of refoulement began to be reported by NGOs, including the non-admission of young single males (Chatty 2016). This was accompanied by a decline in reported Syrian refugee arrivals into Jordan from more than 1,800 per day in 2013 to fewer than 200 in 2014 (NRC 2014).

As for the final stage, which came in the wake of the border attack in June 2016, admission into Jordan was denied to all Syrian refugees except for humanitarian cases (C. Smith 2017). This official and complete border closure was considered by rights groups as a case of systematic refoulement (NRC 2014). As a result of this closure, satellite imagery along the Syrian-Jordanian border captured an estimated 70,000–80,000 Syrians stranded in the desert border area of Ruqban in 2016 (De Bel Air 2016). The main border crossing between the two countries (the Nassib-Jaber border) was only reopened in October 2018, allowing once again the entry of Syrians into Jordan (Morris 2019). Nonetheless, entry is conditioned upon a "security clearance" granted by Jordanian authorities (Al-Khalidi and Barrington 2018). Similar to other nations, Jordan closed most of its borders (except for cargo traffic) in March 2020 in order to contain the spread of COVID-19 (FAO 2020). As a result, new cases of Syrians stranded in the Ruqban crossing area without access to humanitarian assistance were reported (Amnesty International 2020). As of July 2020, most border crossings (including the Nassib-Jaber border) remained closed to the entry of Syrians.

With regard to the type of asylum granted to the refugee population, in the case of mass refugee situations governments are faced with two alternatives: either to consider the incoming group as prima facie refugees or to grant them temporary protection. Prima facie status identifies its holders officially as refugees, has no predetermined duration, and entitles its holders, after RSD, to local integration and voluntary repatriation. Temporary protection is time constrained and allows its holders, after RSD, either voluntary repatriation, when conditions in the home country are deemed safe, or resettlement to a third country, but not local integration (UNHCR 2001b).

Although Jordan's admission of Syrian refugees and the degree to which it adhered to non-refoulement evolved over time, the kingdom's stance on how to legally regulate the residence of Syrian refugees in Jordan did not. According to the GoJ's agreement with UNHCR, upon recognition, Syrian refugees were granted temporary protection for an initial period of six months, subject to renewal upon the government's discretion (UNHCR 2014a).[3] Therefore, Syrians who sought asylum in Jordan and underwent RSD were considered refugees. They were allowed to enter without a visa and to reside in the country for a period of six months, after which they were expected to return to their home country or be resettled to a third country (Fakih and Ibrahim 2016).[4] However, rather than revoke the residence of Syrian refugees whose permits expired after the six-month period, the GoJ constantly renewed the majority of their permits (Bank 2016). While this practice ensured that refugees were not deported, it placed them in a precarious situation in which their legal status was constantly uncertain.

Policy on Livelihoods

A government's policy choices do not end after the granting of asylum and the admission of refugees. The government needs to make choices regarding their type of settlement, the restriction of their movement and employment provisions, and the implementation mode through which it will govern their protection and access to services.

TYPE OF SETTLEMENT ALLOWED

With regard to the type of settlement allowed, practices have historically varied between housing refugees in camps and allowing them to self-settle in urban areas. According to Bakewell (2014), encamping refugees in designated sites has been the more common practice adopted in mass refugee situations. The GoJ's policy regarding Syrian refugees' settlement changed from resisting the building of camps to allowing incoming refugees to choose their place of settlement, in or outside designated camp areas.[5] In 2016 almost 80 per cent of Syrian refugees were self-settled in rural, urban, and peri-urban areas, whereas only 20 per cent were housed in the five camps created specifically for the Syrian refugee population.[6] Despite an initial reluctance to build camps and there being a greater share of self-settled refugees, since 2015 the GoJ has incentivized Syrians to stay in camps (Beaujouan and Rasheed 2019).

SERVICE PROVISION AND FREEDOM OF MOVEMENT

Although the 1951 Convention gives refugees the right to freedom of movement and the right to education, public relief, and assistance, governments may impose restrictions on both rights (UNHCR 2011). Jordan is not party to the Convention, but its MOU with UNHCR allows registered Syrian refugees in Jordan the right to food assistance, subsidized health care, and access to public education for an initial period of six months (Bank 2016). Until 2014, Syrian refugees in and outside of camps were allowed access to such services for free by showing their UNHCR registration card and MOI identification card.[7] Their movement was also unrestricted between camps and urban areas (UNHCR 2021a).[8]

In 2014, however, authorities started to scale back the services to Syrian refugees and to restrict their freedom of movement.[9] Non-camp inhabitants were no longer able to access free health care and were required to pay the equivalent of non-insured Jordanian citizens.[10] New regulations were also placed whereby camp inhabitants could not exit designated camp areas for short- or long-term periods unless a sponsor "bailed" them out and a permit was issued for their exit (Francis 2015). Nevertheless, this "bail out" scheme was cancelled in 2016, and Syrians who had left camps without official permission could not renew their MOI cards or asylum seeker certificates with UNHCR. It is worthy of note that by August 2016 around one-third of UNHCR-registered Syrian refugees who were living outside camps lacked a new MOI service card (Yahya and El-Hariri 2018). Later, in 2018, the GoJ began an amnesty program allowing Syrians under these circumstances to regularize their documentation (Sieverding and Calderón-Mejía 2020), and camp inhabitants were authorized to work outside camp areas for up to one month before returning to renew their paperwork (Beaujouan and Rasheed 2019).

In 2020, in response to the COVID-19 pandemic, Syrian refugees were also included in Jordan's National Health Response Plan (UNHCR 2020c). Similar to other countries, in March 2020 the GoJ imposed curfews and restrictions on travel between cities in order to tackle the spread of COVID-19. Nonetheless, these were not targeted specifically at Syrians and affected the overall population in the country (FAO 2020). These restrictions remained in place until August 2021 (at the time of writing).

ACCESS TO THE LABOUR MARKET

Another important decision a government has to make regarding the status of refugees is whether or not to allow them lawful employment and access to the labour market. The Syrian civil war brought with it implicit changes to how the authorities handled Syrians' engagement in the labour market. While officially Syrians could apply for work permits, they were costly, and authorities no longer readily provided them.[11] Instead, authorities turned a blind eye to Syrians' recourse to working in the informal sector as a means of supplementing the insufficient humanitarian assistance being provided to them (Francis 2015).

Such was consistently the case until the "Supporting Syria and the Region" conference, which was held in London on 4 February 2016. The conference brought about a profound change to the GoJ's policy on labour-market inclusion of Syrian refugees. An agreement, dubbed the Jordan Compact, was forged between donors and Jordanian authorities, whereby in return for easing regulatory restrictions on Syrian employment, donors would increase investments in the Jordanian economy (to EUR 747 million in 2016–17), help build new special industrial zones (SEZ) in Jordan, and ease rules of origin (ROO) on Jordanian exports to European markets (European Commission 2017).[12] This scenario was to be piloted through the issuance of 200,000 free work permits to Syrian refugees in specific sectors, which would not crowd out the Jordanian labour force.[13]

Work permits issued to Syrians were generally tied to one employer and did not allow workers to switch (Gordon 2019), with the exception of "flexible" work permits that were introduced in 2016 for agricultural and construction sectors, which can be requested through agricultural cooperatives and/or the General Federation of Jordanian Trade Unions (UNHCR 2020j).[14] In July 2017, considering that only 60,000 permits had been issued to that point (Barbelet, Hagen-Zanker, and Mansour-Ille 2018), tensions arose between Jordan and international donors, who expected a faster rollout of the work-permit program. Amidst that scenario, and in an attempt to reach the 200,000 mark, the GoJ started allowing each Syrian to carry more than one work permit (Tsourapas 2022). By mid-2022, 305,000 permits had been issued, a number well beyond the initial 200,000 target. As a whole, most of these permits have been issued to Syrians working in agriculture, construction, and manufacturing (UNHCR 2022k). This is because, while Syrian refugees have a diverse skill set and professional abilities, the GoJ initially limited their employment to these sectors. This scenario partially improved in mid-2021 when Syrian refugees became eligible to get work permits in all sectors open to non-Jordanians, meaning that they could now work in sales, crafts, basic industries, and as skilled agricultural, forestry, and fishery workers and plant and machine workers. Moreover, during the COVID-19 pandemic some Syrians were given exemptions to work in the health-care sector to help fight the virus. During that period new "flexible" work permits that allowed Syrians to switch between employment opportunities in all the sectors open to them were also introduced. As of mid-2022, over 30,000 of these permits had been issued (UNHCR 2022d).

While the new ROO scheme for Jordanian exports to the EU ended up being satisfactory to both parties of the agreement, which led to a 2018 revision that extended the scheme until the end of 2030 (ILO 2019), the SEZ model was considered by observers to be ill suited to the realities on the ground. That is, although potentially transformative in theory, the SEZs remained far from where most Syrian refugees were located and offered working conditions and wages that were often unsatisfactory (Almasri 2021; Lenner and Turner 2019). As such, the SEZ model is seen to have stalled, and the new ROO scheme was extended to qualifying companies outside these special zones (Huang and Gough 2019). Meanwhile, EU financial assistance to the GoJ continued, totalling EUR 3.5 billion during the 2011–22 period (European Commission 2022).

Despite recent achievements, the EU and other international donors continue to call the GoJ to open more sectors for the employment of Syrian refugees (Council of the European Union 2022). In particular, the sectors open to Syrians were significantly affected by the economic impact of COVID-19, which led many to lose their jobs. In tandem, these sectors also mainly employ men, which has led women to account for only 6 per cent of all work permits issued to date (UNHCR 2022k). Syrians applying for work permits are also required to pass background security checks, which is a challenging and daunting task that often deters them from applying (Wilson and Casswell 2018). Unpredictability of regulations and implementation gaps at the local level were considered some of the reasons behind the slow formalization of Syrian refugee employment and the issuance of work permits to refugees (World Bank 2020). In this regard, an official mentioned the following:

The formalization of the labour market is not an easy thing since most Syrian refugees are working informally and feel comfortable with it and may even earn more that way. Many manage to earn income through activities and occupations that the government does not allow under formal regulations. This applies to all non-Jordanian workers. Syrians are specifically exempt of the cost of the permit, according to the Jordan Compact agreement. The cost of the permit depends on the occupation (min. JOD 400–500 or USD 600, which is unaffordable to most). However, only registered Syrian refugees are exempt from work-permit cost. Those who have an MOI card only can still apply but would not be exempt from the cost – this is a small portion of the refugee population, though.[15]

With regard to self-employment, before 2018, operating a business as "self-employed" required Syrian refugees to apply for an "investor card," which was generally difficult to obtain (Verme et al. 2015). However, in 2018 the government relaxed regulations; allowing Syrians to register and operate home-based businesses (HBBs) (REACH 2020). Accordingly, Syrians living in camps could operate HBBs in any sector, while those living in urban areas could establish HBBs in specific sectors including food processing, tailoring, and handicrafts (AUB 2020). Nevertheless, financial requirements to register HBBs are high (around JOD 50,000), and those who cannot meet them must enter in joint ventures with Jordanians (Blumont 2020). In addition, Syrians need to present a valid passport for registration (AUB 2020). Hence, most Syrian refugees do not meet the criteria for registering (JIF 2020). Hence, the rate of registration is extremely low. A Jordanian government official explained the following:

By 2021, around forty HBBs have been registered to Syrians. During implementation we found difficulties including access to documentation. This is why the rate of registration and formalization is very low. An exception was made for Syrians to use their MOI cards in early 2020. But due to COVID, everything was slower, which reflected on work permit issuance and registration of HBBs. There is also an incentive problem for HBBs. Owners are not incentivized to formalize their businesses. Why would they create a licence and pay taxes if they can avoid it? The main reason they would do it is if they need invoices as part of their operations. Also, if they need access to finance, which would need them to legalize. This is not very common, so informality is rampant.[16]

With regard to work-related social security coverage, subscription is mandatory for all employees including non-Jordanians (excluding household helpers and unskilled agricultural workers). While vital, especially during the COVID-19 pandemic, it remains a challenge because many employers do not comply, and many more Syrians work informally and are thus not included. Social security covers work-related injuries, retirement, disability insurance, death insurance, maternity insurance, and unemployment insurance where applicable. The subscription is a joint responsibility of the employer and the employee and is payable on a monthly basis (UNHCR 2020k). Syrian workers in the construction sector (registered through the General Federation of Jordanian Trade Unions) are exempt from social-security subscription payments (UNHCR 2020k). The GoJ outlined plans to reform social-security coverage to include improvements enabling the government to attract the self-employed and informal workers, who are particularly vulnerable to shocks (World Bank 2020).

MODE OF IMPLEMENTATION

The mode by which a government chooses to implement its refugee policy is a particularly relevant issue to discuss, especially in the context of mass displacement. Two issues have been mentioned in the literature, including the type of bureaucratic structure to which refugee matters are assigned, and the inclusion of civil society actors.

With regard to the bureaucratic structure, Jordan has relied on a mostly civilian structure to manage the affairs of the Syrian refugee movement, with an Inter-ministerial Coordination Committee (IMCC) reporting directly to the Cabinet and overseeing the work of MOPIC (figure 6.1).[17] With the exception of the border, which is manned by the army, Jordan's MOI is the main body in charge of Syrian refugee affairs.[18] The creation of a specific directorate within the MOI, namely the Syrian Refugee Affairs Directorate, as a response to the displacement, points to the high importance the government placed on this specific refugee population.

The government has also maintained a collaborative relationship with international and local NGOs, allowing them to work

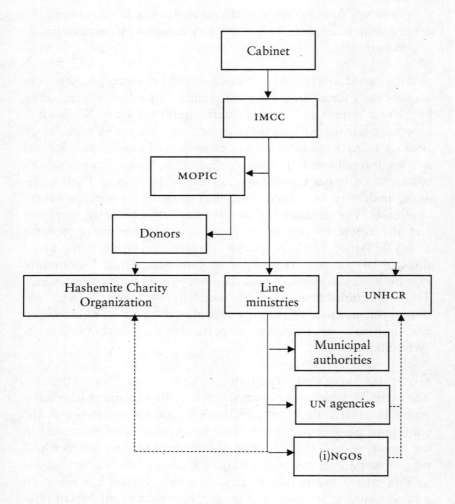

Figure 6.1 | Jordan's institutional framework for the Syrian refugee response

and involving them in the policy formulation process.[19] As opposed to other countries, such as Turkey, where the government often restricted the work of international organizations, including UNHCR (Stupp 2017), Jordan relied heavily on their assistance, especially in the emergency phase, to respond to the rapidly deteriorating situation.[20] The largest providers of humanitarian assistance to Syrian refugees in Jordan are UNHCR and the World Food Program (WFP), which provide mainly cash assistance and food vouchers (Hanmer et al. 2020). Only Syrians registered with UNHCR have access to humanitarian assistance delivered by both organizations. The WFP uses iris-scan data collected with UNHCR to distribute its assistance to Syrians (Baah 2020). To determine eligibility and household need, UNHCR uses guidelines from its Vulnerability Assessment Framework (VAF), which considers a number of indicators, including predicted welfare, documentation status, coping strategies, dependency ratio, and basic needs (Brown et al. 2019). For the years of 2014 and 2015, the government reportedly limited access to international humanitarian assistance by increasing the evidentiary basis for eligibility, where UNHCR was asked not to provide asylum seeker certificates (which enable access to humanitarian services) to refugees who left camps after July 2014 without obtaining official permission to exit (NRC 2016; Kvittingen et al. 2018).

Significant to Jordan's implementation mode was that the way Jordanian authorities managed the displacement evolved over time from a more ad hoc approach to a more centralized one in which they took the lead in formulating the response. This centralized management approach was evident in their decision to issue the Jordan Response Plan for the Syria Crisis (JRPSC), which consolidated the needs and target areas for assistance into one plan that was agreed upon by partners and which provided a more accountable mechanism for tracking fund usage and project implementation.[21] More on this will follow in the section describing the phases of policy evolution.

Policy on Durable Solutions

Upon cessation of refugee or temporary protection status, refugees are no longer allowed to reside in their host country; in this case a solution that resolves their situation must be reached. Three conventional "durable solutions" exist, which are advocated by the international refugee regime: repatriation, local integration, and/or resettlement. The type of durable solution allowed by a government may also be directly linked to the type of asylum granted to the refugee population, or the decision may transpire later as the condition in the home country evolves.

126   The Politics of Refugee Policy in the Global South

With regard to durable solutions, the GoJ had a consistent policy position that allowed Syrian refugees to be resettled or eventually returned to their country of origin upon cessation of hostilities.[22] Syrian refugees were to be "accommodated" but not allowed local integration in Jordan. This stance was best reflected by an adviser at the Royal Court who expressed the following: "we would never allow Syrian refugees to be locally integrated in the legal sense. They can stay for as long as they want, but they will still be refugees."[23] However, with the signing of the Jordan Compact, which facilitates the access of Syrian refugees to the labour market, Jordan's policy made a turn towards some form of local integration, since inclusion in the labour market is considered one of the pillars of local integration (Crisp 2004).

With regard to resettlement, Jordan is considered to have one of the largest resettlement operations in the world. In 2016 alone 17,956 Syrian refugees living in Jordan were resettled to Canada, the United States, and other countries. Nevertheless, from 2017 to the end of 2019 the number of resettled refuges per year ranged from 4,473 (in 2017) to 4,843 individuals (in 2019). In 2020, largely because of COVID-19–related travel restrictions, the number of resettled refugees was significantly reduced, reaching 1,419 Syrians only. However, in 2021 and 2022 the numbers were stabilized, reaching 3,778 and 3,396 individuals (by mid-2022), respectively (UNHCR 2022e). Although discussions on repatriation were initiated, the government during the period of examination did not implement a repatriation operation for the Syrian refugee population, because conditions in their home country had not yet allowed for a "safe and voluntary return," as stipulated by international law.[24]

PHASES OF POLICY EVOLUTION

As argued earlier, the GoJ's response to the Syrian refugee population on its territory evolved and changed shape over the course of the displacement. The shifts in the response can be grouped mainly into three phases that also reflect shifting paradigms. Figure 6.2 shows the evolutionary phases through which Jordan's policy response went between 2011 and 2022. In the following subsections I explain the characterization of each phase in more depth.

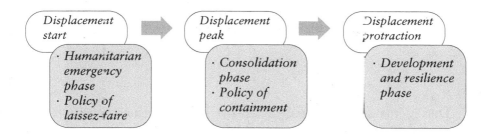

Figure 6.2 Phases of Jordan's policy evolution on Syrian displacement (2011–22)

Displacement Start: Humanitarian Emergency Phase and Policy of Laissez-Faire

During the early emergency phase (2011–13) the government's response to the movement was largely non-restrictive in nature, as evidenced by the mosaic of policy elements that the government adopted towards Syrian refugees, including allowing them open admission and temporary protection in Jordan, abiding by the principle of non-refoulement, allowing Syrian refugees freedom of movement and choice of settlement, providing them with non-relief services such as school enrolment and subsidized health care, and relying on civilian agencies to be in charge of the Syrian refugee population, with the exception of border control. The government was also highly collaborative with local and international NGOs. The restrictive features of Jordan's policy towards Syrian refugees at this stage included prohibiting Syrian refugees' access to the formal labour market and the possibility of their local integration as a durable solution.

During this stage the government focus was primarily on the humanitarian aspect of the displacement, as refugee needs took centre stage. The rhetoric used by the government emphasized the importance of coming to the rescue of fleeing "brothers," as a Muslim and Arab duty. This phase also reflected the government's low capacity to respond to the displacement because decision-making

128 The Politics of Refugee Policy in the Global South

was characterized by being "ad hoc" and "short-term."[25] This initial "hands-off" policy included leaving the displacement and crisis response largely to society and NGOs.

Displacement Peak: Consolidation Phase and Policy of Containment

During the second phase (2014–15) the government's response started to evolve in terms of its degree of restrictiveness towards the Syrian refugee population and its mode of implementation. Although most of the policy choices remained the same, the government started to impose restrictions on admission of Syrian refugees, the provision of non-relief services, and freedom of movement in and out of camps. Refugees were allowed to self-settle only if they had sponsorship outside designated camp areas. Cases of refoulement were reported, albeit not systematic. During this phase Jordan's policy towards Syrian refugees began to take on more restrictive undertones, as the government attempted to contain the crisis. To consolidate the efforts in responding to the crisis, the government launched the JRPSC and created a new institution at the MOI dedicated to Syrian refugee affairs. The JRPSC signified a more planned and organized response. Further, while the government continued to collaborate with NGOs, this phase saw it starting to lead the response rather than allow NGOs to work haphazardly. Additionally, the government rhetoric began to change from one of open hospitality to one of the need for more international assistance in carrying the burden of hosting Syrian refugees.

Displacement Protraction: Development and Resilience Phase

As the displacement entered its protracted stage, starting in 2016 the GoJ moved away from its focus on the refugee population towards building host-community resilience. This approach was reflected in a statement made by a high-ranking officer at the Syrian Refugee Affairs Directorate, who noted that "if we cannot win from hosting this refugee population, then we at least should not lose out on our own development goals."[26]

Further, the government's response towards the Syrian refugee population increased in terms of restrictiveness. While the policy could still be considered semi-restrictive in nature, the closure of the border

Table 6.1 | Jordan's policy choices on Syrian displacement and their evolution

		Displacement start phase (2011–13)	Displacement peak phase (2014–15)	Displacement protraction phase (2016–22)
Policy on entry and stay	Admission choice and adherence to non-refoulement	Open admission and adherence to non-refoulement	Restrictions imposed on admission and non-systematic refoulement	Non-admission and systematic refoulement
	Type of legal residence / asylum granted	De facto temporary protection	De facto temporary protection	De facto temporary protection
Policy on livelihoods	Type of settlement	Non-encampment → followed by choice of settlement type allowed (between camp or urban residence)	Choice of settlement type allowed, subject to sponsorship	Controlled settlement and end of sponsorship scheme
	Labour market access	Access to labour market not allowed	Access to labour market not allowed	Restricted access to labour market
	Freedom of movement	Freedom of movement allowed	Restrictions on movement imposed	Restrictions on movement imposed
	Service provision	Non-relief services provided	Restrictions imposed on service provision	Restrictions imposed on service provision
	Implementation mode	Collaboration with IOs, with IOs leading response	Collaboration with IOs, with state leading response	Collaboration with IOs, with state leading response
		Mixed civilian and military management of refugee population/ operations	Mixed civilian and military management of refugee population/ operations	Mixed civilian and military management of refugee population/ operations
Policy on durable solutions	Repatriation, local integration and resettlement	Only repatriation and resettlement allowed	Only repatriation and resettlement allowed	Only repatriation and resettlement allowed

and the adoption of systematic refoulement gave it an even more restrictive character compared to the previous phases. This stance was reflected in the government's rhetoric that stressed the impact that the hosting of Syrian refugees was having on Jordan. The end of the "bail-out" scheme for refugees wishing to leave camps in 2016 also meant that Syrians were no longer encouraged to self-settle in Jordanian cities. However, in a contrary move, the government launched the Jordan Compact agreement with the EU, whereby it relaxed restrictions on Syrian refugees' access to the formal labour market, and in 2018 the GoJ started to allow the registration of HBBs.

Table 6.1 gives a more detailed account of Jordan's policy on Syrian displacement, broken down into the three main policy elements and their evolutions over the three phases. The policy elements and sub-elements are derived from this book's analytical framework proposed in chapter 2. The table shows the three displacement phases, as discussed previously, including how each policy element evolved during the three phases. To take one example of how to read this table: the policy on admission choice and adherence to non-refoulement began during the displacement start phase (2011–13) with open admission and adherence to non-refoulement, and evolved during the displacement peak phase (2014–15) to restrictive admission with non-systematic refoulement, followed by border closure and non-admission – constituting systematic refoulement during the displacement protraction phase (2016–22). I will discuss in the coming section the drivers and factors behind the change and continuity of Jordan's policies towards Syrian displacement.

DRIVERS OF JORDAN'S POLICY RESPONSE TO SYRIAN DISPLACEMENT: BETWEEN HUMANITARIANISM AND REALISM

The previous section discussed in detail how the GoJ responded to the Syrian refugee movement during the period (2011–22). Using process tracing over that period and relying on primary and secondary data obtained in the field, this section provides an analytical discussion of the main drivers behind the government's policy adoption and implementation. In this section I explain continuity and change in Jordan's policy response over the course of the eleven-year period.

Displacement Start (2011–13)

During the early emergency phase Jordan's adoption of a non-restrictive policy towards the Syrian movement was the result of the coupling of several factors in its international, domestic, and displacement arenas. First, the government's decision to maintain an open-border policy towards Syrian refugees was influenced by the regime's desire to act in accordance with international norms of refugee protection including the principle of non-refoulement. Jordan's being a member of the UN, and its need to abide by the obligations of customary international law, were both cited by government officials as reasons behind their decision to allow in Syrian refugees unregulated.[27] However, the government was also reacting to a developing reality on the ground. The humanitarian nature of the displacement crisis and the government's weak capacity to respond on its own compelled it to seek assistance from UNHCR under the auspices of their MOU, which was previously created to respond to the Iraqi displacement. The need for UNHCR's assistance, specifically with RSD, gives the international organization leverage to advocate for the GoJ's adherence to international norms.

Further, the kinship ties that exist at the horizontal social level between the two societies, as well as the pre-existing no-visa regime for Syrians, facilitated the border movement and created a de facto situation on the ground as Syrians increasingly entered Jordan via formal and informal entry points and were hosted by the local community.[28] The kinship ties to the local communities, especially in the border towns, and the local norms that necessitate both extending hospitality to guests and aiding refugees, contributed to raising society's receptiveness to Syrians' plight. The social solidarity reflected on the government's initial "open" stance to the Syrian refugee movement.[29] The influence of norms on government policy was evident in government rhetoric citing "brotherhood" and "humanitarian obligations" as an impetus for its admission of Syrians.

Until 2013 there was an overlap between international obligations – which Jordan is bound to respect because they are ingrained in customary international law – and local norms. The discourse embraced by the government (e.g., in the king's speeches) facilitated the framing of the humanitarian crisis in public opinion as justified in religious terms, ethnic terms as "Arab brothers," and in tribal relations. This was reflected in the local rhetoric. These are the three sources of framing, which relate with local norms. For example, you will find that government officials were very reluctant to describe the borders as closed because that to them would be shameful at the tribal and monarchy levels. Jordan has an ambition to depict itself as a religious and Arab leader regionally, so it has to uphold these norms.[30]

Such dynamics, however, did not apply in the same manner to Palestinian refugees from Syria, whose admission was subject to more stringent regulations (Abu Zayd et al. 2015). The regime's desire not to tip the demographic balance against Transjordanians ("East Bankers") was behind the aversion to this sub-component of the refugee movement. Fear of regime imbalance, due to Palestinians gaining more political power in Jordan, has underlined many of Jordan's policies, including its electoral distribution laws (Kumaraswamy and Singh 2017). While Jordan's desire to maintain its delicate demographic balance applies to other nationalities as well, including Syrians, it is more pronounced in the regime's dealings with Palestinian refugees. This is especially the case, because the Jordanian authorities expect Syrians to eventually return to their country, but this is more problematic with regard to the Palestinians.[31]

Further, in line with the American diplomatic position on Syria, and Jordan's internal popular support of the Syrian uprising, the king's official statements were in favour of Assad stepping down and giving way for peaceful transfer of power (Mahmoud 2014). The perceived temporariness of the conflict and what was considered as the inevitability of Asaad's ouster reflected on the government's "relaxed" admission of Syrian refugees. An expert mentioned: "At the start, the king was calling for a political solution in Syria and the stepping down of Asaad. Therefore, accepting refugees was a way of displaying that Asaad was hurting his people. It is a form of political accusation."[32]

While Jordan granted open admission to Syrian refugees, it provided them with temporary protection upon recognition, rather than considering them prima facie refugees. According to interview respondents, this policy position was influenced by the regime's need to maintain their refuge in Jordan as a temporary situation that excluded their local integration as an eventual durable solution.[33] This policy stance was specifically influenced by

Jordan's protracted hosting of Palestinian refugees since 1948, and the government's attempt to avoid having to eventually naturalize another refugee population.[34]

Further, the government's decision to create camps to host the Syrian refugee population, while allowing them choice of settlement, was influenced by three major considerations: volume, composition of the refugee movement, and UNHCR advocacy.[35] Refugee camps were not created for Iraqi refugees, but the volume of the Syrian refugee population surpassed the Iraqi refugee population (Marfleet and Chatty 2009). In an interview an informed observer cited the following:

> The regime was reluctant to build camps at the start for reasons such as the traumatic memory of the Palestinian refugee experience for both the public and the regime. The hosting of Palestinian refugees had demographic and political repercussions. It was feared that the influx of Syrian refugees may produce the same dynamics. Yet this changed very soon because of the exponential increase in the numbers, which caused the army and the government to experience logistical difficulties in dealing with the influx. There were complaints at the societal level of refugees' overwhelming numbers, so it was a way to isolate them from the population.[36]

Further, the socio-economic composition of the Syrian refugee population differed from its Iraqi predecessor. According to Chatelard (2010), the Iraqi refugee movement of 2005 comprised mainly urban, educated, and middle- to upper-class Iraqis, who refused the government's suggestion that they settle in camps, preferring to self-settle in Jordanian cities. The Syrian refugee population, however, was of predominantly rural origin and had a lower socio-economic profile (Stave and Hillesund 2015). While government officials cite the movement's socio-economic profile as one of the drivers behind encampment, Turner (2015) argues that Jordan was in part using encampment strategically to raise the visibility of the Syrian refugee presence on its territory. An expert mentioned: "Camps were not created for previous Iraqi refugees. This is part of Jordan's learning experience. Most of the refugees from the Syrian region of Deraa were socio-economically vulnerable. Therefore, it was seen that their presence in urban areas would be challenging for them." [37]

Additionally, UNHCR advocacy played a role in convincing Jordanian authorities to open the Zaatari camp, following negotiations with tribal leaders in the North (UNHCR 2013). "International organizations were also pressing for camp creation to make it logistically easier for them to provide aid and for the government to manage the influx. The perception of camps then changed from being a risk to a solution."[38]

With regard to Jordan's provision of non-relief services to Syrian refugees, including subsidized access to public health care and education, government officials have stated that international obligations towards refugees prompted this specific policy.[39] Such obligations were codified in the MOU with UNHCR, which acted as the alternative legal framework governing Jordan's management of the movement (UNHCR 2014a).

Prohibiting Syrian refugees' access to the formal labour market was attributed by respondents to the high unemployment rate among Jordanians and the government's fear that Syrians would push down wages and compete with the Jordanian labour force.[40] The government's ad hoc implementation and management of the response during this initial stage, as discussed earlier, was influenced by the unexpected volume of the movement, which overwhelmed the government's capacity to respond.[41] This compelled the government to coordinate the response with international organizations and local NGOs as the number of incoming Syrians continued to increase.[42]

Jordan's policy on durable solutions was mainly influenced by the kingdom's historical experience with Palestinian refugee hosting and its desire to prevent Jordan from becoming a permanent country of refuge for Syrians, as well as its need to maintain demographic balance in favour of Transjordanians, as mentioned earlier. Speaking on the topic, an officer at a local NGO mentioned the following: "The government does not want to grant citizenship to Syrian refugees, or for Jordan to become an alternative home to them. Therefore, it acts in accordance with the Geneva Convention but refuses to sign it so as not to commit to obligations it does not want to meet, such as local integration."[43]

Displacement Peak (2014–15)

When the displacement peaked, Jordan's management of the Syrian refugee population became increasingly restrictive, as evidenced by the change in several of its policy components discussed in the previous sections. As elaborated in our previous discussion, the GoJ began to restrict admission of Syrian refugees arriving at its formal and informal border crossings. Further, as discussed, it began to scale back non-relief services offered to Syrian refugees. The change in these two policy sub-elements pertaining to entry and livelihoods, according to respondents, was attributed to the strain that the refugee population was placing on economic, fiscal, and environmental resources. An MOPIC official reflected on this change as follows:

> The influx created a strain on municipalities, whose capacity was limited even before the crisis. Jordan is also one of the most water-scarce countries in the world. Syrian refugees have been allowed to enrol in public schools free of charge, which meant that the government had to rent school buildings, increase teacher intake, rely on double shifts, and increase the number of students per classroom. Jordan also provides health services to the injured. At first it was free, but they are treated now like uninsured Jordanians. There has also been an impact on the state budget and the public transport system. All this reflected on the country's capacity to sustain itself and the refugee presence.[44]

Another main driver behind these shifts towards adopting a more restrictive stance with regard to the Syrian refugee movement, as compared to the government's initial open stance, was cited to be due to the fear of social tensions motivated by rising perceptions among the host communities that Syrian refugees were receiving preferential treatment from the government and NGOs. Further, fear of Jordan's witnessing demographic imbalance as a result of the prolonged presence of the refugee population caused a revisiting of the approach that the GoJ was taking.[45] An adviser to the Royal Court stated: "Over time the welcoming approach among the local host community changed a bit to a perception that Syrian refugees are a threat to their own livelihoods or a burden. There are many Jordanians who sympathize with them, but it will most likely vary with the extent that they are personally affected by their presence. This affected government decisions. We also expect that there may be significant demographic changes in the coming decade as a result."[46]

According to government statistics, Jordan's macroeconomic indicators also started to witness sharp decline. While the trade deficit increased by 57 per cent, the GDP growth rate was reported to have decreased by 60 per cent during 2011–15, compared to the country's macroeconomic performance from 2006 to 2010 (JRPSC 2017). In 2014 Jordan moved from fourth to second place in terms of water scarcity in the world (Namrouqa 2014). Although it is difficult to attribute the cause directly to Syrian refugee presence, it lends some support to respondents' claims that reduced resource capacity influenced the government's approach to the Syrian refugee crisis, especially with regard to admission and service provision. Such resource stress was exasperated by the refugee movement's increased volume and length of stay, coupled with the lack of the international assistance originally pledged to Jordan.

By end of 2015 the registered Syrian refugee population in Jordan had increased to 633,466 (UNHCR 2018c),[47] whereas government sources cite a much higher number (1.3 million) (JRPSC 2017). The total resident population of Jordan had increased to 9.46 million (Kumaraswamy and Singh 2017). In addition, Jordan's funding appeals were coming short of the announced response requirements. In 2015, only 36 per cent of Jordan's funding appeal had been met (JRPSC 2016). In the following statement a high-ranking official at the MOI mentioned resource capacity and realism as the main drivers to the shift in Jordan's response during this time: "One of the pillars of our approach to this crisis is 'realism,' i.e., working with what is possible or managing according to capacity. If you take on more than your capacity, you endanger everyone, even the displaced."[48]

Displacement Protraction (2016–22)

As the conflict in Syria and the refugee presence in Jordan became protracted, the perceived outcome of the Syrian conflict (as being short-termed) among Jordanian policy-makers changed. Realization set in that the Assad regime may not fall, and the opposing factions represented a threat to Jordan's security. Such factors, coupled with the implications of the border attack and conflict spillover for Jordan's security, caused a shift in government policy towards adopting de facto border closure and systematic refoulement of further refugees arriving at the border to seek asylum in Jordan; the adoption of stricter camp regulations; and the placing of restrictions on freedom of movement. During this phase the government started to securitize the refugee presence.[49] In an interview an informed observer mentioned the following: "The main expectations at the start were for

Assad to quickly fall, but then a sense of awareness started to develop that this was not going to happen, and fighting rebels in Deraa were not welcome by the Jordanian regime. This resulted in tougher border procedures such as restricting access of young males and making family reunification more difficult. However, following the border attack the border became effectively closed to any new arrivals."[50]

In a contrary move to adopting a more restrictive policy on entry, the government eased its policy on livelihoods, specifically regarding allowing Syrian refugees access to the Jordanian formal labour market. According to interview respondents, the government's decision to ease restrictions on the employment of Syrian refugees was facilitated by the provision of international assistance dedicated to this specific issue and the advocacy of international organizations.[51] The London conference, which pledged USD 1.7 billion in concessional financial support to Jordan, provided an incentive for the government to regulate Syrians' access to the labour market by granting 200,000 employment permits to Syrian refugees as a pilot project. The Jordan Compact was cited by respondents to have also been motivated by concerns over social tensions arising from the prolonged presence of Syrian refugees, and the perception that refugees were receiving preferential treatment from international organizations that nationals were not receiving.[52] According to respondents, this provided an impetus for the government to modify its response to target the host communities as well as the refugee population.[53] An informed observer on the motivation behind this shift to host-community resilience cited the following:

> There are two aspects of integration: naturalization and economic integration. With regard to economic integration, Jordan was reluctant to give Syrian refugees the right to employment because of fear of competition with Jordanians. International actors (e.g., UNHCR, ILO, and the EU) pressured for this because the Syrian presence was becoming long term. Syrians had to work or else they would become dependent long term. Plus, it had economic benefits for Jordan (e.g., special economic zones). Even if the conflict ends today, it will still take time for Syrians to go back, and it would be contingent on security, reconstruction, and other factors. So, we are speaking about a medium-term situation. Therefore, there is no alternative to economically integrating them. Having a poor destitute population in Jordan would pose a threat to the country's social stability.[54]

138   The Politics of Refugee Policy in the Global South

On the shift to a focus on raising host-community resilience in the government's approach, a livelihoods specialist at an international NGO mentioned the following: "The idea of assisting the host community as well as the refugee population was considered a win-win situation. The government wanted to learn from the previous Iraqi refugee influx into Jordan. They did not want Jordan to lose the development gains it made since then. For NGOs, they wanted to ensure Syrian refugees were not perceived negatively by the local population, which would have reduced social cohesion. Equitable treatment was considered the solution as many Syrians face the same vulnerabilities as Jordanians."[55]

Further, while the government started to allow Syrian refugees access to employment in 2016 and self-employment later in 2018, it was also trying to regulate and restrict some aspects of Syrian refugees' labour-market inclusion in response to reduced social receptiveness. It did so by allowing the employment of non-Jordanians in sectors that, according to government respondents, did not compete with the Jordanian labour force. "The government placed some limitations on the type of sectors and jobs available to non-Jordanians, including Syrians, because of the high unemployment rate among the Jordanian population. So, they allow them to work in occupations that supposedly do not compete with the Jordanian labour force."[56]

Although the government attempted to reopen the Nassib-Jaber border crossing in October 2018 as the Syrian regime regained control of the border region, entry was still conditional, as mentioned earlier, upon obtaining a security clearance granted by Jordanian authorities (Al-Khalidi and Barrington 2018; Reuters 2018c). Security – this time in the form public health security – was again behind the reclosure of the border in March 2020 as a result of the COVID-19 pandemic. Movement restrictions, while imposed on Jordanians as well, were specifically difficult for Syrians. Speaking on the issue, a MOPIC official stated: "One of the main implications of the COVID-19 pandemic happened in Azraq and Zaatari camps. Before the pandemic, if a Syrian refugee had a work permit, they could exit the camp using a thirty-day renewable permit to go outside. But when the pandemic hit, we were afraid that the virus would spread in the camps, causing a humanitarian disaster. Therefore, the government restricted the number of days for leave permits (to fourteen days). It became more difficult to get leave permits."

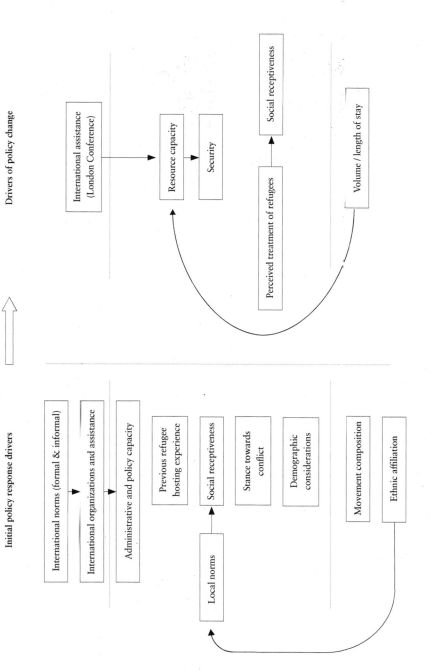

Figure 6.3 | Systemic visualization of Jordan's key response drivers (2011–22)

Further, potentially as a reflection of an improvement in relations between the government of Jordan and its Syrian counterpart, and of the recent policies and discourses of neighbouring countries (particularly Lebanon and Turkey), discussions on the promotion of safe and voluntary return were initiated in 2022. So far, it has involved discussion within the GoJ and with potential key partners in this process, such as Syrian and Turkish authorities (Intelligence Online 2022; The New Arab 2022). Nevertheless, to this date, no concrete actions to promote voluntary return have yet been taken by the GoJ, and UNHCR has not declared Syria safe for voluntary repatriation.

Figure 6.3 displays a dynamic and systemic visualization of how the main drivers behind Jordan's policy response towards the Syrian refugee movement changed and evolved over time. On the left of the diagram are the initial response drivers in the international, domestic, and displacement arenas. The arrows signify the direction of interactions among the various factors. On the right of the diagram are the drivers behind the policy change over time.

CONCLUSION

The implications of the Syrian war and the displacement of hundreds of thousands of Syrians to Jordan may prove detrimental to the future of the kingdom for years to come. This chapter has examined the particular path that the GoJ undertook in response to the mass displacement of Syrian refugees to its territory. Using process tracing over the period from 2011 to 2022, and relying on primary and secondary data, this chapter has demonstrated that the GoJ's response to the Syrian refugee movement started as largely non-restrictive in nature. During this phase Jordan's policy was influenced by the coupling of arrangements in its international, domestic, and displacement system arenas. According to the findings, while international norms of refugee protection may have compelled the government to adhere to the principle of non-refoulement, its open-border policy was facilitated by the existence of local norms and kinship ties at the social level, which raised the local Jordanian community's receptiveness to the plight of Syrian refugees. Such factors were coupled with the perceived temporariness of the conflict and inevitability of Asaad's ouster, which was reflected in the government's "relaxed" response towards the refugee movement. During this stage, humanitarianism was the main policy-response driver.

However, as arrangements in Jordan's international, domestic, and displacement system arenas evolved, Jordan's response to the Syrian refugee movement increased in restrictiveness. Realism and security became the main response drivers. As the size of the refugee population continued to increase, and the displacement became more protracted, social tensions started to mount. The economic, environmental, and fiscal stress reflected on the government's decision to restrict admission of Syrian refugees and to scale back non-relief services. Further, the change in perceived outcome of the Syrian conflict, and the 2016 border attack, caused the GoJ to impose a de facto border closure from 2015 to 2018 and to adopt stricter camp regulations.

As the Assad regime regained control of the border region, some signs of normalization and rapprochement became evident as signalled by the opening of the Nassib-Jaber border crossing and the Jordanian parliamentary delegation's visit to Damascus. This visit had been unprecedented since the start of the conflict. However, security again took centre stage as the COVID-19 pandemic imposed further public-health-security threats on the Jordanian regime, and attempts to open the Nassib-Jaber border crossing with Syria were quickly undone, with no translation in terms of policy on the refugee presence.

7

Syrian Refugee Displacement in Lebanon: A Descriptive Narrative

INTRODUCTION

Since the outbreak of the Syrian civil war in 2011 the Republic of Lebanon has been subject to a mass displacement of Syrians seeking refuge on its territory. As this refugee movement unfolded and intensified over time, Lebanese policy responses evolved, passing through several stages. This chapter provides both a chronological account of the events of this displacement as they unfolded on the ground in Lebanon and a descriptive account of the government's policy response as it evolved over time.

As in the case of Jordan, the evolution of the displacement and the government's policy response were traced using two analytical techniques, namely process tracing and chronologies, over the period from 2011 to 2022. Also, building on primary and secondary data, a road map of events, actions, decisions, and the major policy actors involved was created to help with the analysis. This descriptive chronological account provides an application of how to unpack and analyze a government's policy response, as well as its changes over time, and the main drivers that shaped the response evolutions, in this instance to the case of Lebanon.

SYRIAN DISPLACEMENT AND LEBANON'S POLICY RESPONSE EVOLUTION: A TIMELINE OF EVENTS

The effect of Syrian refugee presence on Lebanon can be all but obvious as one lands in Beirut airport and travels to the heart of the Lebanese capital. The eleven years in which the country wit-

Syrian Refugee Displacement in Lebanon   143

nessed the mass flight of Syrians (2011–22) left a clear mark on a country already brimming with tension and bearing the smears of decades of conflict. Informal tented settlements can be seen scattered along the way, a hallmark of the Syrian refugee presence in Lebanon. It was on the eve of 28 April 2011 that Lebanon witnessed the first trickle of what would soon become a mass displacement of Syrians fleeing regime crackdown and civil strife in the bordering country.

According to interview respondents, Syrians were following kinship and social ties into a country that just decades ago had been one with their own.[1] A high-level official at Lebanon's Ministry of Refugee Affairs (MORA) recounted witnessing and responding to the earliest flows of refugees as part of the informal local community effort:[2] "Syrians are not perceived by the local population as different from Lebanese. The history and the common language made people perceive of them as similar. Many Lebanese living in the border towns also remembered having to seek refuge in Syria themselves, when war broke out with Israel in 2006. Therefore, the local community was receptive of the movement, and many were hosted in Lebanese homes."[3]

However, as Syrians flowed into the border towns and were hosted in locals' homes, pro- and anti-Syrian political factions were divided as to what to do about the refugee inflows. Until December 2011 the government refused to acknowledge them as "refugees" in the legal sense, or to declare the movement an emergency situation.[4] Fear that the Syrian conflict would spill over into the Lebanese arena drove the government to adopt a disassociation policy, whereby political groups agreed to remain neutral towards events happening in Syria (AlSharq Al-Awsat 2017). A MORA high-level official noted the following: "The expectation and hope among political groups, at that stage, was that the Syrian conflict would be a temporary situation that would end soon. The state was almost in denial and there was no official response. The response was mainly societal."[5] Another interviewee stated: "During the early influx stage the borders were left open. There was no filtering of incoming Syrians occurring at the border. Fleeing Syrians were just given stamps on their passports at the official entry points and were allowed in."[6]

As policy elites were adopting a "wait-and-see" approach, however, a situation was evolving on the ground that was creating a new reality. The border movement continued, bringing more people in need of emergency assistance into some of the country's poorest and least equipped localities. A MORA adviser recounted the following: "From 2011 to 2013 there was negligence and avoidance in the management of the situation and non-regulation of refugee inflows. Initial reception was done by society itself. That was the case in Baalbek, Beqaa Valley, Akaar, and the border areas. But the state was not present."[7] According to a local informed observer, "the Ministry of Social Affairs had an umbrella presence, but there was no institution dedicated to responding to the situation, and NGOs were filling in for the state's absence."[8]

Although initially the government refused to let it register them, UNHCR started to register incoming Syrians, under the provisions of its MOU with the government of Lebanon (GoL) signed in 2003.[9] However, Syrian refugees were obliged to arrange for housing on their own or with the help of civil society actors, as the government had turned down negotiations with UNHCR for camps to be created to host the large number of incoming refugees.[10] Speaking on the issue, a Progressive Socialist Party member recounted the following: "The Minister for Social Affairs, who was in charge at the time the crisis broke out, suggested the creation of camps to contain the displaced population in a certain area and facilitate aid provision. However, this caused disagreement. Some political groups were against camps in fear that this would become a protracted situation that would lead to Syrian naturalization, while others were worried camps would become an organized front for Syrian opposition. Both groups were influenced to a large extent by our experience of hosting of Palestinian refugees."[11]

Informal tented settlements and makeshift structures became the housing alternative for Syrians who could not afford private rentals or had no social connections to host them. However, such informal settlements were largely "unfit for human habitation," and their tenants were under constant threat of eviction by police forces.[12] In some municipalities, especially those dominated by non-Sunni communities, curfews were imposed on the largely Sunni refugee movement (HRW 2014b).[13] On the issue of curfews and movement restrictions, an adviser to the Prime Minister's Office mentioned the following: "There are significant variations in implementation of policy across municipalities because the central government does not have as much implementation control everywhere. There is discretionary behaviour, including in imposing movement restrictions on Syrians in certain localities."[14]

The year 2013 brought to Lebanon not only more Syrians seeking refuge on its territory but also internal political turmoil. Disagreements between pro- and anti-Assad political camps led to the resignation of the Mikati government in March 2013 (Salem 2013). Soon afterwards, Hezbollah's leader, Hassan Nasrallah, announced in a televised address that the militant group was coming to the aid of the Assad regime in Syria to "prevent the Middle East from plunging into a dark period" (*The Guardian* 2013). This overt military intervention was in discord with Lebanon's disassociation policy. In addition, the country's parliamentary elections, due to take place in June 2013, were postponed, and the parliament's term in office was extended for an exceptional period. This extension, which was the first the country had witnessed since the end of the civil war, was cited by officials to be due to "political gridlock and the neighboring civil war in Syria" (Jalabi 2013).

In September of that same year the World Bank issued a report assessing the economic and social impact of the Syrian conflict on Lebanon, at the request of the government (World Bank 2013).[15] According to a MORA official, this report sounded the first alarm bell that the situation would soon be unsustainable for the small country, and it became a key document for the government.[16] The report estimated that the decline in trade, tourism, and investment resulting from the conflict in Syria would push an additional 170,000 Lebanese below the poverty line, double the unemployment rate, and cost the country USD 2.5 billion in economic losses during 2012–14.

By April 2014 the number of Syrians registered with UNHCR had reached a peak of 1 million, excluding those who were unregistered or awaiting registration (UNHCR 2014b). Every day, 2,500 new refugees were being registered. Meanwhile, the international humanitarian appeal for Lebanon was only 13 per cent funded (UNHCR 2014b). An official at the Ministry of Finance pointed out that the government started to "wake up from its stupor," specifically with the issuance of the World Bank report and the Syrian refugee population reaching its highest peak since the beginning of the conflict.[17] However, government interventions were described by several informants as being "ad hoc," "fragmented," and "based on individual ministerial efforts."[18] Speaking on the issue, an informed observer noted: "Faith-based organizations and NGOs were doing a lot of uncoordinated work. It was almost a laboratory-like situation. Donors were adopting a 'shopping list' attitude by choosing specific projects to fund according to their own agendas, and the state was muddling through."[19] According to a MORA high-level official, the "government felt that UN agencies were leading the response and national institutions were being bypassed."[20] Therefore, in an effort to have a more active role, an inter-ministerial crisis cell was created, with the Ministry of Social Affairs (MOSA) responsible for coordinating the work of the different line ministries, UN agencies, and local civil society organizations.[21]

As the crisis became protracted, hopes that it would be temporary or short-lived had dissipated. The month of August 2014 also brought further developments, which proved fateful for the refugee movement and its host. In the northern city of Aarsal, ISIL and Al-Nusra fighters stormed Lebanese army checkpoints and abducted hostages, leading to a full-blown five-day showdown with the Lebanese army. What came to be known as the Battle of Aarsal culminated in the death of seventeen Lebanese soldiers and was the first major cross-border incursion to occur since the start of the conflict (Holmes 2014). According to a MORA officer, this security spillover represented a "turning point" for the government. It changed the government's perception of the movement from being a humanitarian problem to being a security problem.[22]

In October 2014 the national unity government, headed by Prime Minister Tammam Salam, issued Lebanon's first official policy document, declaring its intent to tackle the Syrian refugee problem head-on by limiting the flow of refugees into the country (Al Jazeera 2014).[23] In January 2015 new regulations started to be implemented, signalling a clear shift in Lebanon's response to the crisis. This shift effectively put an end to Lebanon's open approach towards the Syrian refugee movement. According to informants, this was the first integrated attempt to regulate the movement.[24]

On 6 May 2015 the government requested UNHCR to stop registering new refugees and to de-register those who had been recorded after the imposition of the January 2015 regulations. It also imposed an annual USD 200 fee on residence renewal for Syrian refugees.[25] These regulations were the subject of negotiations between UNHCR and other rights groups who were advocating with the government to waive the fees and allow in those who met humanitarian criteria, such as minors and those with medical needs.[26] In an interview with UNHCR, the situation was described: "Before the May 2015 policy change, admission was still open for Syrian refugees. Afterwards, those entering were considered to be entering illegally, and there was no proper registration. Without UNHCR registration, new entrants could still reside in Lebanon but would need another reason for their residence."[27]

The Lebanon Crisis Response Plan (LCRP) was issued in partnership with UN agencies and reflected the government's shifting focus from the refugee crisis as a humanitarian emergency to the need for addressing host-community-development needs as well.[28] The two-year crisis response plan identified strategic objectives, which were broken down into key indicators and sectoral targets. One of the objectives was to strengthen the capacity of national institutions and systems to provide services and to respond effectively to the increased demand for waste management, water, education, and health services (LCRP 2016).

One of the key challenges we were facing was how to provide education to Syrians, who were part of a different educational system. Many students had dropped out of school because of the war and had stayed out of school for years, so they were expected to enrol in classes with much younger students. We created an accelerated program for them. We also created double shifts for teachers. We coordinate with UNICEF on this specific aspect of our response. The LCRP helped us coordinate among line ministries and with UN agencies better.[29]

In tandem with developments in Lebanon's response to Syrian refugees, the political climate in the country started to deteriorate. On 21 July 2015, when Lebanon's main landfill was shut down, mounds of garbage started piling up in the streets of Beirut. This led over 100,000 Lebanese to go into the streets and manifest their discontent with the government's corruption; this also marked the beginning of a political turmoil that would last for years (Geha 2019b). In February 2016 the "Supporting Syria and the Region" conference took place in London, during which donor governments, including Germany, Kuwait, Norway, and the United Kingdom, pledged USD 12 billion in support of countries hosting Syrian refugees, including Lebanon (UK Government 2016). Following, in June 2016, the government relaxed restrictions on Syrian refugees' employment by replacing the required pledge not to work, which was demanded of them, with a clause that restricted their work to three sectors, namely agriculture, construction, and environment.[30]

In the same year, after a twenty-nine-month period of political vacuum that had started in April 2014 due to the failure to reach political agreement in Parliament and the failure of any presidential candidate to reach a two-thirds majority vote, Michel Aoun became president, backed by Hezbollah. President Aoun signed a decree appointing Saad Hariri to serve as prime minister for a second time (Karam 2017).

In November 2017, during a trip to Saudi Arabia, Prime Minister Saad Hariri resigned from office, citing Iran's and Hezbollah's over-extension in the Middle East and fears of assassination as the main reasons (Barnard and Abi-Habib 2017). Later on, it was understood that his move could have been coerced by Saudi authorities, and on 22 November Hariri put his resignation on hold (Levy 2017). Originally scheduled for 2013, Lebanon's parliamentary elections were held in 2018 after three postponements caused by the country's security situation, the delayed presidential elections, and other technical issues. The elections, which had a low voter turnout, were held after a year replete with crises, strikes, and demonstrations over many issues and resulted in the growth of the Shiite bloc in the country (Shavit 2018). After the elections Prime Minister Saad Hariri was reappointed by President Michel Aoun to serve. Nevertheless, the new government would only be formed nine months later, in 2019, as the prime minister had to reconcile various political factions in a national unity government (El-Deeb 2019).

In 2018 Lebanon's largest Christian party in Parliament, the Free Patriotic Movement, created its own local refugee-return committee, looking to inform refugees about return pathways and to facilitate returns to Syria's "safe zones." This was done in coordination with Lebanon's General Security Office (GSO) and municipalities. Following warnings issued by UNHCR that conditions in Syria were still not conducive to return, Lebanon's Ministry of Foreign Affairs accused the agency of meddling with the country's sovereignty (Fakhoury and Ozkul 2019). Later that year Hezbollah's leader, Hassan Nasrallah, said the party was also establishing an independent mechanism to return "the biggest possible number" of Syrians wishing to return home safely and voluntarily (Reuters 2018a). An informed observer on the extent of voluntariness of such returns mentioned the following: "In Lebanon there have been some forced returns arranged, especially in areas where there is collaboration between the Syrian army and Hezbollah."[31]

On 13 May 2019 the GSO issued a statement that all Syrians who had entered Lebanon irregularly after 24 April of that year would be deported, in contravention of the principle of non-refoulement (Fakhoury and Ozkul 2019). These deportations came into effect starting on 20 May. According to UNHCR, the agency attempted to intervene in all cases that came to its attention. However, while "some interventions led to a suspension of deportation ... others did not" (2019g). The year 2019 also saw growing economic and political turmoil in Lebanon. In August the country started experiencing a liquidity crisis. As fears that the country would be incapable of covering its maturing debt grew, foreign exchange inflows were halted, and dollars exited Lebanon. As a result, its currency also lost significant value vis-à-vis the US dollar (Matalucci 2019). Furthermore, in October, protests broke out following a proposal to introduce new taxes on gasoline, tobacco, and VOIP calls on applications such as WhatsApp. The protests quickly expanded and started to encompass the condemnation of widespread corruption, unemployment, and the sectarian rule in the country (Nowacka 2019). As a result of these protests, commonly referred to as the 17 October Revolution, Prime Minister Hariri resigned and dissolved the Cabinet on 29 October, leaving one "coalition" in power (represented by President Aoun and Speaker of Parliament Nabih Berri) (Haidar 2020). In December, Hassan Diab was appointed to serve as prime minister by President Michel Aoun, and a new Cabinet was formed on 21 January 2020 (BBC 2020a, 2020b).

On 4 August 2020 one of the largest non-nuclear explosions in history destroyed Beirut's port and damaged over half of the city. The explosion, caused by the detonation of tonnes of mismanaged chemicals, resulted in the death of 218 people and left 7,000 injured (HRW 2021). A few days later, on August 10, amidst growing public anger at the government's negligence and corruption, Hassan Diab and his Cabinet were forced to resign (BBC 2020a, 2020b). Starting in 2020, Lebanon was also seriously hit by the COVID-19 pandemic. Although the country reported from zero to a hundred daily cases between March and July, cases began to soar following the Beirut explosion, in which four major hospitals were destroyed, with Lebanon reporting well over a thousand cases on most days since mid-September. By 30 October 2022 the country had 1.21 million confirmed cases and 10,668 deaths (WHO 2022a). Since the majority of the refugees live in the host community, their level of exposure was high due to close interaction with the wider population. There was no systematic COVID-19 testing for refugees in informal settlements and collective shelters (Fouad et al. 2021). As of mid-2022, 328,380 Syrians had received at least one dose of the COVID-19 vaccine, and 233,558 were deemed to be fully vaccinated (with at least two doses) (UNHCR 2022j).

In a series of violent incidents, which were often triggered by the spread of hate rhetoric against Syrian refugees on the part of political parties and media channels, an incident occurred between Syrian workers and their local employers regarding payment. In the dispute an informal Syrian settlement in northern Lebanon was burned to the ground, forcing over three hundred refugees to flee the place (DW 2020). Over the following two years (2021–22) the Syrian refugee and host communities in Lebanon were embroiled in triple crises, including what is considered to be "the country's largest peace-time economic and financial crisis," the COVID-19 pandemic; and the Port of Beirut explosion, as well as ongoing governance deficits. In 2021 food security was considered the largest threat and the largest target for assistance in dealing with the sharp rise in poverty and food insecurity experienced as a result of the country's deepening economic collapse (Brun et al. 2021).

On 8 September 2021 a sign of possible rapprochement between the Syrian and Lebanese regimes took place as energy ministers convened in Jordan to discuss possible collaboration to help Lebanon with its electricity crisis (Schaer 2021). This was followed by a decline in Hezbollah's electoral position in the May 2022 parliamentary elections, with Hezbollah retaining its dominant position among Shiite Muslims but losing support among its Christian and Sunni Muslim allies. There was also an observed shifting of its decade-long focus on Syria back to a focus on Israel (Byman 2022). In September 2022, one of the country's worst incidents of sea deaths occurred, in which seventy-seven people died attempting to leave Lebanon because of deteriorating conditions (Strzyżyńska 2022). By October 2022, UNHCR had reported the return of 6,489 Syrian refugees to Syria, compared to almost half that number (3,620) in the previous year (UNHCR 2022b).

CONCLUSION

The displacement of hundreds of thousands of Syrians to Lebanon has posed significant economic, social, and political challenges to the country. This chapter has provided a chronological account of the events of the displacement as they unfolded on the ground in Lebanon, and a descriptive account of the government's policy response as it evolved over time. To construct this descriptive timeline of events, primary and secondary data were analyzed as to the key actions and reactions that took place in the three analytical arenas presented in chapter 2 with respect to the Syrian refugee movement in Lebanon. As in the case of Jordan, this descriptive, chronological account is necessary to help us unpack and analyze the government of Lebanon's policy response, as well as its changes over time, and the main drivers that shaped the response evolutions. I will proceed to do this analytically and to apply this book's framework to the case of Lebanon in the coming chapter. In doing so, I will answer the book's second question: how has the government of Lebanon responded to the mass influx of Syrian refugees over time, and what has influenced its policy decisions?

8

Unpacking Lebanon's Policy Response to Syrian Displacement: "Policy of No Policy"

INTRODUCTION

The previous chapter provided a detailed account of both the dynamics of Syrian displacement in Lebanon as it unfolded on the ground over the course of eleven years, including a description of the interplay between the key policy actors, and the critical events that transpired as a result of the Syrian refugee movement. This chapter aims to build on the previous descriptive account by applying to the Lebanese case the analytical framework proposed in chapter 2. As was the case of Jordan, this chapter aims to answer the book's second key research question on *how* Lebanon responded to the Syrian refugee influx on its land and *why* this policy response came about. Using process tracing and chronologies over the period from 2011 to 2022, and relying on primary and secondary data, I analyze the GoL's response in terms of three policy components: entry and stay, livelihoods, and durable solutions.

The chapter is divided into three main sections, starting with an analytical breakdown of Lebanon's policy response to Syrian displacement, followed by characterization of policy-response evolution. In this sense, the first two sections analytically provide an answer to how Lebanon responded to the refugee influx and presence over the eleven-year period. The third section discusses Lebanon's response drivers.

ANALYTICAL BREAKDOWN OF LEBANON'S POLICY RESPONSE TO SYRIAN DISPLACEMENT

In this section, and relying on the literature on refugee-policy choices discussed in chapter 2, Lebanon's policy is analyzed in terms of its three main components: policy on entry and stay, policy on livelihoods, and policy on durable solutions.

For the purpose of this analysis, Lebanon's policy elements, and their evolution over the course of the displacement, have been derived from several sources of data. First, seven in-depth elite interviews were conducted in 2017 and 2021 with both government officials and representatives of political groups, who were asked about the process by which each policy choice was made and how the policy evolved. Second, to triangulate government officials' answers and obtain an accurate picture of any unannounced policies being implemented, twelve in-depth interviews were conducted with NGOs and experts (in 2017 and 2021). It is worth noting that, as in the case of Jordan, both local and international NGOs were interviewed to increase the reliability of the data. International governmental organizations, such as UNHCR, may be more involved in policy formulation, whereas local NGOs may be more involved in implementation; therefore, both views had to be considered. Third, facts mentioned in the interviews were further checked through analysis of secondary data including reports of leading NGOs, scholarly articles, and grey literature.

Policy on Entry and Stay

One of the earliest decisions a government witnessing a mass influx situation has to make is whether to open its borders to admit those seeking refuge on its territory or to close its borders and turn them away. While normatively governments are required by customary law to admit asylum seekers who are fleeing a well-founded fear of persecution in their country of origin (UNHCR 1981), in practice instances of both border closures and openings have historically occurred. A government's policy on entry can be broken down for analytical purposes into three issues: its admission choice, its adherence to the principle of non-refoulement, and the type of asylum it grants to the refugee population.

Over the course of the crisis the GoL's admission choice and adherence to the principle of non-refoulement has gone through two main stages. From 2011 to 2014, the GoL adopted a de facto open-border policy towards the refugee movement.[1] Syrians were allowed in at official entry points with passports stamps.[2] Their entry was facilitated by the pre-existing no-visa regime for Syrians under the bilateral cooperation agreement between Syria and Lebanon. The government was by and large adhering to the principle of non-refoulement.[3]

In January 2015, however, a policy shift occurred, whereby all Syrian refugees wishing to enter Lebanon had to justify the purpose of their visit.[4] Six visa categories were introduced for Syrians: tourism, business, study, medical treatment, economic migrant entering with a Lebanese sponsor, and transit.[5] Syrians entering Lebanon had to fall within one of these categories. According to a Norwegian Refugee Council official, exceptions made for humanitarian cases were rare and inconsistent (Shawaf and El Asmar 2017).[6] Under the new regulations the number of Syrians able to cross legally into Lebanon diminished. Increased border control also reduced the number of informal crossings (UNHCR 2020h; Fakhoury and Ozkul 2019; Berti 2017).[7] This policy change, thus, represented a practical border closure and refoulement of Syrian refugees (UNHCR 2020a).[8] Several officers at UNHCR mentioned the following regarding Lebanon's entry policy: "Since then, the government's policy on entry of Syrians remained to a large extent the same. Minor amendments were periodically made regarding the time allowed for certain categories of residence, for instance, but there were no major changes since the 2015 policy shift regarding new entries. In 2019 the Higher Defense Council and the General Security Office changed the regulation regarding deportations of unregulated residents. We advocated [that] Lebanon's policy on deportations should align with Lebanese law. This mostly occurred in the context of a larger restrictive policy."[9]

With regard to the type of asylum granted to the refugee population, in the case of mass influx situations governments are faced with two alternatives: either to consider the incoming group as "prima facie refugees" or to grant them temporary protection. Prima facie status identifies its holders officially as "refugees"; has no predetermined duration; and entitles its holders, following RSD, to local integration and voluntary repatriation. Alternatively, temporary protection is time constrained and allows its holders, following RSD, either voluntary repatriation when conditions in the home country are deemed safe or resettlement to a third country – but not local integration (UNHCR 2001b).

Syrian refugees in Lebanon are stuck in a legal grey area between being considered by the state as "displaced" and being treated as de facto "refugees" (Janmyr 2018; UNHCR 2014c).[10] The government has steered away from using the internationally acknowledged notion of "refugee."[11] During the early years of the crisis legal residency for Syrian refugees could be obtained based on UNHCR registration. This allowed Syrians six months of temporary residence, subject to renewal by authorities. Those unregistered by UNHCR, or failing to renew their legal residency based on it, were otherwise regulated by the Law on Entry and Exit of Foreigners in Lebanon.[12] From 2013 to 201, an average of 47,000 refugees were being registered every month in the country (Janmyr and Mourad 2018; Janmyr 2018).

In 2015, authorities implemented a new residency-renewal scheme whereby Syrian refugees were required to pay a USD 200 annual fee and present valid travel documentation and a housing pledge (Sieverding and Calderón-Mejía 2020; Janmyr and Mourad 2018).[13] Further, the government requested UNHCR to halt registration of Syrians and to deregister those who approached it after 2015.[14] Accordingly, Syrians who were not registered with UNHCR had to legalize their stay in Lebanon based on one of the six categories created for them.[15] Speaking on the issue, a high-ranking official at the MORA noted the following: "we are currently categorizing Syrians according to status, to differentiate between the displaced, the people in transit, and so on. We have noticed that there has been a cross-border movement. There are also workers, who should not be categorized as displaced. This is an attempt to regulate the influx."[16] As of July 2020, the ban on UNHCR registrations was still in place. A UNHCR official said, "In 2015, the government requested that we stop registering refugees with a post-facto effect. Those who were allowed in after 2015 and who were registered had to be deregistered. Now we record them, but this does not grant them a UNHCR certificate. They do not have access to the same services, and they do not appear on UNHCR's registration database."[17]

Human rights groups condemned the policy change under the pretext that it was pushing Syrians into further vulnerability, because renewal fees were unaffordable for the majority of refugees who depended on humanitarian assistance (HRW 2016b). According to a Norwegian Refugee Council official, this policy change puts Syrians in a precarious legal situation, in which they are vulnerable to deportation and thus have to stay "invisible" to authorities. Without legal

156 The Politics of Refugee Policy in the Global South

residency they are also unable to register new births, putting their children at risk of becoming stateless.[18] In 2021 the percentage of Syrian refugees over fifteen years of age with legal residency was reported to be declining each year, reaching 16 per cent, and 31 per cent of new births are registered at the Foreigners' Registry, according to the Vulnerability Assessment Survey conducted jointly by UN agencies, including UNHCR, UNICEF, and WFP (UNHCR 2022j).

Policy on Livelihoods

A government's policy choices do not end after the granting of asylum and the admission of refugees. The government needs to make choices regarding their type of settlement, the restriction of their movement and employment provisions, and the institutional framework through which it will govern their protection and access to services.

TYPE OF SETTLEMENT ALLOWED

With regard to the type of settlement allowed, practices have historically varied between housing refugees in camps and allowing them to self-settle in urban areas. According to Bakewell (2014), encamping refugees in designated sites has been the more common practice adopted in mass influx situations. The GoL's policy regarding the settlement of Syrian refugees was firm on not allowing camps to be created on its territory.[19] Instead, refugees were left to self-settle. A later discussion will take place about the rationale behind this decision from the authorities' perspective. In 2015 an estimated 18 per cent of refugees were residing in substandard informal settlements, which were subject to routine removals by authorities (LCRP 2016; Limoges 2017). UNHCR has been monitoring collective evictions in the country. During the 2018–20 period, approximately 160 evictions occurred, affecting more than 12,600 Syrian refugees. In most cases refugees were living in tents, and the evictions were justified by "environmental reasons" or the owner's desire to repurpose the land (UNHCR 2019a, 2020i). "There are no camps allowed, so refugees have to lease private property or are hosted by locals. There are some 4,000 informal tented settlements, but refugees still pay rent to the owners of the land. These tented settlements evolved. They started with migrant Syrian workers coming for agricultural work, and then bringing the rest of their families to join them after the war broke out. They have middlemen or 'Shaweesh' who would be Syrian and would coordinate their affairs."[20]

UNHCR mentioned the following regarding changes to Lebanon's policy on settlement of Syrian refugees: "Starting 2016–2017, some restrictions were removed by the government such as the need for housing pledges for Syrians from landowners. Instead, a housing attestation could be issued by UNHCR as proof of residence. However, the no-camp policy has not changed since the start of the refugee presence. In all cases, UNHCR itself is moving away from encampment globally. Authorities try to prevent permanent settlement, so whenever any cement walls are built in the informal settlements, they ask for them to be removed."[21]

In 2021 the Vulnerability Assessment Survey reported that almost 57 per cent of Syrian refugee families lived in shelters that were deemed overcrowded, below humanitarian standards, and/or in danger of collapse (UNHCR 2022i).

SERVICE PROVISION AND FREEDOM OF MOVEMENT

While the 1951 Convention gives refugees the right to freedom of movement and the right to education, public relief, and assistance, governments may impose restrictions on both rights (UNHCR 2011). With regard to movement, Syrian refugees were not restricted as per any government policy. However, discretionary behaviour in certain localities was reported, and in some cases curfews were imposed by municipal police or host communities on Syrians' movement after six o'clock in the evening (HRW 2014b).[22] In 2020 alone, approximately 330 municipalities had imposed curfews on Syrian refugees (HRW 2020). An adviser to the prime minister noted: "We have witnessed differences in implementation at the local level with regard to restricting Syrians' movement. This is mainly because central authorities are unable to impose policies on municipalities effectively. Consequently, there has been discretionary behaviour with regard to implementation of policies, including restricting their movement."[23]

With regard to the provision of basic assistance, health care, and education, the Lebanese government provided registered Syrian refugees with access to health care and education. An estimated 35 per cent of the Syrian refugee influx comprises school-aged children (five to seventeen years old) (Ghalayini, Ismail, and El-Ghali 2016). They belonged to an educational system where the language of instruction and curriculum were different,[24] and many of them had been out of school for years (Brun and Shuayb 2020; Buckner and Moznyah 2019).[25] In 2014 the Ministry of Education and Higher Education issued the "Reaching All Children with Education" (RACE I) plan, a three-year program (2014–16) that committed the government to provide Syrian refugee children with access to the Lebanese public education system (HRW 2016a; LCRP 2016; Abla and Al-Masri 2015).[26] In 2017 the program was renewed for its second phase, under the name RACE II, and it was set to continue until 2021. Similar to its predecessor, the RACE II program is financially supported by both multilateral donors (such as UNHCR, UNICEF, and the EU) and bilateral donors (such as the UK government) (Buckner and Mozynar 2019). The Lebanese government also implemented a cash-transfer program, titled "No Lost Generation" (NLG), to cover the costs of school commuting and income forgone from child employment. It was specifically targeted to Syrian children enrolled in afternoon primary school shifts (De Hoop, Morey, and Seidenfeld 2019).

The need to create double shifts to accommodate the exponential rise in student numbers and to adapt to their specific needs placed an extra burden on Lebanon's already overstretched system.[27] An adviser to MORA noted: "The Lebanese government is keen to sustain the provision of public education to Syrian refugee children because not educating them would make them a ticking bomb, whether they stay or leave."[28]

Syrian refugees who are registered with UNHCR have also been allowed access to the public primary health-care system. Speaking on the issue, a member of Parliament's health committee noted the following: "Every 'displaced' Syrian costs the government USD 400 per year in health expenses. The main problem lies in the number and availability of hospital beds. Lebanon has around 4,000–5,000 beds, which are not enough to accommodate the high volume of Syrian refugees in the country. The second main problem is with the provision of dialysis services for refugees. The Ministry of Health partners with UNHCR to cover the costs of birth-giving, dialysis, and services for seniors."[29] However, Lebanon's health-care system is largely privatized and based on user fees. Refugees registered with the UNHCR have access to selected primary health-care centres with subsidized fees (UNHCR 2019f).[30] Unregistered refugees have access to subsidized fees at a smaller number of health-care centres and may have to pay the same fees as Lebanese citizens (UNHCR 2019f). During the 2020 COVID-19 pandemic Syrian refugees without legal residency in Lebanon were afraid to approach health services. However, the GSO reassured refugees and the UNHCR that refugees would not be punished for lacking legal residency amidst the pandemic.

A food cash program was also provided in cooperation with the World Food Program. However, this program was curtailed in 2015 due to lack of funding (Miller 2016). Material assistance provided in cooperation with UNHCR became increasingly limited, targeted to those considered the most vulnerable based on the Vulnerability Assessment Survey (UNHCR 2020e).[31] To make ends meet, refugees instead rely on loans or assistance from humanitarian organizations.[32]

It is worth noting that residence status affects refugees in many ways, including their freedom of movement and access to services, which are both linked to their legal residence status. In Lebanon, the absence of legal residency for Syrians, which became much harder to obtain after the 2015 regulations, reflected negatively on their livelihoods including their ability to register new births (Elmolla 2019). In 2018 an estimated 250,000 school-age children who were registered with the UNHCR did not have access to education due to issues related to birth registrations (IDS 2018). According to UNHCR, more than half of the Syrian refugee children (aged three to seventeen) were still out of school in 2019 (UNHCR 2019e). Between 2020 and 2021, primary school attendance was reported at 53 per cent, with costs of education material and transportation being the most prominent reasons that refugee children did not attend the school year 2020–21 (UNHCR 2022i).

ACCESS TO THE LABOUR MARKET

Another important decision a government has to make regarding the status of refugees is whether or not to allow them lawful employment and access to the labour market. Given that Lebanon had a pre-existing bilateral agreement with Syria, the agricultural and construction sectors were traditionally large employers of seasonal Syrian labour. However, the Syrian civil war brought with it changes to how the authorities handled Syrians' engagement in the labour market. While Syrians are allowed to engage in the Lebanese labour market as per the 1994 bilateral agreement between the two countries, Syrian refugees who are registered with UNHCR sign a pledge not to work.[33] This prohibition consequently pushed many to

160   The Politics of Refugee Policy in the Global South

engage in the informal labour market and to adopt negative coping mechanisms to survive, such as child labour and street begging.[34]

In June 2016 the GSO issued a regulation that lifted the ban on formal employment of Syrian refugees and replaced it with a clause that restricted their work to three sectors: agriculture, environment, and construction.[35] Nevertheless, the process of securing work permits is still arduous, and most Syrian refugees do not have access to the formal labour market. In order to obtain a permit, Syrians need to be sponsored by a Lebanese employer and to pay a fee according to the category of employment (Verme et al. 2015). In 2019 the Lebanese Labour Minister reportedly said that only 1,733 Syrians had valid work permits in the country (HRW 2019). Speaking on the issue, a MORA adviser noted that "restricting their work is an attempt to regulate the labour market, because reduced economic growth and decreased job opportunities cause tensions between the refugees and the host communities."[36] A representative of the Progressive Socialist Party mentioned the following: "This policy change is based on an economic perspective. Syrian labour can be resorted to for public works and large infrastructural projects funded by incoming aid. This would benefit the refugee and host community; turning the refugee population from a burden into an added value."[37]

Speaking on this, UNHCR officers mentioned that every year the Ministry of Labour publishes a list of sectors that are restricted to Lebanese nationals, with some exemptions made for Syrians. According to the officers, this policy was followed even before the Syrian refugee presence.[38] Although the EU-Lebanon Compact negotiations called for job creation for Syrian refugees, the final agreement did not include provisions for that, but instead focused on the Lebanese community, under the assumption that it would indirectly create jobs for Syrian refugees (El-Daif 2022). In 2021, labour-force participation of Syrian refugees was 47 per cent, with 53 per cent of the refugee population being inactive (UNHCR 2022i).

MODE OF IMPLEMENTATION

The mode by which a government chooses to implement its refugee policy is a particularly relevant issue to discuss, especially in the context of mass displacement. Two issues have been mentioned in the literature, including the type of bureaucratic structure to which refugee matters are assigned and the inclusion of civil society actors.

With regard to the bureaucratic structure, Lebanon has relied on a civilian structure to manage the affairs of the Syrian refugee movement. The institutional structure relied upon to manage the influx has evolved over the course of the crisis. According to an official at MORA, during the early years of the crisis two main institutions were in charge: MOSA, which was responsible for coordinating the efforts of NGOs and government offices, and the GSO, which was in charge of border management.[39] She mentioned: "MOSA at the start was leading the response. The government was present but had an umbrella presence only. There was no unified response, only individual ministerial efforts, not whole of government."[40]

In March 2013, a crisis management unit was created (as a sub-unit in MOSA) to respond more fully to security, health, and shelter issues (Miller 2016). Following, an inter-ministerial committee was created to include the key line ministries.[41] This committee was in charge of jointly examining projects and issues before raising them to the prime minister.[42] It also included working groups for different sectors, such as health and sanitation, where relevant UN agencies were present. A MORA official noted: "We felt that we needed to move away from 'shopping list' attitude adopted by some NGOs and donors, where they came and just decided which areas they wanted to fund, to a results-based approach that included much more involvement by the government." [43]

A Ministry of Refugee Affairs (MORA) was also created, geared for the Syrian refugee crisis.[44] "A ministry was needed to be dedicated specifically to do the work that was beyond what separate ministries could do. It is in charge of policy design and coordination," noted a high-ranking MORA official.[45] However, at the time of creation the ministry still had no clear mandate or budget,[45] and it was not included in 2021 Cabinet formations. On this, officers at UNHCR stated: "The ministry was not achieving what it was intended for. The responsibilities, therefore, were shifted back to the Ministry of Social Affairs – especially regarding non legal matters."[47]

With regard to the inclusion of civil society actors in responding to the refugee influx, tens of international and local non-governmental organizations operate on the ground in Lebanon, providing various forms of assistance to Syrian refugees. They cooperate with the government and each other in a loose and fragmented network-like structure.[48] Line ministries work with 112 partners including designated UN agencies and NGOs, and UNHCR coordinates with other humanitarian actors.[49] LCRP, which forms this structure, is divided into ten sectors: health, social stability, protection, water, basic assistance, shelter, energy, food security and agriculture, education, and livelihoods (El-Daif 2022).

Policy on Durable Solutions

Upon cessation of refugee or temporary protection status, refugees are no longer allowed to reside in their host country, in which case a solution that resolves their situation must be reached. Three conventional "durable solutions" exist that are advocated by the international refugee regime: voluntary repatriation, local integration, and resettlement. The type of durable solution allowed by a government may also be directly linked to the type of asylum granted to the refugee population, or the decision may transpire later as the condition in the home country evolves.

With regard to durable solutions the GoL did not alter its policy position throughout the course of the eleven-year period of analysis. Syrian refugees were to be resettled to a third country or preferably repatriated to their country of origin, but not to be locally integrated in Lebanon under any circumstances.[50] According to an adviser to MORA, there has been general consensus among political parties that Syrian refugees should not be allowed permanent settlement in Lebanon under any circumstances, but there has been disagreement on the logistics and time of their return.[51] Pro-Syrian parties, including the Free Patriotic Movement (Maronite) and Hezbollah (Shiite), advocated for dialogue to be opened with the Assad regime to return the refugees to safe zones within Syria,[52] while other parties, including the Progressive Socialist Party, advocated for their return only when it was deemed safe.[53] In practice, sporadic but few forcible returns were recorded by human rights groups (HRW 2016c), while the self-organized return of some 5,006 Syrians was recorded by UNHCR in 2016 (UNHCR 2018e). Moreover, in April 2018 the GSO started facilitating group returns to Syria through seventeen of its centres (UNHCR 2018b).[54] However, in 2020, due to the border restrictions imposed during the COVID-19 pandemic, both group movements facilitated by the GSO and deportations were paused. Such pause was later undone when caretaker Minister of the Displaced Issam Charafeddine announced in July 2022 the government's plan to deport 15,000

Syrian refugees per month, in coordination with Syrian authorities, under the pretext that "the war was over and Syria was now safe" (Sewell 2022).

With regard to resettlement, which is the responsibility of UNHCR, between 2011 and 2022 the resettlement submissions made by UNHCR amounted to 107,793. Out of this total figure, 75,848 Syrians were resettled, with the highest resettlement occurring in 2016–17 (UNHCR 2022e). However, resettlement figures are low in comparison to the actual refugee population that Lebanon is hosting (UNHCR 2021b).[55] According to a UNHCR officer, opportunities for resettlement to third countries are scarce and can only be applied to registered refugees or the extremely "vulnerable" humanitarian cases.

PHASES OF POLICY EVOLUTION

As is evident from the earlier discussion, the Lebanese government's response to the Syrian refugee influx on its territory evolved and changed shape over the course of the crisis. The shifts in the response can be grouped mainly into two phases that also reflect shifting paradigms. Figure 8.1 shows the evolutionary phases through which Lebanon's policy response went between 2011 and 2022. In the following subsections I explain the characterization of each phase in more depth.

Displacement Start: State Disengagement and Policy of Laissez-Faire

During the initial emergency phase (2011–14) the government's response to the influx was non-restrictive in nature, as evidenced by the mosaic of policy choices that the government adopted towards Syrian refugees, including allowing them open admission and de facto temporary protection in Lebanon; abiding by the principle of non-refoulement; allowing them freedom of movement and choice of settlement; and providing them with non-relief services such as school enrolment and access to public health care. The reliance on civilian institutions to handle refugee affairs, and the autonomy given to civil society organizations to respond to the crisis, are also elements of a non-restrictive approach. The restrictive features of the GoL's policy towards Syrian displacement were largely repre-

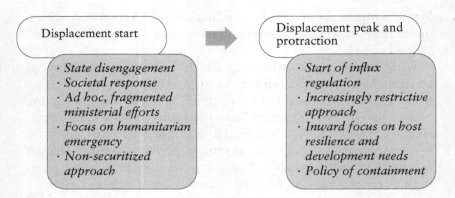

Figure 8.1 | Phases of Lebanon's policy evolution on Syrian displacement (2011–22)

sented in its ban on Syrian refugee employment and local integration as a durable solution.

During this stage, focus was primarily on the humanitarian aspect of the crisis, as refugee needs took centre stage. The state's reluctance to engage with the situation led to decision-making paralysis, with civil society actors, including host communities, filling in for state absence. While this "hands-off" approach was a symptom of dysfunction, it paradoxically provided the refugee movement with some respite to enter and settle without restrictions. However, it also meant that they were largely left to fend for themselves with the aid of humanitarian actors, whose assistance could be sporadic and inconsistent.

*Displacement Peak and Protraction:
Influx Regulation and Policy of Containment*

As the displacement peaked (2015–16) and protracted (2017–21), the government's response started to evolve in terms of its degree of restrictiveness towards the Syrian refugee population and its mode of implementation. The government began to adopt measures to regulate the influx and dissuade Syrian refugees from staying in Lebanon. While Lebanon's approach could still be considered semi-re-

Table 8.1 | Lebanon's policy choices on Syrian displacement and their evolution

		Displacement start (2011–14)	Displacement peak and protraction (2015–22)
Policy on entry and stay	Admission choice and adherence to non-refoulement	Open admission and non-refoulement	Restrictions imposed on admission (practical border closure) and refoulement
	Type of asylum granted	De facto temporary protection	Restrictions imposed on renewal of residency, and ban on new UNHCR registrations
Policy on livelihoods	Type of settlement	Non-encampment	Non-encampment and collective evictions
	Access to labour market	Not allowed (pledge not to work signed with registration)	Allowed but restricted to 3 sectors
	Freedom of movement	Allowed	Allowed (curtailed by discretionary behaviour at local level and curfews specifically targeting Syrian refugees)
	Service provision	Non-relief services provided	Non-relief services scaled back
	Mode of implementation	Collaboration with IOs	Collaboration with IOs
		Civilian management of refugee population	Civilian management of refugee population
Policy on durable solutions	Repatriation, local integration & resettlement	Only repatriation and resettlement allowed	Only repatriation (facilitated by GSO) and resettlement allowed

strictive in nature, the closure of the border and the adoption of systematic refoulement gave it an even more restrictive character compared to the previous phase. Contrarily, the government relaxed the complete ban on Syrian refugee employment by allowing them to work in the three sectors that had traditionally relied on them. During this stage the government turned its focus inward, considering the situation a "Lebanon crisis, not a refugee crisis."[56] The LCRP was created to address host and refugee needs by targeting assistance to refugees and vulnerable host communities and injecting investments into Lebanese infrastructure.[57]

Despite the protraction of the crisis, during the period of 2017–21 no significant changes occurred to the GoL's approach to the governance of Syrian displacement in terms of the three policy elements under examination. The major change could be considered to be in the halting of any further entries, while attempting to use a variety of restrictive measures aimed at preventing permanence of the present refugee presence. Although a new ministry dedicated to the Syrian refugee file was initially created to consolidate the projects and efforts of ministries and civil society actors, it was later abandoned, signalling the potential start of a new era of phasing out the refugee presence. However, at the time of writing of this book, it was too early to tell.

Table 8.1 gives a more detailed account of Lebanon's policy on Syrian displacement, broken down into policy elements and their evolution over the different phases. The policy elements and sub-elements are derived from this book's analytical framework proposed in chapter 2. The table shows the two phases discussed earlier, including the evolution of each policy element across the three phases. To take one example of how this table should be read, the policy on admission choice and adherence to non-refoulement began during the displacement start phase (2011–14) with open admission and adherence to non-refoulement, and evolved during the displacement peak and protraction phase (2015–16 and 2017–21) to restrictive admission with non-systematic refoulement, followed by border closure and non-admission – constituting systematic refoulement. I will discuss in the coming section the drivers and factors behind the change and continuity of Lebanon's policies towards Syrian displacement.

DRIVERS OF LEBANON'S POLICY RESPONSE TO SYRIAN DISPLACEMENT: BETWEEN FRAGMENTATION AND PARALYSIS

The previous section discussed in detail how the GoL responded to the Syrian refugee movement during the period 2011–22. Using process tracing over the period from 2011 to 2022 and relying on primary and secondary data obtained in the field, this section provides an analytical discussion of the main drivers behind the government's policy adoption and implementation. In this section I explain continuity and change in Lebanon's policy response over the course of the eleven-year period.

Displacement Start Phase (2011–14)

During the displacement start phase (2011–14) Lebanon's adoption of a non-restrictive policy towards the Syrian influx was the result of the coupling of several factors in its international, domestic, and displacement arenas. The triangulated data extracted from the field indicates that the "non-securitized" and "hands-off" policy approach adopted by the Mikati government was more a de facto reaction to the situation developing on the ground than a policy of choice or design. As political groups were divided on the conflict and were adopting a wait-and-see approach, the refugee movement was growing in scale, aided by historical ties between the two communities and religious affiliation. The humanitarian nature of the crisis also raised society's receptiveness to the flight of Syrians, who in in this case were also considered "Arab brothers" according to local norms. Besides the presence of porous borders, Syrians' entry into Lebanon was also facilitated by the no-visa regime and the seasonal labour movement, which had existed prior to the crisis, allowing Syrians to follow previous work and social pathways. A high-ranking MORA official said, "I was one of the many people who opened their homes in Akkar province to receive displaced Syrians. We refused to receive any compensation in return because we considered these people as our brothers and guests. They were also fleeing for their lives and were in need of urgent assistance and shelter."[58]

Syrian refugee presence, however, was the subject of internal political discord as the stances of the major political groups differed

168   The Politics of Refugee Policy in the Global South

depending on their demographic considerations and their relationship with the Syrian regime – and, by corollary, what they stood to gain or lose from the outcome of the conflict. Such considerations influenced each group's perception of the problem and how to manage it. As the dominant political groups were hesitant to take action, the political gridlock reflected on the government's ability to take action. The vacuum left by the state compelled civil society actors to step in to fill the void and provide humanitarian assistance in the municipalities most affected. The state's inability to formulate a unified policy resulted in a shifting of responsibility to civil society and UN agencies (Kagan 2012). A member of Parliament mentioned: "Lebanon could not close its border to incoming Syrians, mainly because there was political indecision. There were political groups and communities that wanted to receive fleeing Syrians and there were those that did not."[59] A Progressive Socialist Party member said, "Everyone looks at this file from a sectarian perspective. There is a fear of demographic imbalance, which is always paramount when dealing with foreigners, not just refugees. Hezbollah, for instance, fears from the Sunni dominance of the refugee movement. The division of Lebanon into sects causes a division in the handling of this file. There is no clear vision."[60]

Hezbollah's supportive stance of the Syrian regime, and later involvement in the conflict, as well as its dominance as a political actor in Lebanon, further complicated the state's ability to have a unified vision. However, while displaced Syrians were "allowed" admission into Lebanon, their conditions of stay, livelihoods, and durable solutions were less "relaxed." To maintain "temporariness" of the situation, the government granted Syrian refugees de facto temporary protection, rather than considering them prima facie refugees, referring to Syrians as "displaced" rather than as "refugees." According to respondents, this use of the legal terminology was to avoid any possibility of their local integration and the repetition of another Palestinian protracted scenario. This aversion to refer to Syrians as refugees was also in line with the government's attempt to dissociate Lebanon from the Syrian conflict; referring to them as refugees would implicate the Syrian regime.

The Mikati government's efforts to disassociate the Lebanese state from events in Syria through maintaining "invisibility" of the crisis included refusal to create camps. The legacy of Palestinian refuge in Lebanon, and fears of a security imbalance occurring as a result of hosting the refugee movement, aligned with Hezbollah's stance against allowing Syrians to be hosted in refugee camps for fear of creating an opposition base against the Syrian regime in Lebanon. The Lebanese government had concerns over policies that might become a back door to the permanent settlement of Syrians in the country (Sanyal 2021). Furthermore, fear of Syrian refugees competing with the Lebanese labour force was reported by respondents to have been the reason behind the government's initial prohibition of Syrian refugee employment. The government considered that those who were already employed in Lebanon or who could secure employment should not be treated as refugees.

While international norms of refugee protection are cited by government respondents as a factor behind their decision to adhere to the principle of non-refoulement and to provide Syrian refugees with non-relief services, in line with its MOU with UNHCR, it is evident in the evolution of Lebanon's response that this factor became irrelevant as the crisis evolved. Political divisions and the nature of Lebanon's confessional political system also reflected on the government's ability to formulate and implement policies effectively. This was especially evident in the restrictions imposed on the movement of Syrian refugees in municipalities, where non-state actors have demographic and political leverage. According to an expert, "The government is playing it by ear – even international organizations. It should be the government leading the way, but there is no central lead agency. The political situation has not allowed going beyond ad hoc measures."[61]

Displacement Peak and Protraction (2015–22)

As the size of the refugee population increased during the period from 2011 to the end of 2015, and the displacement became protracted, Lebanon's response took on more restrictive undertones. The increasingly restrictive measures adopted by the government, including border closure and scaling back of services, were adopted to stem the flow of the movement and restrict Syrian refugees' ability to maintain legal residency in Lebanon. Syrian refugees already residing in Lebanon were to be "tolerated," but new refugee flows were not to be permitted entry. According to respondents, Lebanon's shifting policy towards Syrian refugees and its attempt to play a more proactive role in managing the crisis were influenced by the formation of the new national unity government, headed by Prime Minister Tammam Salam. The new government issued the first official policy document with the objective of tackling the refugee crisis based on security and economic imperatives. The LCRP was created, and an institutional structure was put in place to manage the crisis more coherently.

This policy shift was also influenced by reduced economic resource capacity. For instance, Lebanon's GDP growth (annual percentage) witnessed decline over the period under investigation, as compared to pre-crisis performance. General government net debt (as a percentage of GDP) increased from 127.6 per cent in 2010 to 142.3 percent in 2016 (IMF 2018). While this may not be directly linked to the Syrian crisis, it lends support to respondents' claim that reduced resource capacity influenced the government's policy change. A World Bank official cited the following:

> In 2013, Lebanon asked the World Bank for help in assessing the impact of the conflict on Lebanon's economic growth, trade, infrastructure, and other areas. This report became a key document. This is not just a humanitarian crisis, but also a development crisis for the host. The point was not to provide direct support to refugees, but to focus on countries impacted. Lebanon has witnessed USD 7.5 billion economic loss from the conflict, not just the refugee burden. This paved the way for the creation of a road map for stabilization with the government and a trust fund for donors to mitigate the impact.[62]

Further, international assistance provided to the GoL was inconsistent and ambivalent. The multiplicity of actors involved, as well as Lebanon's weak and fragmented state apparatus, led donors to bypass funds through civil society actors and UN agencies, rather than government channels. Funding pledges were also under-fulfilled, which reduced the resource capacity of the government to respond to the needs of the refugee population as well as the host community. A member of the Parliamentary Commission for Health, Labour, and Social Affairs mentioned the following: "The international community does not contribute as much to face the needs of this refugee population. It only provides a fraction of what is promised, which disrupts our ability to plan ahead and respond effectively."[63]

Further, decreased social receptiveness over time, and the security spillover, especially in Aarsal, also compelled the government to rethink its approach in handling the refugee movement. According to the 2017 report *Regular Perceptions Surveys on Social Tensions throughout Lebanon,* 92 per cent of respondents felt that the presence of Syrian refugees placed a strain on resources, and 48.8 per cent believed that relations with Syrian refugees had worsened since 2014 (MOSA 2017). On the impact of reduced social receptiveness on government decision-making, officials at UNHCR, NRC, and MORA reported the following: "There has been a heavy burden on municipalities. Some remotes areas have more refugees than Lebanese. The complaints prompted a need to regulate a situation that was getting out of hand."[64] "Lebanon was not ready, in terms of infrastructure or service provision capacity, for this sudden rise in its population. The areas most affected by the influx are the poorest areas, which adds vulnerability to vulnerability. We have been witnessing a rise in social tensions between host communities and refugees."[65] "Especially in areas where host communities are already vulnerable, they feel that they are receiving less assistance than refugees, which causes social friction."[66]

However, according to respondents, the London conference and the advocacy efforts of international organizations and civil society actors provided an impetus for adopting the Lebanon Compact and opening up the Lebanese labour market to Syrian refugee employment. Speaking on the issue, MORA and NRC officials further stated: "There was ambiguity in relation with international organizations because of political and ministerial tensions. The Supporting Syria and the Region conference, which took place in London, created a momentum for a master plan and for host support."[67] "We do not have leverage to criticize the government, so we flag issues with donors and other actors, who can influence the government. It depends on which part of the government you want to influence; there are so many divided interests and stances. It is a difficult policy environment. We advocated for different issues including employment, registration of new births, and other protection concerns."[68]

Despite the significant impact that later developments, including COVID-19 and the Beirut blast (El-Taliawi and Fakhoury 2020), had on Lebanon at large, they did not change much of the composition of Lebanon's governance of Syrian displacement. No major shift was witnessed to classify it as a different phase. The main policy elements regarding entry and residence, livelihoods, and durable solutions remained for the most part the same. While it would have been expected that such drastic pressures would increase pressures

172   The Politics of Refugee Policy in the Global South

on the government to engage in promoting and engaging in involuntary return operations, this did not occur on any wide or systematic scale that would be enough to consider it the start of an end to the Syrian refugee presence in Lebanon. In the coming chapter I will discuss why that may have been the case by taking a macro-perspective of the system components in Lebanon. On this issue, officials at UNHCR also recounted the following based on their informed and involved observations:

> The blast, along with the other challenges such as the economic collapse and financial devaluation, contributed to the country's difficult situation as a whole. These developments have made life more difficult at the social, household, and individual level for Syrian refugees, as well as Lebanese nationals. Return has been under discussion by authorities for many years, but so far there has been limited implementation even on the part of the General Security Office. This was of course made more difficult by COVID-19, but also because of the inability to reach a consensus on it politically. Hezbollah's majority government would make it easier to adopt such a policy, but we also undertake a lot of advocacy efforts to ensure refugee rights are protected including the need to maintain the voluntariness of return. COVID-19 also suspended some deadlines that the government placed on renewal of residencies and legal documents, since there was a lockdown. It made things practically more difficult, but perhaps legally better. Also, there have been major incidents of social tensions, but the level of hostility has not necessarily increased. Mostly, people are focused on the governance deficits in Lebanon, rather than the Syrian presence right now.[69]

Figure 8.2 demonstrates a systemic visualization of the drivers of Lebanon's response and their change over time (including the influence of national and political group considerations). On the left of the diagram are the initial policy response drivers in the international, domestic, and displacement arenas. The arrows signify the direction of interactions among the various factors. On the right of the diagram are the drivers behind the policy change over time.

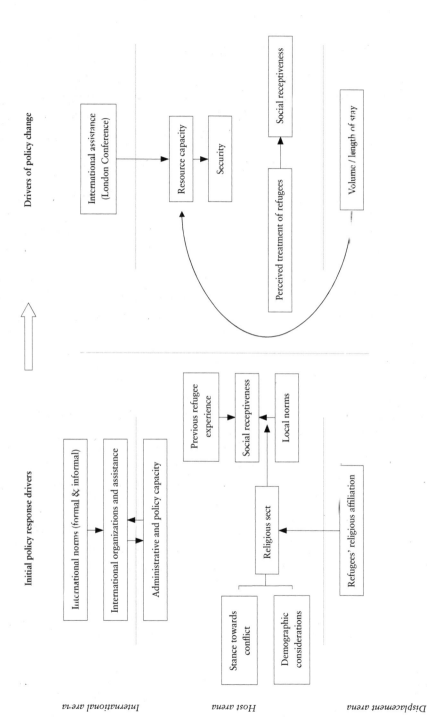

Figure 8.2 | Systemic visualization of Lebanon's key response drivers (2011–22)

CONCLUSION

The displacement of hundreds of thousands of Syrians to Lebanon has posed significant economic, social, and political challenges to the country. This chapter has examined how and why the successive governments of Lebanon have responded to Syrian displacement. Using process tracing over the period from 2011 to 2022 and relying on primary and secondary data, I have analyzed Lebanon's response to the crisis, and its evolution over time, in terms of its three main policy components: policy on entry and stay, livelihoods, and durable solutions. The findings indicate that Lebanon's response to the Syrian refugee influx evolved over the course of the crisis, passing through two main stages. During the initial stage (2011–14) the response was non-restrictive in nature. The government's "non-securitized" response was influenced by several factors, including political parties' divided stances towards the conflict in Syria.

The political gridlock, as well as perceptions among policy elites that this would be a temporary situation, translated into a decision "not to do anything" about the border movement. As the state's capacity to respond was weakened by political indecision, civil society was relied upon to fill the vacuum. Local norms of hospitality and kinship ties between the two societies, especially in the border towns, and the humanitarian nature of the crisis raised society's receptiveness to the refugee movement, which continued unrestrained. The pre-existing no-visa regime for Syrians, and the seasonal labour movement, which traditionally existed, facilitated the entry of thousands of Syrians into Lebanon, creating a new reality on the ground. While international norms of refugee protection are cited by government respondents as a factor behind their adherence to non-refoulement, it is evident in the evolution of their response that this factor does not take precedence over other concerns.

Further, while the state "allowed" the admission of displaced Syrians into its territory, its stance on their conditions of stay, livelihoods, and durable solutions was less "relaxed." Influenced by the legacy of Palestinian refuge in Lebanon, as well as fears that labour competition and demographic and political imbalance would occur as a result of the Sunni-dominated refugee movement, the government adopted measures aimed largely at maintaining "temporariness" of the situation. This was evident in its decision not to allow camps to be created, its prohibition of Syrian refugee employment, and its refusal to ever consider local integration a durable solution for Syrians.

However, as the size of the influx continued to increase and the displacement became more protracted, social receptiveness towards the refugee population decreased. Overstretched public services, economic losses, and security spillovers compelled the government to rethink its approach. Lebanon's response in 2015–22 took on more restrictive undertones, with the government adopting measures to stem the flow of the influx and restrict Syrian refugees' ability to maintain legal residency in Lebanon. Lebanon's shifting policy towards Syrian refugees and its attempt to play a more proactive role in managing the crisis were the result of a coupling of several factors, including the formation of a new unity government whose mandate was to tackle the refugee crisis based on security and economic imperatives. While further external and internal pressures took place, including the global pandemic, political instability, and protests, as well as economic and financial collapse, the main components of Lebanon's governance of Syrian displacement remained largely the same. Calls for return, which may have accelerated, were halted by COVID-19 and the advocacy efforts of UNHCR and other actors. With this chapter, discussion of the Lebanese case comes to an end, paving the way for comparative analysis of the two cases in the coming chapter.

9

One Displacement, Two Responses: Comparative Analysis and Discussion

INTRODUCTION

As a result of the Syrian civil war, both the Kingdom of Jordan and the Republic of Lebanon have been simultaneously subject to a mass influx of displaced Syrians seeking refuge in their territories. As this refugee crisis unfolded and intensified over time, host policy responses evolved and took shape. In the previous four chapters each country's policy response was discussed in depth based on analysis of primary and secondary data over the period of eleven years. This chapter aims to build on the earlier discussion by comparing and contrasting the host responses in light of the analytical framework proposed by this book.

This chapter zooms out and compares the policy responses of Lebanon and Jordan across spatial geographies and over time from a holistic and dynamic perspective. It looks at the elements of convergence and divergence in both countries' policy approaches to Syrian refugees. In doing so, it answers the book's third and final research question: What explains the variations in policy outputs between Lebanon and Jordan, despite the similarities in the displacement features and their contexts? Finally, this chapter demonstrates how the book's analytical framework and adoption of a complex systems lens was useful in analyzing and understanding variation between the two host countries in responding to the same refugee movement at the same time, and how such variations evolved over time. The chapter ends with a brief discussion of the book's scope and case limitations.

One Displacement, Two Responses

CONVERGENCE AND DIVERGENCE IN JORDAN'S AND LEBANON'S POLICY RESPONSES TO SYRIAN DISPLACEMENT

As Jordan and Lebanon were simultaneously faced with the mass influx of refugees from Syria, their responses to the influx exhibited elements of convergence and divergence. This section compares their responses in terms of four main aspects: the policy elements adopted by each host, their formulation and implementation processes, the response focus, and the overall degree of restrictiveness exhibited in responding to the influx. Each of these aspects is analyzed over the course of the period under examination (2011–22) to note similarities and differences in host governments' initial responses and their evolutionary developments. The analysis is enabled by the analytical framework presented in chapter 2. This approach, based on complex systems thinking, allows for a more holistic understanding of refugee policy-making, enabling researchers to move beyond direct causality analysis and to explore processes and systematic factors driving responses, as well as their effects on policy outcomes over time.

As it will be argued, responses in Jordan and Lebanon converged in terms of their overall degree of restrictiveness towards the Syrian refugee movement. This is explained by the shape of the hosts' system arrangements in the international, domestic, and displacement arenas. Jordan's and Lebanon's policy responses can be understood by "zooming out" and looking at the macro-shape of each system and how its component arenas evolved and interacted with one another over time. Table 9.1 presents a useful comparative tabulation of responses adopted by both hosts, broken down into convergent and divergent elements. It is followed by key comparative observations.

Policies on Entry and Stay, Livelihoods, and Durable Solutions

In terms of policy elements adopted by the respective hosts, Jordan and Lebanon converged on their policies of entry and durable solutions, while they diverged on their policies of stay and livelihoods.

The previous chapters demonstrated how Jordanian and Lebanese authorities converged on adopting an open-border policy towards the Syrian refugee movement and on adhering to the principle of non-refoulement during their early response stage. Further, their admission

178   The Politics of Refugee Policy in the Global South

Table 9.1 | Comparative tabulation of Lebanon's and Jordan's policy responses to Syrian displacement (2011–22)

		Jordan	Lebanon
Main elements of convergence	Policy on entry	Open border and non-refoulement adherence, followed by border closure and systematic refoulement	
	Policy on durable solutions	Only resettlement and voluntary repatriation allowed, but no local integration	
	Response focus	Shift from refugee focus to host focus	
	Degree of restrictiveness	Move from a non-restrictive response to a semi-restrictive one	
Main elements of divergence	Policy on stay	* De facto protection for a temporary period of six months, subject to renewal by national authorities * No policy change	* De facto protection for a temporary period of six months, subject to renewal by national authorities * Policy change: residency restrictions and UNHCR registration suspension
	Policy on livelihoods	* Encampment * Service provision; employment ban; collaborative mode of governance; civilian structure. * Policy change: restricted employment; scaling back of services	
	Policy formulation and implementation process	* Coherent decision-making and implementation	* Fragmented decision-making and implementation

One Displacement, Two Responses

policies both shifted following direct security spillovers from the Syrian conflict. The policy change put an end to the open-border movement, and Syrian refugees became subject to refoulement at official border-entry points. Both countries also cancelled pre-existing visa-waiver policies for Syrians and stepped up border security to limit informal border entries. While Jordanian and Lebanese authorities justified this move by claiming that it did not apply to humanitarian cases, no clear criteria existed for decisions on who qualified for this target group, which left room for discretionary decisions. In Jordan, following the 2016 border attack, the main border crossing with Syria was closed until October 2018, leaving thousands stranded in the desert area of Ruqban (De Bel Air 2016; Morris 2019). Following this, entry into Jordan became conditioned upon a security clearance granted by Jordanian authorities (Al-Khalidi and Barrington 2018). In Lebanon six visa categories were created for Syrians in early 2015, and, albeit inconsistently, a few exceptions were made for humanitarian cases (Shawaf and El Asmar 2017). Similar to other countries, both Jordan and Lebanon closed their land borders in early 2020 in order to contain the spread of COVID-19 (UNHCR 2020a).

Additionally, both countries consistently converged on their refusal of local integration as a durable solution to ever be considered for Syrian refugees, preferring refugees to be repatriated to Syria. However, assisted returns, approved by UNHCR, were not conducted during the period of examination in either country's case. While Lebanese political groups converged on the inevitability of the return of Syrian refugees, they disagreed on the timing and the logistics (Atallah and Mahdi 2017). Although UNHCR has not yet promoted voluntary returns from either Lebanon or Jordan, the Lebanese government has been organizing returns in collaboration with the Syrian government since April 2018 (UNHCR 2018b). Following an initial period of disagreement in regard to the timing and logistics of returns among political groups in Lebanon, the GSO started to facilitate group movements under the supervision of UNHCR and in collaboration with Syrian authorities (Atallah and Mahdi 2017; UNHCR 2020f).[1] So far, in Jordan, government officials publicly acknowledge that there are no conditions for a safe and dignified return (UNHCR 2020d).

However, despite Lebanon and Jordan granting Syrian refugees, upon recognition, de facto protection for a temporary period of six months, subject to renewal by national authorities, the Lebanese government started to impose residency restrictions in 2015 and requested that Syrian refugees pay residency-renewal fees, hold valid travel documents, and sign housing pledges. It also requested UNHCR to stop registering new Syrian refugees and to de-register those who approached it after 2015.

With regard to the policy on livelihoods, the major difference between the two countries under examination lies in the type of settlement allowed for Syrian refugees. In the Jordanian case, although there was initial trepidation at the idea of creating more refugee camps, which would be reminiscent of Palestinian refugee history, the government opted for their creation in cooperation with UNHCR. Over time, five refugee camps were created to house the Syrian refugees and the Palestinian refugees from Syria, with refugees being given the choice to self-settle outside of designated camp areas. However, in Lebanon's case, the construction of refugee camps to house incoming Syrian refugees was prohibited by the successive governments despite the informal settlements created by refugees, the large volume of the influx, the mounting pressures on host communities, and UNHCR advocacy.

With regard to freedom of movement, which was allowed during the early years of the crisis in both countries, the movement of camp inhabitants in Jordan became increasingly curtailed following the border security attack, as the government considered camps a security hot spot. Jordanian authorities started to impose restrictions on camp inhabitants, who were no longer able to exit designated camp areas without sponsorship. Since then the government has instructed UNHCR to stop issuing asylum-seeker certificates to those who left camps without government authorization (Achilli, Yassin, and Erdogan 2017). Freedom of movement also became curtailed in Lebanon, mostly by local authorities and non-state actors. According to Mourad (2017), imposing curfews on Syrian refugees, while informal, was a common form of community policing at the local level. As of January 2020, approximately 330 municipalities had imposed curfews on Syrian refugees (HRW 2020).

As for labour-market access, both countries started with a complete ban on Syrian refugee employment, which was eased for a few sectors following the London conference, during which the Jordan and Lebanon compacts were signed. Nevertheless, the process of securing work permits is still arduous, and most Syrian refugees do not have access to the formal labour market in either country (Gordon 2019;

Verme et al. 2015). Both countries also allowed Syrian refugees access to non-relief services, including education and health care. However, as the crisis became protracted, both countries started to scale back service provision to Syrian refugees. Since 2014, non-camp inhabitants in Jordan have had to pay the same health-care fees as uninsured citizens pay (UNHCR 2019d). In Lebanon, while refugees registered with UNHCR have had access to subsidized fees at selected primary health-care centres, those unregistered had to pay the same fees as Lebanese citizens paid (UNHCR 2019c).

Finally, with regard to mode of implementation, both countries relied on a mostly civilian structure to manage Syrian refugee affairs, with the exception of border control. Both countries also adopted collaborative approaches to the management of the influx through partnering with a wide array of UN agencies, iNGOs, and local NGOs. The JRPSC outlines that it "maintains collaborative and transparent principles to develop the interventions under the plan, by working hand in hand with more than 150 national and international partners" (MOPIC 2022), while the LCRP is introduced by the GoL as a "joint plan between the Government of Lebanon and its international and national partners" (LCRP 2022; MOPIC 2022).

Policy Formulation and Implementation Processes

Jordan's and Lebanon's responses diverged significantly in terms of policy formulation and coherence in the way policies were implemented (implementation coherence).

Both countries' policy formulation and implementation processes were highly influenced by their different political systems and refugee-policy subsystem structures. A policy subsystem, according to Howlett and Ramesh (2003), is the interplay between actors, institutions, and ideas found in a specific policy sector, which affects the dynamics and policy outcomes in that sector. The structure and functioning of the Lebanese and Jordanian states reflected significantly on their response coherence. Jordan's management of the Syrian influx was more centralized, hands on, and effective, compared to Lebanon's, owing to the existence of one dominant policy actor with monopoly over decision-making and implementation. The Royal Court serves as adviser to the king, who has an upper hand on issues of political matters, including refugee affairs. The government institutions execute rather than formulate major policy decisions.

182   The Politics of Refugee Policy in the Global South

Otherwise, the number of actors in the refugee-policy subsystem is limited. Jordan's stable working relationship with international organizations and the international donor community is also facilitated by the presence of one dominant actor with which to negotiate. A UNHCR official noted: "The political scene in Jordan is politically stable. The degree to which parliamentary changes impact UNHCR's operations is limited. It would have more impact perhaps if it were high-level army or intelligence changes. The Jordanian government is fairly responsive and open to discussion. They may stand their ground at first, but they become incrementally responsive to us."[2]

Meanwhile, the confessional political system in Lebanon led to the evolution of a fragmented refugee-policy subsystem with many policy actors who had divergent demographic considerations and stances towards the Syrian conflict. This resulted in decision-making paralysis during the early crisis stage and delayed policy formulation as the crisis progressed. Further, implementation of policies was undermined by the weak capacity of the state to implement policies at the local level: local communities and non-state actors have the capacity to obstruct and carry out discretionary policies in districts where they have substantial political power and demographic presence. For instance, while freedom of movement was the government's policy of choice, it was curtailed by discretionary behaviours at the local level, as discussed earlier. Given each political group's competition over power, and Hezbollah's presence as a powerful actor, there is no incentive to strengthen the state institutions. The state fragmentation and fragility also reflect on Lebanon's relationship with international organizations and donors. An NRC officer mentioned: "We do not have leverage to criticize the government, so we flag issues with donors and other actors, who can influence the government. It depends on which part of the government you want to influence; there are so many divided interests and stances. It is a difficult policy environment. We advocated for different issues regarding Syrian refugees, including employment, registration of new births, and other protection concerns."[3]

Changes in Focus

Both responses evolved from focusing on refugee assistance to focusing on raising host resilience. The initial focus in both countries was handling the influx from a humanitarian-emergency standpoint, but as the crisis became more protracted, their responses became geared towards adopting a developmental approach to managing the influx. The LCRP and the JRPSC were created, and the Jordan and Lebanon compacts were signed, signalling a more consolidated attempt on the part of the respective governments to manage and regulate the refugee influx and its aftermath on the host community. This move was the result of reduced resource capacity and mounting social tensions arising from the movement's prolonged stay.

Degree of Response Restrictiveness

While Jordan and Lebanon varied on their mix of policy choices towards the Syrian influx, the overall degree of restrictiveness of their policy responses was similar.

Degree of response restrictiveness, as discussed in chapter 2, is the degree by which a host government adheres to normative prescriptions of refugee protection as measured by the policy components of its response. Despite differences between the two hosts, both started with a largely non-restrictive policy towards the refugee movement, which increased in restrictiveness as the crisis became protracted. However, despite their responses taking on more restrictive features, such as border closures, both responses remained semi-restrictive to the Syrian refugee population. Neither hosts responded completely restrictively to the Syrian refugee population, despite the security spillovers and resource constraints that arose from the protracted refugee presence.[4] This indicates that features of the displacement, as well as the common arrangements in hosts' domestic and international arenas, including norms of refugee protection, were highly relevant in influencing the hosts' degree of restrictiveness towards the refugee population, despite the different mix of policy elements adopted by the hosts. Jordan's and Lebanon's varying political regime types and other contextual differences influenced features of their responses, specifically with regards to encampment, but they did not influence the overall degree of response restrictiveness (table 9.2). According to Dowding (2015), a foundational premise of systems theory is that open systems, such as social and biological systems, can exhibit "equifinality," where the same outcomes may be reached through different means or pathways. The concept of equifinality may explain why Lebanon's and Jordan's responses converged in such a way, despite their varying inputs, processes, and policy elements adopted.

184   The Politics of Refugee Policy in the Global South

Table 9.2 | Differences and similarities in Lebanon's and Jordan's system inputs, process, and outputs

	Input variables	Process	Output variables
Similar	* International legal framework * Local norms, social receptiveness, security considerations, resource capacity, and demographic constraints * Displacement features	None	* Degree of restrictiveness * Policies on entry and exit / durable solutions
Different	* Political-regime type and policy-subsystem structure * Relationship with international donor community * Geopolitical position * Stance towards the conflict * Palestinian refuge experience	Policy formulation and implementation coherence	* Policies on stay and livelihoods (encampment)

Note: Table 9.2 organizes input variables, process, and output variables according to their similarities or differences across the two cases. However, it does not imply a linear connection in this table from inputs to outputs.

Further, such convergence in host responses occurred because the system arenas of both hosts were in harmony during the initial crisis stage and started to diverge as the crisis became prolonged (figure 9.1). During the initial stage of the crisis, factors in the international and host arenas (including international and local norms) overlapped with favourable features of the displacement (including ethnic and religious ties) and the socio-economic character of the movement, which made it exceptionally vulnerable and in need of assistance. Such overlapping resulted in a non-restrictive response towards the refugee movement in the form of maintaining an open-border policy, adhering to the principle of non-refoulement, and providing non-relief services, such as public education and subsidized health care.

As the crisis became protracted, however, the three arenas moved further apart. Security considerations took centre stage, as both hosts were subject to violent spillovers from the conflict, which effectively put an end to the open-border movement and reflected on stricter camp regulations in Jordan. Further, the hosts' reduced resource capacity and the low degree of international burden sharing reflected on the scaling back of service provision and the attempt of Lebanese authorities to make it exceptionally difficult for Syrian refugees to stay in the country. As the influx volume became unsustainable for either host, domestic stability, in the form of the economy, society, security, and politics, took overriding importance, and features of the displacement became less paramount as social receptiveness was eroded. Such dynamics also reflected on the shifting of response focus from refugee assistance to host resilience.

The concept of emergence in systems theory posits that the whole has properties that come about or emerge due to interactions among its parts. Therefore, the whole is larger than the sum of the parts and cannot be understood by examining the parts in isolation from each other (Sawyer 2005). In this case, Jordan's and Lebanon's policy responses can be understood by zooming out and looking at the macro-shape of each system and how its component arenas evolved and interacted with one another over time. In sum, during the initial stage, the following key factors helped in creating a conducive environment to allow a non-restrictive response to the Syrian refugee movement: international norms of refugee protection and international assistance provided by UN agencies and the international donor community; and local norms, which overlapped with features of the displacement (including the common Arab and Muslim identity, the humanitarian nature of the crisis, and its highly visible political nature).

As the crisis evolved, other factors became predominant in influencing the relatively increased restrictiveness of host responses towards the Syrian refugee population. Security considerations took centre stage, as both hosts were subject to violent spillovers from the conflict, which reflected on stricter admission regulations. Further, both countries' reduced resource capacity reflected on the scaling back of service provision, and on residency restrictions in

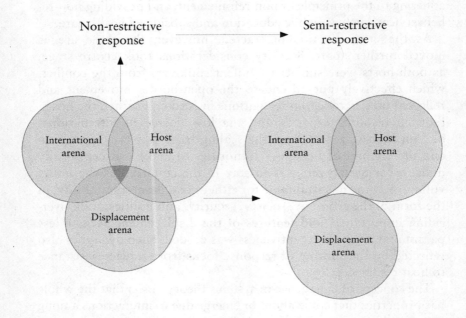

Figure 9.1 | Evolution of Lebanon's and Jordan's input arena interactions and responses (2011–22)

Lebanon. The increased volume and protracted stay, which reduced social receptiveness, reflected on the shifting of focus from refugee assistance to host resilience. Additionally, international assistance, while coming short of funding pledges and appeals, facilitated the signing of the Jordan and Lebanon compacts to ease employment restrictions on Syrian refugees and contain the refugee influx within the region.

CASE SYNOPSIS, SIGNIFICANCE, AND LIMITATIONS

The cases of Syrian displacement in Jordan and Lebanon, explored in depth in chapters 4–8, validate this book's analytical approach and also add to the literature a detailed empirical examination of these countries' responses to one of the twenty-first century's largest refugee movements. Lebanon and Jordan were specifically chosen for this study due to their comparable nature from a research perspective. They are both border-sharing countries to Syria and have been countries of first entry to Syrian refugees. They rank second and fourth respectively in hosting the largest proportion of refugees to the population, including non-Syrians. Further, they have both witnessed the same refugee influx (exogenous shock) at the same time and share the same regional context of the "Arab Spring." Lebanon and Jordan also served as key cases to examine because they both are developing countries that are non-signatory to the Geneva Convention. They also have varying arrangements including their political-regime types, geopolitical positions in the MENA region, relationship with the international donor community, involvement in and stance on the Syrian conflict, and relations with the Syrian regime.

The findings of this book indicate that, as Lebanon and Jordan were faced with the mass influx of Syrian refugees, their responses evolved over the course of the crisis (2011–22) from being non-restrictive to semi-restrictive in nature, as evidenced by their mix of policy choices. Although their varying contextual features, including their political-regime types and their refugee-policy subsystem structures, influenced their policy formulation and implementation processes and policy choices differently, their responses converged in terms of their overall degree of restrictiveness towards the Syrian refugee movement.

In terms of policy elements adopted by the respective hosts, Jordan and Lebanon converged on their policies of entry and durable solutions, while they diverged on their policies of stay and livelihoods particularly with regards to encampment. In terms of focus, both responses evolved from focusing on refugee assistance to focusing on raising host resilience. The findings also indicate that Lebanon's fragmented policy subsystem reduced its policy and administrative capacity to respond coherently and effectively to the refugee crisis (Nassar and Stel 2019), whereas Jordan's homogenous policy subsystem raised its ability to formulate and implement a more coherent and effective response. The systems analysis revealed that the equifinality of outcomes witnessed was due to the shape of both hosts' system arenas and their evolutions over the course of the crisis. During the initial response stage the conditions were favourable for both hosts to respond non-restrictively towards the Syrian refugee movement as interacting arenas overlapped. However, as the arenas became in tension, both hosts recalibrated their responses to ensure that domestic stability was not undermined.

Thus, the examination of Syrian displacement in Lebanon and Jordan has helped in demonstrating the use of the framework presented in chapter 2. Applying the framework to these cases was useful in analyzing and understanding Lebanon's and Jordan's responses to Syrian displacement individually and comparatively. It has allowed us to zoom in and out and to trace the evolutions in the system arenas of both countries over time. Thus, the cases helped in demonstrating how the framework is useful, not only in describing variation observed between both cases but also in exploring the causes of such variation. As such, this book's framework and the use of a complexity lens have proven useful in lending nuance to the analysis of refugee policy-making across space and time. The framework's policy inputs and outputs, which were derived from the norm and practice of refugee protection in the context of mass displacement, are specifically useful to replication in other Global South contexts. In the coming chapter I will further demonstrate how the hypothetical propositions derived from the framework were validated in the cases of Lebanon and Jordan, including the propositions that were confirmed and those that were refuted, and what this means for the study of refugee policy-making in the South.

Scope and Limitations

As with every research, this book and the cases presented in it have limitations that are important to note. The cases represent cases of border-sharing, first-asylum countries that have witnessed a conflict-induced mass influx situation, which incapacitated their ability to conduct individual status-determination procedures. Thus, it is not within the scope of this book to generalize its analytical approach to cases of responses by non-border-sharing countries or to reasons for mass flight other than violent conflict. Such cases may have differing dynamics and should be explored further, but with adaptation of the framework drivers to their specific conditions.

Furthermore, no Syrian refugee-camp visits or interviews with Syrian refugees were conducted for the purpose of this book. While these visits and interviews may have provided more insight into the cases, they were excluded from the research design owing to inaccessibility and permit constraints. Instead, interviews with NGO

One Displacement, Two Responses 189

personnel were considered a vital substitute to gathering many of the important details related to the implemented policies, based on their close experiences and daily encounters with Syrian refugees. This book has also excluded non-Syrian refugees from the analysis, including Palestinian refugees from Syria. Although they are a sub-component of the same refugee movement, they fall under a different institutional and legal framework. Therefore, this study has mainly used Palestinian refugees from Syria as a counterfactual during data collection and analysis, but it did not try to address them in answering the research questions.

While the book attempts to examine the influence of policy actors beyond the government on the policy-making process, its scope does not include conducting actor-centred analysis; that is, it does not attempt to present a comprehensive mapping of the relevant policy actors and their specific policy positions but builds on their insights to inform its analysis and findings. Further, during qualitative interviews, respondents often provided anecdotal and/or conflicting responses. This was especially problematic in the Lebanese context, where government officials have other political and sectarian affiliations that influence their world views. To overcome such bias, I corroborated their insights by referring to secondary sources. Interviews conducted with experts and non-governmental actors were also used as a mechanism to provide a more accurate and balanced picture. However, the subjective nature of responses was also taken into consideration because they revealed significant intricacies of each policy-making process and context, as well as political groups' own stances.

Since, at the time of writing, this refugee displacement was still ongoing, analysis of the case is limited to the period 2011–22. Developments that happened after this period are excluded from the book. Finally, this study aims for analytic expansion of theory (i.e., analytic generalization) rather than statistical generalization (Yin 2009). Considering that case studies engage with a smaller number of units of analysis, their findings are not generalizable in a conventional sense, but their theoretical propositions may be transposed beyond the original sites of study (Hodkinson and Hodkinson 2001; Yin 2009). Therefore, this book can be used as an analytical and methodological research manual by scholars and researchers aiming to explore and analyze refugee-policy processes in other similar contexts of the Global South.

CONCLUSION

This chapter has discussed the responses of Lebanon and Jordan to Syrian displacement in comparative perspective by applying the analytical framework presented in chapter 2. It compared and contrasted their responses in terms of four main aspects: the policy choices adopted by the successive governments; the response's overall degree of restrictiveness towards the refugee movement; the response focus; and the formulation and implementation processes. Each of these aspects was analyzed over the course of the period under examination (2011–22). Following, this chapter has shed light on why Jordan and Lebanon responded to the Syrian refugee population with the same degree of restrictiveness despite their contextual differences.

While their varying contextual features, including their political-regime types and their refugee-policy subsystem structures, influenced their policy formulation and implementation processes and policy choices differently, their responses converged in terms of their overall degree of restrictiveness towards the Syrian refugee movement. The systems thinking approach demonstrated that the equifinality of outcomes witnessed between the two hosts could be attributed to the evolution in the shape of their system arrangements over time. During the initial stage the conditions were conducive to non-restrictive responses towards the Syrian refugee movement. However, over time, as the hosts' system arenas became in tension, both hosts recalibrated their response strategies, with domestic stability as their primary goal.

Finally, the outcomes of this comparison serve to validate the analytical framework proposed in chapter 2 and show us that a complex systems thinking approach was successful in explaining variation between Jordan and Lebanon. From the analysis presented, in the coming chapter I will discuss how far the cases have confirmed or refuted the propositions presented in chapter 2, and I will derive theoretical and conceptual implications for the broader field of forced migration and refugee studies, and particularly for the study of refugee policy.

10

Similar but Different: Understanding Refugee-Policy Variation in the Global South

INTRODUCTION

This book has examined the policy responses of the Hashemite Kingdom of Jordan and the Republic of Lebanon to one of the twenty-first century's largest refugee movements to date, the Syrian refugee crisis. Its goal was not only to understand how these countries have responded to the crisis per se but also to advance the way in which we understand how states in the Global South respond to the arrival of refugees. The proposed analytical framework for understanding refugee responses in the South was applied and tested in the cases of Jordan and Lebanon.

When responding to mass refugee influxes, Global South countries tend to be loci for the unique dynamics created through dependency on humanitarian assistance, reduced state capacity, limited adherence to international protection standards, *inter alia*. As presented in the cases of Jordan and Lebanon, refugee policies are also the result of not a single overriding factor but a constellation of factors that interact with each other and are in constant change. Hence, it is important for scholars to realize the complexity at play while analyzing national policy responses to refugee movements and to avoid presenting overly simplistic and static notions of asylum.

Even though the existing literature has advanced our understanding of factors influencing public policies during the arrival of refugees en masse, it is not yet adequate for explaining variation between countries and over time. Moreover, while the field of forced migration studies is said to be closely informed by policy practices, it has rarely drawn upon the tools of public policy to inform its analysis.

Notably, the use of frameworks and analytical tools provided by the field of public policy can contribute to a more nuanced understanding of refugee policy-making. Therefore, this book argues that complex systems thinking is a conceptual tool that enables a more holistic and nuanced understanding of refugee policy-making in the context of mass refugee movements in the Global South. By doing so, it not only provides a point of reference for scholars researching refugee policy-making in the South but also bridges the fields of refugee studies and public policy, which have been long disconnected. This book has also contributed to the literature by advancing on previous scholarship, including Jacobsen's seminal work (1996) that allows for the breakdown of state policy responses into elements, and the analysis of state responses according to their degree of adherence to normative standards of refugee protection. Through its use of a complexity lens, this approach can allow researchers to move beyond simple dichotomous or static assessments and to evaluate refugee responses in a more nuanced and dynamic manner. This is particularly important in countries that are not party to the 1951 Geneva Convention and thus do not operate strictly according to international refugee norms and standards. This subset of countries is unique and has, thus far, been under-examined by scholarship.

This final chapter of the book is divided into six sections. Following the introduction, the first section reflects on the broader theoretical implications for the study of refugee policy in the context of the Global South. The second section discusses what can be inferred from the cases of Lebanon and Jordan for the politics of refugee-policy variation. This discussion paves the way for the third section, a recap of the book's contributions, including its original typology of host-government behaviour in mass influx situations, and directions for future research. Finally, this chapter ends with a reflection on the broader lessons learned from the governance of Syrian displacement, for policy and practice (in the fourth section), and with an overall conclusion to the book (in the last section).

IMPLICATIONS FOR THE STUDY OF REFUGEE POLICY IN THE GLOBAL SOUTH

In this section I examine the implications of the findings from the studies examined for our current understanding of refugee policy-making in the context of mass refugee movements in the Global

Understanding Refugee-Policy Variation

South. The analytical framework presented fills a gap in the scholarly literature and provides a tool kit that can be applied to other case studies of refugee-hosting states across the Global South. This framework encompasses the nuances of policy contexts in the South and allows researchers to explore a wider range of direct and indirect systemic factors, as well as their effects on policy outcomes over time. Moreover, this dynamic perspective is especially important in the analysis of a crisis situation because changes are expected to occur at a faster pace.

Scholars who have examined mass displacement have identified determinant factors that are said to drive countries' policy responses to mass influx situations (Gottwald 2014; Zolberg, Suhrke, and Aguayo 1986; Harper 2008). For the purpose of this study, such factors have been grouped broadly into three categories of arenas: international, host, and displacement. According to the theoretical and empirical literature discussed in chapter 2, the following set of propositions were formulated to guide the research. This section discusses each of them to confirm or refute the hypothesized propositions in light of the empirical findings of Lebanon's and Jordan's responses to the Syrian refugee influx. From these most recent and up-to-date empirical findings, I derive implications for the study of refugee policy in similar contexts of the Global South.

Influence of International Regime

The first proposition suggested that a host government's policy response to a mass refugee influx is influenced by the international regime via assistance, advocacy, and the setting of protection standards.

The findings from Jordan's and Lebanon's responses to the Syrian refugee crisis indicate that the international refugee regime played a role in raising both governments' reception standards and in reducing their restrictiveness. This was evidenced by the easing of employment restrictions after the London conference and by the provision of relief and non-relief assistance. The regional response plan (3RP) put in place by UNHCR acted as an overall framework for hosts' planning and coordination efforts (Petzoldt 2016). International organizations, including UNHCR, also raised Syrian refugees' protection standards through the propagation of refugee-protection norms. This included negotiating with Lebanese authorities to allow the registration of new births to Syrian refugee parents and the repeal of Syrian refugees' employment prohibition (Janmyr 2018). This finding confirms Loescher's (2014) argument that international and intergovernmental organizations, including UNHCR, supplement their lack of political power by using means such as advocacy to encourage governments in the Global South to adopt more favourable policies towards refugees. Therefore, we continue to see this influence.

Khalil (2011) argues that international conventions establish standards for the treatment and protection of refugees, even if countries are not party to them. In line with that argument, the findings from my study indicate that international norms acted as a constraint on Lebanon's and Jordan's responses to the Syrian refugee movement, despite neither country being party to the Geneva Convention. However, the influence of this factor was more predominant during the initial response stage. As resource capacity and security were undermined, Lebanon and Jordan responded more restrictively to the Syrian refugee population. This was especially the case because burden sharing, in the form of financial assistance and resettlement of refugees, fell short of the Convention's preamble (UNHCR 2021b).[1] In both cases, the failure to deliver on pledged assistance was cited to have influenced the government's restrictions on service provision. Ward's (2014) and Mogire's (2009) arguments are, therefore, confirmed. When inadequate international assistance is received, governments in the Global South become less willing to host refugees.

Moreover, Gordenker (2015) argues that developing countries' lack of capacity to manage large refugee flows provides the international refugee regime with an advantage because it is relied upon for help. This was found to be true in responses to Syrian displacement in Lebanon and Jordan as international organizations' influence was mediated by the low capacity of the two hosts that requested assistance from UNHCR to respond to the crisis. Therefore, both countries' low administrative capacity functioned as an intermediary mechanism for international organizations' leverage and advocacy. Atallah and Mahdi (2017) further argue that Hezbollah's tacit approval to delegate to the UN the coordination of Syrian refugees' return to Syria was due to the unwillingness of the Lebanese government to jeopardize the international community's financial, humanitarian, and logistical support, which it desperately needed.

Additionally, findings from this study have indicated that the extent of the international regime's influence was mediated by each host's relationship to the international donor community. Lebanon's fragmented and weak state apparatus reduced trust in the ability of the government or municipal authorities to utilize funds effectively and neutrally (Boustani et al. 2016). However, in the Jordanian case, the monarchy's stable and collaborative relationship with international actors allowed for a more effective partnership. This was evidenced, for instance, by the Jordan Compact, which was more elaborate than its Lebanese counterpart. Jordan's position as a strategic ally to the West, and as a neighbour to Israel, also meant that the United States and other donor governments had a strong interest in helping the monarchy avoid potential instability arising from the Syrian refugee presence (Satloff and Schenker 2013).

Therefore, the extent of the influence of the international refugee regime on Lebanon's and Jordan's responses towards the Syrian refugee influx was mediated by three issues: the extent of burden sharing provided to host governments; the capacity of the Jordanian and Lebanese governments to respond to the crisis alone; and their relationship to the international donor community. In this specific arena, imbalances in power dynamics between actors in the global refugee regime particularly come into play. Such imbalances play out clearly in European–Middle East relations, specifically in the area of migration policy. They are also reflected in the politicization of burden sharing, and the cooperation in migration management between EU and MENA countries through adoption and promotion of externalization policies that attempt to contain refugees outside of Europe (Afailal and Fernandez 2018). The compacts signed between Lebanon, Jordan, and European donors, discussed in the case chapters 5–8, could be construed as examples of such "bargaining" attempts. Their hidden goals of containing the "refugee problem" in the region of origin and their lack of coherent designs, given the realities on the ground in both countries, were key reasons for their ineffectiveness in achieving their announced objectives of improving Syrian refugee livelihoods in the host countries.

In the words of Canefe (2017, 19), who contextualizes European responses to Syrian forced migration, "when migration as a necessity is the entry point, ethical perspectives that conjure state sovereignty are not enough." However, a "global methodology of redistributive and restorative justice, and an adjuvant legal ethics pertaining to forced migration, is needed to care for the ordeals of those, who are not seen as a 'natural' part of the political community" (Canefe 2017, 20). While this perspective on the ethics of refugee governance sounds welcome, the reality is far removed from this ideal. This was never as pronounced as in responses to the 2022 Ukrainian refugee movement. Comparisons of responses between Ukrainian and Syrian displacement, especially with regards to European countries, have shed valuable insights on the debate on the efficacy of the international refugee regime and its ability to provide impartial protection to refugees – regardless of nationality, ethnicity, or other markers (Diab 2022). The positive response to the Ukrainian displacement to date on the part of European countries signals how the impetus of the international system remains politically vulnerable, which further highlights the arguments made in this book. There are clear binaries in the international response system that have been amplified by comparing responses to Syrian and Ukrainian displacement in the continent where the global refugee regime was first established. This movement also confirms that refugee movements are often politicized, and support for refugees may depend on the political visibility and value of the conflict to those countries that have the most power, resources, and capacity to provide assistance and responsibility sharing (Jackson Sow 2022; Mützelburg 2022).

Influence of Domestic Considerations

The second proposition suggested that a host government's policy response to a mass refugee influx is influenced by domestic considerations, including foreign policy and stance towards the conflict, previous refugee experience, social receptiveness, and economic, environmental, demographic, and security considerations.

According to Zolberg et al. (1986), refugee movements may have adverse effects on relations between host and sending countries. Therefore, asylum decisions are usually influenced by a state's stance towards the conflict. This has been especially evident in Lebanon's and Jordan's responses to the Syrian refugee population. As discussed previously, Hezbollah and the desire of the Mikati government to maintain invisibility of the crisis reflected on their refusal to acknowledge the refugee problem during the early stage so as not to incriminate the Syrian regime. According to Fakhoury (2017), the Lebanese government's aversion to camps was not a reflection of inclusion of Syrian refugees, but rather a desire to avoid the threat of refugee camps' turning into conflict enclaves for anti-Assad militants. Alternatively, Turner (2015) argues that the Jordanian authorities' decision to create camps for Syrian refugees was an attempt to raise the visibility of the crisis and to capitalize on the refugee presence through funding appeals. This was facilitated by Jordan's relative detachment from the internal conflict in Syria. While the security of the kingdom's northern border and the threat of radical groups spilling over into Jordan were important policy concerns (Mahmoud 2014), the Jordanian regime saw the crisis as an opportunity, as it consistently tried to disassociate itself from the conflict.

Further, both countries' previous refugee experiences influenced their responses to the Syrian refugee movement. One of the main contextual differences between Jordan and Lebanon is their experiences with Palestinian refugee hosting. This factor specifically influenced their different policy choices with regard to the type of settlement allowed to Syrian refugees. Both countries have been hosting considerable Palestinian refugee populations since 1948. This refuge experience, as discussed earlier, has had a deep impact on both countries' socio-economic and political fabric. Militant activism among the Palestinian refugee population posed security challenges, as the Palestine Liberation Organization used these host countries as bases for its fight against Israel. The refugee camps constructed over the years had become frequent sites of violent conflict. However, this militant activism was eliminated in Jordan in the events of Black September in 1971 (Milton-Edwards and Hinchcliffe 2009). In Lebanon the camps are still sites of recurrent violence, and Palestinians are still being blamed for involvement in Lebanon's fifteen-year-long civil war. Furthermore, Turner (2015) argues that the Jordanian regime's centralized and strong surveillance ability has made it less fearful about Syrian refugee camps, despite its history of militarized Palestinian presence.

With regard to social receptiveness, Jacobsen (1996) argues that the way in which a community receives refugees is influenced by the cultural meaning it ascribes to them. In the Jordanian and Lebanese cases, the role of local norms as a constraining device on policy actors was significant. For instance, despite its supportive stance of the Assad regime, Hezbollah was careful to maintain its popular image as a resistance movement. This was done by differentiating between the humanitarian and political aspects of the Syrian refugee presence in Lebanon (ICG 2017; Fakhoury 2017; *The Daily Star* 2012). Tribal support is also an important source of political legitimacy for the Hashemite regime (Francis 2015). Therefore, upholding Islamic and Arab traditions of extending aid to refugees, who were also considered "brothers" in this case, acted as a constraining device on the behaviour of both regimes towards the Syrian refugee movement. "We should deal with the Syrian refugees with purely humanitarian responsibility, without politicization of the issue. Attention must be paid to the displaced families, whatever their political background" (Hassan Nasrallah, quoted in Muzaffar 2013).

Further, Jordan's and Lebanon's shifts in border policies confirm previous arguments presented by Lischer (2008) and Salehyan (2008). They have pointed to the role that a conflict spillover has on states' rising securitization and adoption of restrictive policies towards refugees. Additionally, economic, environmental, and social considerations were all significant factors in influencing Lebanon's and Jordan's responses. The lower degree of resource capacity, which was exacerbated by the protracted situation and the overwhelming and unexpected volume of the influx, created a conducive environment to adopt a more restrictive approach towards the Syrian refugee population. This finding confirms Crisp's (2000) argument that deteriorating environmental and economic conditions caused by large refugee populations, and the failure of the international community to address the problem, led to reduced willingness, over time, of African countries to host refugees. This was especially the case because social receptiveness towards the Syrian refugee movement became eroded over time. Ensuring that domestic stability was not undermined was a high priority in Lebanon's and Jordan's responses to Syrian displacement.

Moreover, demographic considerations have also played a significant role in influencing host responses to the Syrian refugee population, especially in the Lebanese case. Although demographic considerations exist in Jordan, in Lebanon they intersect heavily with the confessional system of governance, where religious communities have historically relied on their demographic balance to vie for political power. The predominant Sunni character of the Syrian refugee movement threatened to tip the demographic balance in Lebanon, deepening tensions between Sunnis, Shiites, and Christian Maronites (Meier 2014; Rainey 2014). Therefore, Syrian refugee policies in Lebanon have been highly influenced by the sectarian cleavages adopted by political actors and embodied by society. Demographic considerations have especially influenced both countries' policies on stay and durable solutions of Syrian refugees. The imposition of residency restrictions on Syrians refugees in Lebanon, for instance, and the refusal of both hosts to allow any opportunity for their local integration, are measures adopted to maintain temporariness of their presence (Davidson 2015).

Influence of Displacement Features

The third proposition suggested that a host government's policy response to a mass refugee influx is influenced by features of the displacement, including the volume, nationality, ethnicity, length of stay, and character of the refugee movement.

Findings indicate that several features of Syrian displacement have influenced Jordan's and Lebanon's policy responses. These include its ethnic and religious affiliations, socio-economic composition, volume, and length of stay. According to scholars (Walzer 2008; Abuya 2007; Harper 2008), an increased influx volume and a protracted presence (Jesse 1998) have a negative influence on host reception standards. This was found to be true in the cases under examination, where host policy responses increased in restrictiveness as the number of Syrian refugees residing in both countries reached significantly high levels in proportion to the population, and the conflict had become protracted.

Furthermore, the ethnic and religious affiliations of the Syrian refugee movement reflected positively on social receptiveness, as hypothesized by Fielden (2008). While social receptiveness in both cases mattered, for instance with regard to admission, the influence of nationality was specifically evident in the more restrictive policies adopted in Jordan and Lebanon towards Palestinian refugees from Syria who were part of the same refugee movement. This highlights that, while ethnic and religious affiliations matter, they may take less precedence depending on other factors, including demographics. With regard to the character of the refugee movement, as discussed earlier, the Syrian refugee influx had a distinct socio-economic profile, which influenced Jordan's response. Camps were considered the suitable policy option for housing Syrian refugees, because of their vulnerable socio-economic profile, as compared to their Iraqi predecessors (Turner 2015).

The empirical findings from the cases of Lebanon's and Jordan's policy responses to Syrian displacement over the course of eleven years have thus advanced our understanding of the dynamics of refugee policy-making in the context of mass displacement. This is specifically relevant for countries in the Global South, where mass movements are predominant and tend to become protracted. We now know more about how and why refugee-host states, particularly those in the Global South, respond to mass refugee movements. The three sets of propositions developed to guide the data collection and analysis conducted for this book can be replicated to examine other similar contexts. This applies whether it be analysis of Turkey's and Iraq's management of Syrian displacement, Kenyan and Ugandan responses to the Somali refugee movement, Colombia's approach to Venezuelan refugees, or other mass displacement situations. In the coming section I specifically reflect on what we learn from the cases examined here about the nature of refugee-policy variation.

THE POLITICS OF VARIATION IN REFUGEE POLICY ACROSS SPACE AND TIME

This book has examined Jordan's and Lebanon's policy responses initially and over time. It has revealed that while the same policy arena may take precedence over other international and displacement arenas, the factors within each arena may have varying significance in different country cases or across time. For example, the host arena may play a predominant role in influencing host behaviour, but because of different sub-arrangements within it, whether across countries or in the same country as the host arena, drivers change over time. We have seen how the host arenas in the cases of Lebanon and Jordan took precedence in influencing the policy output as the crisis became protracted, owing to varying factors across both countries and over time. This book has demonstrated that when the three interacting arenas were in initial harmony, Jordan's and Lebanon's policy responses were less restrictive; when the arenas were in tension, hosts' policy responses increased in restrictiveness. A given factor's significance may also change as the crisis evolves, indicating that it is not a static situation. Certain factors may take precedence over time, as is evident from the Jordanian and Lebanese responses. Therefore, in our understanding of refugee policy and governance we need to consider that certain factors may play a role in influencing host responses up to a certain point, after which other factors may take precedence.

The complex systems framework used in analyzing the cases of Lebanon and Jordan is useful in conceptualizing host behaviour. This is not just in terms of policy choices, but also in terms of the degree of adherence to normative standards of refugee protection. This feat allows for more accurate understanding of what it means for a host to be responding restrictively or otherwise to a certain refugee population. It allows for assessment of host responses in terms of a continuum, rather than binary choices. This is especially relevant because host governments may alter their mix of policy choices to balance the complex policy trade-offs and constraints on their behaviour, while still responding with the same degree of restrictiveness to the refugee population. As the empirical cases in this book have revealed, although Lebanon's and Jordan's mix of policy choices varied, they responded to the Syrian refugee movement with the same overall degree of restrictiveness.

Furthermore, the framework developed to examine the cases is useful in conceptualizing a host's refugee-policy-making system in terms of arenas, comprising policy inputs, process, and outputs. This exploration would help shed light on the influence that policy-making processes may have in producing variations in policy output and outcomes, even among countries that share similar contexts in the Global South. The processes in the Global South can be explored further by examining their countries' ability to produce coherently formulated policies that can be implemented effectively. Using relevant indicators and methods, such as policy-impact evaluation, scholars may help us further understand how policy-making in Southern contexts can influence policy-outcome variations.

The findings in this book also shed light on the diverse sources of norms as constraining devices on host behaviour. Although other scholars have discussed the influence of international norms of refugee protection on host policies (Khalil 2011), this study has highlighted the role of local norms in influencing policy variations across countries and over time. Specifically, the empirical evidence has revealed that while local norms have mostly acted as a constraining device against government action, they have done so as an interaction with the displacement features, not in isolation. As I zoomed out, I found that this constraining device also changed over time. Therefore, the extent of influence of local norms can produce variations among cases, even among those sharing similar contexts.

Finally, it is clear that governments witnessing mass influx situations pick and choose the elements that they can "mix" to cater to their needs in light of the constraints. The strategies used by the hosts examined in this book to navigate the complex policy terrain in light of the constraints on their behaviour included shifting of responsibility to UN agencies to reduce resource pressures; "accommodating" the existing refugee population on a temporary basis while preventing new flows; and maintaining visibility or invisibility of the refugee presence. The common fault line, however, which remained unaltered throughout, was the prohibition of local integration as a durable solution. Scholars examining refugee policy in the Global South should thus be comfortable with witnessing and expecting variation in host policy responses and, rather than attempting to homogenize refugee hosts, analytically examine their policy-making processes using a holistic and dynamic lens. Only through adopting complexity can we begin to understand host policies in mass displacement settings.

A Typology of Variation in Host Government Behaviour

Political scientists have long attempted to use typologies to classify political systems, states, and regimes into groups or types with common sets of attributes and to be able to compare between them (McCormick, Hague, and Harrop 2019). One of this book's original contributions is the following typology, which may be tested to guide analysis of host government behaviour, depending on two criteria: degree of constraints on host behaviour, and host involvement in the conflict (figure 10.1). In the cases examined in this book, on the one hand, Jordan's attempt to capitalize on the humanitarian crisis may be understood in the light of its high international and domestic constraints but marginally low involvement in the conflict. On the other hand, Lebanon's high stake in and interconnectedness to the conflict in Syria, and the high constraints on its behaviour, have reflected on its attempt to contain the crisis, from both political and humanitarian perspectives. It can therefore be expected, subject to empirical testing, that a host government with high involvement in a conflict, but with low constraints, would use a crisis as a

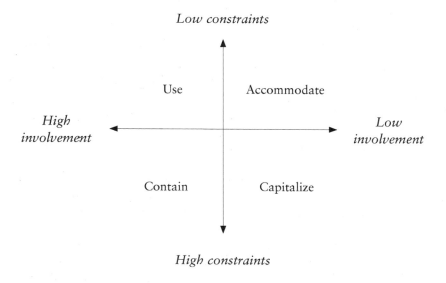

Figure 10.1 | Hypothesized typology of host behaviour

political tool (Greenhill 2011). This can be understood in Turkey's attempts to utilize the Syrian refugee population as a political tool (Okyay and Zaragoza-Cristiani 2016). However, a host government with low involvement and low constraints would merely be accommodating of the movement. Iraq's management of the Syrian movement provides demonstration of this specific merely accommodating dynamic (Yassen 2019; Bahram 2018).

This typology adds to the conversation on the migration-management approaches of states, as discussed by international relations and migration studies scholars. Such approaches have been analyzed in terms of being nationalizing, developmental, and/or neoliberal models of migration management (Adamson and Tsourapas 2020). Secen (2021) also proposes a classification of hosts in terms of securitization. This book proposes analyzing the hosts' forced-migration-management models according to the degree of constraints on a government's policy behaviour, and the involvement in the conflict of origin. The typology can help us analytically describe and characterize how governments may behave in cases of mass influx situations. Predicting behaviour would require further empirical testing but would help us advance both theoretically and practically.

CONTRIBUTIONS AND DIRECTIONS FOR FUTURE RESEARCH

The process of policy-making has been studied widely by scholars from various disciplines and using varying conceptual tools. Scholars who have analyzed policy-making from a rational perspective posit that policies are the outcome of rational and technical decision-making on the part of policy actors (Weimer and Vining 1998). This argument is echoed by proponents of the rational actor model, who argue that political actors and decision-makers are "rational" beings who design policies that achieve maximum social gain based on comprehensive information about the problem, its causes, and solutions (Dye 1992). However, this perspective falls short of examining the nuances and complexity involved during policy-making. Howlett and Ramesh (2003) argue that policy choices do not result from government will alone but interact with the many constraints imposed by actors, structures, and ideas.

The application of a complex systems lens to the analysis of refugee policy-making in Jordan and Lebanon confirmed the importance of analyzing policy responses to complex and intractable policy dilemmas from a holistic, dynamic, and non-reductionist perspective. Such a perspective has allowed for consideration of system components and their role in shaping outcomes. This is especially important for analysis of crisis situations. The empirical findings revealed how Lebanon's and Jordan's policy responses to the Syrian refugee crisis were not the result of intentional policy-design decisions but were emergent from the system dynamics. This book has, thus, advanced the current state of the refugee-policy literature; it utilizes complex systems theory and explains refugee-policy outcomes as resulting from a constellation of multifactorial and non-linear elements in interaction, rather than from rational calculated decisions (Checkland 1999; De Greene 2012; Stewart and Ayres 2001; El-Taliawi and Hartley 2021). It has also contributed to the refugee-policy formulation and implementation literature (O'Toole 2000; Hill and Hupe 2014; DeLeon 1992), by providing empirical evidence of two cases of refugee-policy formulation and implementation processes in response to mass displacement.

Furthermore, it has added the examination of two empirical cases of refugee policy-making in the Global South context. The current state of the refugee-policy literature is skewed towards examining refugee-policy-making processes in the Global North. Less attention is given in the literature to countries in the Global South, in which refugee-policy-making dynamics are expected to be different due to their different capacities and resource endowments (Colebatch and Radin 2006). This book has also advanced the empirical literature on crisis policy-making at large (Crotty 2003; Rosenthal and Hart 1991). According to Dror (2017), policy-making in crisis situations tends to differ from policy-making in non-crisis times. However, the former is currently under-researched especially in the context of developing countries of the South.

Additionally, the analysis in this book has shed light on the role of the refugee-policy subsystem in influencing policy-making in terms of process and outputs. Policy subsystems are composed of networks of policy participants in a particular policy sector and geographical area (Sabatier 1987). They have been previously discussed by Milward and Walmsley (1985), Baumgartner and Jones (1991), Jochim and May (2010), and others. According to Weible (2008), three types of subsystems exist based on the degree of cohesiveness of subsystem members: unitary, collaborative and adversarial. The empirical findings from this book have revealed how Jordan's and Lebanon's different refugee-policy-subsystem structures influenced their policy formulation and implementation processes. In the Jordanian case, the king and UNHCR are the dominant policy actors causing the subsystem to be unitary and homogeneous. In contrast, the policy subsystem in the Lebanese case is heterogeneous, fragmented, and adversarial. This reflected on each host's capacity to formulate and implement policies effectively, also referred to by Painter and Pierre (2004) as policy and administrative capacity.

Therefore, while study book has relied on macro-level analysis, the findings echo the need for meso-level analysis by zooming in on the policy subsystem. This is especially relevant in cases where the government is not the primary agent of policy-making and does not have the sole means of policy enforcement, such as in the Lebanese scenario. This analytical approach can capture the influence of interest groups in the policy subsystem, where non-state actors have considerable power and the government holds more of a symbolic position, resulting in a complex web of interactions making up the policy-making process. Future studies may examine the shape of policy-subsystem structure using social network analysis (Shivakoti 2017). The policy and administrative capacity required to formulate and implement policies coherently and effectively has emerged as a key factor of influence in the cases of Lebanon and Jordan, as mentioned earlier in this chapter. Therefore, this specific variable requires further exploration in other cases.

This work has also shed light on the role of policy legacies, norms, and the international regime on domestic policy-making (Hernes 2018). According to Thelen (1999), policy legacies are said to constrain new policies. Path dependence in policy-making has previously been examined by P. David (2005), Kato (2003), and Clemens and Cook (1999). This book has demonstrated how hosts' experiences with Palestinian refugee hosting reflected on decisions related to Syrian refugees, especially with regard to encampment and local integration. The policy legacy of the Palestinian refugees constrained the choices available to the host governments in responding to new refugee flows, confirming Thelen's argument (1999). Furthermore, the study has demonstrated the role of local norms and the international regime in shaping and constraining host policies, thereby contributing to similar studies including those of Semb (2001), Surel (2000), and Checkel (1997). In terms of methodology, this book has advanced the comparative-policy-analysis literature (Freeman 1985; Capano and Howlett 2009) and the use of process tracing in policy studies (Kay and Baker 2015).

Future research can build on this book by comparing and contrasting border-sharing versus non-border-sharing host government responses to the same refugee movement. This would shed light on the differing dynamics of both contexts, while holding the refugee nationality constant. It can also incorporate a longitudinal comparative perspective by comparing responses to various mass influx situations in the same host context. For instance, a comparative study can be conducted between Jordan's responses to the Syrian, Iraqi, and Palestinian refugee crises. This may shed light on how host governments learn from previous refugee experiences and how this reflects on their future responses. The approach of this book may also be extended by including Turkey and Iraq as border-sharing, first-asylum countries to the Syrian refugee movement.

Future studies may also be supplemented with local-level analysis, which was beyond the scope of this book. Findings indicate that local-level dynamics in both Lebanon and Jordan influenced policy implementation and coherence of policy responses to the Syrian refugee crisis. Given municipal differences, central-level analysis may not be enough to capture fully the phenomenon. Therefore, it would be significant to examine such dynamics by interviewing municipal authorities. Such micro-level analysis would help supplement our understanding of the role that street-level bureaucrats and other local actors can play in shaping policy outcomes beyond the Global North (Lowndes and Polat 2022; Chopra 2020; Marshall and Béland 2019).

Furthermore, while this book provides an in-depth analysis of how Lebanon and Jordan have responded to the same refugee movement, it does not attempt to prove causality. The conceptual framework developed was useful in examining the responses. However, future research may be conducted to determine causality, based on examination of more mass displacement situations to determine the validity and reliability of the framework. Finally, future research may also build on this analysis by including other significant policy actors who were not included in this study for accessibility reasons. The analysis may be supplemented with interviews and focus group discussions conducted with refugees, who were excluded from this study due to permit constraints. As discussed previously, refugee identities tend to be homogenized in works on refugees. Such homogenization may obfuscate how identity plays a key role in refugees' lived experiences and often intersects with policy. Future research on policy responses can shed light on how policy intersects with refugee identities, including how governments may vary their reception and assistance by gender, sexual orientation, age, religious identity, and other issues, to the detriment of the importance of impartiality in refugee protection (Joseph et al. 2022).

IMPLICATIONS FOR EFFECTIVE REFUGEE GOVERNANCE IN THE GLOBAL SOUTH

Based on Jordan's and Lebanon's experiences in hosting the Syrian refugee population, this section outlines implications for the policy and practice of responding to mass displacement in other contexts of the Global South. It is meant neither to be prescriptive nor to disrespect contextual specificity. However, it builds on the experiences of

The Politics of Refugee Policy in the Global South

Lebanon's and Jordan's governance of the mass movement of Syrian refugees for over a decade, to provide actionable lessons for practice. Like all lessons derived from external experiences, policy recommendations should be contextualized, rather than merely copied, as there are no bullet-proof or one-size-fits-all solutions to complex policy problems. The implications and lessons learned here are based on two rounds of field reflections (2017 and 2021), as well as on the works of other scholars and practitioners. It is meant to encapsulate some of the key lessons learned for more effective governance of mass refugee movements, but it does not purport to be a comprehensive discussion, which could be the subject of a new book. It also highlights some of the policy successes and shortcomings of the governance of Syrian displacement in Lebanon and Jordan.

Firstly, stakeholders, including international organizations, can take this crisis opportunity to invest in strengthening national host institutions instead of creating completely parallel systems of service provision. This could be done through enhancing the capacity of central and municipal authorities to deliver services to refugees and local communities. Field interviews conducted for this book revealed that one of the problematic aspects of national institutions engaging with international organizations, specifically in an emergency, is the feeling of being "overwhelmed" and sidelined by international organizations coming to the stage to aid and raise the capacity of national agencies. Therefore, building the capacity of national and already existing institutions, rather than providing parallel technical support or investing resources in new ones, emerged as one of the key lessons. This was especially evident in conversations with Lebanese and Jordanian officials regarding the chosen mode of policy implementation and collaboration; they often referred to the arrival of international NGOs to the scene as a "mass influx of NGOs."[2] Jordan's more coordinated and nationally led (but collaborative) approach to the management of the influx, which came later on as their policy response evolved, can be seen as a positive manner of policy learning in this regard.

However, it should also be noted that the power imbalance between stakeholders can be problematic. There needs to be a mechanism for safeguarding refugees from potential class-discrimination and xenophobia that can emerge in their interactions with government personnel, as well as in service-provision contexts where nationals and refugees interact. The potential of discrimination on the part of street-level bureaucrats is, of course, a hazard that is existent everywhere – even in non-refugee settings. However, its propensity to happen may increase in mass displacement settings, especially in the case of protraction. This is particularly the case due to the political marginality of refugees. For instance, UNHCR attempted to include refugees in Lebanon's state education system as a way of promoting their access to quality education. However, the manner in which inclusion was pursued and enacted, on the part of teachers and principals, often led to the reproduction of educational inequities, rather than the opposite (Kelcey and Chatila 2020). Therefore, potential class discrimination and bureaucratic xenophobia needs to be addressed by stakeholders, despite potential reservations that may arise from host governments.

Furthermore, coordination and participatory planning between civil society actors and government institutions at the local and central levels are paramount to delivering an effective and coherent crisis response. We learn from the Lebanese case that local-level dynamics matter for policy coherence. Central governments may lose touch with developments on the ground in remote regions, and so coordination with municipal authorities is important. Municipalities and mayors are often at the forefront of engaging with refugees, especially in remote localities (Betts, Memişoğlu, and Ali 2021). Coordination can ensure that policies implemented at the local level are better aligned with central policy-making, and deviations in practice are reduced. In the Lebanese case, as discussed in chapter 9, freedom of movement of refugees was often curtailed at the local level, in contrast to government policy, often due to lack of coordination, communication, and capacity to implement policy away from the centre.

This book's findings and the cases of Lebanon and Jordan have also revealed that while security and sovereignty are important national considerations, they cannot be a host government's only response drivers. Neither can humanitarianism be relied upon to be the only impetus driving host governments. A third way needs to be forged, one that realizes the interest of the host as well as the needs of the refugee population. This rationale, for instance, served as an impetus behind the shift in policy approaches in both countries over time – from an emergency response that focused on the refugee population to a more developmental response that targeted both refugees and the host communities.[3] Adopting solutions that address the needs of host governments for security and sovereignty, as well as the humanitarian needs of those who flee, can ensure more realistic and effective asylum governance, especially in the long run. To this end, there is a need for forced-migration scholars, researchers, and academics to engage with policy-makers, and vice versa. While it is often the case that refugee policies lack reliance on evidence and tend to be politically motivated, policy-makers' current lack of engagement with scholars on refugee issues can and should be addressed. One of the central aims of this book is to highlight the need for policy to engage with academic work, and vice versa. The aim of such engagement is to help raise the capacity of host governments to respond effectively to mass refugee situations, while improving their refugee-reception standards.

As the popular saying goes, crises provide opportunities. Governments witnessing mass refugee movements can take mass influx situations as an opportunity to improve pre-crisis services by targeting aid for humanitarian as well as development purposes (Dahi 2014). Such was the learned experience of Jordan as it altered its approach to the protracted stay of Syrian refugees.[4] This developmental approach can ensure that host development plans are not disrupted as a result of hosting any refugee population. It can also reduce social tensions, compassion fatigue, and perceived preferential treatment of refugees on the part of the local host community, as they are not excluded from crisis-mitigation efforts. Furthermore, governments at the crossroads of recurrent refugee movements need to be proactive in developing their crisis-management capacities, instead of responding reactively to crises. The burden of responding to refugee movements should not fall on them alone, however, and this call should not be understood as putting the entire responsibility on the shoulders of those surrounded by refugee crises (Türk 2018). All governments need to be prepared for future movements. This is critically important as climate migration becomes more of a reality in the future. Lebanon's and Jordan's inability to learn from previous refugee experiences, and their limited crisis learning, did not prepare them for another mass displacement (in this case, from neighbouring Syria).

Other important lessons for practice can be derived from one of the key policy innovations that have emerged during this displacement, namely the Jordan Compact. We learn that reinforcing policy dialogue between stakeholders, including refugees and host communities, is key to ensuring that the refugee population is not excluded from the management of its own affairs and that the host government listens to the most affected. While the reality is that not all stakeholders are of equal position of influence, wealth, or legal-status recognition, refugees as policy-takers can shed important insights onto the policies designed to address them. Attention needs to be paid to overcoming the power imbalances between stakeholders if policy success is desired. The Jordanian case provides lessons for this, specifically with regard to the efficacy of the Jordan Compact in promoting livelihoods for Syrian refugees. As refugees were not systematically consulted on the policy, the agreement had major design flaws that had an impact on its ability to achieve its goals (Al-Mahaidi 2021). It is well established that regulating refugees' access to livelihood mechanisms can reduce their dependence on aid and engagement in the informal economy, in which they are likely to be exploited. It can also reduce their need to resort to negative coping mechanisms to support their livelihoods. This can occur especially as a conflict becomes prolonged. While this is important, how refugee-employment policies are designed is again key for policy success (Kraftt, Malaeb, and Al Zoubi 2022). While the Jordan Compact is considered a positive policy on the part of the Jordanian government, it has not been able to meet the target objective of issuing employment permits to Syrian refugees. Implementation and design flaws, including the capacity of the Jordanian economy to create new jobs, and the desire of Syrian refugees not to restrict themselves to the prescribed sectors, have undermined program objectives (Cole, Al-Ma'aitah, and Al Hasan 2022). Therefore, host governments need to ensure that policies and programs are designed with realistic and achievable goals and to include refugees in decision-making processes.

Lebanon's experiences and developments in the post-2016 era, and the agreement made after the London conference, can also provide lessons for practice. The EU-Lebanon Compact, for instance, was considered to be out of sync with the political reality and landscape of refugee politics in Lebanon and, therefore, failed to be implemented and to produce its desired effects. This again signals that the transformational potential of cooperation agreements, such as those forged between the EU and Jordan, and the EU and Lebanon, may ideally provide positive incentive schemes for host governments. However, for such agreements to work they need to reflect coherence with the reality that they are addressing (Fakhoury 2020). They should also not be an attempt to contain a refugee movement within a specific geography, away from others, in return for financial assistance and can instead be supplemented with a mix of policy measures, including the provision of resettlement opportunities, to ensure credibility (Fakhoury 2022).

With regard to other lessons, interviews with respondents in Lebanon highlighted how the ad hoc, ambiguous, and constantly changing government policies and regulations regarding refugees, including their arbitrary and discretionary implementation at the local level, problematized refugees' living conditions and placed them in constant legal limbo. To overcome this, the notion of "crisis communications" can be a useful tool for government agencies in situations of mass refugee displacement (Coombs and Holladay 2022). Changes in regulations need to be communicated effectively to the refugee community. This can be done through formal and informal channels, including the development of communication networks with refugee representatives and local civil society actors. Governments may also consider the need to reduce the pace with which such regulations are changed because fast-paced and poorly communicated policy changes can reduce the effectiveness of any crisis management (Carlson, Jakli, and Linos 2018).

Furthermore, a main driver of host-community and refugee tensions can be political groups and media outlets spreading hate rhetoric. This politicizing of the refugee issue by associating refugees with political interests and/or religious affiliation was especially evident in the Lebanese case. The push for premature refugee returns, as I demonstrated in chapter 3, deviates from the necessary conditions for voluntary and safe return of refugees and is often used as a political agenda on the part of political actors. While regulating this misuse of rhetoric regarding refugees may be difficult, the use of evidence in debunking myths can be a useful tool for governments (Brun and Fakih 2022). Academia can be supported in developing evidence-based policies and research that debunks popular stereotypes related to refugees. A good example of this comes from Lebanon, where a scholarly initiative was spearheaded by Yassin and Khodor (2019) to debunk myths surrounding Syrian refugees in Lebanon through the use of evidence. However, in one of the few studies that examined whether research evidence was used to inform humanitarian policy-making in Lebanon (and Canada) in response to the Syrian refugee crisis, Khalid et al. (2019) found that evidence had limited influence on policy-making, in comparison to the influence of other factors in Lebanon and Canada; this can be remedied with the help of the scholarly and practitioner community.

Based on Jordan's and Lebanon's experiences, I also deduce the need for a concrete mechanism for ensuring that donor pledges and international obligations of burden sharing are fulfilled. Funding shortages, such as those witnessed by the two countries examined in this book, can disrupt the implementation of national response plans – to the detriment of both refugee and host communities. This was especially evident in interviews with Jordanian and Lebanese officials. Resettlement programs are also an essential element of responsibility sharing. Increasing resettlement opportunities by countries in the North and the South can help ease the burden on host countries. Chapters 6 and 8 of this book highlighted the rise in restrictive policies towards refugees over time. This was due to the lack of responsibility sharing, to funding shortages despite pledges, and to low resettlement opportunities offered to refugees hosted in Lebanon and Jordan. Alternatively, incentive mechanisms can be put in place to harmonize better the policy input arenas of host governments by capitalizing on resources, such as international assistance, and to reduce the constraints on the ability of host governments to respond favorably to refugee movements. For instance, governments that lack legal frameworks for refugee affairs, such as Lebanon and Jordan, can be incentivized to develop national legislation that provides refugees with a well-defined status that protects their rights. However, this cannot happen without proper responsibility sharing on the part of the international community. Global compacts can play a role here and are a positive demonstration of global cooperation (Clark-Ginsberg et al. 2022). However, the Global Compact on Refugees, adopted in 2018, has been heavily criticized by observers for lacking mention of third states' responsibility for recent refugee outflows that are linked to their acts of intervention, in particular Western states (Chimni 2018). It proposes a set of new mechanisms for global cooperation, including the Global Refugee Forum, Comprehensive Response Framework, and support platforms, which should help in responding to mass outflows of refugees (Türk 2018). However, the Global Compact on Refugees has shortcomings, including the lack of real commitment from states in the Global North to admit asylum seekers and to

214   The Politics of Refugee Policy in the Global South

prevent walls from being erected in "Fortress Europe" (Aleinikoff 2018). Further, it dilutes established principles of international refugee law and weakens the protection of children and women (Chimni 2018). It is also considered to lack a concrete mechanism for responsibility sharing (Ineli-Ciger 2019).

CONCLUSION

It has been this book's aim to demonstrate and argue that the responses of host governments to refugees are not inevitable. They are conditioned by many interacting and complex factors that change over time and between one state and the other. Therefore, the more that researchers, scholars, and practitioners understand why host governments respond in the way they do to mass refugee movements, and why variations exist, the more that they can do about it. This is especially important in the context of the Global South, where states witness most refugee flows and where international refugee norms and protection instruments may be lagging behind in addressing the contextual trends evident in the region. The specific contexts of Southern displacement, and the propensity for refugee studies to be influenced by the voices of scholars and institutions in the North, require us to step back and question the extent to which we examine refugee policy issues in the Global South with sufficient nuance.

Adopting a reductionist approach to the study of asylum, through attributing asylum provision and the behaviour of host governments to single overriding policy considerations, fails to address the complexity of mass refugee contexts in the Global South. This book has argued that analysis of refugee policy-making in the Global South requires a unique set of tools and methods that recognize the complexity of policy-making amidst highly fluid, dynamic, and volatile humanitarian emergency settings such as mass displacement situations. It has also highlighted the need to distinguish between North and South contexts and to advance our understanding of refugee policy-making in the under-examined contexts of the Global South. The shared contexts of host states in the Global South, and the distinct set of constraints that are placed on governments responding to mass displacement, require a holistic and dynamic perspective that recognizes that refugee-policy responses are multifactorial. They are also characterized by high interdependence between international, host, and displacement arenas.

It has been this study's aim to advocate that as scholars, researchers, and practitioners aiming to improve the lives of those who flee, and the host communities that take them in, we should not simply engage in criticizing and pathologizing host states, because this constitutes an easy way out. Alternatively, we need to understand the reasons and causes behind their policies to help improve them. Conducting complex systemic analysis should be at the very heart and centre of our engagement with major refugee-hosting states. To do so, this book has provided the necessary methodological and analytical tools that can be applied to understand the unique dynamics of refugee policy-making in the Global South and to analyze the politics of refugee-policy variations in such contexts.

Notes

KEYWORDS, DEFINITIONS, AND ABBREVIATIONS

1 UNHCR (2014d).
2 This differs from the principle of *country of first asylum*, which refers to countries that allow refugees to enter their territory to seek asylum pending repatriation or resettlement.
3 Albert (2010).
4 Hansen (2014).
5 Rutinwa (2002).
6 Definition of the 1951 Convention Relating to the Status of Refugees, http://www.unhcr.org/3b66c2aa10.
7 UNHCR (2023).

CHAPTER ONE

1 Wicked policy problems are characterized by being difficult to define and resolve, owing to contestation between stakeholders over causes, effects, and possible solutions.
2 Asylum seekers make up 4.6 million, and internally displaced people account for 53.2 million of the total displaced population.
3 This figure includes refugees under the mandates of both UNHCR and UNRWA.
4 In Africa the 1969 Organisation of African Unity (OAU) Convention Governing the Specific Aspects of Refugee Problems in Africa broadened the regional refugee definition to also cover individuals affected by "external aggression, occupation, foreign domination or events seriously disturbing public order" (UNHCR 2006b). In 2009, African states also

218 Notes to pages 7–43

strengthened the African Union Convention for the Protection and Assistance of Internally Displaced Persons in Africa (Kampala Convention) to assert guidelines for the protection of IDPs (African Union 2009). In the Americas the 1984 Cartagena Declaration on Refugees expanded the regional refugee definition to cover victims of "massive violations of human rights or circumstances of seriously disturbed public order" (UNHCR 2006a).

5 Complex systems thinking is the multidisciplinary investigation of phenomena from a holistic approach.

6 Relative to their national populations, the island of Aruba hosted the largest number of refugees in 2021 (one in six inhabitants being a refugee).

7 The Syrian refugee crisis has become a "protracted refugee situation," which is defined as a situation in which twenty-five thousand or more refugees of the same nationality have been in exile for five years or longer in a given asylum country (UNHCR 2016).

8 This is in contrast to the most different, most similar comparative method, which analyzes systems with the same dependent variables to identify the independent variables causing the outcome in common.

9 Whenever possible, administrative personnel were interviewed as street-level bureaucrats who can provide a view from "the bottom." This was important in order to note any divergence between policies and their actual implementation.

10 Triangulation refers to the use of a variety of sources, including persons, data, and time, in order to corroborate findings. For more on this, check Nightingale (2020).

11 For further discussion refer to Maxwell's (2013) checklist for combating threats to validity in qualitative case study research.

CHAPTER TWO

1 While this work focuses on conflict-induced displacement, as opposed to displacement caused by economic deprivation or environmental factors, I recognize the complex nature of mass movements that often comprise a variety of migrant categories, including refugees, asylum seekers, and economic migrants. For the purpose of my analysis, conflict is seen as the primary instigator of the movement, rather than the only cause, which may in reality be due to a multiplicity of factors.

2 A combination of the three solutions may occur (Moretti 2015).

3 The displacement arena may be replaced by a "home arena" conceptualization, which refers to the input variables related to the displaced

Notes to pages 52–86

movement's country of origin. For the purposes of this book I am focusing on host processes that interact with the "home" via the displacement arena (e.g., movement nationality).

4 Even though Talib's (2012) analysis is based on individual asylum applications, its results lend more strength to the idea that increased influx volume is coupled with increased restrictive attitudes towards refugees.

5 These could also be understood as features of the displacement.

6 For atheoretical comparative works, cf. Snoubar and Tanrisever (2019).

CHAPTER THREE

1 For a more in-depth debate on sectarianism in Syria as an authoritarian tool, see Daher (2018).

2 Between 2001 and 2020, agriculture value-added share of GDP in Syria ranged between 25 and 20 per cent. For more details see FAOSTAT (2022).

3 For further information on the link between water scarcity and mismanagement, see Daher (2022b).

4 According to Ferris and Kirişci (2016), Sunni Muslims comprised 65 per cent of the pre-war population in Syria. Other religious minority groups included Christians, Druze, Ismailis, ethnic (Sunni) Kurds, and Alawites (from which the House of Assad originates).

5 Interview SYR-C-01 by the author on 16 August 2021.

6 Interview SYR-C-01 by the author on 16 August 2021.

7 Interview SYR-C-01 by the author on 16 August 2021.

8 Interview ESC-EXP-05 by the author on 23 February 2021.

9 While it is difficult to verify this claim, most of this study's interview respondents in Lebanon and Jordan confirmed that the refugee population was composed mainly of Sunni Muslims. Also see Ferris, Kirişci, and Shaikh (2013).

10 Interview SYR-C-01 by the author on 16 August 2021.

11 Interview SYR-C-01 by the author on 16 August 2021.

12 Despite being party to the Geneva Convention and its 1967 Protocol, Turkey maintains a geographical limitation, restricting formal refugee status to Europeans.

13 Interview SYR-C-01 by the author on 16 August 2021.

14 Interview SYR-C-01 by the author on 16 August 2021.

15 Interview SYR-C-01 by the author on 16 August 2021.

16 Interview ESC-NGO-04, international NGO, by the author on 22 February 2021.

Notes to pages 86–106

17 Interview ESC-EXP-06 by the author on 4 March 2021.
18 Interview ESC-EXP-06 by the author on 4 March 2021.
19 Interview SYR-C-01 by the author on 16 August 2021.
20 Interview SYR-C-01 by the author on 16 August 2021.
21 According to an expert, Hezbollah's collaboration with the army was effectively an attempt at non-voluntary return (interview SYR-C-01 by author on 16 August 2021).
22 For a more in-depth discussion of motivations behind Turkish-Syrian rapprochement, see EUI (2022).

CHAPTER FOUR

1 These figures are close to the ones reported in the US Department of State's *International Religious Freedom Report* on Lebanon (US Department of State 2017).
2 Nonetheless, the agreement is considered by experts to be an incomplete process in many ways, in which certain parts including transitional justice were either left out or unimplemented.
3 Based on 2005 estimates (Faour 2007).
4 Figures of PRS in Lebanon vary by source, which may be due to the presence, or lack, of official documentation. In 2016 a report by the Danish Institute for International Studies reported it to be 53,000 (DIIS 2016).

CHAPTER FIVE

1 Interview JD-A-06, Jordan's Ministry of Interior (MOI), by the author on 21 June 2017.
2 Interview JD-C-02 by the author on 14 June 2017.
3 Interview JD-C-02.
4 Interview JD-B-02, UNHCR, by the author on 12 June 2017.
5 Interview JD-A-06, Jor lldan's MOI, by the author on 21 June 2017.
6 Interview JD-A-06.
7 Interview JD-A-07, Jordan's MOPIC, by the author on 31 July 2017.
8 Interview JD-A-06, Jordan's MOI, by the author on 21 June 2017.
9 Interview JD-A-07, Jordan's MOSD, by the author on 31 July 2017.
10 Interview JD-B-02, UNHCR, by the author on 12 June 2017.
11 Interview JD-A-06, Jordan's MOI, by the author on 21 June 2017.
12 Interview JD-A-04, Jordan's Ministry of State for Media Affairs and Communication, by the author on 8 June 2017.

Notes to pages 106–18

13 Interview JD-A-03, Jordan's MOPIC, by the author on 8 June 2017.

14 Interview JD-A-06, Jordan's MOI, by the author on 21 June 2017.

15 Interview JD-A-03, Jordan's MOPIC, by the author on 8 June 2017.

16 Interview JD-B-04, Caritas, by the author on 15 June 2017.

17 Interview JD-B-08, JHCO, by the author on 6 August 2017

18 Interview JD-C-04 by the author on 19 July 2017.

19 Interview JD-A-03, Jordan's MOPIC, by the author on 8 June 2017.

20 Interview JD-A-06, Jordan's MOI, by the author on 21 June 2017.

21 Interview JD-C-04 by the author on 19 July 2017.

22 Interview JD-A-06, Jordan's MOI, by the author on 21 June 2017.

23 Interview JD-C-05 by the author on 28 July 2017.

24 Transcript JD-A-09 of a tri-sectoral workshop organized by Jordan's MOI.

25 Interview JD-A-02, Adviser to the Jordanian Royal Court, by the author on 20 June 2017.

26 Interview JD-A-06, Jordan's MOI, by the author on 21 June 2017.

27 Interview JD-B-06, Oxfam, by the author on 20 July 2017.

28 Interview JD-A-08, Jordan's MOL, by the author on 2 August 2017.

29 Interview JD-B-05, Danish Refugee Council, by the author on 19 June 2017.

30 Interview JD-B-02, UNHCR, by the author on 12 June 2017.

31 Interview JD-A-03, Jordan's MOPIC, by the author on 8 June 2017.

32 At that time, the Nassib border crossing (Syria) was controlled by insurgent forces. The region was captured from the Syrian government on 1 April 2015 and retaken in July 2018.

33 Interview JD-C-01 by the author on 13 June 2017.

34 Interview JD-B-06, Oxfam, by the author on 20 July 2017; and interview JD-C-06 by the author on 8 March 2017.

35 Interview JD-C-01; expert, by the author on 13 June 2017.

36 Interview SYR-EXP-01 by the author on 16 February 2021.

37 Interview ESC-GOV-02 by the author on 16 February 2021.

38 Interview ESC-EXP-02-B by the author on 3 February 2021.

CHAPTER SIX

1 Interview JD-C-01, an expert, by the author on 13 June 2017.

2 Interview JD-B-01, UNDP, by the author on 11 June 2017.

3 Interview JD-C-03, an expert, by the author on 21 June 2017.

4 Interview JD-A-06, MOI, by the author on 21 June 2017.

5 Interview JD-A-01, Foreign Affairs Parliamentary Commission, by the author on 14 June 2017; JD-A-03, MOPIC, by the author on 8 June 2017; JD-A-07, MOSD, by the author on 31 July 2017.

6 Interview JD-B-06, Oxfam, by the author on 20 July 2017; JD-C-01, an expert, by the author on 13 June 2017.

7 Syrians can only access public health-care facilities that fall under the area of registration of their MOI cards, generating difficulties for those who relocate within Jordan (Salemi, Bowman, and Compton 2018). Interview JD-B-03, ARDD, by the author on 14 June 2017.

8 Interview JD-B-02, UNHCR, by the author on 12 June 2017.

9 Interview JD-B-03, ARDD, by the author on 14 June 2017.

10 In February 2018, Syrian refugees outside camps were required to pay even higher fees (the equivalent of what most foreigners paid), but the government rolled back this measure in April 2019 (UNHCR 2019d). Interview JD-A-03, MOPIC, by the author on 8 June 2017.

11 The fees were originally JOD 700 (approximately USD 1000) (Beaujouan and Rasheed 2019). Interview JD-B-01, UNDP, by the author on 11 June 2017; and Interview JD-C-05, an expert, by the author on 28 July 2017.

12 Interviews by the author: JD-A-03, MOPIC, on 8 June 2017; JD-A-06, MOI, on 21 June 2017; JD-A-08, MOL, on 2 August 2017.

13 Formal employment of Syrians in Jordan is possible in five sectors: agriculture, construction, food and beverage services, manufacturing, and wholesale and retail trade (Mencutek and Nashwan 2020). Interview JD-B-04, Caritas, by the author on 15 June 2017; JD-C-01, an expert, by the author on 13 June 2017.

14 Approximately 45,000 Syrians hold active work permits. In some sectors, such as agriculture, cooperatives and unions can be used as proxy employers, allowing Syrians to move between individual employers (Gordon 2019); Interview ESC-NGO-06, international NGO, by the author on 2 March 2021.

15 Interview ESC-NGO-02, intergovernmental NGO, by the author on 22 February 2021.

16 Interview ESC-GOV-02, government official, by the author on 25 February 2021.

17 Interview JD-B-01, UNDP, by the author on 11 June 2017.

18 Interviews by the author: JD-A-06, MOI, on 21 June 2017; JD-C-01, an expert, on 13 June 2017.

19 Interview JD-B-02, UNHCR, by the author on 12 June 2017.

20 Interviews by the author: JD-C-02, an expert, on 14 June 2017; JD-B-02, UNHCR, on 14 June 2017.

21 Interviews by the author: JD-A-07, MOSD, on 31 July 2017; JD-C-03, an expert, on 21 June 2017.

22 Interview JD-A-01, Foreign Affairs Parliamentary Commission, by the author on 14 June 2017.

23 Interview JD-A-02, adviser to the Jordanian Royal Court, by the author on 20 June 2017.

24 Interview JD-A-01, Foreign Affairs Parliamentary Commission, by the author on 14 June 2017.

25 Interviews by the author: JD-C-05, an expert, on 28 July 2017; JD-B-04, Caritas, on 15 June 2017; and JD-B-08, JHCO, on 6 August 2017.

26 Interview JD-A-06, MOI, by the author on 21 June 2017.

27 Interviews by the author: JD-A-01, Foreign Affairs Parliamentary Commission, on 14 June 2017; JD-A-06, MOI, on 21 June 2017; JD-A-07, MOSD, on 31 July 2017; JD-A-09, Tri-sectoral workshop organized by MOI; JD-A-05, Foreign Affairs Parliamentary Commission.

28 Interviews by the author: JD-B-01, UNDP, on 11 June 2017; JD-A-01, Foreign Affairs Parliamentary Commission, on 14 June 2017.

29 Interview JD-A-02, adviser to the Jordanian Royal Court, by the author on 20 June 2017.

30 Interview JD-C-05, an expert, by the author on 28 July 2017.

31 Interview JD-A-02, adviser to the Jordanian Royal Court, by the author on 20 June 2017.

32 Interview JD-C-05, an expert, by the author on 28 July 2017.

33 Interview JD-A-02, adviser to the Jordanian Royal Court, by the author on 20 June 2017.

34 Interview JD-B-04, Caritas, by the author on 15 June 2017.

35 Interviews by the author: JD-A-01, Foreign Affairs Parliamentary Commission, on 14 June 2017; JD-A-07, MOSD, on 31 July 2017.

36 Interview JD-C-05, an expert, by the author on 28 July 2017.

37 Interview JD-C-03, an expert, by the author on 21 June 2017.

38 Interview JD-C-05, an expert, by the author on 28 July 2017.

39 Interview JD-A-01, Foreign Affairs Parliamentary Commission, by the author on 14 June 2017.

40 Interviews by the author: JD-A-08, MOL, on 2 August 2017; JD-C-03, an expert, on 21 June 2017; JD-C-05, an expert, on 28 July 2017; JD-C-02, an expert, on 14 June 2017.

41 Interview JD-C-02, an expert, by the author on 14 June 2017.

42 Interview JD-B-01, UNDP, by the author on 11 June 2017.

43 Interview JD-B-03, ARDD, by the author on 14 June 2017.

44 Interview JD-A-03, MOPIC, by the author on 8 June 2017.

45 Interview JD-B-01, UNDP, by the author on 11 June 2017.

224 Notes to pages 135–44

46 Interview JD-A-02, adviser to the Jordanian Royal Court, by the author on 20 June 2017.
47 Adapted from UNHCR (2018c).
48 Interview JD-A-06, MOI, by the author on 21 June 2017.
49 Interviews by the author: JD-A-01, Foreign Affairs Parliamentary Commission, on 14 June 2017; and JD-A-06, MOI, on 21 June 2017.
50 Interview JD-C-05, an expert, by the author on 28 July 2017.
51 Interviews by the author: JD-A-03, MOPIC, on 8 June 2017; JD-B-05, Danish Refugee Council, on 19 June 2017.
52 Interview JD-B-01, UNDP, by the author on 11 June 2017.
53 Interviews by the author: JD-A-07, MOSD, on 31 July 2017; JD-A-06, MOI, on 21 June 2017.
54 Interview JD-C-05, an expert, by the author on 28 July 2017.
55 Interview ESC-NGO-06, international NGO, by the author on 2 March 2021.
56 Interview ESC-NGO-02, intergovernmental NGO, by the author on 22 February 2021.

CHAPTER SEVEN

1 Interview LB-C-03, an expert, by the author on 11 April 2017.
2 Interview LB-A-05, high-ranking official of MORA and Future Movement, by the author on 12 April 2017.
3 Interview LB-C-03, an expert, by the author on 11 April 2017.
4 Interview LB-A-05, a high-ranking official of MORA and Future Movement, by the author on 12 April 2017.
5 Interview LB-A-01, a MORA high-level official, by the author on 28 March 2017.
6 Interview LB-B-05, Norwegian Refugee Council, by the author on 12 April 2017.
7 Interview LB-A-04, a MORA adviser, by the author on 11 April 2017.
8 Interview LB-A-01, a MORA high-level official, by the author on 28 March 2017.
9 Interview LB-A-01.
10 Interview LB-A-01.
11 Interview LB-A-07, Progressive Socialist Party, by the author on 27 April 2017.
12 Interview LB-B-06, URDA / Leb4Refs, by the author on 26 April 2017.
13 Interview LB-B-01, UNHCR, by the author on 21 March 2017.

Notes to pages 144–54

14 Interview LB-A-06, adviser to the prime minister, by the author on 13 April 2017.
15 Interview LB-B-03, World Bank, by the author on 10 April 2017.
16 Interview LB-A-03, Ministry of Finance, by the author on 11 April 2017.
17 Interview LB-B-03, World Bank, by the author on 10 April 2017.
18 Interview L3-A-01, a MORA high-level official, by the author on 28 March 2017.
19 Interview LB-C-02, an expert, by the author on 27 March 2017.
20 Interview LB-A-01, a MORA high-level official, by the author on 28 March 2017.
21 Interview LB-A-06, an adviser to the prime minister, by the author on 13 April 2017.
22 Interviews by the author: LB-A-01, a MORA high-level official, on 28 March 2017; LB-B-06, URDA / Leb4Refs, on 26 April 2017.
23 Interview LB-A-01.
24 Interview LB-A-01.
25 Interview LB-B-05, Norwegian Refugee Council, by the author on 12 April 2017.
26 Interview LB-B-02, UNHCR, by the author on 24 March 2017.
27 Interview LBLB-B-01, UNHCR; by the author on 21 March 2017.
28 Interview LB-A-01, a MORA high-level official, by the author on 28 March 2017.
29 Interview LB-A-06, adviser to the prime minister, by the author on 13 April 2017.
30 Interview LB-B-02, UNHCR, by the author on 24 March 2017.
31 Interview SYR-EXP-01, by the author on 16 February 2021.

CHAPTER EIGHT

1 Interview LB-B-01, UNHCR, by the author on 21 March 2017.
2 Interview LB-B-05, Norwegian Refugee Council, by the author on 12 April 2017.
3 Interview LB-B-01, UNHCR; by the author on 21 March 2017.
4 Interviews by the author: LB-A-02, Parliamentary Commission for Health, Labour, and Social Affairs; LB-C-02, an expert, on 27 March 2017.
5 Interview LB-B-05, Norwegian Refugee Council, by the author on 12 April 2017.
6 The MOSA developed a category of humanitarian exceptions aimed at unaccompanied and separated children (under sixteen years of age) whose

226 Notes to pages 154–5

parents or legal guardians were confirmed to be displaced in Lebanon; persons with disabilities dependent on family or relatives who were confirmed to be displaced in Lebanon; persons in need of life-saving medical treatment not usually available in Syria; and individuals pursuing resettlement or transitioning through Lebanon to a third country with proof of onward travel outside Lebanon. Interview LB-B-05, Norwegian Refugee Council, by the author on 12 April 2017.

7 In May 2019 the GSO declared that all Syrians who entered or resided in Lebanon irregularly in the period after 24 April 2019 would be handed over to the Syrian immigration authorities. Interview LB-A-02, Parliamentary Commission for Health, Labour, and Social Affairs, by the author.

8 Similar to other countries, amidst the outbreak of the COVID-19 pandemic in 2020, Lebanon imposed restrictions on access to its territory. As of July 2020 the Lebanon-Syria border was closed (except for trucks) in both directions. Despite calls from the UNHCR asking for states to maintain individuals' rights to seek asylum amidst global border closures, the Lebanese borders remained closed to Syrians trying to cross to its territory or go back to Syria.

9 Interview LB-B-07, UNHCR.

10 Despite limitations related to the 2003 MOU, Syrians in Lebanon are treated as de facto prima facie refugees by the UNHCR, and proper RSD interviews only occur during resettlement procedures. The "merged" RSD/resettlement was initiated in 2014 when the UNHCR concluded that conducting individual RSD interviews for all Syrians would not be feasible due to the large scale of displacement. In its 2015–16 Lebanon Crisis Response Plan document, UNHCR used the term de facto refugees to refer to "Syrian nationals who are registered with UNHCR or seeking registration."

11 Interview LB-A-01, a MORA high-level official, by the author on 28 March 2017.

12 Interviews by the author: LB-B-05, Norwegian Refugee Council, on 12 April 2017; LB-B-01, UNHCR, on 21 March 2017.

13 Interview LB-B-01, UNHCR, by the author on 21 March 2017. A waiver of the fee was announced in early 2017 for Syrian refugees who had registered with UNHCR prior to January 2015. Refugees registered with the UNHCR in Lebanon receive an asylum-seeker certificate, valid for two years. Nevertheless, the document has not exempted refugees from penalties associated with irregular entry or a lack of residency in the country.

14 Interviews by the author: LB-B-05, Norwegian Refugee Council, on 12 April 2017; LB-B-01, UNHCR, on 21 March 2017.

15 In 2020, amidst the COVID-19 pandemic, the GSO temporarily paused its procedures for renewing residency permits. The Lebanese government

Notes to pages 155–60

declared that residency permits expiring between 11 March 2020 and 30 June 2020 would be exempted from overstay fees and would be renewed for a period starting from the expiry date. Interview LB-B-01, UNHCR, by the author on 21 March 2017.

16 Interview LB-A-05, a MORA high-ranking official/Future Movement, by the author on 12 April 2017.

17 Interview LB-B-02, UNHCR, by the author on 24 March 2017.

18 In May 2020 the Syrian embassy in Lebanon announced that Syrians in Lebanon may obtain any civil status document (including individual civil extract, family civil extract, and marriage certificate) through the embassy. Interview LB-B-05, Norwegian Refugee Council, by the author on 12 April 2017.

19 Interview LB-B-01, UNHCR, by the author on 21 March 2017.

20 Interview LB-B-05, Norwegian Refugee Council, by the author on 12 April 2017.

21 Interview LB-B-07, UNHCR.

22 Interviews by the author: LB-B-01, UNHCR, on 21 March 2017; LB-A-06, adviser to the prime minister, on 13 April 2017.

23 Interview LB-A-06, adviser to the prime minister, by the author on 13 April 2017.

24 Arabic is the language of instruction in Syria, as opposed to English and French in Lebanon.

25 Interview LB-A-06, adviser to the prime minister, by the author on 13 April 2017.

26 Less than a third of the Lebanese school-aged children enrolled in public schools, where education is largely privatized.

27 Interview LB-B-02, UNHCR, by the author on 24 March 2017.

28 Interview LB-A-04, a MORA adviser, by the author on 11 April 2017.

29 Interview LB-B-02, UNHCR, by the author on 24 March 2017.

30 As of December 2019, the UNHCR had a network of ten primary health-care centres and forty hospitals to provide health services with subsidized fees for refugees in Lebanon.

31 The UNHCR estimated that 84,000 severely vulnerable Syrian refugee families were in need of its multi-purpose cash assistance program in 2020, but approximately only 35,000 families would be prioritized and receive the assistance.

32 Interviews by the author: LB-B-05, Norwegian Refugee Council, on 12 April 2017; LB-B-02, UNHCR, on 24 March 2017.

33 Interview LB-A-03, Ministry of Finance, by the author on 11 April 2017.

34 Interviews by the author: LB-A-01, a MORA high-level official, on 28 March 2017; LB-B-03, World Bank, on 13 April 2017.

228 Notes to pages 160–6

35 Interview LB-B-02, UNHCR, by the author on 24 March 2017.

36 Interview LB-A-04, a MORA adviser, by the author on 11 April 2017.

37 Interview LB-A-07, Progressive Socialist Party, by the author on 27 April 2017.

38 Interview LB-B-07, UNHCR.

39 Interview LB-A-01, a MORA high-level official, by the author on 28 March 2017.

40 Interview LB-A-01.

41 Ministries of Interior, Foreign Affairs, Social Affairs, Refugee Affairs, Planning, Health, Education, and Finance.

42 Interview LB-A-06, adviser to the prime minister, by the author on 13 April 2017.

43 Interview LB-A-01, a MORA high-level official, by the author on 28 March 2017.

44 Interview LB-A-01.

45 Interview LB-A-05, a high-ranking official of MORA and Future Movement, by the author on 12 April 2017.

46 Interview LB-B-05, Norwegian Refugee Council, by the author on 12 April 2017.

47 Interview LB-B-07, UNHCR.

48 Interview LB-C-02, an expert, by the author on 27 March 2017.

49 Interview LB-B-05, Norwegian Refugee Council, by the author on 12 April 2017.

50 Interview LB-B-05

51 Interview LB-A-04, a MORA adviser, by the author on 11 April 2017.

52 Interview LB-A-04.

53 Interview LB-A-07, Progressive Socialist Party, by the author on 27 April 2017.

54 The GSO assists refugees to register their interest to return, and seeks clearance with the Syrian authorities. Refugees wishing to return to Syria have any overstay fees waived and are not issued a re-entry ban.

55 Despite the small number of resettled refugees vis-à-vis the overall refugee population in the country, Lebanon has been the country with the second-most resettlement submissions since the beginning of the crisis in Syria (2011), only lagging behind Turkey. Together with Turkey, Jordan, Iraq, and Egypt, resettlement out of Lebanon is among UNHCR's key priorities. Interview LB-B-01, UNHCR, by the author on 21 March 2017.

56 Interview LB-A-01, a MORA high-level official, by the author on 28 March 2017.

57 Interview LB-A-05, a high-ranking MORA official / Future Movement, by the author on 12 April 2017.

Notes to pages 167–210

58 Interview L3-A-05.
59 Interview L3-A-02, Parliamentary Commission for Health, Labour, and Social Affairs.
60 Interview L3-A-07, Progressive Socialist Party, by the author on 27 April 2017.
61 Interview L3-C-05, an expert, by the author on 14 April 2017.
62 Interview L3-B-03, World Bank, by the author on 10 April 2017.
63 Interview L3-A-02, Parliamentary Commission for Health, Labour, and Social Affairs.
64 Interview L3-B-02, UNHCR, by the author on 24 March 2017.
65 Interview L3-A-01, a MORA high-level official, by the author on 28 March 2017.
66 Interview LB-B-05, Norwegian Refugee Council, by the author on 12 April 2017.
67 Interview LB-A-04, a MORA adviser, by the author on 11 April 2017.
68 Interview LB-B-05, Norwegian Refugee Council, by the author on 12 April 2017.
69 Interview LB-B-07, UNHCR.

CHAPTER NINE

1 UNHCR has been present at all departure points across the country during GSO-facilitated group return movements.
2 Interview JD-B-02, UNHCR, by the author on 12 June 2017.
3 Interview LB-B-05, Norwegian Refugee Council, by the author on 12 April 2017.
4 Notably, in Lebanon, curfews were implemented in several municipalities, and during the COVID-19 pandemic they affected Syrians disproportionally (HRW 2020).

CHAPTER TEN

1 Despite low numbers, Lebanon and Jordan have been among the three countries of asylum with the most UNHCR resettlement referrals during recent years (with Turkey being number one). Jordan and Lebanon were among UNHCR's resettlement priorities for 2021.
2 Interview JD-C-04, an expert, by the author on 19 July 2017.
3 For more on this shift, refer back to chapters 6 and 8 of this book.
4 For more on this, refer to chapters 5 and 6 of this book.

References

Abdelaaty, L. 2020. "RSD by UNHCR: Difficulties and Dilemmas." *Forced Migration Review* 65 (November): 21–3.

– 2021a. "Refugees and Guesthood in Turkey." *Journal of Refugee Studies* 34 (3): 2827–48.

– 2021b. "Rivalry, Ethnicity, and Asylum Admissions Worldwide." *International Interactions* 47 (2): 346–73.

Abdulrahim, S., and M. Khawaja. 2011. "The Cost of Being Palestinian in Lebanon." *Journal of Ethnic and Migration Studies* 37 (1): 151–66.

Aberman, T. 2013. "Gendered Perspectives on Refugee Determination in Canada." *Refuge* 30 (2): 57–66.

Abla, Z., and M. Al-Masri. 2015. "Better Together: The Impact of the Schooling System of Lebanese and Syrian Displaced Pupils on Social Stability." Paper written for International Alert. https://data2.unhcr.org/en/documents/download/44275.

Abouzeid, R. 2018. *No Turning Back: Life, Loss, and Hope in Wartime Syria*. New York: W.W. Norton.

Abuya, E.O. 2007. "Past Reflections, Future Insights: African Asylum Law and Policy in Historical Perspective." *International Journal of Refugee Law* 19 (1): 51–95.

Abu Zayd, Karen, Denis J. Sullivan, Susan M. Akram, and Sara Roy. 2015. "The Syrian Humanitarian Crisis: What Is to Be Done?" *Middle East Policy* 22 (2): 1–29.

Achilli, L., Nasser Yassin, and M. Murat Erdogan. 2017. "Neighbouring Host-Countries' Policies for Syrian Refugees: The Cases of Jordan, Lebanon, and Turkey." Working paper, Migration Policy Centre. https://cadmus.eui.eu/handle/1814/44904.

References

ACRPS Policy Analysis Unit. 2014. *Geneva Conference II: Challenges Faced in Syria and the Region*. Doha, Qatar: Arab Center for Research and Policy Studies.

Adamson, F.B., and G. Tsourapas. 2019. "Migration Diplomacy in World Politics." *International Studies Perspectives* 20 (2): 113–28.

– 2020. "The Migration State in the Global South: Nationalizing, Developmental, and Neoliberal Models of Migration Management." *International Migration Review* 54 (3): 853–82. https://doi.org/10.1177/0197918319879057.

Admirand, P. 2014. "The Ethics of Displacement and Migration in the Abrahamic Faiths: Enlightening Believers and Aiding Public Policy." *Journal of Ethnic and Migration Studies* 40 (4): 671–87.

Afailal, H., and M. Fernandez. 2018. "The Externalization of European Borders: The Other Face of Coloniality Turkey as a Case study." *Athens Journal of Mediterranean Studies* 4 (3): 215–22.

African Union. 2009. *African Union Convention for the Protection and Assistance of Internally Displaced Persons in Africa (Kampala Convention)*. UNHCR. https://www.unhcr.org/about-us/background/ae9bede9/african-union-convention-protection-assistance-internally-displaced-persons.html.

Akgündüz, Y., M. Van den Berg, and W. Hassink. 2015. "The Impact of Refugee Crises on Host Labor Markets: The Case of the Syrian Refugee Crisis in Turkey." Institute for the Study of Labor (IZA), Bonn, Discussion Paper No. 8841.

Akpinar, S. 2007. "Hospitality in Islam." *Religion East and West* 7 (1): 23–7.

Alakoc, B.P., G.U. Göksel, and A. Zarychta. 2022. "Political Discourse and Public Attitudes toward Syrian Refugees in Turkey." *Comparative Politics* 54 (3): 547–71.

Alam, S., N.K.A. Siddique, and R. Akhtar. 2022. "Social Interaction between 'Host' and 'Guest': Rohingya Refugee Context in Bangladesh." *Asian Journal of Social Sciences and Legal Studies* 4 (3): 85–93.

Albert, M. 2010. "Governance and Prima Facie Refugee Status Determination: Clarifying the Boundaries of Temporary Protection, Group Determination, and Mass Influx." *Refugee Survey Quarterly* 29 (1): 61–91.

Alden, Chris, and Marco Antônio Vieira. 2005. "The New Diplomacy of the South: South Africa, Brazil, India, and Trilateralism." *Third World Quarterly* 26 (7): 1077–95.

Aleinikoff, T.A. 2018. "The Unfinished Work of the Global Compact on Refugees." *International Journal of Refugee Law* 30:611.

References

Alexander, P., and Ahlam. 2021. *Syria's Economic Collapse and Its Impact on the Most Vulnerable*. Center for Strategic and International Studies, 18 February 2021. https://www.csis.org/analysis/syrias-economic-collapse-and-its-impact-most-vulnerable.

Alfred, C. 2018. "Dangerous Exit: Who Controls How Syrians in Lebanon Go Home." *New Humanitarian*, 8 August 2018. https://deeply.thenewhumanitarian.org/refugees/articles/2018/08/08/dangerous-exit-who-controls-how-syrians-in-lebanon-go-home.

Alink, F., Arjen Boin, and Paul T'Hart. 2001. "Institutional Crises and Reforms in Policy Sectors: The Case of Asylum Policy in Europe." *Journal of European Public Policy* 8 (2): 286–306. https://doi.org/10.1080/13501760151146487.

Al Jazeera. 2014. "Lebanese PM Unveils National Unity Cabinet." 15 February 2014. https://www.aljazeera.com/news/middleeast/2014/02/lebanese-pm-unveils-national-unity-cabinet-201421511275434 3666.html.

– 2016. "Jordan Declares Border with Syria Military Zone." 21 June 2016. https://www.aljazeera.com/news/2016/06/jordan-declares-border-syria-military-zone-160621172026984.html.

– 2018. "Syria: The Endgame." 19 October 2018. https://www.aljazeera.com/podcasts/2018/10/19/syria-the-endgame.

– 2020. "Russia and China Veto UN Extension of Cross-Border Aid to Syria." 8 July 2020. https://www.aljazeera.com/news/2020/7/8/russia-and-china-veto-un-extension-of-cross-border-aid-to-syria.

Al-Khalidi, S. 2021a. "Syrian Rebels Attack Army Outposts in Southern Syria." Reuters, 29 July 2021. https://www.reuters.com/world/middle-east/syrian-rebels-attack-army-outposts-southern-syria-2021–07–29/.

– 2021b. "Jordan Fully Reopens Border Crossing with Syria, Seeks Trade Boost." Reuters, 30 September 2021. https://www.reuters.com/world/middle-east/jordan-fully-reopens-main-crossing-with-syria-2021–09–29/.

– 2021c. Jordan's Abdullah Receives First Call from Syria's Assad since Start of Conflict." Reuters, 3 October 2021. https://www.reuters.com/world/middle-east/jordans-abdullah-receives-first-call-syrias-assad-since-start-conflict-2021–10–03/.

Al-Khalidi, S., and L. Barrington. 2018. "Jordan and Syria Reopen Nassib Border Crossing." Reuters, 15 October 2018. https://www.reuters.com/article/us-mideast-crisis-syria-jordan/jordan-and-syria-reopen-nassib-border-crossing-idUSKCN1MP0L4.

References

Al Khouri, R. 2007. "Aspects of Migration and Development in Jordan." Paper prepared for Migration and Refugee Movements in the Middle East and North Africa, Forced Migration and Refugee Studies Program, the American University in Cairo, 23–25 October 2007. https://fount.aucegypt.edu/faculty_journal_articles/5052.

Al-Kilani, S. 2014. "A Duty and a Burden on Jordan." *Forced Migration Review* 47:30.

Al-Makahleh, S. 2017. "The Case for Safe Zones in Syria." *Fair Observer*, 13 May 2017. https://www.fairobserver.com/region/middle_east_north_africa/military-intervention-syria-jordan-middle-east-news-analysis-71330/.

– 2018. "The Diplomatic Overtures of Jordan and Syria." *Alarabiya News*, 23 December 2018. https://english.alarabiya.net/views/news/middle-east/2018/12/23/The-diplomatic-overtures-of-Jordan-and-Syria.

Almasri, S. 2021. "The Political Economy of Nationality-Based Labor Inclusion Strategies: A Case Study of the Jordan Compact." *Middle East Critique* 30 (2): 185–203.

Almohamad, H., and A. Dittmann. 2016. "Oil in Syria between Terrorism and Dictatorship." *Social Sciences* 5 (2): 20.

Al-Momnei, F., A. Athamna, and Y. El-Radayda. 2016. "نحو اللجوء السوري تصورات الأردنيين نحو." Al-Yarmouk University, Irbid, Jordan.

Al-Sharq Al-Awsat. 2017. "Lebanese Government Renews Commitment to Disassociation Policy." 5 December 2017. https://aawsat.com/english/home/article/1104211/lebanese-government-renews-commitment-disassociation-policy.

Alvarez-Ossorio, I. 2019. "The Sectarian Dynamics of the Syrian Conflict." *Review of Faith & International Affairs*, 17 (2): 47–58.

Amnesty International. 2020. "Jordan: Authorities Must Allow Urgent Medical Care for Displaced Syrians in Rukban during COVID-19." 7 May 2020. https://www.amnesty.org/en/latest/news/2020/05/jordan-authorities-must-allow-urgent-medical-care-for-displaced-syrians-in-rukban-during-covid19/.

Anckar, C. 2020. "The Most-Similar and Most-Different Systems Design in Comparative Policy Analysis." In *Handbook of Research Methods and Applications in Comparative Policy Analysis*, edited by B. Guy Peters and Guillaume Fontaine, 33–48. Cheltenham, UK: Edward Elgar.

Anderson, J.E. 2001. *Public Policymaking: An Introduction*. Boston: Houghton.

Andrew, F.A., and N.M. Lukajo. 2005. "Golden Opportunities – Reality or Myth? Horn of Africa Female Migrants, Refugees, and Asylum

Seekers in the Netherlands." *Community Development Journal* 40 (2): 224–31. https://doi.org/10.1093/cdj/bsio33.

Androff, D.K. 2022. *Refugee Solutions in the Age of Global Crisis: Human Rights, Integration, and Sustainable Development.* Oxford: Oxford University Press.

Apps, P. 2012. "Analysis: Syria's Assad Faces Growing Rebel, Foreign Threat." Reuters, 27 June 2012. https://www.reuters.com/article/uk-syria-escalation-idUKBRE85Q11C20120627.

Arar, R., and D.S. FitzGerald. 2022. *The Refugee System: A Sociological Approach.* Cambridge: Polity Publishing.

Aras, N.E.G., and Z.Ş. Mencütek, 2015. "The International Migration and Foreign Policy Nexus: The Case of Syrian Refugee Crisis and Turkey." *Migration Letters* 12 (3): 193–208.

Aslan, M. 2019. "Turkey's Reconstruction Model in Syria." SETA. https://setav.org/en/assets/uploads/2019/04/R139Syria.pdf.

Asseburg, M. 2020. *Reconstruction in Syria: Challenges and Policy Options for the EU and Its Member States.* Berlin: Stiftung Wissenschaft und Politik.

Assi, A. 2016. *Democracy in Lebanon: Political Parties and the Struggle for Power since Syrian Withdrawal.* London: Bloomsbury Publishing.

Assi, A. 2019. "International Politics of Syrian Refugee Return: The Case of Lebanon." Middle East Institute. https://www.mei.edu/publications/international-politics-syrian-refugee-return-case-lebanon.

Atallah, S., and D. Mahdi. 2017. "Law and Politics of Safe Zones and Forced Returns to Syria: Refugee Politics in Lebanon." The Lebanese Center for Policy Studies. https://www.lcps-lebanon.org/articles/details/2248/law-and-politics-of-%E2%80%9Csafe-zones%E2%80%9D-and-forced-return-to-syria-refugee-politics-in-lebanon.

AUB (American University of Beirut). 2020. "Timeline of Major Policies Influencing the Livelihoods of Syrian Refugees in Jordan." Issam Fares Institute of Public Policy and International Affairs, December 2020. https://www.aub.edu.lb/ifi/Documents/publications/infographics/2019–2020/20210208_timeline_of_major_policies_influencing_the_livelihoods_of_Syrian_refugees_in_Jordan_infog.pdf.

Aubone, A., and J. Hernandez. 2013. "Assessing Refugee Camp Characteristics and the Occurrence of Sexual Violence: A Preliminary Analysis of the Dadaab Complex." *Refugee Survey Quarterly* 32 (4): 22–40.

Awad, I. 2014. "Population Movements in the Aftermath of the Arab Awakenings: The Syrian Refugee Crisis between Regional Factors and State Interest." In *Migration in the Mediterranean: Human Rights, Security and Development Perspectives*, edited by O. Grech and M. Wohlfeld, 24–39. Malta: Mediterranean Academy of Diplomatic Studies.

Baah, B. 2020. *Humanitarian Cash and Voucher Assistance in Jordan: A Gateway to Mobile Financial Services*. London: GSMA.

Bacik, G. 2007. *Hybrid Sovereignty in the Arab Middle East: The Cases of Kuwait, Jordan, and Iraq*. Berlin: Springer.

Badalič, V. 2019. "Rejected Syrians: Violations of the Principle of 'Non-Refoulement' in Turkey, Jordan and Lebanon." *Dve domovini*, 49. In Slovenian.

Bahram, H. 2018. "Kurdish Guests or Syrian Refugees? Negotiating Displacement, Identity and Belonging in the Kurdistan Region." Master's diss., Linköping University.

Baines, E., and L.R. Gauvin. 2014. "Motherhood and Social Repair after War and Displacement in Northern Uganda." *Journal of Refugee Studies* 27 (2): 282–300.

Bakewell, O. 2014. "Encampment and Self-Settlement." In Fiddian-Qasmiyeh et al., *The Oxford Handbook of Refugee and Forced Migration*, 127–38.

Balanche, F. 2018. *Sectarism in Syria's Civil War*. Washington, DC: Washington Institute for Near East Policy.

Bank, A. 2016. *Syrian Refugees in Jordan: Between Protection and Marginalisation*. GIGA Focus Nahost 03. Hamburg: GIGA German Institute of Global and Area Studies, Leibniz-Institut für Globale und Regionale Studien, Institut für Nahost-Studien.

Banki, S. 2004. *Refugee Integration in the Intermediate Term: A Study of Nepal, Pakistan, and Kenya*. Geneva: UNHCR, Evaluation and Policy Analysis Unit.

Banks, J. 2008. "The Criminalisation of Asylum Seekers and Asylum Policy." *Prison Service Journal* 175: 43–9.

Barbelet, V., J. Hagen-Zanker, and D. Mansour-Ille. 2018. *The Jordan Compact: Lessons Learnt and Implications for Future Refugee Compacts*. London: Overseas Development Institute.

Barnard, A., and M. Abi-Habib. 2017. "Why Saad Hariri Had That Strange Sojourn in Saudi Arabia." *New York Times*, 24 December 2017.

Barnes, J. 2009. "Managing the Waters of Ba'th Country: The Politics of Water Scarcity in Syria." *Geopolitics* 14 (3): 510–30.

References

Barron, R., and J. Barnes. 2018. "Trump Policy in the Middle East: Syria." Issue Brief 3. Barker Institute for Foreign Policy.

Bashford, A., and J. McAdam. 2014. "The Right to Asylum: Britain's 1905 Aliens Act and the Evolution of Refugee Law." *Law and History Review* 32 (2): 309–50. https://doi.org/ 10.1017/S0738248014000029.

Baumgartner, F.R., and B.D. Jones. 1991. "Agenda Dynamics and Policy Subsystems." *Journal of Politics* 53 (4): 1044–74.

Baylouny, A.M. 2020. *When Blame Backfires: Syrian Refugees and Citizen Grievances in Jordan and Lebanon*. Ithaca, NY: Cornell University Press.

BBC. 2011. "Syria Protests: Bashar al-Assad Lifts Emergency Law." 21 April 2011. https://www.bbc.com/news/world-middle-east-13161329.

– 2016. "Jordanian Troops Killed in Bomb Attack at Syria Border." 21 June 2016. https://www.bbc.com/news/world-middle-east-36584885.

– 2017. "Syria Conflict: Jordanians at 'Boiling Point' Over Refugees." 2 February 2016. http://www.bbc.com/news/world-middle-east-35462698.

– 2020a. "Lebanon Protests: New Government Ends Months of Deadlock." 22 January 2020. https://www.bbc.com/news/world-middle-east-51189782.

– 2020b. "Beirut Explosion: Lebanon's Government Resigns as Public Anger Mounts." 10 August 2020. https://www.bbc.com/news/world-middle-east-53722909.

– 2023. "Why Has the Syrian War Lasted 12 Years?" 2 May 2023. https://www.bbc.com/news/world-middle-east-35806229.

Beaujouan, J., and A. Rasheed. 2019. "The Syrian Refugee Policy of the Jordanian Government." In *Syrian Crisis, Syrian Refugees: Voices from Jordan and Lebanon*, 47–64. London: Springer Nature.

Belanger, D., and C. Saracoglu. 2020. "The Governance of Syrian Refugees in Turkey: The State-Capital Nexus and Its Discontents." *Mediterranean Politics* 25 (4): 413–32.

Bellintani, V. 2021. "Putting Families' Needs at the Center: A Humanitarian Approach to Disappearance in Syria." The Tahrir Institute for Middle East Policy, 23 July 2021. https://timep.org/explainers/putting-families-needs-at-the-center-a-humanitarian-approach-to-disappearance-in-syria/.

Ben Mimoune, N. 2020. "Policy and Institutional Responses to COVID-19 in the Middle East and North Africa: Jordan." Brookings. https://www.brookings.edu/wp-content/uploads/2020/12/MENA-Covid-19-Survey-Jordan-12-20-.pdf.

References

Bennett, A., and J.T. Checkel, eds. 2014. *Process Tracing: From Metaphor to Analytic Tool.* Cambridge: Cambridge University Press.

Berry, L. 2008. "The Impacts of Environmental Degradation on Refugee–Host Relationships." *African Security Studies* 17 (3): 125–31.

Berti, B. 2017. *Lebanon's Short Sighted Refugee Policy.* Washington, DC: Carnegie Endowment for International Peace.

Berti, B., and J. Paris. 2014. "Beyond Sectarianism: Geopolitics, Fragmentation, and the Syrian Civil War." *Strategic Assessment* 16 (4): 21–34.

Betts, A. 2010a. "The Refugee Regime Complex." *Refugee Survey Quarterly* 29 (1): 12–37.

– 2010b. "Survival Migration: A New Protection Framework." *Global Governance* 16 (3): 361.

– 2013. "Conclusion: Implementation Matters." In *Survival Migration: Failed Governance and the Crisis of Displacement,* 188–98. Ithaca, NY: Cornell University Press.

Betts, A., L. Bloom, J. D. Kaplan, and N. Omata. 2017. *Refugee Economies: Forced Displacement and Development.* Oxford: Oxford University Press.

Betts, A., and G. Loescher. 2011. *Refugees in International Relations.* Oxford: Oxford University Press.

Betts, A., F. Memişoğlu, and A. Ali. 2021. "What Difference Do Mayors Make? The Role of Municipal Authorities in Turkey and Lebanon's Response to Syrian Refugees." *Journal of Refugee Studies* 34 (1): 491–519.

Beydoun, Z., S. Abdulrahim, and G. Sakr. 2021. "Integration of Palestinian Refugee Children from Syria in UNRWA Schools in Lebanon." *Journal of International Migration and Integration* 22 (4): 1207–19.

Bhardwaj, M. 2012. "Development of Conflict in Arab Spring Libya and Syria: From Revolution to Civil War." *Washington University International Review* 1 (1): 76–99.

Bianchi, S. 2014. "Advocating 'Dignity' and 'Return' for Lebanon's Palestinians: Imagining a Diasporic Project." *Refugee Survey Quarterly* 33 (3): 118–38.

Bidinger, S., A. Lang, D. Hites, Y. Kuzmova, E. Noureddine, S. Akram, and T. Kistner. 2014. *Protecting Syrian Refugees: Laws, Policies, and Global Responsibility Sharing.* Boston: Boston University School of Law, International Human Rights Clinic.

Black, I. 2012. "Syrian President Assad Blames 'Foreign Conspiracies' for Crisis." *The Guardian,* 10 January 2012. https://www.theguardian.com/world/2012/jan/10/syrian-president-assad-foreign-conspiracies.

References

Blair, C.W., G. Grossman, and J.M. Weinstein. 2022. "Forced Displacement and Asylum Policy in the Developing World." *International Organization* 76 (2): 337–78.

Bloch, A., and L. Schuster. 2005. "Asylum Policy under New Labour." *Benefits* 13 (2): 115–18.

Blumont. 2020. *Legal Framework for HBBs in Jordan*. Amman, Jordan: Blumont.

Boustani, M., E. Carpi, H. Gebara, and Y. Mourad. 2016. "Responding to the Syrian Crisis in Lebanon: Collaboration between Aid Agencies and Local Governance Structures." IIED Working Paper. http://pubs.iied.org/10799IIED.

Bradley, M. 2009. "Obstacles to Realising Guiding Principle 29 in Afghanistan." *Forced Migration Review*, 24–5.

– 2011. "Unlocking Protracted Displacement: Central America's 'Success Story' Reconsidered." *Refugee Survey Quarterly* 30 (4): 84–121.

Britannica. 2022. "Baáth Party." Accessed 4 December 2022. https://www.britannica.com/topic/Bath-Party.

Brown, H., N. Giordano, C. Maughan, and A. Wadeson. 2019. "Vulnerability Assessment Framework: Population Study 2019." UNHCR, April 2019. https://data.unhcr.org/en/documents/download/68856.

Brun, C., and A. Fakih. 2022. "Debunking the Dangerous Myth That Refugees Are an Economic Burden in Lebanon." *The New Humanitarian*, 26 September 2022. https://www.thenewhumanitarian.org/opinion/2022/09/26/Syrian-refugees-Lebanon-economics.

Brun, C., A. Fakih, M. Shuayb, and M. Hammoud. 2021. *The Economic Impact of the Syrian Refugee Crisis in Lebanon: What It Means for Current Policies*. World Refugee & Migration Council Research Report. https://wrmcouncil.org/wp-content/uploads/2021/09/Lebanon-Syrian-Refugees-WRMC.pdf.

Brun, C., and M. Shuayb. 2020. "Exceptional and Futureless Humanitarian Education of Syrian Refugees in Lebanon: Prospects for Shifting the Lens." *Refuge: Canada's Journal on Refugees* 36 (2): 20–30.

Buckner, E., and N. Mozynah. 2019. "The Educational Response to Syrian Displacement: A Professionalizing Field in a Politicized Environment." In *Comparative Perspectives on Refugee Youth Education*, edited by A. Wiseman, L. Damaschke-Deitrick, E. Galegher, and M. Mark, 50–69. London: Routledge.

Bulos, N. 2019. "U.S. Punishes Syria with Sanctions – But Allies Like Jordan Also Pay a Price." *Los Angeles Times*, 10 September 2019.

https://www.latimes.com/world-nation/story/2019–09–09/u-s-ally-jordan-suffers-alongside-syria-under-sanctions-caused.

Butt, U. 2020. "Remembering Bashar Al-Assad Becoming President of Syria." *Middle East Monitor,* 17 July 2020. https://www.middleeast-monitor.com/20200717-remembering-bashar-al-assad-becoming-president-of-syria/.

Byman, D. 2022. "Hezbollah's Dilemmas." Brookings policy brief, November 2022. https://www.brookings.edu/articles/hezbollahs-dilemmas/.

Çakmak, C., and M. Ustaoğlu. 2015. "The Arab Spring and the Emergence of the Syrian Crisis." In *Post-Conflict Syrian State and Nation Building: Economic and Political Development,* edited by C. Çakmak and M. Ustaoğlu, 17–22. New York: Palgrave Pivot.

Calabrese, J. 2019. "China and Syria: In War and Reconstruction." Middle East Institute. https://www.mei.edu/publications/china-and-syria-war-and-reconstruction.

Camarena, K.R. 2015. "Refugee Policy as Foreign Policy: Third Party Intervention in Civil War." Annual Meeting of the American Political Science Association, San Francisco.

Canefe, N. 2017. "Migration as a Necessity: Contextualising the European Response to the Syrian Exodus." *Refugee Watch,* no. 48.

Capano, G., and M. Howlett. 2009. "Introduction: The Determinants of Policy Change; Advancing the Debate." *Journal of Comparative Policy Analysis* 11 (1): 1–5.

Carlson, M., L. Jakli, and K. Linos. 2018. "Rumors and Refugees: How Government-Created Information Vacuums Undermine Effective Crisis Management." *International Studies Quarterly* 62 (3): 671–85. https://doi.org/10.1093/isq/sqy018.

Carpenter, T. 2013. "Tangled Web: The Syrian Civil War and Its Implications." *Mediterranean Quarterly* 24 (1): 1–11. DOI: 10.1215/10474552-2018988.

Chalcraft, J. 2005. "Of Specters and Disciplined Commodities: Syrian Migrant Workers in Lebanon." *Middle East Report,* no. 236 (Fall 2005): 28–33.

Chatelard, G. 2010. "Jordan: A Refugee Haven." *Migration Information Source,* 31 August 2010. https://www.migrationpolicy.org/article/jordan-refugee-haven.

Chatty, D. 2016. "The Syrian Humanitarian Disaster: Disparities in Perceptions, Aspirations, and Behavior in Jordan, Lebanon and Turkey." *IDS Bulletin* 47 (3):10.

References

Chatty, Dawn, and Nisrine Mansour. 2011. "Unlocking Protracted Displacement: An Iraqi Case Study." *Refugee Survey Quarterly* 30 (4): 50–83.

Checkel, J.T. 1997. "International Norms and Domestic Politics: Bridging the Rationalist-Constructivist Divide." *European Journal of International Relations* 3 (4): 473–95.

Checkland, P. 1999. *Systems Thinking, Systems Practice.* Hoboken, NJ: John Wiley.

Chemali, L. el-. 2019. "Lebanon's Political Discourse and the Role of the UNHCR in the 'Safe and Secure Return' of Syrian Refugees from Lebanon into the So-Called 'Secure' Zones in Syria." In *Recent Migrations and Refugees in the MENA Region*, 81–97. London: Transnational Press.

Chetail, V. 2004. "Voluntary Repatriation in Public International Law: Concepts and Contents." *Refugee Survey Quarterly* 23 (3): 1–32.

Chimni, B.S. 2018. "Global Compact on Refugees: One Step Forward, Two Steps Back." *International Journal of Refugee Law* 30 (4): 630–4. https://doi.org/10.1093/ijrl/eey067.

Chopra, V. 2020. "'We're Not a Bank Providing Support': Street-Level Bureaucrats and Syrian Refugee Youth Navigating Tensions in Higher Education Scholarship Programs in Lebanon." *International Journal of Educational Development* 77 (September): 102216.

Chorev, Nitsan. 2023. "South–South Technology Transfer: the Case of Pharmaceutical Know-How in Kenya, Tanzania and Uganda." *Socio-Economic Review* 21 (1): 119–57.

Chulov, M. 2021. "Syrian Economy Lies in Ruins and China Sniffs Opportunity." *The Guardian*, 21 July 2021. https://www.theguardian.com/world/2021/jul/21/syrian-economy-ruins-china-sniffs-opportunity-assad.

CIA. 2004. *The World Factbook.* Retrieved from https://www.cia.gov/static/aceo93e73a538c79f31907a2a2b891fe/jordan-transport.jpg.

– 2007. *The World Factbook.* Retrieved from https://www.cia.gov/static/acbe10cc121dc36181dfc4074f3a8fc1/Syria_Transportation.jpg.

– 2018. *The World Factbook.* Retrieved from https://www.cia.gov/static/d91746419fac591fdb125d7cdd2cfee4/Lebanon_Transporation.jpg.

– 2020. *Syria: The World Factbook.* Accessed 19 August 2020, https://www.cia.gov/library/publications/the-world-factbook/geos/sy.html.

– 2022a. *Lebanon: The World Factbook.* Accessed 14 February 2024, https://www.cia.gov/the-world-factbook/countries/lebanon/.

– 2022b. *Jordan: The World Factbook.* Accessed 14 February 2024, https://www.cia.gov/the-world-factbook/countries/jordan/.

Clark-Ginsberg, A., J. Balagna, C.S. Nam, M. Casagrande, and O. Wilkinson. 2022. "Humanitarian Policymaking as Networked Governance: Social Network Analysis of the Global Compact on Refugees." *Journal of International Humanitarian Action* 7 (1): 1–13.

Clemens, E.S., and J.M. Cook. 1999. "Politics and Institutionalism: Explaining Durability and Change." *Annual Review of Sociology* 25 (1): 441–66.

Clemot, E.C. 2022. *Discerning Welcome: A Reformed Faith Approach to Refugees*. Eugene, OR: Wipf and Stock Publishers.

CMRS. 2018a. *Jordan Country Profile: Legal Instruments*. Accessed 16 June 2021, https://www4.aucegypt.edu/CMRS/ViewCountry.aspx?Country=Jordan.

– 2018b. *Lebanon Country Profile: Legal Instruments*. Accessed 16 June 2021, https://www4.aucegypt.edu/CMRS/ViewCountry.aspx?Country=Lebanon.

Cobban, H. 2019. *The Making of Modern Lebanon*. Milton Park, UK: Routledge.

Cole, Rosanna, Noor Al-Ma'aitah, and Rima Al Hasan. 2022. "Integrating Syrian Refugee Workers in Global Supply Chains: Creating Opportunities for Stable Trade." *Journal of Humanitarian Logistics and Supply Chain Management* 12 (3): 404–24.

Colebatch, H.K., and B.A. Radin. 2006. "Mapping the Work of Policy." In *The Work of Policy: An International Survey*, edited by W.T. Coombs and S.J. Holladay, 19–44. Lanham, MD: Lexington Books.

Collett, E. 2016. "The Paradox of the EU-Turkey Refugee Deal." Migration Policy Institute. https://www.migrationpolicy.org/news/paradox-eu-turkey-refugee-deal.

Collin, K. 2018. "7 Years into the Syrian War, Is There a Way Out?" Brookings. https://www.brookings.edu/blog/order-from-chaos/2018/03/16/7-years-into-the-syrian-war-is-there-a-way-out/.

Coombs, W.T., and S.J. Holladay, eds. 2022. *The Handbook of Crisis Communication*. Hoboken, NJ: John Wiley.

Corstange, D., and E. York. 2018. "Sectarian Framing in the Syrian Civil War." *American Journal of Political Science* 62 (2): 441–55.

Council of the European Union. 2022. *European Union's Position for the Association Council's 14th meeting*. Brussels: Council of the European Union.

Crawford, N.J.W. 2021. *The Urbanization of Forced Displacement: UNHCR, Urban Refugees, and the Dynamics of Policy Change*. Montreal: McGill-Queen's University Press.

References

Crea, Thomas M., Rocío Calvo, and Maryanne Loughry. 2015. "Refugee Health and Wellbeing: Differences between Urban and Camp-Based Environments in Sub-Saharan Africa." *Journal of Refugee Studies* 28 (3): 319–30.

Crisp, J. 2000. "Africa's Refugees: Patterns, Problems, and Policy Challenges." *Journal of Contemporary African Studies* 18 (2): 157–78. https://doi.org/10.1080/02589000050080986.

– 2004. "The Local Integration and Local Settlement of Refugees: A Conceptual and Historical Analysis." UNHCR, New Issues in Refugee Research, working paper no. 102. https://www.unhcr.org/media/local-integration-and-local-settlement-refugees-conceptual-and-historical-analysis-jeff-crisp.

– 2010. "Forced Displacement in Africa: Dimensions, Difficulties, and Policy Directions." *Refugee Survey Quarterly* 29 (3): 1–27.

Crisp, J., and K. Long. 2016. "Safe and Voluntary Refugee Repatriation: From Principle to Practice." *Journal on Migration and Human Security* 4 (3): 141–7. https://doi.org/10.1177/233150241600400305.

Crotty, W. 2003. "Presidential Policymaking in Crisis Situations: 9/11 and Its Aftermath." *Policy Studies Journal* 31 (3): 451–64.

Dados, N., and R. Connell. 2012. "The Global South." *Contexts* 11 (1): 12–13. https://doi.org/10.1177/1536504212436479.

Daher, J. 2018. "Popular Oral Culture and Sectarianism, a Materialist Analysis." *Syria Untold*, 31 October 2018. https://syriauntold.com/2018/10/31/popular-oral-culture-and-sectarianism-a-materialist-analysis/

– 2020. "The 'Caesar Bill': A Step towards Accountability in Syria, or a Worsening Economic Crisis?" *Syria Untold*, 27 January 2020. https://syriauntold.com/2020/01/27/the-caesar-bill-a-step-towards-accountability-in-syria-or-a-worsening-economic-crisis/.

– 2021. "The Private Banking Sector in Syria: Between Survival and Opportunity." Technical report, Middle East Directions, European University Institute.

– 2022a. "The Enemy of My Enemy: Hamas and the Syrian Regime." *Al-Araby*, 11 July 2022. https://english.alaraby.co.uk/opinion/enemy-my-enemy-hamas-and-syrian-regime.

– 2022b. "Water Scarcity, Mismanagement and Pollution in Syria." Research project report: Wartime and Post-Conflict in Syria, issue 2022/10, 27 June 2022. Middle East Directions Program, Robert Schuman Centre, EUI. Cadmus. https://cadmus.eui.eu/bitstream/handle/1814/74678/QM-09-22-308-EN-N.pdf?sequence=1&isAllowed=y.

Dahi, Omar. 2014 "The Refugee Crisis in Lebanon and Jordan: The Need for Economic Development Spending." *Forced Migration Review* 47 (September 2014): 11–13.

Daif, C. el-. 2022. *Access to Legal Stay and Labor for Syrians in Lebanon: Status and Prospects.* Beirut: Heinrich Böll Stiftung Beirut.

The Daily Star. 2012. "Hezbollah Sends First Aid Delegation to Refugees." Accessed 23 September 2018. http://www.dailystar.com.lb/News/Lebanon-News/2012/Sep-11/187468-hezbollah-sends-first-aid-delegation-to-refugees.ashx.

Dakroub, H. 2007. "Three-Month Battle Ends as Army Takes Over Refugee Camp." *The Guardian,* 3 September 2007. https://www.theguardian.com/world/2007/sep/03/syria.lebanon.

Daoudy, M. 2020. *The Origins of the Syrian Conflict: Climate Change and Human Security.* Cambridge, UK: Cambridge University Press.

David, A., M.A. Marouani, C. Nahas, and B. Nilsson. 2020. "The Economics of the Syrian Refugee Crisis in Neighboring Countries: The Case of Lebanon." *Economics of Transition and Institutional Change* 28 (1): 89–109.

David, P.A. 2005. "Path Dependence in Economic Processes: Implications for Policy Analysis in Dynamical Systems Contexts." In *The Evolutionary Foundations of Economics,* edited by J.S. Metcalfe and R. Ramlogan, 149–94. Cambridge, UK: Cambridge University Press.

Davidson, C. 2015. "The Temporary Permanence of Syrian Refugees in Jordan." PhD diss., University of Arkansas.

De Bel Air, F. 2016. "Jordan's Migration Profile." Migration Policy Centre. https://cadmus.eui.eu/bitstream/handle/1814/46504/RSCAS_PB_2017_12_MPC.pdf.

– 2017. "Migration Profile: Lebanon." Migration Policy Centre. Policy brief, issue 2017/12, May 2017.

De Greene, K.B., ed. 2012. *A Systems-Based Approach to Policymaking.* Berlin: Springer Science & Business Media.

De Hoop, J., M. Morey, and D. Seidenfeld. 2019. "No Lost Generation: Supporting the School Participation of Displaced Syrian Children in Lebanon." *Journal of Development Studies* 55 (sup1): 107–27.

DeLeon, P. 1992. "Policy Formulation: Where Ignorant Armies Clash by Night." *Review of Policy Research* 11 (3–4): 389–405.

Deng, N. 2022. "Refugees in Kenya's Kakuma and Dadaab Camps Are Still in Limbo." Al Jazeera, 28 May 2022. https://www.aljazeera.com/opinions/2022/5/28/refugees-in-kenyas-kakuma-and-dadaab-camps-are-still-in-limbo.

References

Devadas, S., I. Elbadawi, and N.V. Loayza. 2019. *Growth after War in Syria*. Policy Research Working Paper 8967. World Bank. August 2019. https://documents1.worldbank.org/curated/en/424551565105634645/pdf/Growth-after-War-in-Syria.pdf.

Devi, S. 2022. "11 Years of War in Syria." *The Lancet* 399 (10329): 1037–8. https://doi.org/10.1016/S0140-6736(22)00474-3.

Diab, Y.L. 2022. "What Ukraine, Afghanistan, and Syria Have Taught Us about the Politics of International Refugee Law." TRC *Journal of Humanitarian Action* 2 (2): 39–44. https://trcjha.com/article/what-ukraine-afghanistan-and-syria-have-taught-us-about-the-politics-of-international-refugee-law/.

DIIS (Danish Institute for International Studies). 2016. *The Neglected Palestinian Refugees in Lebanon and the Syrian Refugee Crisis*. Copenhagen and Beirut: The Danish Institute for International Studies and the Institute for Migration Studies, Lebanese American University. https://pure.diis.dk/ws/files/739488/DIIS_Report_2016_12_Web.pdf

Dionigi, F. 2016. *The Syrian Refugee Crisis in Lebanon: State Fragility and Social Resilience*. LSE Middle East Centre paper series 15. London: LSE Middle East Centre.

DoS (Jordan Department of Statistics). 2011. "Jordan in Numbers Report." Accessed 16 June 2021, http://dosweb.dos.gov.jo/DataBank/JordanInFigures/2011.pdf.

Dowding, K. 2015. *The Philosophy and Methods of Political Science*. London: Macmillan International Higher Education.

Dror, Y. 2017. *Policymaking under Adversity*. Milton Park, UK: Routledge.

Durieux, J.F. 2013. "Three Asylum Paradigms." *International Journal on Minority and Group Rights* 20 (2): 147–77.

DW. 2020. "Syrian Refugee Camp Burned to Ground in Northern Lebanon." 27 December 2020. https://www.dw.com/en/syrian-refugee-camp-burned-to-ground-in-northern-lebanon/a-56068640.

Dye, T.R. 1992. *Understanding Public Policy*. Englewood Cliffs, NJ: Prentice Hall.

EASO (European Asylum Support Office). 2020. *Syria Internally Displaced Persons, Returnees and Internal Mobility*. https://euaa.europa.eu/sites/default/files/publications/easo-coi-report-syria-idps-returnees-internal-mobility.pdf.

ERBD (European Bank for Reconstruction and Development). 2020. "Support to the Jordan Investment Commission: Terms of Reference." https://www.ebrd.com/sites/BlobServer?blobtable=MungoBlobs&

blobwhere=1399793887713&blobkey=id&blobcol=urldata&blobno
cache=true.

The Economist. 2015. "Europe's Crisis: Strangers in Strange Lands."
12 September 2015. https://www.economist.com/news/briefing/
21664217-worlds-institutional-approach-refugees-was-born-europe-
seven-decades-ago.

– 2021. "Who Controls Syria?" 26 May 2021. https://www.economist.
com/the-economist-explains/2021/05/26/who-controls-syria.

– 2022. "Democracy Index." 9 February 2022. https://www.economist.
com/graphic-detail/2022/02/09/a-new-low-for-global-democracy.

Edwards, B., and M. Cacciatori. 2018. "The Politics of International
Chemical Weapon Justice: The Case of Syria, 2011–2017."
Contemporary Security Policy 39 (2): 280–97.

El-Deeb, S. 2019. "Lebanon Announces the Formation of a New
Government after 9-Month Deadlock." *Time*, 31 January 2019. https://
web.archive.org/web/20190201014147/http://time.com/5517759/
lebanon-new-government/.

El-Hariri, K.E. 2020. "Analysing the Evolution of Lebanon's Syrian
Refugee Policy: The Role of Foreign Policy." In *Syrian Crisis, Syrian
Refugees*, edited by H. Altinay and S. Stetter, 65–82. Cham,
Switzerland: Palgrave Pivot.

Elmolla, J.H. 2019. "Birth Registration in Crisis: Exploring a Rights-
Based Approach to Birth Registration through the Experience of Syrian
Refugees." *International Journal of Refugee Law* 31 (4): 541–66.
https://doi.org/10.1093/ijrl/eez043.

El-Taliawi, O.G. Forthcoming. "Caught between Covid-19 and Sanctions:
What Policy Options Exist for Syrian Remittances in Jordan? An
Exploratory Study." UN ESCWA.

El-Taliawi, O.G., and T. Fakhoury. 2020. "What the Beirut Blast Means
for Lebanon's Refugees." *Cairo Review*, 11 September 2020. https://
www.thecairoreview.com/essays/what-the-beirut-blast-means-for-
lebanons-refugees/.

El-Taliawi, O.G., and K. Hartley. 2021. "The COVID-19 Crisis and
Complexity: A Soft Systems Approach." *Journal of Contingencies and
Crisis Management* 29 (1): 104–7.

El-Taliawi, Ola G., Luiz Leomil, and James Milner. 2021. "Where Is the
Policy in Refugee Studies? Enhancing the Role of Policy Studies in the
Study of Refugee Policy." Paper presented at the International
Conference on Public Policy, Panel T20P02 – Bridging the Gap between

Public Policy and Refugee Studies: Tools, Concepts and Frameworks for the Study of Refugee Policy, Barcelona, July 2021.

El-Taliawi, O.G., S. Nair, and Z. van der Wal. 2021. "Public Policy Schools in the Global South: A Mapping and Analysis of the Emerging Landscape." *Policy Sci* 54:371–95. https://doi.org/10.1007/s11077-020-09413-z.

El-Taliawi, O.G., and Z. van der Wal. 2019. "Developing Administrative Capacity: An Agenda for Research and Practice." *Policy Design and Practice* 2 (3): 243–57.

Enab Baladi. 2021. "Jordan and Syria Reoperate Jaber-Nassib Border Crossing." 29 July 2021. https://english.enabbaladi.net/archives/2021/07/jordan-and-syria-reoperate-jaber-nassib-border-crossing-here-are-the-details/.

Enders, D. 2018. "Lebanese Foreign Minister Battles UNHCR over Refugee Policy on Return." *The National*, 11 June 2018. https://www.thenationalnews.com/world/mena/lebanese-foreign-minister-battles-unhcr-over-refugee-policy-on-return-1.739062.

Eran, O. 2018. *Demonstrations in Jordan: A Bona Fide Threat to the Regime?* INSS Insight No. 1065.

– 2020. *Jordan: A New Political System Faces Longstanding Problems.* INSS Insight No. 1393.

ESCWA (Economic and Social Commission for Western Asia). 2016. *Syria at War: Five Years On.* United Nations, January 2016. https://www.unescwa.org/publications/syria-war-five-years.

– 2020. *Syria at War: Eight Years On.* United Nations. https://www.unescwa.org/publications/syria-war-eight-years.

– 2021. *Multidimensional Poverty in Lebanon (2019–2021): Painful Reality and Uncertain Prospects.* Policy brief. https://www.unescwa.org/sites/default/files/news/docs/21-00634-_multidimentional_poverty_in_lebanon_-policy_brief_-_en.pdf.

EUI (European University Institute). 2022. "Turkish-Syrian Rapprochement: Rhetoric and Motivations." *MEDirections Blog*, 7 October 2022. https://blogs.eui.eu/medirections/turkish-syrian-rapprochement-rhetoric-and-motivations/.

European Commission. 2017. *The EU-Jordan Partnership: The Compact.* https://ec.europa.eu/neighbourhood-enlargement/sites/near/files/jordan-compact.pdf.

– 2018. *European Civil Protection and Humanitarian Aid Operations: Lebanon Fact Sheet.* https://ec.europa.eu/echo/where/middle-east/lebanon_en.

- 2022. "Responding to the Syrian Crisis: EU Support in Jordan." https://neighbourhood-enlargement.ec.europa.eu/system/files/2022-05/06052022_factsheet_eu_support_jordan.pdf.

European Parliament. 2017. "Syrian Crisis: Impact on Iraq." https://www.europarl.europa.eu/thinktank/en/document.html?reference=EPRS_BRI%282017%29599387.

Fakhoury, T. 2017. "Governance Strategies and Refugee Response: Lebanon in the Face of Syrian Displacement." *International Journal of Middle East Studies* 49 (4): 681–700. https://doi.org/10.1017/S0020743817000654.

- 2020. "Refugee Governance in Crisis: The Case of the EU-Lebanon Compact." Migration Governance and Asylum Crises. https://www.magyc.uliege.be/wp-content/uploads/2021/01/D2.3-v1December2020.pdf.

- 2021. "Refugee Return and Fragmented Governance in the Host State: Displaced Syrians in the Face of Lebanon's Divided Politics." *Third World Quarterly* 42 (1): 162–180.

- 2022. "The External Dimension of EU Migration Policy as Region-Building? Refugee Cooperation as Contentious Politics." *Journal of Ethnic and Migration Studies* 48 (12): 2908–26. https://doi.org/10.1080/1369183X.2021.1972568.

Fakhoury, T., and D. Ozkul. 2019. "Syrian Refugees' Return from Lebanon." *Forced Migration Review* 62 (October): 26–8.

Fakih, A., and M. Ibrahim. 2016. "The Impact of Syrian Refugees on the Labor Market in Neighboring Countries: Empirical Evidence from Jordan." *Defence and Peace Economics* 27 (1): 64–86.

FAO (Food and Agriculture Organization of the United Nations). 2020. *GIEWS Country Brief: Jordan.* https://reliefweb.int/sites/reliefweb.int/files/resources/JOR_8.pdf.

FAOSTAT. 2022. *Syria Data.* https://www.fao.org/faostat/en/#search/agriculture%20GDP%20Syria.

Faour, M.A. 2007. "Religion, Demography, and Politics in Lebanon." *Middle Eastern Studies* 43 (6): 909–21.

Fee, M. 2022. "Lives Stalled: The Costs of Waiting for Refugee Resettlement." *Journal of Ethnic and Migration Studies* 48 (11): 2659–77.

Feller, E. 2006. "Asylum, Migration, and Refugee Protection: Realities, Myths, and the Promise of Things to Come." *International Journal of Refugee Law* 18 (3–4): 509–36.

Ferdinand, P. 2013. *The Positions of Russia and China at the UN Security*

Council in the Light of Recent Crises. European Parliament, 5 March 2013. https://op.europa.eu/en/publication-detail/-/publication/8548d4c3-e486-42e7-9462-7e3ed914a470.

Ferris, E., and K. Kirişci. 2016. *The Consequences of Chaos: Syria's Humanitarian Crisis and the Failure to Protect*. Washington, DC: Brookings Institute.

Ferris, E., K. Kirişci, and S. Shaikh. 2013. "Syrian Crisis: Massive Displacement, Dire Needs and a Shortage of Solutions." Brookings, 18 September 2013. https://www.brookings.edu/research/syrian-crisis-massive-displacement-dire-needs-and-a-shortage-of-solutions/.

Fiddian-Qasmiyeh, E. 2011. "The Pragmatics of Performance: Putting 'Faith' in Aid in the Sahrawi Refugee Camps." *Journal of Refugee Studies* 24 (3): 533–47.

Fiddian-Qasmiyeh, E., G. Loescher, K. Long, and N. Sigona, eds. 2014. *The Oxford Handbook of Refugee and Forced Migration Studies*. Oxford: Oxford University Press.

Fiddian-Qasmiyeh, E., and J. Pacitto. 2019. "Southern-Led Faith-Based Responses to Refugees: Insights for the Global North." In *Religion and European Society: A Primer*, edited by B. Schewel and E. Wilson, 195–214. Hoboken, NJ: John Wiley.

Fielden, A. 2008. *Local Integration: An Under-Reported Solution to Protracted Refugee Situations*. UNHCR, Policy Development and Evaluation Service. https://www.unhcr.org/media/local-integration-under-reported-solution-protracted-refugee-situations-alexandra-fielden.

FitzGerald, D.S., and R. Arar. 2018. "The Sociology of Refugee Migration." *Annual Review of Sociology* 44:387–406.

Forrester, J.W. 1993. "System Dynamics and the Lessons of 35 Years." In *A Systems-Based Approach to Policymaking*, edited by K.G. De Greene, 199–240. Berlin: Springer.

Fouad, F.M., S.J. McCall, H. Ayoub, L.J. Abu-Raddad, and G.R. Mumtaz. 2021. "Vulnerability of Syrian Refugees in Lebanon to COVID-19: Quantitative Insights." *Conflict and Health* 15:13. https://doi.org/10.1186/s13031-021-00349-6.

FOX News. 2016. "Interview with Queen Rania of Jordan." https://www.youtube.com/watch?v=EoPyFyi_Wt8.

France24 News. 2022. "Hamas Resumes Syria Ties in Damascus Visit." 19 October 2022. https://www.france24.com/en/live-news/20221019-hamas-resumes-syria-ties-in-damascus-visit.

Francis, A. 2015. *Jordan's Refugee Crisis*. Vol. 21. Washington, DC: Carnegie Endowment for International Peace.

Frangieh, G. 2016. "Relations between UNHCR and Arab Governments: Memoranda of Understanding in Lebanon and Jordan." *LSE Middle East Centre Blog*, 23 September 2016. https://blogs.lse.ac.uk/mec/2016/09/23/relations-between-unhcr-and-arab-governments-memoranda-of-understanding-in-lebanon-and-jordan/.

Freedman, J., Z. Kıvılcım, and N. Baklacıoğlu, eds. 2017. *A Gendered Approach to the Syrian Refugee Crisis*. Abingdon, UK: Routledge.

Freedom House. 2022a. *Freedom in the World 2022*. Accessed 12 December 2022. https://freedomhouse.org/explore-the-map?type=fotn&year=2022&country=JOR.

– 2022b. *Freedom in the World 2022: Lebanon*. Accessed 12 December 2022. https://freedomhouse.org/country/lebanon/freedom-world/2022.

Freeman, G.P. 1985. "National Styles and Policy Sectors: Explaining Structured Variation." *Journal of Public Policy* 5 (4): 467–96. http://www.jstor.org/stable/3998398.

Freier, L.F., N.R. Micinski, and G. Tsourapas. 2021. "Refugee Commodification: The Diffusion of Refugee Rent-Seeking in the Global South." *Third World Quarterly* 42 (11): 2747–66.

Geddes, B. 1990. "How the Cases You Choose Affect the Answers You Get: Selection Bias in Comparative Politics." *Political Analysis* 2:131–50.

Geha, C. 2019a. *Political Complexities of Return: Syrian Refugees in Lebanon*. Middle East Institute, 14 May 2019. https://www.mei.edu/publications/political-complexities-return-syrian-refugees-lebanon.

– 2019b. "Politics of a Garbage Crisis: Social Networks, Narratives, and Frames of Lebanon's 2015 Protests and Their Aftermath." *Social Movement Studies*, 78–92.

Geha, C., and J. Talhouk. 2019. "From Recipients of Aid to Shapers of Policies: Conceptualizing Government–United Nations Relations during the Syrian Refugee Crisis in Lebanon." *Journal of Refugee Studies* 32 (4): 645–63.

George, A.L., and A. Bennett. 2005. *Case Studies and Theory Development in the Social Sciences*. Cambridge, MA: MIT Press.

Gerring, J. 2006. *Case Study Research: Principles and Practices*. Cambridge, UK: Cambridge University Press.

Geukjian, O. 2016. *Lebanon after the Syrian Withdrawal: External Intervention, Power-Sharing and Political Instability*. Milton Park, UK: Routledge.

Ghalayini, N., G. Ismail, and H.A. El-Ghali. 2016. "Responding to Crisis: Syrian Refugee Education in Lebanon." Policy Brief 7/2016. American University in Beirut Policy Institute.

References

Ghazal, M. 2017. "Jordan Hosts 657,000 Registered Syrian Refugees." *Jordan Times*, 21 March 2017. https://jordantimes.com/news/local/jordan-hosts-657000-registered-syrian-refugees.

Gibson, I. 2015. "An Analysis of Jordan's 2013 Policy Regarding Iraqi Refugees." *Social Identities* 21 (3): 199–210.

Gifkins, J. 2012. "Briefing: The UN Security Council Divided; Syria in Crisis." *Global Responsibility to Protect* 4 (3): 377–93. https://doi.org/10.1163/1875984X-00403009.

Gil-Bazo, M.T. 2015. "Refugee Protection under International Human Rights Law: From Non-refoulement to Residence and Citizenship." *Refugee Survey Quarterly* 34 (1): 11–42. https://doi.org/10.1093/rsq/hduo21.

Gill, N. 2010. "New State-Theoretic Approaches to Asylum and Refugee Geographies." *Progress in Human Geography* 34 (5): 626–45.

Gilsinan, K. 2015. "The Confused Person's Guide to the Syrian Civil War." *The Atlantic*, 29 October 2015.

Giorgio, C. 2020. *China Plays the Long Game on Syria*. Middle East Institute, 10 February 2010. https://www.mei.edu/publications/china-plays-long-game-syria.

Gleick, P. 2014. "Water, Drought, Climate Change, and Conflict in Syria." *American Meteorological Society* 6 (3): 331–40. https://doi.org/10.1175/WCAS-D-13-00059.1.

GoJ (Government of Jordan). 2018. "About Jordan." Accessed 21 September 2018. https://jordan.gov.jo/wps/portal/Home/AboutJordan.

Goodwin-Gill, G.S., and J. McAdam. 2007. *The Refugee in International Law*. 3rd ed. Oxford: Oxford University Press.

Göransson, M.B., L. Hultin, and M. Mähring. 2020. "'The Phone Means Everything': Mobile Phones, Livelihoods, and Social Capital among Syrian Refugees in Informal Tented Settlements in Lebanon." *Migration and Development* 9 (3): 331–51.

Gordenker, L. 2015. *International Aid and National Decision: Development Programs in Malawi, Tanzania, and Zambia*. Princeton, NJ: Princeton University Press.

Gordon, J. 2019. *Refugees and Decent Work: Lessons Learned from Recent Refugee Jobs Compacts*. International Labour Organization, 17 December 2019. https://www.ilo.org/employment/Whatwedo/Publications/working-papers/WCMS_732602/lang--en/index.htm

Gottwald, M. 2014. "Burden Sharing and Refugee Protection." In Fiddian-Qasmiyeh et al., *The Oxford Handbook of Refugee and Forced Migration*, 525–38.

Goldberg, J. 2013. "The Modern King in the Arab Spring." *The Atlantic*, April 2013. https://www.theatlantic.com/magazine/archive/2013/04/monarch-in-the-middle/309270/.

Greenhill, K.M. 2011. *Weapons of Mass Migration: Forced Displacement, Coercion, and Foreign Policy*. Ithaca, NY: Cornell University Press.

Grütters, C. 2007. "System Dynamics Methodology and Dutch Asylum Policy." Working Paper for "Migration Control and Societal Steering" Workshop, Edinburgh, Scotland.

The Guardian. 2013. "Hezbollah Leader Vows to Stand by Syrian Regime in Fight against Rebels." 25 May 2013. https://www.theguardian.com/world/2013/may/25/hezbollah-leader-syria-assad-qusair.

– 2014. "Syrian Refugee Killed in Riot at Camp in Jordan." 6 April 2014. https://www.theguardian.com/world/2014/apr/06/damascus-opera-house-syrian-rebels-shelling.

Guild, E. 2006. "The Europeanisation of Europe's Asylum Policy." *International Journal of Refugee Law* 18 (3–4): 630–51.

Haddad, E. 2008. *The Refugee: The Individual between Sovereigns*. Cambridge: Cambridge University Press.

Haidar, N. 2020. "Radical Lawyering in Times of Revolution: Dispatches from Lebanon." *Socialist Lawyer*, no. 84: 20–34. https://doi.org/10.13169/socialistlawyer.84.0030.

Hajdukowski-Ahmed, M., N. Khanlou, and H. Moussa. 2008. *Not Born a Refugee Woman: Contesting Identities, Rethinking Practices*. New York: Berghahn Books.

Hamadeh, S. 2019. "A Critical Analysis of the Syrian Refugee Education Policies in Lebanon Using a Policy Analysis Framework." *Journal of Education Policy* 34 (3): 374–93.

Hamlin, R. 2022. "Institutional Analyses of Refugee Protection." *Journal of Refugee Studies* 36 (3): 584. https://doi.org/10.1093/jrs/feaco45.

Hammerstad, A. 2014. "The Securitization of Forced Migration." In Fiddian-Qasmiyeh et al., *The Oxford Handbook of Refugee and Forced Migration*, 265–77.

Hammond, L. 2014. "'Voluntary' Repatriation and Reintegration." In Fiddian-Qasmiyeh et al., *The Oxford Handbook of Refugee and Forced Migration*, 499–511.

Hanmer, L., E. Rubiano, J. Santamaria, and D.J. Arango. 2020. "How Does Poverty Differ among Refugees? Taking a Gender Lens to the Data on Syrian Refugees in Jordan." *Middle East Development Journal* 12 (2): 208–42.

References

Hansen, R. 2014. "State Controls: Borders, Refugees and Citizenship." In Fiddian-Qasmiyeh et al., *The Oxford Handbook of Refugee and Forced Migration*, 253–64.

Hardan, M. 2021. "Is Opening of Jordanian-Syrian Crossing Politically Motivated?" *Al-Monitor*, 25 April 2021. https://www.al-monitor.com/originals/2021/04/opening-jordanian-syrian-crossing-politically-motivated.

Harper, A. 2008. "Iraqi Refugees: Ignored and Unwanted." *International Review of the Red Cross* 90 (869): 169–90.

Harrell-Bond, B. 2008. "Building the Infrastructure for the Observance of Refugee Rights in the Global South." *Refuge* 25:12.

Harris, W. 2005. "Bashar al-Assad's Lebanon Gamble." *Middle East Quarterly* 12:33–44.

Harvey, C. 2015. "Time for Reform? Refugees, Asylum-Seekers, and Protection under International Human Rights Law." *Refugee Survey Quarterly* 34 (1): 43–60.

Harvey, William S. 2011. "Strategies for Conducting Elite Interviews." *Qualitative Research* 11 (4): 431–41.

Hassan, H. 2018. "The True Origins of ISIS." *The Atlantic*, 30 November 2018. https://www.theatlantic.com/ideas/archive/2018/11/isis-origins-anbari-zarqawi/577030/.

Head, B.W. 2008. "Wicked Problems in Public Policy." *Public Policy* 3 (2): 101–18.

Heale, Roberta, and Alison Twycross. 2018. "What Is a Case Study?" *Evidence-Based Nursing* 21 (1): 7–8.

Henriksen, A. 2018. "Trump's Missile Strike on Syria and the Legality of Using Force to Deter Chemical Warfare." *Journal of Conflict & Security Law* 23 (1): 33–48.

Hernes, V. 2018. "Cross-National Convergence in Times of Crisis? Integration Policies before, during and after the Refugee Crisis." *West European Politics* 41 (6): 1305–29.

Heydemann, S. 2020. "Pity the Nation: Assessing a Half-Century of Assadist Rule." Brookings, 14 December 2020. https://www.brookings.edu/blog/order-from-chaos/2020/12/14/pity-the-nation-assessing-a-half-century-of-assadist-rule/.

Hill, M.J., and P.L. Hupe. 2014. *Implementing Public Policy: An Introduction to the Study of Operational Governance*. 3rd ed. Thousand Oaks, CA: Sage.

Holmes, O. 2014. "Militants Pull Out of Lebanese Border Town with Captives." Reuters, 7 August 2014. https://www.reuters.com/article/

us-lebanon-security-arsal/militants-pull-out-of-lebanese-border-town-with-captives-idUSKBN0G70HC20140807.

Hokayem, E. 2012. "Syria and Its Neighbours." *Survival: Global Politics and Strategy* 54 (2): 7–14.

Hokayem, E. 2014. "Iran, the Gulf States and the Syrian Civil War." *Adelphi Papers* 54 (447–8): 39–70. https://doi.org/10.1080/19445571.2014.995937.

Hollenbach, D. 2014. "Religion and Forced Migration." In Fiddian-Qasmiyeh et al., *The Oxford Handbook of Refugee and Forced Migration*, 447–59.

Holliday, J. 2011. *The Struggle for Syria in 2011: An Operational and Regional Analysis*. Washington, DC: ISW.

Holzer, B., F. Kastner, and T. Werron. eds. 2014. *From Globalization to World Society: Neo-Institutional and Systems-Theoretical Perspectives*. Milton Park, UK: Routledge.

Hovil, L. 2007. "Self-Settled Refugees in Uganda: An Alternative Approach to Displacement?" *Journal of Refugee Studies* 20 (4): 599–620. https://doi.org/10.1093/jrs/fem035.

– 2014. "Local Integration." In Fiddian-Qasmiyeh et al., *The Oxford Handbook of Refugee and Forced Migration*, 488–98.

Hovil, L., and N. Maple. 2022. "Local Integration: A Durable Solution in Need of Restoration?" *Refugee Survey Quarterly* 41 (2): 238–66.

Howlett, M., and M. Ramesh. 2003. *Studying Public Policy: Policy Cycles and Policy Subsystems*. 2nd ed. Don Mills, ON: Oxford University Press.

HRW (Human Rights Watch). 2011. "Syria: Jailed for 'Weakening National Sentiment.'" Accessed 17 August 2023. https://www.hrw.org/news/2011/01/27/syria-jailed-weakening-national-sentiment.

– 2012. "Syria Neighbors Keep Borders Open for Refugees." Accessed 21 September 2018. https://www.hrw.org/news/2012/08/29/syria-neighbors-keep-borders-open-refugees.

– 2014a. "Jordan: Syrians Blocked, Stranded in Desert." Accessed 21 September 2018. https://www.hrw.org/news/2015/06/03/jordan-syrians-blocked-stranded-desert.

– 2014b. "Lebanon: At Least 45 Local Curfews Imposed on Syrian Refugees." Accessed 21 September 2018. https://www.hrw.org/news/2014/10/03/lebanon-least-45-local-curfews-imposed-syrian-refugees.

– 2016a. "Growing Up without an Education: Barriers to Education for Syrian Refugee Children in Lebanon." Accessed 26 May 2020. https://

www.hrw.org/report/2016/07/19/growing-without-education/
barriers-education-syrian-refugee-children-lebanon.

– 2016b. "Lebanon: Residency Rules Put Syrians at Risk." Accessed
22 September 2018. https://www.hrw.org/news/2016/01/12/
lebanon-residency-rules-put-syrians-risk.

– 2016c. "Lebanon: Stop Forcible Returns to Syria." Accessed 20 August
2023.https://www.hrw.org/news/2016/01/11/lebanon-stop-forcible-returns-
syria.

– 2017. "Jordan: Syrian Refugees Being Summarily Deported." Accessed
5 December 2022. https://www.hrw.org/news/2017/10/02/jordan-syrian-
refugees-being-summarily-deported.

– 2019. "Lebanon: Syrian Refugee Shelters Demolished." Accessed 20
May 2019.https://www.hrw.org/news/2019/07/05/lebanon-syrian-refugee-
shelters-demolished.

– 2020. "Lebanon: Refugees at Risk in COVID-19 Response." Accessed 26
May 2020. https://www.hrw.org/news/2020/04/02/lebanon-refugees
risk-covid-19-response.

– 2021. "They Killed Us from the Inside: An Investigation into the August
4 Beirut Blast." Accessed 5 December 2022. https://www.hrw.org/
report/2021/08/03/they-killed-us-inside/investigation-august-4-beirut-
blast.

– 2022. "Forced Return of Syrians by Lebanon Unsafe and Unlawful."
https://www.hrw.org/news/2022/07/06/forced-return-syrians-lebanon-unsafe-
and-unlawful.

Huang, C., and Gough, K. 2019. *The Jordan Compact: Three Years
on; Where Do We Stand?* Washington, DC: Center for Global
Development.

Hudson, M.C. 1997. "Palestinians and Lebanon: The Common Story."
Journal of Refugee Studies 10 (3): 243–60.

Hughes, G. 2014. "Syria and the Perils of Proxy Warfare." *Small Wars &
Insurgencies* 25 (3): 522–38.

Hultin, L., L. De Introna, M.B. Göransson, and M. Mähring. 2022.
"Precarity, Hospitality, and the Becoming of a Subject That Matters:
A Study of Syrian Refugees in Lebanese Tented Settlements."
Organization Studies 43 (5): 669–97.

Içduygu, A., and D.B. Aksel. 2022. "Vulnerable Permanency in Mass
Influx: Refugees on the Move; Crisis and Response in Turkey and
Europe." In *Refugees on the Move: Crisis and Response in Turkey and
Europe,* vol. 45, edited by Erol Balkan and Zümray Kutlu-Tonak, 133.
New York: Berghahn Books, 2022.

Içduygu, A., and M. Nimer. 2020. "The Politics of Return: Exploring the Future of Syrian Refugees in Jordan, Lebanon and Turkey." *Third World Quarterly* 41 (3): 415–33.

ICG (International Crisis Group). 2017. *Hizbollah's Syria Conundrum.* Middle East Report No. 175. https://www.crisisgroup.org/middle-east-north-africa/eastern-mediterranean/lebanon/175-hizbollah-s-syria-conundrum.

IDMC (Internal Displacement Monitoring Centre). 2020. "Syria: Reconstruction and Challenges around Housing and Property." https://www.internal-displacement.org/publications/syria-reconstruction-and-challenges-around-housing-land-and-property.

– 2022. "Syria Country Profile." Accessed 6 December 2022. https://www.internal-displacement.org/countries/syria.

Idris, A. 2012. "Malaysia and Forced Migration." *Intellectual Discourse* 20 (1). https://journals.iium.edu.my/intdiscourse/index.php/id/article/view/276.

IDS (Institute of Development Studies). 2018. "Urban Refugees in Lebanon: Housing, Residency, and Wellbeing." Accessed 20 May 2020. https://www.ids.ac.uk/publications/urban-refugees-in-lebanon-housing-residency-and-wellbeing.

Ihlamur-Öner, S.G. 2013. "Turkey's Refugee Regime Stretched to the Limit? The Case of Iraqi and Syrian Refugee Flows." *Perceptions* 18 (3): 191.

ILO (International Labour Organization). 2019. "EU-ILO Collaboration in the Monitoring of Labour Aspects in the Implementation of the EU's Rules of Origin Initiative for Jordan (Phase II)." https://www.ilo.org/beirut/projects/WCMS_713067/lang--en/index.htm.

Ineli-Ciger, M. 2019. "The Global Compact on Refugees and Burden Sharing: Will the Compact Address the Normative Gap Concerning Burden Sharing?" *Refugee Survey Quarterly* 38 (2): 115–38.

Intelligence Online. 2022. "Amman and Damascus Coordinate Intelligence to Bring Refugees Home." Accessed 14 September 2022. https://www.intelligenceonline.com/government-intelligence/2022/09/14/amman-and-damascus-coordinate-intelligence-to-bring-refugees-home,109812586-art.

IMF (International Monetary Fund). 2018. *World Economic Outlook Database.* Accessed 21 September 2018. https://www.imf.org/external/pubs/ft/weo/2017/02/weodata/weorept.aspx?pr.x=20&pr.y=3&sy=2010&ey=2016&scsm=1&ssd=1&sort=country&ds=.&br=1&c=446&s=GGXWDN_NGDP&grp=0&a=.

References

– 2022. *World Economic Outlook Database: General Government Gross Debt.* Accessed 15 December 2022. http://www.imf.org/external/datamapper/GGXWDG_NGDP@WEO/OEMDC/ADVEC/WEOWORLD/JOR.

IRIN. 2015. "A Timeline of Syria's Closing Border." *IRIN News,* 8 January 2015. http://newirin.irinnews.org/syrian-refugees-restrictions-timeline.

ISDR (International Strategy for Disaster Reduction). 2011. "Drought Vulnerability in the Arab Region: Case Study – Drought in Syria – Ten Years of Scarce Water (2000–2010)." Cairo: United Nations, Secretariat of the International Strategy for Disaster Reduction. https://www.undrr.org/publication/drought-vulnerability-arab-region-case-study-drought-syria-ten-years-scarce-water-2000.

Issawi, C. 1983. *An Economic History of the Middle East and North Africa.* New York: Columbia University Press.

Jackson Sow, M. 2022. "Ukrainian Refugees, Race, and International Law's Choice between Order and Justice." *American Journal of International Law* 116 (4): 698–709. https://doi.org/10.1017/ajil.2022.56.

Jacobsen, K. 1996. "Factors Influencing the Policy Responses of Host Governments to Mass Refugee Influxes." *International Migration Review* 30 (3): 655–78.

– 2002. "Livelihoods in Conflict: The Pursuit of Livelihoods by Refugees and the Impact on the Human Security of Host Communities." *International Migration* 40 (5): 95–123.

– 2014. "Livelihoods and Forced Migration." In Fiddian-Qasmiyeh et al., *The Oxford Handbook of Refugee and Forced Migration,* 99–111.

Jadarat, H. 2010. "Jordan's Economy: Crisis, Challenge and Measures." Accessed 16 June 2021, https://www.oecd.org/gov/budgeting/46382448.pdf.

Jaji, R. 2014. "Religious and Ethnic Politics in Refugee Hosting: Somalis in Nairobi, Kenya." *Ethnicities* 14 (5): 634–49.

Jalabi, R.. 2013. "Lebanon's Government to Postpone Elections until November 2014." *The Guardian,* 31 May 2013. https://www.theguardian.com/world/2013/may/31/lebanon-elections-postponed-2014.

Jamail, D. 2013. "Jordan to Host Largest Refugee Camp." Al Jazeera. Accessed 21 September 2018. http://www.aljazeera.com/humanrights/2013/05/20135136445430108.html.

James, C.C., and Ö. Özdamar. 2009. "Modeling Foreign Policy and Ethnic

Conflict: Turkey's Policies towards Syria." *Foreign Policy Analysis* 5 (1): 17–36. https://doi.org/10.1111/j.1743–8594.2008.00081.x.

Janmyr, M. 2018. "UNHCR and the Syrian Refugee Response: Negotiating Status and Registration in Lebanon." *International Journal of Human Rights* 22 (3): 393–419. https://doi.org/10.1080/13642987.2017.1371140.

Janmyr, M., and L. Mourad. 2018. "Modes of Ordering: Labelling, Classification, and Categorization in Lebanon's Refugee Response." *Journal of Refugee Studies* 31 (4): 544–65.

Jasser, M.Z. 2014. "Sectarian Conflict in Syria." *PRISM* 4:58–67. http://www.jstor.org/stable/26469777.

Jesse, J.K. 1998. "Policy Networks and Resource Dependencies: Third World Governments, International Organizations, and Refugee Policy Making." PhD diss., University of Wisconsin-Milwaukee.

JIF (Jordan INGO Forum). 2020. *Walk the Talk for the Jordan Compact: Progress and Challenges in Implementing the Commitments Made in the Brussels Conference 2019 by Jordan and the International Community (June 2020).* Amman, Jordan: JIF.

Jochim, A.E., and P.J. May. 2010. "Beyond Subsystems: Policy Regimes and Governance." *Policy Studies Journal* 38 (2): 303–27.

Jordan, A., S. Akil, and K. Shaar. 2022. "Data Shows Nowhere in Syria Is Safe for Return." Washington, DC: Middle East Institute.

Jordan. Ministry of Water and Irrigation. 2009. *Water for Life: Jordan's Water Strategy (2008–2022).* 19 May 2009. http://www.emwis.org/thematicdirs/news/2009/05/jordan-jd586b-water-strategy-finalized.

Jordan Times. 2016a. "Jordan to Respond with Iron Fist to Threat, King Says, as 6 Troops Killed in Border Terror Attack." 22 June 2016. http://www.jordantimes.com/news/local/jordan-respond-iron-fist-threat-king-says-6-troops-killed-border-terror-attack.

– 2016b. "2015 Budget Deficit up by JD346m as Revenues Drop." 21 March 2016. http://www.jordantimes.com/news/local/2015-budget-deficit-jd346m-revenues-drop.

Joseph, J., S. Henderson, M. Withers, and R. Shivakoti. 2022. "Regulation through Responsibilisation: Gendered Exit Policies and Precarious Migration from India and Sri Lanka." *International Migration* special issue, 1–14. https://doi.org/10.1111/imig.13074.

JRPSC (Jordan Response Plan for the Syria Crisis). 2013. *Needs Assessment Review.* http://www.undp.org/content/dam/rbas/doc/SyriaResponse/Jordan%20Needs%20Assessment%20-%20November%202013.pdf.

– 2016. *The Jordan Response Plan for the Syria Crisis: Executive Summary (2016–2018).* http://www.jrp.gov.jo/Files/JRP2016.pdf.

– 2017. *The Jordan Response Plan for the Syria Crisis (2017–2019).* https://www.susana.org/en/knowledge-hub/resources-and-publications/library/details/3356#.

Jubilut, L.L., and W.P. Carneiro. 2011. "Resettlement in Solidarity: A New Regional Approach towards a More Humane Durable Solution." *Refugee Survey Quarterly* 30 (3): 63–86.

Kaduri, E., and J. Essa. 2022. *11 Years of War in Syria: Situation Assessment.* Tel Aviv: INSS.

Kagan, M. 2002. "Assessment of Refugee Status Determination Procedure at UNHCR's Cairo Office, 2001–2002." 1–49. https://fount.aucegypt.edu/faculty_journal_articles/5050.

– 2012. "The UN 'Surrogate State' and the Foundation of Refugee Policy in the Middle East." *U.C. Davis Journal of International Law & Policy* 18 (2): 307.

Kaiser, T. 2005. "Participating in Development? Refugee Protection, Politics, and Developmental Approaches to Refugee Management in Uganda." *Third World Quarterly* 26 (2): 351–67.

Kalia, K. 2006. "Crisis in Lebanon Displaces Lebanese, Foreign Workers, and Refugees." *Migration Policy Institute*, 1 December 2006.

Kaltmeier, O. 2015. *Concepts of the Global South.* Cologne, Germany: Global South Studies Center, University of Cologne.

Karam, J. 2017. "Beyond Sectarianism: Understanding Lebanese Politics through a Cross-Sectarian Lens." Brandeis University, April 2017. https://www.brandeis.edu/crown/publications/middle-east-briefs/pdfs/101–200/meb107.pdf.

Karasapan, O. 2022. *Forcibly Displaced Ukrainians: Lessons from Syria and Beyond.* Washington, DC: Brookings.

Kato, J. 2003. *Regressive Taxation and the Welfare State. Path Dependence and Policy Diffusion.* Cambridge, UK: Cambridge University Press.

Kaunert, C. 2009. "Liberty versus Security? EU Asylum Policy and the European Commission." *Journal of Contemporary European Research* 5 (2): 148–70.

Kay, A., and P. Baker. 2015. "What Can Causal Process Tracing Offer to Policy Studies? A Review of the Literature." *Policy Studies Journal* 43 (1): 1–21.

Kelberer, V. 2017. "Negotiating Crisis: International Aid and Refugee Policy in Jordan." *Middle East Policy* 24 (4): 148–65.

Kelcey, J., and S. Chatila. 2020. "Increasing Inclusion or Furthering Fragmentation? How the Global Strategy to Include Refugees in National Education Systems Has Been Implemented in Lebanon." *Refuge: Canada's Journal on Refugees* 36 (2): 9–19. https://doi.org/10.25071/1920-7336.40713.

Kenner, D. 2018. "No Matter Who Wins the Syrian Civil War, Israel Loses." *The Atlantic*, 29 August 2018. https://www.theatlantic.com/international/archive/2018/08/israel-gamble-assad-syria/568693/.

Kessler, O. 2011. "Jordan's Abdullah Calls on Assad to Resign." *Jerusalem Post*, 14 November 2011.

Khalid, A.F., J.N. Lavis, F. El-Jardali, and M. Vanstone. 2019. "The Governmental Health Policy-Development Process for Syrian Refugees: An Embedded Qualitative Case Study in Lebanon and Ontario." *Conflict and Health* 13 (1): 1–11.

Khalil, A. 2011. "Socioeconomic Rights of Palestinian Refugees in Arab Countries." *International Journal of Refugee Law* 23 (4): 680–719.

Kheiralla, K.A., B.F. Ababneh, H. Bendak, A.R. Alsuwaidi, and I. Elbarazi. 2022. "Exploring the Mental, Social, and Lifestyle Effects of a Positive COVID-19 Infection on Syrian Refugees in Jordan: A Qualitative Study." *International Journal of Environmental Research and Public Health* 19 (9): 12588. https://doi.org/10.3390/ijerph191912588.

Kikano, F., G. Fauveaud, and G. Lizarralde. 2021. "Policies of Exclusion: The Case of Syrian Refugees in Lebanon." *Journal of Refugee Studies* 34 (1): 422–52.

Kikano, F., and G. Lizarralde. 2019. "Settlement Policies for Syrian Refugees in Lebanon and Jordan: An Analysis of the Benefits and Drawbacks of Organized Camps." In *Resettlement Challenges for Displaced Populations and Refugees*, edited by Ali Asgary, 29–40. New York: Springer, Cham.

Kloß, S.T. 2017. "The Global South as Subversive Practice: Challenges and Potentials of a Heuristic Concept." *The Global South* 11 (2): 1–17.

Knudsen, A.J., and M. Kerr, eds. 2013. *Lebanon: After the Cedar Revolution*. Oxford: Oxford University Press.

Kothari, U. 2005. *A Radical History of Development Studies: Individuals, Institutions, and Ideologies*. London and New York: Zed Books.

Krafft, C., B. Malaeb, and S. Al Zoubi. 2022. "How Do Policy Approaches Affect Refugee Economic Outcomes? Insights from Studies of Syrian Refugees in Jordan and Lebanon." *Oxford Review of Economic Policy* 38 (3): 654–77. https://doi.org/10.1093/oxrep/graco19.

References

Kraft, M., M. Al-Mazri, H. Wimmen, and N. Zupan. 2008. "Walking the Line: Strategic Approaches to Peacebuilding in Lebanon." Working Group on Development and Peace. Bonn: FriEnt.

Küçükkeleş, M. 2012. *Arab League's Syrian Policy*. Ankara, Turkey: Foundation for Political, Economic and Social Research.

Kumaraswamy, P.R., and M. Singh. 2017. "Population Pressure in Jordan and the Role of Syrian Refugees." *Migration and Development* 6 (3): 412–27.

Kunz, E.F. 1981. "Exile and Resettlement: Refugee Theory." *International Migration Review* 15 (1/2): 42–51.

Kvittingen, A., M. Valenta, H. Tabbara, D. Baslan, and B. Berg. 2018. "The Conditions and Migratory Aspirations of Syrian and Iraqi Refugees in Jordan." *Journal of Refugee Studies* 32 (1) (2019): 106–24.

Landau, L.B. 2003. "Beyond the Losers: Transforming Governmental Practice in Refugee-Affected Tanzania." *Journal of Refugee Studies* 16 (1): 19–43.

– 2014. "Urban Refugees and IDPs." In Fiddian-Qasmiyeh et al., *The Oxford Handbook of Refugee and Forced Migration*, 1:139–50.

Landau, L.B., and R. Amit. 2014. "Wither Policy? Southern African Perspectives on Understanding Law, 'Refugee' Policy and Protection." *Journal of Refugee Studies* 27 (4): 534–52. https://doi.org/10.1093/jrs/feuoo5.

Laub, Z., and J. Masters. 2013. "Syria's Crisis and the Global Response." Council of Foreign Relations, 11 September 2013. https://www.cfr.org/backgrounder/syrias-crisis-and-global-response.

LCRP (Lebanon Crisis Response Plan). 2016. *Lebanon Crisis Response Plan 2015: Annual Report*. UNHCR, 21 March 2016. https://reliefweb.int/report/lebanon/lebanon-crisis-response-plan-2015-annual-report.

– 2021. The *Lebanon Crisis Response Plan (2017–2021)*. UNHCR, 12 March 2021. https://data2.unhcr.org/en/documents/details/85374.

– 2022. *The Lebanon Crisis Response Plan (2022–2023)*. UNHCR, 16 February 2022. https://data.unhcr.org/en/documents/details/90915.

Lee, S.K. 2014. "Security, Economy and the Modes of Refugees' Livelihood Pursuit: Focus on Karen Refugees in Thailand." *Asian Studies Review* 38 (3): 461–79. https://doi.org/10.1080/10357823.2014.931345.

Leenders, R. 2008. "Iraqi Refugees in Syria: Causing a Spillover of the Iraqi Conflict?" *Third World Quarterly* 29 (8): 1563–84.

Lenner, K. 2020. "'Biting Our Tongues': Policy Legacies and Memories in the Making of the Syrian Refugee Response in Jordan." *Refugee Survey Quarterly* 39 (3): 273–98.

Lenner, K., and L. Turner. 2019. "Making Refugees Work? The Politics of Integrating Syrian Refugees into the Labor Market in Jordan." *Middle East Critique* 28 (1): 65–95.

Leomil, L. 2022. "Displaced Venezuelans and the Politics of Asylum: The Case of Brazil's Group Recognition Policy." *Carta Internacional* 17 (1): 1–22.

Levy, J. 2017. *The Political Crisis in Lebanon: An Opportunity to Strengthen Israeli-Saudi Cooperation against Iran.* Begin-Sadat Center for Strategic Studies, Israel. Retrieved from https://policycommons.net/ artifacts/2032643/the-political-crisis-in-lebanon/2785086/.

Lilly, D. 2019. "UNRWA's Protection Mandate: Closing the 'Protection Gap.'" *International Journal of Refugee Law* 30 (3): 444–73.

Limoges, B. 2017. "Thousands of Syrians Face Eviction from Lebanon Camps." Al Jazeera, 15 April 2017. https://www.aljazeera.com/indepth/ features/2017/04/thousands-syrians-face-eviction-lebanon-camps-170415042553730.html.

Lischer, S. 2005. *Dangerous Sanctuaries: Refugee Camps, Civil War, and the Dilemmas of Humanitarian Aid.* Ithaca, NY: Cornell University Press.

– 2008. "Security and Displacement in Iraq: Responding to the Forced Migration Crisis." *International Security* 33 (2): 95–119.

Loescher, G. 2001. "The UNHCR and World Politics: State Interests vs. Institutional Autonomy." *International Migration Review* 35 (1): 33–56.

– 2014. "UNHCR and Forced Migration." In Fiddian-Qasmiyeh et al., *The Oxford Handbook of Refugee and Forced Migration,* 215–26.

Loescher, G., A. Betts, and J. Milner. 2008. UNHCR: *The Politics and Practice of Refugee Protection into the Twenty-First Century.* London: Routledge.

Long, K. 2012. "In Search of Sanctuary: Border Closures, 'Safe' Zones and Refugee Protection." *Journal of Refugee Studies* 26 (3): 458–76.

– 2014. "Rethinking 'Durable Solutions.'" In Fiddian-Qasmiyeh et al., *The Oxford Handbook of Refugee and Forced Migration,* 475–87.

Lopez, A.J. 2007. "Introduction: The (Post)Global South." *The Global South* 1 (1): 1–11.

Lowndes, V, and R.K. Polat. 2022. "How Do Local Actors Interpret, Enact, and Contest Policy? An Analysis of Local Government Responses to Meeting the Needs of Syrian Refugees in Turkey." *Local Government Studies* 48 (3): 546–69.

Lundgren, M. 2016. "Mediation in Syria: Initiatives, Strategies, and Obstacles, 2011–2016." *Contemporary Security Policy* 37 (2): 273–88.

References

Lupieri, S. 2020. "When 'Brothers and Sisters' Become 'Foreigners': Syrian Refugees and the Politics of Healthcare in Jordan." *Third World Quarterly* 41 (6): 958–75.

Lust-Okar, E. 2009. "Reinforcing Informal Institutions through Authoritarian Elections: Insights from Jordan." *Middle East Law and Governance* 1 (1): 3–37.

Magid, A. 2016. "Jordan's Elections: Voting in a Weak Parliament." Middle East Institute, 28 September 2016. https://www.mei.edu/publications/jordans-elections-voting-weak-parliament.

Al-Mahaid, A. 2021. "Securing Economic Livelihoods for Syrian Refugees: The Case for a Human Rights-Based Approach to the Jordan Compact." *International Journal of Human Rights* 25 (2): 203–30. https://doi.org/10.1080/13642987.2020.1763314.

Mahmoud, K. 2014. "Where Does Jordan Stand on Syrian Crisis." *Middle East Monitor.* https://www.middleeastmonitor.com/20140124-where-does-jordan-stand-on-the-syrian-crisis/.

Malaeb, B. 2018. *State Fragility in Lebanon: Proximate Causes and Sources of Resilience.* London: International Growth Centre's Commission on State Fragility, Growth and Development.

Malkki, L. 1992. " National Geographic: The Rooting of Peoples and the Territorialization of National Identity amongst Scholars and Refugees." *Cultural Anthropology,* 22–44.

– 1995. "Refugees and Exile: From 'Refugee Studies' to the National Order of Things." *Annual Review of Anthropology* 24:495–523.

Mandić, D. 2022. *The Syrian Refugee Crisis: How Democracies and Autocracies Perpetrated Mass Displacement.* Milton Park, UK: Taylor & Francis.

Marcus, J. 2015. "Islamic State: Where Key Countries Stand." BBC, 3 December 2015. https://www.bbc.com/news/world-middle-east-29074514.

Marfleet, P., and D. Chatty. 2009. *Iraq's Refugees: Beyond "Tolerance."* Oxford: University of Oxford, Refugee Studies Centre.

Marshall, A., and D. Béland. 2019. "Street-Level Bureaucrats, Policy Learning, and Refugee Resettlement: The Case of Syrian Refugees in Saskatoon, Canada." *Canadian Public Administration* 62 (3): 393–412.

Martin, A. 2005. "Environmental Conflict between Refugee and Host Communities." *Journal of Peace Research* 42 (3): 329–46.

Martin, P. 2017. "Trump and U.S. Immigration Policy." *California Agriculture* 71 (1): 15–17. DOI: 10.3733/ca.2017a0006.

Matalucci, S. 2019. "Lebanon Faces a Race against Time to Avoid Financial Collapse." DW, 1 October 2019. https://www.dw.com/en/lebanon-faces-race-against-time-to-avoid-financial-collapse/a-50655866.

Maxwell, J. 2013. *Qualitative Research Design: An Interactive Approach*. 3rd ed. Thousand Oaks, CA: Sage.

Mccarthy, A. 2021. "Turning Crisis into Opportunity? The Syrian Refugee Crisis and Evolution of Welfare Policy for Refugees in Turkey from a Public Choice Theory Perspective." *Critical Social Policy* 41 (1): 111–27.

McConnachie, K. 2022. "Refugee Policy as Border Governance: Refugee Return, Peacebuilding, and Myanmar's Politics of Transition." *Modern Asian Studies* 56 (2): 661–90.

McCormick, J., R. Hague, and M. Harrop. 2019. *Comparative Government and Politics: An Introduction*. London: Bloomsbury Publishing.

Mehchy, Z. 2019. "The Syrian Pound Signals Economic Deterioration." Chatham House. https://www.chathamhouse.org/2019/09/syrian-pound-signals-economic-deterioration.

Meier, D. 2014. "Lebanon: The Refugee Issue and the Threat of a Sectarian Confrontation." *Oriente Moderno* 94 (2): 382–401. https://doi.org/10.1163/22138617–12340063.

Memişoğlu, F., and B. Yavçan. 2022. "Beyond Ideology: A Comparative Analysis of How Local Governance Can Expand National Integration Policy – The Case of Syrian Refugees in Istanbul." *Journal of Ethnic and Migration Studies* 48 (3): 503–23.

Mencütek, Z. 2018. *Refugee Governance, State and Politics in the Middle East*. Milton Park, UK: Routledge.

– 2020. "Conducting Comparative Migration Research in MENA: Are the Regional Countries Too Unique or Too Similar for Comparisons of Refugee Policies?" *Perceptions* 25 (1): 12–34.

– 2022. "The Geopolitics of Returns: Geopolitical Reasoning and Space-Making in Turkey's Repatriation Regime." *Geopolitics* 28 (3): 1079–1105. https://doi.org/10.1080/14650045.2022.2081550.

Mencütek, Z., and A. Nashwan. 2020. "Perceptions about the Labor Market Integration of Refugees: Evidences from Syrian Refugees in Jordan." *Journal of International Migration and Integration* 22:615–33.

Messari, N., and J. Van der Klaauw. 2010. "Counter-Terrorism Measures and Refugee Protection in North Africa." *Refugee Survey Quarterly* 29 (4): 83–103.

Meyer, S. 2008. "Research Guide on Local Integration." *Forced Migration Online*. http://www.forcedmigration.org/guide/fmo045/.

Middle East Monitor. 2020. "UN: Over 80% of Syria Refugees are Women and Children." 5 March 2020. https://www.middleeastmonitor.com/20200305-un-over-80-of-syria-refugees-are-women-and-children/.

Middle East Monitor. 2022. " Turkey, Jordan Agree to Cooperate in the Voluntary Return of Syria Refugees." 2 March 2022. https://www.middleeastmonitor.com/20220302-turkey-jordan-agree-to-cooperate-in-the-voluntary-return-of-syria-refugees/.

Miller, S.D. 2014. "Lessons from the Global Public Policy Literature for the Study of Global Refugee Policy." *Journal of Refugee Studies* 27 (4): 495–513.

– 2016. *Political and Humanitarian Responses to Syrian Displacement*. London: Taylor & Francis.

Millett, P. 2021. "Jordan: A Palace Coup?" *Asian Affairs* 52 (3): 521–28.

Milner, J. 2009. *Refugees, the State and the Politics of Asylum in Africa*. Dordrecht, Netherlands: Springer.

– 2014. "Can Global Refugee Policy Leverage Durable Solutions? Lessons from Tanzania's Naturalization of Burundian Refugees." *Journal of Refugee Studies* 27 (4): 553–73.

Milton-Edwards, B., and P. Hinchcliffe. 2009. *Jordan: A Hashemite Legacy*. Milton Park: Routledge.

Milward, H.B., and G.L. Wamsley. 1985. "Policy Subsystems, Networks, and the Tools of Public Management." In *Policy Implementation in Federal and Unitary Systems*, edited by K. Hanf and T.A.J. Toonen, 105–30. Springer.

Mitroff, I. 2000. *Managing Crises before They Happen: What Every Executive and Manager Needs to Know about Crisis Management*. AMACOM/American Management Association.

Mogire, E. 2009. " Refugee Realities: Refugee Rights versus State Security in Kenya and Tanzania." *Transformation* 26 (1): 15–29. https://doi.org/10.1177/0265378809102173.

MOPIC (Ministry of Planning and International Cooperation, Jordan). 2015. *The Jordan Response Plan for the Syria Crisis 2015*. UNDP, 17 December 2014. https://www.undp.org/sites/g/files/zskgke326/files/migration/jo/88450d1edc83883d0049c8eaae3741c4c34825c979d01c-7742836112cbbb25f1.pdf.

– 2022. *The Jordan Response Plan for the Syria Crisis (2020–2022)*. UNHCR, 26 July 2020. https://data.unhcr.org/en/documents/details/77959.

Moretti, S. 2015. "The Challenge of Durable Solutions for Refugees at the Thai–Myanmar Border." *Refugee Survey Quarterly* 34 (3): 70–94.

Morris, J. 2019. " The Politics of Return from Jordan to Syria." *Forced Migration Review* 62:31–4.

MOSA (Ministry of Social Affairs, Lebanon). 2017. *Regular Perception Surveys on Social Tensions throughout Lebanon Wave II: Interim Results.* 26 September 2017. https://data2.unhcr.org/es/documents/download/60885.

Mourad, L. 2017. "Standoffish" Policy-Making: Inaction and Change in the Lebanese Response to the Syrian Displacement Crisis." *Middle East Law and Governance* 9 (3): 249–66.

MSF (Médecins Sans Frontières). 2021. "A Decade of War in Syria: The Needs of Millions Haven't Vanished." 3 March 2021. https://reliefweb.int/report/syrian-arab-republic/decade-war-syria-needs-millions-haven-t-vanished.

Muhammad, R.K. 2011. "International Forced Migration and Pak-Afghan Development Concerns: Exploring Afghan Refugee Livelihood Strategies." *Journal of Social and Development Sciences* 2 (4): 181–7.

Musarat-Akram, S. 1999. "The World Refugee Regime in Crisis: A Failure to Fulfill the Burden-Sharing and Humanitarian Requirements of the 1951 Refugee Convention." In *Proceedings of the Annual Meeting (American Society of International Law)*, 213–16. The American Society of International Law.

Mützelburg, I. 2022. "NGOs in Ukraine's Multi-Scalar Asylum Governance: Between Influence and Dependence on State Authorities." *Journal of Intercultural Studies* 44 (1): 125–42. https://doi.org/10.1080/07256868.2022.2146664.

Muzaffar, S. 2013. "Hezbollah Chief Urges Lebanon to Help in Syrian Crisis." *New York Times*, 4 January 2013. https://www.nytimes.com/2013/01/04/world/middleeast/syria-hezbollah-lebanon-Nasrallah-.html.

Namrouqa, H. 2014. "Jordan World-Second Water Poorest Country." *Jordan Times*, 22 October 2014.

Nassar, J., and N. Stel. 2019. "Lebanon's Response to the Syrian Refugee Crisis: Institutional Ambiguity as a Governance Strategy." *Political Geography* 70:44–54.

Neang, L., R. McNally, and N. Rahim. 2022. "Who Has Published in the *Journal of Refugee Studies*? Examining Author Affiliation and Geographic Representation in Articles and Book Reviews." *LERRN*, 12 May 2022. https://carleton.ca/lerrn/2022/jrs-analysis/.

The New Arab. 2022. "Jordan, Syria Foreign Ministers Discuss 'Voluntary Refugee Returns' at UNGA Sidelines." 23 September 2022. https://english.alaraby.co.uk/news/jordan-syria-fms-discuss-voluntary-refugee-returns.

Nisan, M. 2017. *Politics and War in Lebanon: Unravelling the Enigma.* New Brunswick, NJ: Transaction Publishers.

Nightingale, A.J. 2020. "Triangulation." In *International Encyclopedia of Human Geography*, 2nd ed., edited by A. Kobayashi. Amsterdam: Elsevier.

Nowacka, S. 2019. "Reforms Prospects in Lebanon in Light of the Mass Protests." *Polski Instytut Spraw Międzynarodowych.* https://www.ceeol.com/search/gray-literature-detail?id=847556.

NRC (Norwegian Refugee Council). 2014. *No Escape: Civilians in Syria Struggle to Find Safety Across Borders.* https://reliefweb.int/report/syrian-arab-republic/no-escape-civilians-syria-struggle-find-safety-across-borders.

– 2016. *Securing Status: Syrian Refugees and the Documentation of Legal Status, Identity, and Family Relationships in Jordan.* https://www.nrc.no/globalassets/pdf/reports/securing-status.pdf.

– 2018. *Dangerous Ground: Syria's Refugees Face an Uncertain Future.* https://www.nrc.no/resources/reports/dangerous-ground---syrias-refugees-face-an-uncertain-future.

OCHA (Office for the Coordination of Humanitarian Affairs). 2020a. *Syrian Arab Republic Humanitarian Response Plan 2020.* https://fts.unocha.org/appeals/924/summary.

– 2020b. *Syrian Arab Republic Refugee Response and Resilience Plan (3RP) 2020.* https://fts.unocha.org/appeals/943/summary.

– 2021. *Syrian Arab Republic Refugee Response and Resilience Plan (3RP) 2021.* https://fts.unocha.org/appeals/1020/summary.

– 2022. *Syrian Arab Republic Refugee Response and Resilience Plan (3RP) 2022.* https://fts.unocha.org/appeals/1072/summary.

OFAC (Office of Foreign Assets Control). 2013. *Syria Sanctions Program.* Washington, DC: OFAC.

OHCHR (Office of the United Nations High Commissioner for Human Rights). 2010. "Human Rights' Compilation Report – Universal Periodic Review: The Republic of Lebanon." 2 September 2010. https://www.ohchr.org/sites/default/files/lib-docs/HRBodies/UPR/Documents/Session9/LB/A.HRC.WG.6.9.LBN.2_Lebanon_eng.pdf.

– 2017. *14th Report of the Commission of Inquiry on the Syrian Arab Republic – A/HRC/36/55.* 6 September 2017. Geneva: OHCHR.

– 2022. "UN Syria Commission Calls on Security Council to Ensure Life-Saving Humanitarian Aid to Syria: 'Unconscionable to Consider Closing Last Border Crossing When Needs Are at Their Highest.'" 26 May 2022. https://www.ohchr.org/en/press-releases/2022/05/un-syria-commission-calls-security-council-ensure-live-saving-humanitarian.

Okyay, A., and J. Zaragoza-Cristiani. 2016. "The Leverage of the Gatekeeper: Power and Interdependence in the Migration Nexus between the EU and Turkey." *International Spectator* 51 (4): 51–66.

Olwan, M.Y., and A. Shiyab. 2012. "Forced Migration of Syrians to Jordan: An Exploratory Study." Migration Policy Centre. Research Report 06. https://cadmus.eui.eu/handle/1814/23502.

O'Neill, A. 2021. "Syria: National Debt from 2000 to 2010 in Relation to Gross Domestic Product (GDP)." *Statisa*, 17 November 2021. https://www.statista.com/statistics/326945/national-debt-of-syria-in-relation-to-gross-domestic-product-gdp/.

Ongpin, P.A. 2009. "Refugees: Asset or Burden?" *Journal of Refugee Studies* 15 (4): 37–8.

Osman, T. 2017. "The Problem with Syria's Demographics: How Population Change Stymies Peace." *Foreign Affairs*, July 2017. https://www.foreignaffairs.com/syria/problem-syrias-demographics.

O'Toole Jr, L.J. 2000. "Research on Policy Implementation: Assessment and Prospects." *Journal of Public Administration Research and Theory* 10 (2): 263–88.

Owen, D. 2020. *What Do We Owe to Refugees?* Cambridge: Polity.

Oztig, L.I. 2022. "Refugee Flows, Foreign Policy, and Safe Haven Nexus in Turkey." *Third World Quarterly* 43 (3): 684–702.

Painter, M., and J. Pierre, eds. 2004. *Challenges to State Policy Capacity: Global Trends and Comparative Perspectives.* Springer.

Paul, O.T., and N. Kuluthum. 2022. "Protracted Refugees: Understanding the Challenges of Refugees in Protracted Refugee Situations in Uganda." *Journal of African Studies and Development* 14 (1): 1–11.

Pearlman, W.R. 2017. *We Crossed a Bridge and It Trembled: Voices from Syria.* New York: Custom House.

Pearson, A., and L. Sanders. 2019. "Syria: What Do Key Foreign Powers Want?" DW, 23 January 2019. https://www.dw.com/en/syria-conflict-what-do-the-us-russia-turkey-and-iran-want/a-41211604.

Pešalj, J., A. Steidl, L. Lucassen, and J. Ehmer. 2022. *Borders and Mobility Control in and between Empires and Nation-States.* Leiden, Netherlands: Brill.

References

Petersen, A. 2016. "Exploring Intersectionality in Education: The Intersection of Gender, Race, Disability, and Class." PhD diss., University of Northern Iowa, Cedar Falls.

Petzoldt, M. 2016. "Refugee Crisis in Lebanon 2013–2016 and the Role of the United Nations High Commissioner for Refugees (UNHCR)." *Bundeszentrale Politische Bildung*, 31 August 2016. https://www.bpb.de/gesellschaft/migration/laenderprofile/233345/refugee-crisis-and-unhcr.

Pipes, D. 1990. "Greater Syria in History." In *Greater Syria: The History of an Ambition*, 13–117. New York: Oxford University Press.

Pirjola, J. 2009. "European Asylum Policy-Inclusions and Exclusions under the Surface of Universal Human Rights Language." *European Journal of Migration and Law* 11 (4): 347–66.

Rabil, R.G. 2003. *Embattled Neighbors: Syria, Israel, and Lebanon.* Boulder, CO: Lynne Rienner Publishers.

– 2016. *The Syrian Refugee Crisis in Lebanon: The Double Tragedy of Refugees and Impacted Host Communities.* Lanham, MD: Lexington Books.

Rafizadeh, M. 2013. "How Bashar Al-Assad Became So Hated." *The Atlantic*, 17 April 2013. https://www.theatlantic.com/international/archive/2013/04/how-bashar-al-assad-became-so-hated/275058/.

Rainey, V. 2014. "Lebanon's Refugee Influx Alarms Christians." *Al Jazeera*, 11 May 2014. https://www.aljazeera.com/news/middleeast/2014/04/lebanon-refugee-influx-alarms-christians-20144191365914 9837.html.

Rana, M.S., and A. Riaz. 2022. "Securitization of the Rohingya Refugees in Bangladesh." *Journal of Asian and African Studies* 58 (7): 1274–90.

Rasmussen, A., and J. Annan. 2009. "Predicting Stress Related to Basic Needs and Safety in Darfur Refugee Camps: A Structural and Social Ecological Analysis." *Journal of Refugee Studies* 23 (1): 23–40.

Razzaz, O. 2019. "Full Thrust Ahead." The Business Year, 24 June 2019. https://www.thebusinessyear.com/interview/full-thrust-ahead/.

REACH. 2020. "Livelihoods Assessment Focused on Micro-Businesses in Jordan." 20 May 2020. https://reliefweb.int/report/jordan/livelihoods-assessment-focused-micro-businesses-jordan.

RefWorld. 2023. "Jordan: Law No. 24 of 1973 on Residence and Foreigners' Affairs, 1 January 1973." UNHCR, 17 August 2023. http://www.refworld.org/docid/3ae6b4ed4c.html.

Reiter, Y. 2004. "The Palestinian-Transjordanian Rift: Economic Might and Political Power in Jordan." *Middle East Journal* 58 (1): 72–92.

Reuters. 2017. "Lebanon Will Coordinate Refugee Returns to Syria Only with U.N.: PM Hariri." 14 July 2017. https://www.reuters.com/article/us-mideast-crisis-lebanon-syria-idUSKBN19Z1M4.

– 2018a. "Lebanon's Hezbollah to Work with Syrian State on Refugee Returns." 29 June 2018. https://www.reuters.com/article/us-mideast-crisis-lebanon-syria-refugees-idUSKBN1JP29Q.

– 2018b. "Syrian Troops Celebrate Seizing Jordan Border Crossing." 7 July 2018. https://www.reuters.com/article/us-mideast-crisis-syria-crossing/syrian-troops-celebrate-seizing-jordan-border-crossing-idUSKBN1JX0VF.

– 2018c. "With Border Open, Jordanians Visit Syria for First Time in Years." 28 October 2018. https://www.reuters.com/article/us-mideast-crisis-syria-jordan-idUSKCN1N20IR.

– 2021. "Jordan Closes Jaber Border Crossing with Syria, State News Agency Says." 31 July 2021. https://www.reuters.com/world/middle-east/jordan-closes-jaber-border-crossing-with-syria-state-news-agency-says-2021–07–31/.

Robinson, C.W. 1998. *Terms of Refuge: The Indochinese Exodus and the International Response.* London: Zed Books.

Ronald, M.A. 2022. "An Assessment of Economic and Environmental Impacts of Refugees in Nakivale, Uganda." *Migration and Development* 11 (3): 433–49.

Rosenthal, U., and P. 't Hart. 1991. "Experts and Decision Makers in Crisis Situations." *Knowledge* 12 (4): 350–72.

Ruiz, I., M. Siegel, and C. Vargas-Silva. 2015. "Forced Up or Down? The Impact of Forced Migration on Social Status." *Journal of Refugee Studies* 28 (2): 183–201.

Ruiz, I., and C. Vargas-Silva. 2013. "The Economics of Forced Migration." *Journal of Development Studies* 49 (6): 772–84.

– 2016. "The Labor Market Consequences of Hosting Refugees." Growth and Labour Markets in Low Income Countries Programme working paper no. 6, March 2016. https://g2lm-lic.iza.org/wp-content/uploads/2017/04/glmlic-wp006.pdf.

Rutinwa, B. 2002. "Prima Facie Status and Refugee Protection." UNHCR.

Ryan, Y. 2011. "The Tragic Life of a Street Vendor." Al Jazeera, 20 January 2011. https://www.aljazeera.com/features/2011/1/20/the-tragic-life-of-a-street-vendor.

Saad, H., A. Barnard, and C. Hauser. 2021. "Divided Kingdom: Jordan Shaken by Split between King and Ex-Crown Prince." *New York Times,*

4 April 2021. https://www.nytimes.com/2021/04/04/world/middleeast/jordan-king-abdullah-royal-dispute.html.

Sabatier, P.A. 1987. "Knowledge, Policy-Oriented Learning, and Policy Change: An Advocacy Coalition Framework." *Knowledge* 8 (4): 649–92.

Salehyan, I. 2008. "The Externalities of Civil Strife: Refugees as a Source of International Conflict." *American Journal of Political Science* 52 (4): 787–801.

Salehyan, I., and K. Gledtisch. 2006. "Refugees and the Spread of Civil War." *International Organization* 60 (2): 277–97.

Salem, P. 2013. "Lebanon Imperiled as Prime Minister Resigns under Duress." Carnegie Middle East Center, 23 March 2013. https://carnegie-mec.org/2013/03/23/lebanon-imperiled-as-prime-minister-resigns-under-duress-pub-51281.

Salemi, C., J. Bowman, and J. Compton. 2018. "Services for Syrian Refugee Children and Youth in Jordan: Forced Displacement, Foreign Aid, and Vulnerability." Economic Research Forum Working Paper Series, no. 1188.

Salloukh, B.F., R. Barakat, J.S. Al-Habbal, L.W. Khattab, and S. Mikaelian. 2015. *The Politics of Sectarianism in Postwar Lebanon.* London: Pluto Press.

Samaddar, R. 2020. *The Postcolonial Age of Migration.* Routledge India.

Sanyal, R. 2021. "Making Urban Humanitarian Policy: The 'Neighbourhood Approach' in Lebanon." *Urban Geography* 42 (7): 937–57.

Sasnal, P. 2016. "The International Dimension of the Fight for Aleppo in Syria." *Polish Institute of International Affairs Bulletin*, 1–3.

Satloff, R., and D. Schenker. 2013. "Political Instability in Jordan." Contingency Planning Memorandum no. 19, Council on Foreign Relations.

Sawyer, R.K. 2005. *Social Emergence: Societies as Complex Systems.* Cambridge: Cambridge University Press.

Schaer, C. 2021. "Lebanon Deal: Beginning of the End of Syria's Isolation?" DW, 22 September 2021. https://www.dw.com/en/lebanon-power-deal-beginning-of-the-end-of-syrias-isolation/a-59263980.

Schillings, T. 2018. "The Macro-Economic Impacts of Syrian Refugee Aid." *Forced Migration Review* 58:42–4.

Secen, S. 2021. "Explaining the Politics of Security: Syrian Refugees in Turkey and Lebanon." *Journal of Global Security Studies* 6 (3): ogaa039. https://doi.org/10.1093/jogss/ogaa039.

Seeberg, P. 2022. "Syrian Refugees in Jordan and Their Integration in the Labour Market: Jordanian Migration Diplomacy and EU Incentives." *Mediterranean Politics* 27 (2): 192–211. https://doi.org/10.1080/13629 395.2020.1758452.

Semb, A.J. 2001. "How Norms Affect Policy: The Case of Sami Policy in Norway." *International Journal on Minority and Group Rights* 8 (2): 177–222.

Şengül, İ. 2022. "Unpacking Temporary Protection of Refugees: Failure of Durable Solutions and Uncertainties." *İnönü Üniversitesi Hukuk Fakültesi Dergisi* 13 (1): 16–28.

Seven, Ü. 2022. "Armed Conflict, Violence, and the Decision to Migrate: Explaining the Determinants of Displacement in Syria." *Migration and Development* 11 (3): 1029–45. https://doi.org/10.1080/21632324.2020. 1859177.

Sewell, A. 2022. "While Refugee Return Plan Flounders, Syrians in Lebanon Face Deportation Risk." *L'Orient Today,* 13 August 2022. https://today.lorientlejour.com/article/1308469/while-refugee-return-plan-flounders-syrians-in-lebanon-face-deportation-risk.html.

Shavit, E. 2018. "The Parliamentary Elections in Lebanon: Hezbollah's Victory within the Political Status Quo Eldad Shavit." Institute for National Security Studies (INSS) Insight, 1–4.

Shawaf, N., and F. El Asmar. 2017. "'We're Not There Yet ...': Voices of Refugees from Syria in Lebanon." Oxfam, 31 May 2017. https://www.oxfam.org/en/research/were-not-there-yet-voices-refugees-syria-lebanon.

Shivakoti, R. 2017. "Multi-layered Migration Governance in Asia: Lessons from Nepal and the Philippines." PhD diss., National University of Singapore.

Sieverding, M., and V. Calderón-Mejía. 2020. "Demographic Profile of Syrians in Jordan and Lebanon." In *Comparative Demography of the Syrian Diaspora: European and Middle Eastern Destinations*, edited by E.D. Carlson and N.E. Williams, 109–38. New York: Springer, Cham.

Singh, M. 2017. "Parliamentary Election in Jordan, 2016." *Contemporary Review of the Middle East* 4 (3): 297–318. https://doi.org/10.1177/2347798917711296.

Singh, N.S., A. Dingle, A.H. Sabra, J. DeJong, C. Pitt, G.R. Mumtaz, A.M. Sibai, and S. Mounier-Jack. 2020. "Healthcare Financing Arrangements and Service Provision for Syrian Refugees in Lebanon." In *Health Policy and Systems Responses to Forced Migration*, edited by K. Bozorgmehr, B. Roberts, O. Razum, and L., Biddle, 53–76. Springer, Cham.

References

Smith, C. 2017. "Between Security and Protection: Refugee Policy Dilemmas in Jordan." Wesleyan University, Connecticut. https://digitalcollections.wesleyan.edu/_flysystem/fedora/2023-03/24005-Original%20File.pdf.

Smith, M. 2004. "Warehousing Refugees." *World Refugee Survey* 38:38–56.

Smith, S.K. 2013. "Education for Repatriation: Refugee Education Policy-Making Globally and for Burundian Refugees in Tanzania." PhD diss., Teachers College, Columbia University.

Snoubar, Y., and O. Tanrisever. 2019. "Response to the Syrian Crisis within the Middle East Region: Comparison of Humanitarian Aid for Syrian Refugees in Jordan and Lebanon." *Review of International Affairs* 70:1176. https://open.metu.edu.tr/handle/11511/71810.

Snyder, J. 2011. "Realism, Refugees and Strategies of Humanitarianism." In *Refugees in International Relations*, edited by A. Betts and G. Loescher, 29–52. Oxford University Press.

Solh, M. 2010. "Tackling the Drought in Syria." *Nature Middle East*, 27 September 2010. https://www.natureasia.com/en/nmiddleeast/article/10.1038/nmiddleeast.2010.206.

Song, L. 2014. "Who Shall We Help? The Refugee Definition in a Chinese Context." *Refugee Survey Quarterly* 33 (1): 44–58.

Sonmez, M. 2019. "Mystery Surrounds Turkey's $40 Billion Refugee Bill." Al-Monitor, 31 October 2019. https://www.al-monitor.com/originals/2019/10/turkey-syria-40-billion-refugee-bill-calls-for-explanation.html.

Spyer, J. 2009. "Israel and Lebanon: Problematic Proximity." *Middle East Review of International Affairs (Online)* 13 (2): 1–16.

Stave, S.E., and S. Hillesund. 2015. *Impact of Syrian Refugees on the Jordanian Labor Market*. Geneva: ILO.

Stelzenmüller, C. 2019. "A European Security Force in Syria Is a Courageous Idea." Brookings, 30 October 2019. https://www.brookings.edu/blog/order-from-chaos/2019/10/30/a-european-security-force-in-syria-is-a-courageous-idea/.

Stewart, J., and R. Ayres. 2001. "Systems Theory and Policy Practice: An Exploration." *Policy Sciences* 34 (1): 79–94.

Stone, D., and K. Moloney, K., eds. 2019. *The Oxford Handbook of Global Policy and Transnational Administration*. Oxford: Oxford University Press.

Strzyżyńska, W. 2022. "Scores Dead in Worst Sinking of Migrant Boat from Lebanon in Recent Years." *The Guardian*, 23 September 2022.

https://www.theguardian.com/world/2022/sep/23/scores-dead-in-worst-sinking-of-migrant-boat-from-lebanon-in-recent-years.

Stupp, C. 2017. "Turkey Blocks UNHCR Access to Syrian Refugees." EURACTIV, 19 January 2017. https://www.euractiv.com/section/global-europe/news/turkey-blocks-unhcr-access-to-syrian-refugees/.

Su, A. 2017. "Why Jordan Is Deporting Syrian Refugees." *The Atlantic*, 20 October 2017. https://www.theatlantic.com/international/archive/2017/10/jordan-syrian-refugees-deportation/543057/.

Sunderland, J. 2022. "Endless Tragedies in the Mediterranean Sea: Europe's Commitment to Rescue Would Save Lives." Human Rights Watch, 13 September 2022. https://www.hrw.org/news/2022/09/13/endless-tragedies-mediterranean-sea.

Surel, Y. 2000. "The Role of Cognitive and Normative Frames in Policy-Making." *Journal of European Public Policy* 7 (4): 495–512.

Sweis, R. 2017. "A Refugee Crisis on Jordan's Border." *The Huffington Post*, 31 May 2016. Updated 30 May 2017. https://www.huffpost.com/entry/a-refugee-crisis-on-jorda_b_10201702.

Tabar, P. 2010. "Lebanon: A Country of Emigration and Immigration." Institute for Migration Studies, American University in Cairo, 1–26. https://fount.aucegypt.edu/faculty_journal_articles/5056.

Taggart, P., and A. Szczerbiak. 2018. "Putting Brexit into Perspective: The Effect of the Eurozone and Migration Crises and Brexit on Euroscepticism in European States." *Journal of European Public Policy* 25 (8): 1194–214. https://doi.org/10.1080/13501763.2018.1467955.

Taha, P. 2019. *Intersectionality and Other Critical Approaches in Refugee Research: An Annotated Bibliography*. Ottawa: Local Engagement Refugee Research Network (LERRN).

Talib, M. 2012. "Numbers versus Rights: State Responsibility towards Asylum Seekers and the Implications for the International Refugee Regime." *Georgetown Immigration Law Journal* 27:405.

Tansey, Oisín. 2009. "Process Tracing and Elite Interviewing: A Case for Non-probability Sampling." *Methoden der vergleichenden Politik-und Sozialwissenschaft: Neue entwicklungen und anwendungen*, 481–96.

Tesfaghiorghis, J.M. 2019. "Refugees, Convenient Bargaining Chips? A Comparative Analysis of Kenyan and Ethiopian Refugee policy." Master's thesis, Norwegian University of Life Sciences, Ås.

Thelen, K. 1999. "Historical Institutionalism in Comparative Politics." *Annual Review of Political Science* 2 (1): 369–404.

Tobin, S.A., F. Momani, and T. Al-Yakoub. 2022. "'The War Has Divided Us More Than Ever': Syrian Refugee Family Networks and Social

Capital for Mobility through Protracted Displacement in Jordan." *Journal of Ethnic and Migration Studies* 48 (18): 4365–82.

Tomlinson, B.R. 2003. "What Was the Third World?" *Journal of Contemporary History* 38 (2): 307–21.

Traboulsi, F. 2007. *A Modern History of Lebanon.* Ann Arbor, MI: Pluto Press.

Trad, S. 2014. "Opportunity to Change Lebanon's Asylum Policy." *Forced Migration Review* 45:87.

TRT World. 2016. "King Abdullah of Jordan Speaks at Syrian Donor Conference." https://www.youtube.com/watch?v=jaxihyo LVYk.

Tsourapas, G. 2019. "The Syrian Refugee Crisis and Foreign Policy Decision-Making in Jordan, Lebanon, and Turkey." *Journal of Global Security Studies* 4 (4): 464–81.

– 2022. *The Jordan Compact.* London: MAGYC.

Türk, V. 2018. "The Promise and Potential of the Global Compact on Refugees." *International Journal of Refugee Law* 30 (4): 575–83. https://doi.org/10.1093/ijrl/eey068.

Türk, V., and R. Dowd. 2014. "Protection Gaps." In Fiddian-Qasmiyeh et al., *The Oxford Handbook of Refugee and Forced Migration,* 278–89.

Turner, L. 2015. "Explaining the (Non-)Encampment of Syrian Refugees: Security, Class and the Labor Market in Lebanon and Jordan." *Mediterranean Politics* 20 (3): 386–404.

UK Government. 2016. *Co-hosts Statement Annex: Fundraising – Supporting Syria and the Region Conference.* Reliefweb, 4 February 2016. https://reliefweb.int/attachments/3f74d6c6-bf29–3c8e-97df-305ea10cf18b/CO-HOST%E2%80%99S_STATEMENT_ANNEX-_FUNDRAISING.pdf.

UN (United Nations). 2021. "The Syrian Golan." Permanent Mission of the Syrian Arab Republic to the United Nations. Accessed 5 December 2022. https://www.un.int/syria/syria/syrian-golan.

UNDP (United Nations Development Programme). 2018. "Human Development Indicators: Jordan Country Profile." Accessed 21 September 2018. http://hdr.undp.org/en/countries/profiles/JOR.

– 2020. "An Introduction to the Regional Refugee and Resilience Plan (3RP)." 30 June 2020. https://www.arabstates.undp.org/content/rbas/en/home/library/crisis-response0/an-introduction-to-the-regional-refugee-and-resilience-plan-3rp.html.

– 2022. "Human Development Insights." Accessed 4 December 2022. http://hdr.undp.org/sites/all/themes/hdr_theme/country-notes/SYR.pdf.

UNHCR (United Nations High Commissioner for Refugees). 1981. "EXCOM Conclusions on the Protection of Asylum Seekers in Situations of Large-Scale Influx." 21 October 1981. http://www.unhcr. org/3ae68c6e10.html.

– 2000. "The State of the World's Refugees: 50 Years of Humanitarian Action." 1 January 2000. http://www.unhcr.org/4a4c754a9.html.

– 2001a. "Practical Aspects of Physical and Legal Protection with Regard to Registration." 19 February 2001. http://www.unhcr.org/cgi-bin/texis/ vtx/home/opendocPDFViewer.html?docid=3ae68f3c8&query=Mass %20influx%20situations.

– 2001b. "Annotated Comments on Council Directive 2001/55/EC of 20 July 2001 on Minimum Standards for Giving Temporary Protection in the Event of a Mass Influx of Displaced Persons and on Measures Promoting a Balance of Efforts between Member States in Receiving Such Persons and Bearing Consequences thereof." 20 July 2001. http:// www.unhcr.org/436620152.html.

– 2006a. "1984 Cartagena Declaration on Refugees." https://www. unhcr.org/about-us/background/45dc19084/cartagena-declaration-refugees-adopted-colloquium-international-protection.html.

– 2006b. "OAU Convention Governing the Specific Aspects of Refugee Problems in Africa." https://www.unhcr.org/about-us/back-ground/45dc1a682/oau-convention-governing-specific-aspects-refugee-problems-africa-adopted.html.

– 2010. "UNHCR Projected Global Resettlement Needs 2011." Sixteenth Annual Tripartite Consultation on Resettlement, Geneva, 6–8 July 2010. http://www.unhcr.org/4c31e3716.html.

– 2011. "The 1951 Convention Relating to the Status of Refugees and Its 1967 Protocol." September 2011. http://www.unhcr.org/4ec262df9. html.

– 2012a. "Global Report 2011." https://www.refworld.org/pdfid/ 50c737241a.pdf.

– 2012b. "Roundtable on Temporary Protection: 19–20 July 2012. International Institute of Humanitarian Law, San Remo, Italy: Summary Conclusions on Temporary Protection." 20 July 2012. http://www. refworld.org/docid/506d908a2.html.

– 2013. "Syrian Refugees Living Outside Camps in Jordan." https://relief-web.int/sites/reliefweb.int/files/resources/HVreport_09MarCS6_small-size.pdf.

– 2014a. "Global Appeal, 2014–2015: Jordan." http://www.unhcr. org/528a0a2c13.pdf.

References

277

- 2014b. "Syrian Refugees in Lebanon Surpass One Million." 3 April 2014. http://www.unhcr.org/news/press/2014/4/533c15179/syrian-refugees-lebanon-surpass-million.html.
- 2014c. "Lebanon Crisis Response Plan, 2015–2016." 15 December 2014. https://data2.unhcr.org/en/documents/download/42701.
- 2014d. "UNHCR Asylum Trends 2014." https://www.unhcr.org/551128679.pdf.
- 2015. "Refugees in the Horn of Africa: Somali Displacement Crisis." Accessed 27 October 2015. http://data.unhcr.org/horn-of-africa/region.php?id=3&country=110.
- 2016. "Global Trends 2015." 20 June 2016. https://www.unhcr.org/statistics/unhcrstats/576408cd7/unhcr-global-trends-2015.
- 2018a. "Fourth Regional Survey on Syrian Refugees' Perceptions and Intentions on Return to Syria (RPIS) (October)." 31 July 2018. https://reliefweb.int/report/lebanon/fourth-regional-survey-syrian-refugees-perceptions-and-intentions-return-syria-rpis.
- 2018b. "Lebanon December Factsheet." December 2018. https://www.unhcr.org/lb/wp-content/uploads/sites/16/2019/07/UNHCR-Lebanon-Operational-Update-Jan-Dec-2018.pdf.
- 2018c. "Population Statistics." Accessed 21 September 2018. http://popstats.unhcr.org/en/overview.
- 2018d. "Syria Regional Refugee Response Platform." Accessed 21 September 2018. https://data2.unhcr.org/en/situations/syria.
- 2018e. "Syria Regional Refugee Response Platform: Durable Solutions." Accessed 21 September 2018. https://data2.unhcr.org/en/situations/syria_durable_solutions.
- 2018f. "Vulnerability Assessment of Refugees of Other Nationalities in Lebanon 2017." 27 June 2018. https://reliefweb.int/report/lebanon/vulnerability-assessment-refugees-other-nationalities-lebanon-2017.
- 2019a. "Collective Evictions: Activity Info Report Covering 2018." 10 October 2019. https://data2.unhcr.org/en/documents/download/71705.
- 2019b. "Fifth Regional Survey on Refugee Return Perceptions and Intentions: March 2019." 17 March 2019. https://data2.unhcr.org/en/documents/details/68443.
- 2019c. "Health Services for Refugees and Asylum Seekers in Lebanon." Accessed 20 May 2020. https://www.refugees-lebanon.org/uploads/poster/poster_152837840982.pdf.
- 2019d. "Jordan Fact Sheet." November 2019. http://reporting.unhcr.org/sites/default/files/UNHCR%20Jordan%20Fact%20Sheet%20-%20November%202019_0.pdf.

278 References

– 2019e. "Lebanon Fact Sheet." January 2019. https://reliefweb.int/sites/reliefweb.int/files/resources/UNHCR-Lebanon-Operational-fact-sheet-January-2019.pdf.
– 2019f. "Lebanon: Health Programme 2019." https://www.unhcr.org/lb/wp-content/uploads/sites/16/2019/04/Health-Factsheet.pdf.
– 2019g. "Lebanon Operational Update (April–June 2019)." https://www.unhcr.org/lb/wp-content/uploads/sites/16/2020/07/Q2–2019-operational-update.pdf.
– 2020a. "Coronavirus Outbreak." Accessed 22 May 2020. https://data.unhcr.org/en/situations/covid-19.
– 2020b. Global Trends in Forced Displacement in 2019. Accessed 4 December 2022. https://www.unhcr.org/statistics/unhcrstats/5ee200e37/unhcr-global-trends-2019.html.
– 2020c. "Jordan Fact Sheet." September 2020. https://reliefweb.int/report/jordan/jordan-unhcr-factsheet-september-2020.
– 2020d. "Jordan Operational Update June 2020." https://reporting.unhcr.org/sites/default/files/UNHCR%20Jordan%20Operational%20Update%20-%20June%202020.pdf.
– 2020e. "Lebanon Covid-19 Update." Accessed 20 May 2020. https://reliefweb.int/sites/reliefweb.int/files/resources/UNHCR%20Lebanon%20COVID-19%20Update%20-%2016APR20_0_0.pdf.
– 2020f. "Lebanon Fact Sheet." January 2020. https://www.unhcr.org/lb/wp-content/uploads/sites/16/2020/02/UNHCR-Lebanon-Operational-Fact-sheet-January-2020.pdf.
– 2020g. "Lebanon: Inter-Agency – Collective Evictions and Eviction Notices in Lebanon – Year-End dashboard Covering January–December 2019." 25 February 2020. https://data2.unhcr.org/en/documents/details/74226.
– 2020h. "Protection (including SGBV and Child Protection) 2019 Mid-Year Dashboard." 12 February 2020. https://reliefweb.int/report/lebanon/lebanon-inter-agency-protection-including-sgbv-and-child-protection-2019-mid-year.
– 2020i. "3RP 2020 Progress Report." August 2020. https://reporting.unhcr.org/sites/default/files/3RP%202020%20Progress%20Report%20-%20August%202020.pdf.
– 2020j. "Working in Jordan (for Syrian Nationals Only)." https://help.unhcr.org/jordan/en/helpful-services-unhcr/working-in-jordan-permits/.
– 2020k. "Work Permits for Syrian Refugees in Jordan." Accessed 4 December 2022. https://help.unhcr.org/jordan/en/frequently-asked-questions-unhcr/work-permit-syrian-faqs/.

References

- 2021a. "Health." Accessed 4 December 2022. https://help.unhcr.org/jordan/en/helpful-services-unhcr/health-services-unhcr/.
- 2021b. "Projected Global Resettlement Needs 2021." https://reliefweb.int/sites/reliefweb.int/files/resources/5ef34bfb7.pdf.
- 2021c. "Sixth Regional Survey on Syrian Refugees' Perceptions & Intentions on Return to Syria." 26 March 2021. https://data2.unhcr.org/en/documents/details/85739.
- 2022a. "COVID-19 Vaccine Compensation for Refugees in Jordan." https://help.unhcr.org/jordan/en/frequently-asked-questions-unhcr/vaccine-incentive-jordan/.
- 2022b. "Global Focus: Lebanon." Accessed 15 December 2022. https://reporting.unhcr.org/lebanon.
- 2022c. "Global Trends Report: Forced Displacement in 2021." Accessed 6 December 2022. https://www.unhcr.org/globaltrends.html.
- 2022d. "Jordan Issues Record Number of Work Permits to Syrian Refugees." 25 January 2022. https://www.unhcr.org/news/news-releases/jordan-issues-record-number-work-permits-syrian-refugees.
- 2022e. "Resettlement Data Finder." Accessed 15 December 2022. https://rsq.unhcr.org/en/#I4wV.
- 2022f. "Syria Emergency." Accessed 6 December 2022. https://www.unhcr.org/syria-emergency.html.
- 2022g. "Syria Regional Refugee Response Platform." Accessed 6 December 2022. https://data.unhcr.org/en/situations/syria.
- 2022h. "Syria Regional Refugee Response Platform: Durable Solutions." Accessed 4 December 2022. https://data.unhcr.org/en/situations/syria_durable_solutions.
- 2022i. "2021 Vulnerability Assessment for Syrian Refugees in Lebanon." https://data2.unhcr.org/en/documents/details/90589.
- 2022j. "UNHCR's Covid-19 Response in Lebanon – Q2 2022." https://reporting.unhcr.org/document/3028.
- 2022k. "Written Evidence Submitted by the UNHCR, the UN Refugee Agency." London: UK Parliament. 18 August 2022. https://committees.parliament.uk/writtenevidence/110629/pdf/.
- 2023. "Resettlement." Accessed 28 August 2023. http://www.unhcr.org/resettlement.html.

UNICEF (United Nations International Children's Emergency Fund). 2022. *Water Stress in Jordan.* https://www.unicef.org/jordan/reports/water-stress-jordan-report.

United Kingdom. Home Office. 2018. "Country Policy and Information Note – Lebanon: Palestinians." June 2018. https://www.refworld.org/docid/5b32026b4.html.

United States. Department of State. 2017. *International Religious Freedom Report on Lebanon.* https://www.state.gov/wp-content/uploads/2019/01/Lebanon-2.pdf.

UNPAN (United Nations Public Administration Network). 2012. *Lebanon Public Administration Country Profile.* http://unpan1.un.org/intradoc/groups/public/documents/un/unpan023179.pdf.

– 2014. *Jordan Public Administration Country Profile.* http://unpan1.un.org/intradoc/groups/public/documents/un/unpan023177.pdf.

UNRWA (United Nations Relief and Works Agency for Palestine Refugees in the Near East). 2011. *Palestine Refugees in Lebanon.* Accessed 1 January 2011. https://www.unrwa.org/sites/default/files/201110023o6.pdf.

– 2022. *Where We Work: Syria.* August 2022. https://www.unrwa.org/where-we-work/syria.

Unutulmaz, K.O. 2019. "Turkey's Education Policies towards Syrian Refugees: A Macro-level Analysis." *International Migration* 57 (2): 235–52.

Van Evera, S. 1997. *Guide to Methods for Students of Political Science.* Ithaca, NY: Cornell University Press.

Van Selm, J. 2014. "Refugee Resettlement." In Fiddian-Qasmiyeh et al., *The Oxford Handbook of Refugee and Forced Migration,* 512–24.

Verme, P., C. Gigliarano, C. Wieser, K. Hedlund, M. Petzoldt, and M. Santacroce. 2015. *The Welfare of Syrian Refugees: Evidence from Jordan and Lebanon.* Washington, DC: World Bank.

Vervliet, M., J. De Mol, E. Broekaert, and I. Derluyn. 2013. "'That I Live, That's Because of Her': Intersectionality as Framework for Unaccompanied Refugee Mothers." *British Journal of Social Work* 44 (7): 2023–41.

Vigil, Y.N., and C.B. Abidi. 2018. "'We' the Refugees: Reflections on Refugee Labels and Identities." *Refuge* 34 (2): 52–60.

Vohra, A. 2019. "Russia's Payback Will Be Syria's Reconstruction Money." *Foreign Policy,* 5 May 2019. https://foreignpolicy.com/2019/05/05/russias-payback-will-be-syrias-reconstruction-money/.

Vrecer, N. 2010. "Living in Limbo: Integration of Forced Migrants from Bosnia and Herzegovina in Slovenia." *Journal of Refugee Studies* 23 (4): 484–502. https://doi.org/10.1093/jrs/feq042.

Walsh, G. 2021. "10 Years on: 10 Facts That Explain Syria's Conflict." *Trócaire,* 12 March 2021. https://reliefweb.int/report/syrian-arab-republic/10-years-10-facts-explain-syria-s-conflict.

Walzer, G. 2008. "UNHCR Operations in Pakistan in the Early 1980s." *Refugee Survey Quarterly* 27 (1): 40–4.

References

Wang, A. 2021. "China Takes Firm Stand against Regime Change in Syria." *South China Morning Post*. Accessed 4 December 2022. https://www.scmp.com/news/china/diplomacy/article/3141576/china-takes-firm-stand-against-regime-change-syria.

Ward, P. 2014. "Refugee Cities: Reflections on the Development and Impact of UNHCR Urban Refugee Policy in the Middle East." *Refugee Survey Quarterly* 33 (1): 77–93.

Webb, P. 2014. "Deadlock or Restraint? The Security Council Veto and the Use of Force in Syria." *Journal of Conflict & Security Law* 19 (3): 471–88.

Weible, C.M. 2008. "Expert-Based Information and Policy Subsystems: A Review and Synthesis." *Policy Studies Journal* 36 (4): 615–35.

Weimer, D.L., and A. Vining. 1998. *Policy Analysis: Concepts and Practice.* 2nd ed. Englewood Cliffs, NJ: Prentice-Hall.

WHO (World Health Organization). 2022a. "COVID-19 Dashboard (Lebanon)." 12 October 2022. https://covid19.who.int/region/emro/country/lb.

– 2022b. "Health Emergency Dashboard (COVID-19 in Jordan)." 13 October 2022. https://covid19.who.int/region/emro/country/jo.

Whyte, Susan Reynolds, Sulayman Mpisi Babiiha, Rebecca Mukyala, and Lotte Meinert. 2013. "Remaining Internally Displaced: Missing Links to Security in Northern Uganda." *Journal of Refugee Studies* 26 (2): 283–301.

Wilson, M., and J. Casswell. 2018. *Recognizing Urban Refugees in Jordan: Opportunities for Mobile-Enabled Identity Solutions.* London: GSMA.

WIPO (World Intellectual Property Organization). 2023. "Constitution of the Hashemite Kingdom of Jordan 1952." Accessed 22 August 2023. http://www.wipo.int/wipolex/en/text.jsp?file_id=227813.

World Bank. 2013. *Lebanon: Economic and Social Impact Assessment of the Syrian Conflict.* United Nations.

– 2018. *Refugee Population by Country.* Accessed 22 December 2018. https://data.worldbank.org/indicator/SM.POP.REFG?end=2010&page=4&start=1990.

– 2020. *Proposed Additional Credit and Restructuring.* 19 May 2020. https://documents.worldbank.org/curated/en/292571592100064307/pdf/Jordan-Economic-Opportunities-for-Jordanians-and-Syrian-Refugees-Program-for-Results-Project-Additional-Financing.pdf.

– 2022a. *Jordan Country Profile.* Accessed 12 December 2022. https://data.worldbank.org/country/jordan?view=chart.

– 2022b. *Lebanon Country Profile*. Accessed 12 December 2022. https://data.worldbank.org/country/lebanon?view=chart.

– 2022c. *Literacy Rate Data: Lebanon; UNESCO Institute for Statistics (UIS)*. 24 October 2022. https://data.worldbank.org/indicator/SE.ADT.LITR.ZS?locations=LB.

– 2022d. *Syrian Arab Republic Data*. Accessed 4 December 2022. https://data.worldbank.org/country/SY.

– 2022e. *Syrian Arab Republic: Poverty Headcount Ratio*. Accessed 4 December 2022. https://data.worldbank.org/indicator/SI.POV.NAHC?end=2007&locations=SY&start=2005.

Xinhua Net. 2020. "Aoun Says Syria's War Costs Lebanon 43 Billion USD." 20 May 2020. http://www.xinhuanet.com/english/2020-05/20/c_139072828.htm.

Yahya, M., J. Kassir, and K. El-Hariri. 2018. "Policy Framework for Refugees in Lebanon and Jordan." In *Unheard Voices: What Syrian Refugees Need to Return Home*, 11–24. Washington, DC: Carnegie Endowment for International Peace.

Yahya, M., and M. Muasher. 2018. "Refugee Crises in the Arab World." In *Arab Horizons: Pitfalls and Pathways to Renewal*, edited by Joseph Bahout, Nathan J. Brown, Perry Cammack, Michele Dunne, Intissar Fakir, Marwan Muasher, Maha Yahya, and Sarah Yerkes, 85–105. Washington, DC: Carnegie Endowment for International Peace.

Yassen, A.O. 2019. "The Prospects for Durable Solutions for Syrian Refugees in the Kurdistan Region of Iraq: A Case Study of Erbil Governorate Camps." *Refugee Survey Quarterly* 38 (4): 448–69.

Yassin, N., and R. Khodor. 2019. *101 Facts & Figures on the Syrian Refugee Crisis*. Vol. 2. Issam Fares Institute for Public Policy and International Affairs.

Yassin-Kassab, R., and L. Al-Shami. 2018. *Burning Country: Syrians in Revolution and War*. London: Pluto Press.

Yin, R. 2009. *Case Study Research: Design and Methods*. 4th ed. Sage.

– 2014. *Case Study Research: Design and Methods*. 5th ed. Thousand Oaks, CA: Sage.

Zeager, L.A. 2002. "The Role of Strategic Threats in Refugee Resettlement: The Indochinese Crisis of 1978–79." *Rationality and Society* 14 (2): 159–91. https://doi.org/10.1177/1043463102014002002.

Zetter, R. 1991. "Labelling Refugees: Forming and Transforming a Bureaucratic Identity." *Journal of Refugee Studies* 4 (1): 39–62.

– 2012. "Are Refugees an Economic Burden or Benefit?" *Forced Migration Review* 41:50.

References

– 2014. "Creating Identities, Diminishing Protection and the Securitization of Asylum in Europe." In *Refugee Protection and the Role of Law: Conflicting Identities*, edited by Susan Kneebone, Dallal Stevens, and Loretta Baldassar, 22–35. New York: Routledge.

Zeus, B. 2011. "Exploring Barriers to Higher Education in Protracted Refugee Situations: The Case of Burmese Refugees in Thailand." *Journal of Refugee Studies* 24 (2): 256–76.

Zisser, E. 2017. "Syria – From the Six-Day War to the Syrian Civil War." *British Journal of Middle Eastern Studies* 44 (4): 545–58.

Zolberg, A.R., A. Suhrke, and S. Aguayo. 1986. "International Factors in the Formation of Refugee Movements." *International Migration Review* 20 (2):151–69. PMID: 12267846.

Zuber, M., and S. Moussa. 2018. "Arab Spring as a Background of Civil War in Syria." *International Conference: The Knowledge-Based Organization* 24 (1): 245–51. https://doi.org/10.1515/kbo-2018-0038.

Index

Abdelaaty, Lamis, 12, 47, 53. *See also* refugee status determination

Adamson, Fiona, 7, 32, 47, 203

administrative capacity, 25, 187, 194, 205–6

advocacy, 193–4. *See also* United Nations High Commissioner for Refugees

Afghanistan, 41

Aflaq, Michel, 69. *See also* Lebanon, Republic of

Africa, 5–6, 25, 32; Horn of, 38; Organisation of African Unity, 45, 217n4. *See also* Global South; Middle East and North Africa

African Union, 217n4. *See also* internally displaced persons

agenda: government, 40; institutional, 34; policy, 48; political, 212; research, 7; UNHCR, 46

al-Asaad, Bashar, 70, 71, 73 78; Asaad regime, 85, 87; civil war outcome, 85, 112; Hafiz al-Assad, 70; House of Asaad, 219n4; perceived war outcome, 132, 140; Syrian president, 77, 111. *See also* Ba'ath Party

Alawite, 70, 72, 219n4

Al Jazeera, 71, 75, 109, 112, 146. *See also* news sources

Al-Khalidi, Suleiman, 111–13, 117, 138, 179

Al-Makahleh, Shehab, 85, 110, 111. *See also* safe zone

Al-Nusra Front, 72. *See also* Syrian rebel groups

Amnesty International, 117

Annan, Kofi, 78

Aoun, Michel, 80, 88, 148–9

Arab League: Syrian civil war, 78–9. *See also* multilateral peace efforts

Arab Spring, 13, 16, 69, 187

asylum seekers, 3, 4, 5, 13, 99

Australia, 37

Ba'ath Party, 69–70. *See also* regimes

bargaining, 6, 40, 46, 85, 195; rent-seeking, 46–7. *See also* Greenhill, Kelly M.

286 Index

Baumgartner, Frank, 205. *See also* agenda

BBC, 70, 74, 75, 109, 149. *See also* news sources

Betts, Alexander, 39, 43–7, 50, 65, 209

Bitar, Salah-al-Din, 69

Black Friday, 197. *See also* Palestinian refugees: in Jordan

blame, 80; scapegoating, 50

borders, 31, 35; admission choice, 37; border-sharing countries, 31, 33, 65, 187; closures, 36, 141; open-border policy, 81, 105, 140, 185

bottom-up perspective, 10–11, 30, 218n9

Bradley, Megan, 52, 87

Brazil, 26, 47

burden sharing, 7, 32, 45, 213; politicization, 195; shortage, 185, 194. *See also* responsibility sharing

bureaucratic structure, 39; Directorate General of Migration Management (Turkey), 40; Disaster and Emergency Management Authority (Turkey), 40. *See also* implementation mode

Burundi, 52

Caesar Act, 77

Cambodia, 41

camps: Azraq, 138; Dadaab, 38; encampment, 38, 46, 63, 133, 157; regulations in Jordan, 141; "warehousing," 38; Zaatari, 105, 134, 138. *See also* settlement types

Canada, 213

capacity: bureaucratic, 9; economic, 49; refugee assistance, 3, 6–7, 9, 20, 36, 40, 45; state, 32. *See also* administrative capacity; policy capacity

Cartagena Declaration on Refugees (1984), 217n4. *See also* Latin America

case study, 14, 17, 20, 24, 218n11; comparative, 14–16, 18, 20–1, 65, 175; qualitative, 20–1, 61, 189, 218n11

causality, 207

character (refugee movement), 51, 63, 184, 198

Chatty, Dawn, 52, 95, 117, 133. *See also* local norms

children: child labour, 160; protection standards, 214; Syrian refugee movement, 80; Syrian refugees in Jordan, 105; Syrian refugees in Lebanon, 156–9

China: asylum policy, 48, 52; Indochinese refugees, 53; Syrian civil war, 75–8. *See also* reconstruction

civil war: Lebanon, 94, 97, 99, 101; Syria, 67–79. *See also* proxy war

climate migration, 210

Cold War, 25, 36, 47, 50

colonialism: anti-colonial liberation struggle, 53–4; European powers, 91, 101; legacy, 26; neo-colonialism, 25; post-colonial, 8

compact agreement, 14; Global Compact on Refugees, 213; Jordan Compact, 108, 120–2, 126, 130, 210–11; Lebanon

Compact, 160, 171, 211, 180, 186. *See also* innovations
compassion fatigue, 52, 210
complex systems, 7, 10, 18–19, 28, 55, 201, 204; complexity, 10, 188, 191–2, 202; policy inputs, 56–9, 188, 201; policy outputs, 8, 29, 55–6; policy process, 59–61. *See also* systems thinking
Comprehensive Response Framework, 213. *See also* global cooperation
constraints, 201–2, 206, 213; constraining devices, 201
containment strategies, 36. *See also* safe zone
Convention for the Protection and Assistance of Internally Displaced Persons in Africa, 217n4
Convention Relating to the Status of Refugees (1951). *See* Geneva Convention
coping mechanisms, 30
country of conflict origin, 31, 41, 67–89
COVID-19, 12, 16, 21; Syria, 83–4, 86, 88. *See also* pandemic
crisis: learning, 210; management, 210; policy-making, 205
Crisp, Jeff: integration, 41–2, 126; international assistance, 45, 58; perceived threat, 49; perceived treatment, 59; reduced reception standards, 198; refugee return conditions, 84
curfews: Syrian refugees in Jordan, 119; Syrian refugees in Lebanon, 144, 157, 180. *See also* freedom of movement

customary international law, 36, 58, 116, 131, 153. *See also* non-refoulement

Daher, Joseph, 70, 72, 219n1, 219n3. *See also* civil war: Syria
data: collection, 16, 23–4, 19, 61; analysis, 23–4, 61; coding, 23; database, 24; interview, 23; primary, 21, 24, 103, 114–15; qualitative, 21; saturation, 22; secondary, 24, 103, 114–15; triangulation, 23
De Bel Air, Françoise, 100, 117, 179
demographic considerations, 58, 168, 182, 198–9. *See also* political considerations
displacement arena, 43, 218n3. *See also* policy response: drivers
displacement features: influence on host refugee policy, 199–200
Druze, 70, 91, 97–8, 219n4

economic concerns, 49–50, 55, 58; currency devaluation, 172; gross domestic product, 70, 86, 93, 98; inflation, 86, 107; poverty, 70, 98, 145, 150
Economist, The, 11, 87, 91, 97. *See also* news sources
education: Geneva Convention, 38, 157; Syrian refugees in Jordan, 119, 134; Syrian refugees in Lebanon, 110, 147, 157–9
Egypt, 46, 69–70
El-Taliawi, Ola G., 15, 17, 18, 204
employment policy, 37–9, 45; research, 12; Syrian refugees in Jordan, 108, 111, 116; Syrian

288 Index

refugees in Lebanon, 147, 156, 158–60, 164

Ensour, Abdullah, 110. *See also* Lebanon, Republic of

environmental concerns, 49, 58, 62–3, 69; drought, 71; water scarcity, 70, 136, 219n3

Eritrea, 41

ethics: refugee governance, 195–6; research, 23. *See also* methodology

Ethiopia, 41

ethnic affiliation, 79; affinity, 53; ethnicity, 63, 91. *See also* religious affiliation

Europe: Brexit, 82–3; European Union, 82–3; "fortress," 214; Syrian civil war, 75–8. *See also* Global North

evidence-based policies, 212; impact evaluation, 201

faith, 50–1; evangelical humanitarian relief providers, 51; faith-based organizations, 98, 145; faith-based responses, 51; Islam, 95. *See also* traditions

Fakhoury, Tamirace, 10, 12, 65, 85, 148

far-right parties, 82; presidential candidate, 83

Fiddian-Qasmiyeh, Elena, 31, 50. *See also* faith

forced migration studies, 192, 203; refugee studies, 192; scholars, 210; scholarship, 33, 192, 214

foreign policy, 3, 12, 47–8, 51, 54. *See also* geopolitics

framework: analytical, 7–8, 12–13,

18–19, 54–61; technique, 23, 113. *See also* complex systems

France: French mandate (Syria), 70; Paris attacks (2015), 81–2; role in Syrian civil war, 76–7

freedom of movement, 38; Syrian refugees in Jordan, 119, 127, 136; Syrian refugees in Lebanon, 157, 159, 163

Friends of Syria, 77–8. *See also* civil war; multilateral peace efforts

fundamentalism, 76

funding shortage, 63, 213. *See also* international assistance

gender: intersectionality, 207; refugee identities, 27, 207; Syrian refugee destination choice, 80; violence, 38, 79

Geneva Agreement (Syria), 78. *See also* Annan, Kofi

Geneva Convention, 5, 15, 44–5, 94–5, 192; Convention Relating to the Status of Refugees (1951, UN), 4, 32, 39, 119, 157; non-signatory countries, 10, 13, 187; Refugee Convention, 20. *See also* Protocol Relating to the Status of Refugees (1961)

Geneva II Conference on Syria, 78

geopolitics: driver of host policy, 48, 89; North-South power relations, 25; Syrian war, 73–7, 187. *See also* foreign policy

Germany, 11, 37, 77, 82, 147

global cooperation: international cooperation, 5, 32; migration management, 195, 211; refugee

Index

protection mechanisms, 213. *See also* compact agreement

global forced displacement, 11, 17

globalization, 25

Global North, 3, 6–9, 17–18, 205, 213; developed countries, 25; first and second worlds, 25; industrialized countries, 9, 17, 42, 82. *See also* Western countries

Global Refugee Forum, 213. *See also* global cooperation

global refugee regime, 5, 9, 17, 20, 32, 55, 193–6

Global South, 5–10, 12–13, 17–20, 25–6, 31–3; developing countries, 6, 25, 45, 187, 205; developing economies, 5; developing world, 8; least-developed countries (LDCs), 3; low-income countries, 3. *See also* Southern displacement; Third World

Greenhill, Kelly M., 48, 203

Guardian, The, 107, 145. *See also* news sources

Gulf War, 36, 94. *See also* proxy war

Hariri, Saad, 88, 148, 149; Rafiq, 101

health care, 181, 227n30. *See also* pandemic

Hezbollah, 73, 87–8, 98, 150, 220n21. *See also* Nasrallah, Hassan

Horn of Africa, 38

host arena, 43, 58, 184, 200. *See also* policy response: drivers

host communities, 39, 49, 62; livelihoods, 11; relations, 85;

sentiments, 50. *See also* perceived treatment

Hovil, Lucy, 38, 41–2

Howlett, Michael, 181, 204, 206. *See also* policy subsystem

humanitarian: crisis, 79, 81, 83, 131; disaster (Syria), 79–81; emergency, 54, 127, 147, 214

humanitarianism, 51, 58, 95, 108, 130; humanitarian norms, 44, 46. *See also* local norms

human rights: Arab Charter on Human Rights, 95, 100; groups, 107, 155, 162; Human Rights Watch, 70, 85; law, 59; record (Jordan), 91; Universal Declaration of Human Rights, 95, 100; violations, 77, 79, 217n4

impartiality, 207

implementation mode, 37, 39; Syrian displacement in Jordan, 118, 123–5, 128; Syrian displacement in Lebanon, 160, 164

Independent International Commission of Inquiry on the Syrian Arab Republic, 77

India, 26

Indochinese refugees, 42, 53

innovations: policy, 12, 14, 210. *See also* compact agreement

integrity: research, 23. *See also* research design

internally displaced persons, 30, 79, 217n2, 217n4

international arena, 43–7, 56–8, 61, 63, 183. *See also* policy response: drivers

Index

international assistance, 61, 63,
185–6, 194, 213; Brussels
Conference, 83; Helsinki
Conference, 83; influence on
host refugee policy, 44–6, 58;
Jordan, 108, 128, 136–7;
Lebanon, 170; London
Conference, 109, 137, 171, 180.
See also funding shortage
international refugee norms, 192,
201; normative standards of
refugee protection, 192, 201
international refugee regime, 9, 20,
26, 40, 43–7, 84; influence on
host refugee policy, 193–6. *See
also* global refugee regime
international relations, 19, 203
International Syria Support Group
(ISSG), 78
intersectionality, 27. *See also*
refugees: identities
Iran, 47, 72–6, 148. *See also* civil
war
Iraq: involvement in Syrian civil
war, 73–4; Iraqi refugees in
Jordan, 51; Iraqi refugees in
Lebanon, 45; Iraqi refugees in
Syria, 49, 51; Iraqi refugees in
Turkey, 36, 48; research design,
16. *See also* Gulf War; Kurds
Ismailis, 70, 219n4

Jacobsen, Karen, 32, 34, 39, 197
Janmyr, Maja, 65, 155, 194
Jess, J.K., 52, 54, 199
Jordan, Hashemite Kingdom of,
91–5, 103–41; Government of
Jordan, 105–7, 111–14; Jordan
Hashemite Charity Organization,
106; Jordan Response Plan for

the Syria Crisis, 106, 108, 125,
128; King Abdullah, 104, 109,
110; Ministry of Interior, 106,
119, 122; Ministry of Planning
and International Cooperation,
123–4, 135, 138, 181

Kagan, Michael, 37, 168
Karen refugees, 48. *See also*
Thailand
Kenya, 26, 37, 53, 200
Kunz, E.F.: model of refugee
movements, 43
Kurds: Kurdish forces in Syrian
Kurdistan, 73; Kurdish Iraqi
refugees, 36; Kurdistan Regional
Government, 81; Kurdish state,
73; Kurdistan Workers' Party,
73. *See also* civil war

Landau, Loren, 5, 28, 50
Latin America, 6, 25, 32, 45
Lebanese-Syrian relations, 100–1;
Ta'ef Agreement, 97
Lebanon, Republic of: Crisis
Response Plan, 147, 162, 170,
181; Free Patriotic Movement,
148, 162; General Security
Office, 148, 154, 172;
Government of Lebanon, 144,
153, 170, 181; Law on Entry
and Exit of Foreigners in
Lebanon, 155; Ministry of
Finance, 145; Ministry of
Foreign Affairs, 48; Ministry of
Refugee Affairs, 143–4, 145–6,
155, 158, 160–1; Ministry of
Social Affairs, 144, 161;
Progressive Socialist Party, 144,
162, 160; Syrian displacement,

142–75. *See also* compact agreement; policy actors

legal framework: governing refugees in Jordan, 94; governing refugees in Lebanon, 99–100; hard laws, 13, 56, 94; international, 56; international refugee law, 214; legal instruments, 58, 94–5, 100; normative frameworks, 90, 94; soft laws, 56, 94. *See also* customary international law; Geneva Convention; humanitarianism

legitimacy, 47

length of stay (refugee movement), 51, 59, 136, 199

linear causal pathway, 33. *See also* framework

Lischer, Sarah, 48–9, 51, 53, 58–9, 198

local integration, 37, 40–3, 52–3; de facto, 42; intermediate, 42; Syrian refugees in Jordan, 117, 125–7, 129, 132, 134; Syrian refugees in Lebanon, 154, 162, 164–5, 168, 175

local-level analysis, 207, 211; localities, 144, 209; mayor, 209; micro-level analysis, 207; municipalities, 209; street-level bureaucrats, 209, 218n9

local norms, 6, 50, 58, 62, 90, 94–5, 102, 131. *See also* traditions

Loescher, Gill, 35, 44–7, 194. *See also* international relations

London Conference, 193; Supporting Syria and the Region conference, 171. *See also* international assistance

Long, Katy: non-refoulement, 84; repatriation, 41; safe zones, 36

mass refugee influx, 36, 191, 192; en masse, 191; mass displacement, 30; mass influx situations, 34, 35, 38, 192

media, 3, 27, 150, 212

memorandums of understanding (MOUS): UNHCR and Jordan, 94, 105, 119, 131; UNHCR and Lebanon, 45, 100, 169, 226n10. *See also* legal framework; United Nations High Commissioner for Refugees

Mencütek, Zeynep Sahin: comparative cases, 14, 16, 18; foreign policy, 12, 58; refugee movement volume, 52; Syrian employment in Jordan, 222n13

methodology, 7, 23, 66, 195, 206; limitations, 186–9; methods, 14–16, 20–3, 201, 214. *See also* research design; Yin, Robert K.

Middle East and North Africa, 14, 19–20, 32, 49

migration diplomacy, 47. *See also* bargaining; strategic tools

migration management, 40, 195, 203; securitization, 49, 198, 203

Migration State, 7

militarization, 53, 59, 63

Miller, Sarah Deardorff, 3, 159

Milner, James, 17–18, 32, 39, 42, 45–6, 50

Ministry of Planning and International Cooperation (Jordan), 105–6, 109, 123–4, 135

most-similar design, 14, 16, 21. *See also* case study

MOUs. *See* memorandums of understanding
Mozambique, 41
Mulki, Hani, 110
multilateral peace efforts, 77–9
Myanmar, 51

Nasrallah, Hassan, 145, 148, 198
Nassib-Jaber border crossing, 138, 141, 117. *See also* borders
nationality: impartial refugee protection, 196; naturalization (Lebanese law), 100; refugee movement, 63, 199
naturalization, 41–2; citizenship, 111, 134. *See also* local integration
news sources, 24. *See also* Al Jazeera; BBC; *Guardian, The*
non-refoulement, 4, 35–6; Syrian refugees in Jordan, 116–17, 127, 130–1, 140; Syrian refugees in Lebanon, 149, 153–4, 163, 166, 169, 174; Syrian refugees in the Middle East, 81, 84. *See also* customary international law; Geneva Convention; global refugee regime
normalization, relations with Syrian regime, 85, 88, 111; rapprochement, 141, 150, 220n22
Norwegian Refugee Council, 154, 155; on Syrian refugees in Lebanon, 171

Palestinian-Israeli conflict, 74–5. *See also* Palestinian resistance groups
Palestinian refugees: Department of Palestinian Refugee Affairs,

39–40; hosting experience of, 16, 51, 133, 143–4; in Jordan, 94, 132–3, 180; in Lebanon, 39–40, 97, 99–100, 144, 168; in the Middle East, 48; from Syria (PRS), 22, 80–1, 99, 189, 199. *See also* policy legacy; refugee-hosting experiences, previous
Palestinian resistance groups: Hamas, 75; Palestine Liberation Organization, 48, 98, 197; Palestinian Islamic Jihad, 75; Popular Front for the Liberation of Palestine – General Command, 75. *See also* militarization
pandemic, 112, 114, 119, 121, 123, 138; public health, 21, 134, 138, 141, 222n7. *See also* COVID-19; health care; service provision
participatory planning, 209
perceived treatment, 59, 107; preferential, 62, 108, 135. *See also* host communities: relations
policy: learning, 210, 133; mix, 202; trade-offs, 201
policy actors, 204–5, 207; interest groups, 205; non-state actors, 68, 87–8, 169, 205–6; policy-makers, 210; stakeholders, 208
policy capacity, 139, 173, 205–6
policy design, 204, 211
policy dialogue, 210–11
policy enforcement, 205
policy evolution, 125–7, 163–4; change, 140, 146, 154–5, 160; over time, 7, 8, 10, 140, 142

policy legacy, 168, 174, 206; path dependence, 206. *See also* Palestinian refugees

policy on durable solutions, 34, 40–3. *See also* local integration; resettlement

policy on entry and stay, 34–7

policy on livelihoods, 34, 37–40

policy recommendations, 9, 17, 208

policy response: drivers, 43–54; host, 10, 27; state, 33–43, 192. *See also* host arena

policy subsystem, 181–2, 187, 190, 205–6. *See also* Baumgartner, Frank

policy success, 211

political considerations, 50, 58, 100. *See also* demographic considerations; stability

political regime type, 58; authoritarian, 50, 69, 91, 97, 219n1; democracy index, 91; Freedom in the World, 91; parliamentary democracy, 97; pluralistic democracy, 79; presidential democracy, 70. *See also* sectarianism: confessionalism

practice, 192; asylum provision, 33–4; effective refugee governance, 207–14; lessons learned, 192; practical implications, 207–14; practitioners, 9, 208, 213–15. *See also* policy recommendations

precariousness of legal status, 118, 155

process tracing, 23, 152, 167, 174, 206. *See also* methodology

protection: quality, 46, 50, 62; standards, 20, 32, 191, 193

Protocol Relating to the Status of Refugees (1961), 4, 13, 36, 219n12

protracted displacement: durable solutions, 52; Palestinian refugees, 51, 133; restrictive refugee policy, 63; Sudanese refugees, 52; Syrian, 107, 128. *See also* length of stay

proxy war, 72–3

perceived conflict outcome, 48, 58, 89, 136, 141. *See also* policy response: drivers

Qatar: Syrian civil war, 73–4. *See also* Gulf War

Rabil, Robert G., 97, 98, 99

rational actor model, 204

Razzaz, Omar, 110. *See also* Lebanon, Republic of

realism, 130, 41

reconstruction: post-war Syria, 74, 76, 88; Syrian refugee returns, 87, 137

refoulement, 35–7, 41. *See also* customary international law; non-refoulement

refugee crisis: Syria, 11–16, 79–83; terminology, 8–9

refugee-hosting experiences, previous, 16, 58–9, 90, 105, 134; historical, 50–1, 134. *See also* policy legacy

refugee-host states: Global South, 40; neighbouring, 28; policy variation, 64; rent-seeking, 46; Syrian refugees, 85, 87, 89

refugee life cycle, 34–5
refugee policy, 34–43; policy-making, 177, 188, 192, 204–5; variation, 192, 200–2. *See also* policy on durable solutions; policy on entry and stay; policy on livelihoods; typology
refugees: categories, 26, 27, 218n1; definition, 4, 217n4; identities, 26, 27, 207; labels, 26–7; livelihoods, 30; rights, 33–5, 38, 41–2
refugee status determination (RSD), 30, 36, 47; Jordan, 131; Lebanon, 154, 226n10
regimes: Asaad, 85, 87; Syria, 14, 70, 73–7, 79, 196. *See also* global refugee regime
religious affiliation, 167, 212, 85. *See also* sectarianism
repatriation, 41. *See also* policy on durable solutions; Syrian refugee returns
research design, 14, 19–20, 188
research questions, 8, 33; hypothetical propositions, 61–4, 193–200
resettlement, 42–3; permanent settlement, 111, 134; Syrian refugees in Jordan, 126; Syrian refugees in Lebanon, 163
responsibility sharing, 5, 44, 61, 196, 213–14
restrictive refugee policy, 52, 57, 62–3; Syrian refugees in Jordan, 131, 137, 183; Syrian refugees in Lebanon, 154, 167, 183. *See also* Crisp, Jeff; Jacobsen, Karen
revolution: economic mismanagement, 71; Egypt, 70; Lebanon,

101, 149; Syria, 71–3. *See also* Arab Spring
rhetoric: anti-refugee, 4; government, 127–8, 130–1, 150
Ruiz, Isabel, 30, 39, 49
Russia: role in Syrian civil war, 73–8; Syrian refugee returns, 87–8
Rwanda, 36, 52

safe zone, 36, 85, 88, 148, 162; haven, 4
Salam, Tammam, 146, 169
Samaddar, Ranabir, 8. *See also* colonialism
sanctions, 73, 77, 79, 86
Saudi Arabia: intervention in Lebanon, 148; Syrian civil war, 73–4, 79. *See also* Arab League
Second World War, 5, 32. *See also* global refugee regime
sectarianism, 71–2, 97–8, 149, 168, 189, 219n1; confessionalism, 97
security, 37–8, 43, 48, 55; considerations, 55, 62, 63; national, 58; threat, 49. *See also* terrorists
service provision: capacity, 16, 171; parallel systems, 208; refugee rights, 38; scaling back, 181, 185, 194. *See also* education; health; xenophobia
settlement types, 37–8, 42, 180, 197; peri-urban, 80, 118; self-settlement, 128, 130, 133, 156; Syrian refugees in Jordan, 118; Syrian refugees in Lebanon, 156; urban, 4, 37, 156; urbanization, 4. *See also* policy on livelihoods

Shiite, 162; coalition, 73, 148; Muslims, 97–8, 150. *See also* Iran

Slovenia, 39

social network analysis, 206

social receptiveness, 58, 62. *See also* ethnic affiliation; host communities: relations

Southern displacement, 5, 214. *See also* Global South

sovereignty, 209–10

spill-over effect, 37–8

stability: domestic, 185, 188, 190, 198; macroeconomic, 93; political, 3, 110; social, 137, 162

strategic tools, 48. *See also* bargaining: rent-seeking; migration diplomacy

study limitations, 186, 188–9; terminological limitations, 25

Sunni Islam, 70; Muslims in Jordan, 15, 91; Muslims in Lebanon, 97–8; Muslims in Syria, 72, 219n4; Syrian civil war, 69–74; Syrian refugee movement, 219n9; Syrian refugees in Lebanon, 144, 150, 168, 174, 198. *See also* host communities: relations

Support Front for the People of Syria, 72. *See also* civil war

Syrian Arab Republic, 67–9; Syrian Golan Heights, 74

Syrian rebel groups: Free Syrian Army, 71, 76; Islamic Caliphate of Abu Bakr al-Baghdadi, 72; Islamic State of Iraq and the Levant (ISIL), 75; Islamic State of Iraq and Syria, 72. *See also*

Support Front for the People of Syria

Syrian refugee returns, 83–8; Hezbollah, 148; promotion of voluntary returns (Turkey), 113; refugee-return committee (Lebanon), 148

Syrian refugees: crisis, 40, 81, 161, 191–3, 204; influx, 152, 157, 163, 174

systems thinking, 10, 18, 54, 190, 192, 218n5; feedback, 59–61; systemic, 10, 14, 19, 55, 66. *See also* complex systems

Tanzania, 26, 36, 42, 46, 52

temporary asylum, 53

temporary protection, 36–7

temporary stay, 37

terrorists: groups, 75, 77; threat, 49, 72

Thailand, 47, 48, 51

theoretical implications: directions for future research, 192, 204–7; policy science, 7, 54; public policy, 12, 15, 17–19, 34, 54; refugee policy, 9–11, 13, 18–21, 30–43, 192–200; refugee studies, 7, 9–10, 190, 192, 214

Third World, 25, 50. *See also* Global South

traditions: generosity, 54, 95, 107; hospitality, 50, 95, 101, 198; Islamic and Arab, 198. *See also* local norms

Tsourapas, Gerasimos, 12, 16, 18, 32

Tunisia, 69

Türk, Volker, 45–6, 210, 213. *See also* compact agreement

Turkey: Geneva Convention, 219n12; Iraqi refugees, 48; research design, 16, 206; resettlement, 228n55, 229n1; Syrian civil war, 73; Syrian refugees, 11 typology, 192, 202–4

Uganda, 26, 38, 52, 200
Ukraine, 20, 196
United Nations High Commissioner for Refugees (UNHCR): cash assistance, 113; data, 79; international refugee regime, 84, 113; memorandum of understanding, 94, 100, 105, 118–19; Regional Refugee & Resilience Plan (3RP), 81, 83, 193; Syrian refugee returns, 84–8
United Nations Relief and Works Agency for Palestine (UNRWA), 80, 94, 99, 217n3. *See also* Palestinian refugees
United Nations Security Council, 75–6, 78–9, 87. *See also* multilateral peace efforts
United States: Cold War, 47; Iraqi refugees, 48; resettlement, 47; Syrian asylum applications, 82; Syrian civil war, 75–8; Syrian refugee returns, 87; temporary protection, 37

validity: conceptual, 21; threats, 16, 23, 207, 218n11. *See also* study limitations

volume (refugee movement), 51–3, 59, 219n4. *See also* policy response: drivers
Vulnerability Assessment: Framework (VAF), 125; Survey, 156–9

Western countries, 17, 30, 73, 75–7, 97, 213
women, 214; Convention on the Elimination of All Forms of Discrimination against Women, 95, 100; refugee identities, 27; Syrian refugee movement, 80; Syrian refugees in Jordan, 105, 121. *See also* gender
World Bank, 70, 93–4, 98, 121, 123; impact of Syrian crisis on Lebanon, 145, 170
World Food Program (WFP), 125, 156

xenophobia, 83, 85, 208–9; discrimination, 95, 100, 208, inclusion, 209. *See also* ethnic affiliation; social receptiveness; women

Yahya, Maha, 20, 119
Yin, Robert K., 21, 23–4, 61, 189. *See also* case study

Zetter, Robert, 26, 39. *See also* refugees: labels; service provision